The
Pullman Strike

The Pullman Strike

THE STORY OF A UNIQUE EXPERIMENT
AND OF A GREAT LABOR UPHEAVAL

ALMONT LINDSEY

THE UNIVERSITY OF CHICAGO PRESS / CHICAGO & LONDON

International Standard Book Number: 0-226-48383-5
Library of Congress Catalog Card Number: 64-23413

THE UNIVERSITY OF CHICAGO PRESS, CHICAGO 60637

The University of Chicago Press, Ltd., London

TO THE MEMORY OF

MY FATHER, ALBERT LINDSEY

WHO EXEMPLIFIED THE FINEST QUALITIES
OF HIS GENERATION

PREFACE

MORE than ten years ago Marcus L. Hansen, professor of history at the University of Illinois, suggested that I investigate the town of Pullman as a social experiment. Out of this study came my doctoral thesis. So fascinating was the subject and so unexplored was the field that I later decided to broaden my research to include the entire scope of the Pullman Strike. My project met with the enthusiastic encouragement of my friend and mentor, Professor Hansen, who felt that there was need for a full treatment of this great upheaval. His unexpected demise in 1938 deprived me of an able counselor, whose scholarly judgment and sympathetic advice I greatly missed in the preparation of this book.

The material of many libraries contributed to the substance of this volume, and to all these institutions I owe a debt of gratitude. In particular I would like to acknowledge the extremely valuable assistance of the Illinois State Historical Library, the Pullman Branch Library, the John Crerar Library, the Metropolitan Library of Chicago, the Illinois State Archives, and the newspaper, legal, and manuscript divisions of the Library of Congress. For permission to use certain quotations I wish to express my appreciation to Charles Scribner's Sons and to Alfred A. Knopf and Company. To George W. Arms, one of my colleagues at Mary Washington College, I am greatly indebted for his painstaking perusal of my manuscript and his many helpful suggestions.

A. L.

Mary Washington College
Fredericksburg, Virginia

vii

TABLE OF CONTENTS

LIST OF ILLUSTRATIONS

CHAPTER I

EMBATTLED LABOR

EIGHTEEN HUNDRED AND NINETY-FOUR was a year of fast-moving drama. Never had the nation witnessed a spectacle of greater despair or more serious labor disturbances. The panic of 1893 paralyzed the industrial structure, demoralized wages, and reduced to idleness three million workers.[1] Added to the growing chorus of national discontent was the voice of the agrarian forces, protesting against forty-nine-cent wheat, seven-cent cotton and twenty-six-cent corn.[2] From hamlet and city the armies of the Commonweal were recruited. Their weapon was the petition; but, to exploited labor, industrial warfare seemed more effective in forcing redress of grievances. Strikes shook the nation to its foundation. All the pent-up bitterness of years found expression in the tragic struggle between the classes and the masses.

John Swinton, journalist and author, wrote of events in that feverish year:

Do we hear cries of distress from a million idle people? The wail of hunger from men, women and children? The groans of anguish from the multitudes who suffer in many a great city? Do we see hordes of men, mingled with women, looking for work by which they may earn their daily bread? Does strife rage between the workers and the capitalists? Do we hear the tramp of a hundred thousand soldiers, bearing guns, with which they are ready to shoot their own countrymen? Do we hear Grover Cleveland ordering his generals to whet their swords for blood? Do we see dread spectacles of human degradation all over the coal area of our country? Have we seen a half million workers on the strike in a single month of the year 1894? Did not the reader feel that our country was "shooting Niagara" while he read the daily reports in the newspapers of June and July? Who can tell the wierd and ghastly story of the last quarter of the nineteenth century? And is this the proud country into which Grover Cleveland was born 57 years ago?[3]

The fury with which labor and capital battled in 1894 was the outgrowth of years of mutual distrust and hate; indeed, from the dawn of the industrial revolution the interests of the two had clashed repeatedly. The bitter strikes and cataclysmic upheavals of labor resolved themselves into an attempt on the part of the employees to improve a standard of living which too often bred tragedy, suffering, and despair. Entrepreneurs of the nineteenth century enjoyed great financial success, but in large measure they failed to understand or appreciate the laborer as he evolved from the domestic worker and sought in unions the only real hope of escaping from the terrors of poverty.

During the nineteenth century the position of labor was not enviable. Rapid growth of the cities led to congested conditions and disgraceful housing facilities. The rise of tenements with their glaring evils followed in the wake of factory expansion, leaving few cities free of sprawling slum areas. Many thousands of workers lived in habitations that were filthy, badly crowded, and poorly ventilated.[4] Tragic proof of such conditions was furnished by the high mortality rate from the dreadful epidemics that swept through the reeking slums of the large cities during the post–Civil War era.[5] The miserable housing facilities furnished to thousands of miners in Pennsylvania were in large part responsible for the Coal Strike of 1873.[6] Under such baleful influences as the slums provided, competence and efficiency among the workers could not easily be developed. Labor was keenly aware of the crying need for clean, livable homes and accorded recognition to this matter in their platform of principles.[7] The manufacturer apparently did not realize that bad home environment militated against his own factory interests.

Wages for the most part were low and inadequate. Following the Civil War the plight of the laborer grew worse, in spite of the industrial boom which made work more plentiful and wages higher. Between 1860 and the close of 1866 wages rose approximately 60 per cent, whereas commodity prices during the same period soared 90 per cent. House rents increased an even greater percentage. Skilled employees in 1868 and 1869 were definitely worse off than they had been in 1860, judging from the shabbier homes in which they lived and the simpler fare which they ate. Pay cuts during the panic of 1873 were severe, and wages did not take a turn for the better until 1880;[8] but in the panic of 1893 wage slashes again reduced the wage-earner to a state of desperation.

Wretched housing and low wages were not the only causes for unrest among labor; long hours, child labor, and dangerous and unsanitary working conditions ranked also as major grievances. The standard factory working day after the Civil War was at least ten hours and frequently more. Before 1860 only skilled artisans and government employees were able to command the ten-hour day, while a large proportion of workers had to toil twelve and fourteen hours. Children under sixteen years then worked twelve or more hours a day; and almost as tragic was the plight of female textile workers, who at Lowell in 1846 were compelled to labor thirteen hours a day during the summer and from dawn to sunset in winter. Wages were often reduced one-half by the truck system of payment, which was especially prevalent in factory towns and mining regions.[9] In view of such conditions it was only natural that the laborer should resort to methods of self-help.

Prior to the Civil War unionism was largely in the embryonic state. In the thirties the first trade-unions of the United States developed but could not muster enough strength to survive the panic of 1837. Numerous attempts to develop unions were made during the next twenty-five years, but none seemed to have any enduring results. Strikes were won and certain gains made, but such basic matters as wages, hours, and housing did not improve materially. The odds against labor were great. Employers' associations developed in order effectively to combat labor organizations. The courts rushed unhesitatingly to the side of capital by prosecuting unions for conspiracy; and not until the famous decision in the case of *Massachusetts Commonwealth vs. Hunt in 1842* were unions held to be legal organizations. Yet during this transitional period the foundation was laid for the powerful labor organizations which later emerged.

Prior to the panic of 1873 there were in the United States no less than thirty national unions, of which the most significant were the National Labor Union and the Knights of Labor. Both of these unions enjoyed meteoric growth only to fade out of the industrial picture. Launched in 1866 as a confederation of all types of labor organizations, the National Labor Union soon possessed six hundred and forty thousand members; but participation in politics destroyed the movement when it was only five years old. Although short-lived, the organization contributed materially to the cause of national amalgamation, the eight-hour-day movement, and the establishment of labor bureaus.

In 1869 the Order of the Knights of Labor was founded by Uriah S. Stephens, a Philadelphia garment-cutter. The movement was at first cloaked in secrecy, and not until this feature was abandoned in 1881 did the organization enjoy rapid growth. It was launched as the first great experiment in industrial unionism, and virtually all workers, irrespective of skill or craft, were eligible to membership. The preamble to the constitution of the union announced: "When bad men combine, the good must associate, else they will fall, one by one, an unpitied sacrifice in a contemptible struggle." Under the leadership of Terence V. Powderly, who became grand master in 1879, the union mushroomed into a membership of over seven hundred thousand. Precipitate strike action in 1886 combined with unmerited public censure arising out of the Haymarket riot contributed to the disintegration of the union, and at the time of the Pullman Strike the organization was but a shadow of its former strength.[10]

Of more enduring character was the American Federation of Labor, which began its slow, steady growth in 1881. Concerned only with the aristocracy of labor, the movement rested on craft lines. Under the resourceful leadership of Samuel Gompers, the organization pursued a conservative course, eschewing all political action and following a cautious policy in industrial warfare.[11] During the tempestuous year of 1894 the federation voiced sympathy for embattled labor but otherwise deemed it better valor to hold aloof from the struggle.[12] So discreetly did this organization conduct itself that the turn of the century found it more strongly established than ever.

The industrialist was inclined to observe the rise of unions with apprehension and to view them as a deadly foe to be resisted and exterminated. The future of labor organizations remained precarious, since they had not yet won a recognized place in the social order. Public opinion still frowned upon all strikes. Nevertheless, labor was grimly determined to compel capital to make concessions through higher wages and shorter hours. During this period the workers were sullen, embittered, and resolved to support their demands with their most effective weapon, the strike. With capital equally determined to thwart labor and destroy unionism, the stage was cleared for the industrial upheavals which shook the country following the Civil War.[13]

Before labor strife is discussed, a few observations about the industrialist are relevant. Prior to 1860 industry was being revolutionized, and the Civil War seemed to accelerate the movement. Through improved means of production and the rapid growth of home and foreign markets, transportation and manufacturing were beginning to broaden out on a nation-wide basis. In 1865 most businesses were conducted on a small scale, but not many years elapsed before consolidation of small competing firms occurred; and, by absorbing and crushing small competitors, giant monopolies evolved, capitalized at tens of millions of dollars.[14] Often the growth of a monopoly was achieved through the shrewd calculations of one tycoon. Principles, honesty, and lawfulness were ruthlessly brushed aside as swollen fortunes were amassed. Industrial anarchy and social confusion prevailed as many of the capitalists, in order to gain their ends, resorted to unethical, illegal practices.[15]

Bribery—perhaps the worst of the prevailing evils—was employed in this ruthless era of industry, but to what extent cannot be determined. But prevalent it was, corrupting officials in both the federal and the state governments. Railway lobbying, for instance, was notorious, the Union Pacific alone disbursing in the national capital by 1868 no less than five hundred thousand dollars. The practice of winning corporate privileges from state legislatures was facilitated with the aid of large money gifts. Both the judiciary and the legislature of New York State in 1870 were conspicuously corrupt;[16] but no less disgraceful were the legislative sessions of Illinois, which were literally swamped with the demands of influential lobbyists, who succeeded in getting what they wanted. In 1869 approximately seven hundred acts of incorporation were jammed through the legislature of this prairie state.[17] Everywhere the situation was ideal for the type of men who dominated industry.

Cornelius Vanderbilt, who typified the ruthlessness of the new era, successfully merged a number of roads into the famous New York Central and, through stock manipulation, boosted his fortune within twelve years from ten million to one hundred and four million dollars. He conducted his business relations upon the theory that the end always justified the means and, without compunction, pursued a policy of crushing small competitors, bribing legislators, corrupting courts, violating laws, and watering stock.[18] But he was no more vicious than Daniel Drew, Jay Gould, and James Fisk, from whom he tried to wrest control of the Erie Railroad in the late sixties. The triumvirate, as officers of the Erie, printed enormous quantities of stock in order to forestall Vanderbilt's attempt to corner the securities of that railroad. Eventually they induced the state legislature of New York to legalize this issue but not without recourse to widespread bribery, in which state senators received all the way from fifteen thousand to one hundred thousand dollars apiece. Vanderbilt resorted to the same strategy but was outgeneraled.[19]

The methods employed by the Standard Oil Company were as unprincipled as they were successful. Competition was anathema to John D. Rockefeller, who crushed competitors by outrageously barbarous means and who ordered agents of the company upon threat of summary dismissal to secure control of the entire oil business in their respective districts. Railroad officials were bribed in order to gain access to the records showing the nature and extent of the business of all competitors; and with this information oil was secretly offered to the dealers of these competitors at greatly reduced prices.[20] The utter ruthlessness of this company was representative of many. It is not difficult to understand why the employers of this era with their untrammeled rights would brook no opposition from labor. Just as the capitalists overcame business competition in a cunning and savage manner, so they tried to overwhelm labor unions in a manner no less pitiless.

Although there was a number of strikes immediately following the Civil War, it was not until the panic of 1873 that they assumed the character of industrial upheavals. As had earlier depressions, this one proved a severe blow to labor. Wages dropped rapidly, and unemployment mounted until it finally reached between two and three million men. In protest against shrinking pay checks, strikes were called; but defeat almost invariably confronted labor. Believing the time ripe to smash unions, the employers resorted to lockouts, blacklists, and legal prosecutions, with the result that labor organizations were greatly weakened.

In July, 1877, the country was shaken by a strike of major proportions. Having suffered from a decline of business, the railroads slashed wages. The managers of the eastern roads felt that the time was auspicious to destroy the powerful Brotherhood of Locomotive Engineers, which, because of some notable victories in 1875, had become very popular among railway employees.[21] Angered by repeated wage cuts, the employees were in a militant mood; and an abrupt 10 per cent slash, effective in June and July on the Baltimore and Ohio Railroad, precipitated the strike. The latent hostility of labor found immediate expression, and the struggle quickly assumed national dimensions. Traffic on all eastern roads was paralyzed, and at such rail junctions as Baltimore, Pittsburgh, Reading, and Chicago there were strife and bloodshed. In Pittsburgh the mob dominated the situation for days, successfully resisting all efforts on the part of the militia to restore order. The infuriated civilians drove out of the city the state troopers who dared to open fire. The destruction here was estimated at three to ten million dollars.

Unable to cope with the growing violence, the governors of Maryland, Illinois, Pennsylvania, and West Virginia requested federal military aid, and regular troops were rushed to the affected areas. For political reasons the executives in Indiana and Missouri hesitated to avail themselves of such aid; but, upon application of the United States marshals, federal troops were ordered into these states—a procedure which was destined to become a vital part of the strategy of the federal government in 1894. Within two weeks the strike was crushed.[22]

While starvation wages forced the struggle, the justification advanced by the railroads for their drastic wage policy was not very convincing. Especially was this true in the case of the New York Central, which throughout that turbulent year paid 8 per cent dividends on stock that had been capitalized at twice its real value. By reducing dividend payments to 6 per cent, Vanderbilt could have avoided the wage reduction of 1877.[23] The indifference of the railroads toward the plight of labor fostered among the workers a new feeling of solidarity. Railway managers were now conscious of the strength possessed by underpaid and dissatisfied laborers. Capital seemed determined to prevent a recurrence of such a cataclysmic outbreak; and to this end conspiracy laws were passed by several states and armories quickly erected in many places.[24]

This strike was followed by many others. The great Anthracite Strike of 1877 furnished evidence that cause for discontent was confined not alone to railroad employees. With earnings reduced to fifteen dollars a month and less, the coal miners struck and forced a 10 per cent advance in wages.[25] The year of 1880 brought a flood of strikes; indeed, the situation became more feverish, culminating in 1886, "the year of the great uprisings."

Labor demonstrated a militant determination to battle for its "rights" in 1886, with the result that the number of strikes in that year doubled any previous record. During the early part of the year the Gould railway system in the Southwest was involved in a serious struggle. The Knights of Labor had gathered strength from two earlier victories on the road and were in no mood to see one of their members discharged for alleged incompetency. Refusal to reinstate him provoked the conflict which quickly paralyzed six thousand miles of railway and led to violence and property destruction. In some states the militia was ordered on duty; but within two months the strike wore itself out and ended disastrously for the Knights of Labor.[26]

Deeming the times right, the American Federation of Labor abandoned for the moment its extreme caution and sponsored a nation-wide movement for the eight-hour day. The general strike called on May 1 was partially effective, and tens of thousands of workers won the shorter day; but for the most part results were discouraging.[27]

It was during this epidemic of strikes that the Haymarket riot in Chicago electrified the nation. On May 3 several strikers were killed and wounded by the police in a fray at the McCormick reaper works; and in protest against the brutality of these agents of the law a meeting was called at Haymarket Place, where violent remarks were uttered by some anarchists. When a bomb was hurled by an unknown hand at the police as they were trying to disperse the crowd, several were killed, and considerably more were wounded. A wave of horror swept the country and feeling ran high. While human passions were thus aroused, eight leading anarchists were placed on trial and pronounced guilty. One took refuge in suicide, four expiated on the scaffold a crime which they probably did not commit, and three languished in prison until pardoned in 1893 by Governor John P. Altgeld. In the considered opinion of this executive the entire trial had been a travesty of justice and was conducted by Judge Gary with "malicious ferocity." For this act of mercy, buttressed by a carefully prepared statement, Altgeld was universally criticized and bitterly denounced. The press raged, referring to him as "anarchist," "demagogue," "socialist," and "fomenter of lawlessness." Finally the storm subsided, but the vested interests did not forget.[28]

In 1892 occurred the famous Homestead Strike which long rankled in the memory of organized labor. The Amalgamated Association of Iron and Steel Workers was then one of the strongest trade-unions in the United States. Prior to 1889 the union was able to maintain friendly relations with the Carnegie Steel Corporation; but in that year Henry C. Frick became general manager of the company, and immediately antiunionism developed as one of its fixed policies. In 1892 the workers were confronted by an unyielding disposition on the part of the corporation to reduce wages; and before their union could take action the company assumed the initiative and declared a lockout. Other mills in the Pittsburgh area were soon involved. Andrew Carnegie hastily departed for Europe, leaving Frick in full command to wage a war to the death against the Amalgamated Association.

Henry Frick acted quickly. He erected around the steel plant at Homestead a wire fence three miles long and fifteen feet high and then entered into an arrangement with the Pinkerton Detective Agency to furnish three hundred armed guards. As they approached Homestead in barges on the Monongahela River during the early morning of July 6, the workers gathered at the landing prepared to contest their arrival. Ten were killed, and many more seriously wounded when rifles blazed and a pitched battle was fought. Pinkerton's men were routed, but the victory of the workers proved illusory. The entire militia of Pennsylvania was soon concentrated at Homestead, where martial law was proclaimed; and under the protection of bayonets the mills gradually resumed production. The troops remained until the latter part of November, when the workers, forced by necessity, were compelled to call off the strike and return to the mills as nonunionists. By this one stroke the Carnegie Company successfully swept unionism out of Homestead and reduced it to a negligible factor in the steel mills throughout the Pittsburgh area.[29]

The Homestead Strike was convincing proof to labor that the steel industry, despite its pretended interest in better living standards for the workers, was supremely indifferent to their fate. Labor beheld one of the most highly protected industries in the nation pursuing a policy of barbarism toward its employees, despite the major contention, long advanced and fostered by steel interests, that high tariff schedules would confer benefits on the workers. The employment of a private army and the militia to protect corporate interests against the demands of workers sharpened class feelings. Labor played a large part in the defeat of the protectionist-minded Republican party in 1892[30] and, in scanning the future, looked more and more to its own weapons of industrial warfare.

The rise of modern corporations and associations of employers was not paralleled by the growth of equally strong combinations in the field of labor. Despite the growing need for organization, the rank and file remained nonunionized. Too often the many unions that existed worked at counterpurposes, defeating the long-range interests of the workers. Their only salvation seemed to lie in the unity and solidarity of a common front; and none realized this better than Governor Altgeld of Illinios, who sympathized profoundly with the cause of labor. In the fall of 1893 he admonished the workers that in the fierce struggle for existence labor could defend its interests only through unity of purpose. He deplored the fact that labor was still largely a scattered force. With emphasis he declared:

This is an age of concentration. Everywhere there is concentration and combination of capital and of those factors which today rule the world. . . . . The world gives only when it is obliged to, and respects only those who compel its respect. . . . . Let all men of America who toil with their hands once stand together and no more complaints will be heard about unfair treatment.[31]

What Altgeld urged and what Eugene Debs and other labor leaders believed to be a necessity[32] loomed on the horizon as a dread specter to the industrialists. What they must have discussed in their inner chambers about the labor menace and the growing class consciousness of the workers has never been fully recorded, but it can hardly be denied that they were apprehensive and fearful about the trends of the times.

Some of these fears were enlarged upon in the summer of 1894 by the editor of the *Railway Age*, Harvey P. Robinson, who was closely in touch with the sentiment of railroad executives. Though he made his observations at the close of the Pullman Strike, in retrospect they shed light on the attitude of some of the corporation executives during the early part of 1894. The editor pointed out that those who were conversant with the objectives of labor had foreseen the gathering storms of industrial conflict. The plans of labor, he affirmed, have "accomplished nothing less than a general industrial rebellion, through which, by force of numbers, the labor organizations of the country proposed to obtain control of the legislative machinery of this government." The chief obstacle to the realization of this goal, it was explained, had been lack of unity, but this difficulty was gradually being overcome. The rise of the American Railway Union was cited as a part of the program to absorb all railroad workers in a formidable combination, which in co-operation with other powerful labor units hoped to become the predominant force in the economic system and "the guiding voice in the government."[33] If the industrial leaders believed that labor was fighting to dislodge them from their complete control of the economic machinery, as was alleged by the editor of the *Railway Age*, then it is easy to understand the ferocity with which the government, the judiciary, and the corporate interests struck back at striking labor in 1894.

Conditions in that year were extremely bad, because of one of the most acute depressions the nation had yet experienced. During 1893 six hundred and forty-two banks failed and twenty-two thousand and five hundred miles of railway went into receivership. The industrial market collapsed, business underwent drastic retrenchment, and unemployment increased sharply as millions of men tramped the streets in search for work. The winter of 1893–94 was filled with tragedy for thousands, and during such a crisis the people grew restless and critical of the economic order.[34]

Discontent found expression in industrial strife and the Commonweal movement. Labor was sullen, moody, and determined to resist further wage reductions. In Illinois, seat of the Pullman Strike, 16 per cent of the employees were thrown out of work in 1894 by virtue of strikes—a record with which not even 1886, notorious in the annals of labor conflict, could compare.[35] The workers could protest against economic injustices by bringing the wheels of industry to a halt, but the unemployed could only beg, march, and petition.

The armies of the Commonweal sought remedial action from Congress. Desperate and forlorn, thousands of idle men believed that a concerted march on Washington, D.C., would impress the government with the need for immediate action; and so from various parts of the United States "Coxeyites" traveled by foot and by rail; but comparatively few of those who resolutely left home ever reached the nation's capital. Their reception in that city was cold and inhospitable; but more discouraging was the complete indifference of Congress to their plea for help. The nation beheld this upsurging of discontent with surprise and dismay.[36]

Organized labor was not oblivious to this expression of unrest. Eugene V. Debs in June of that dramatic year portrayed the movement in vivid language:

Out of work, out of money and without food, ragged, friendless and homeless, these Commonwealers began their march to the capital city of the nation while Congress is in session. . . . . Faster and still faster they rallied as the bugle call echoed through the land. They walk, they ride, they float; the storms beat upon them, their tent their skins; their couch the mother earth, their pillows stones. Some fall by the way and are buried by their comrades, unknelled and unsung, to sleep their last sleep in unknown and forgotten graves. But the survivors press forward to Washington, and as they march, recruits start up from almost every center of population in all of the land, from mountain and valley, from hill and dale, from abandoned mine and silent factory, shop and forge—they come and tramp to the muffled drum—funeral march of their throbbing hearts. The cry is, "on to Washington," where, on the marble steps of the nation's capitol, in their rags, and barefooted, they would petition Congress to enact laws whereby they might perpetuate their wretched existence by toil—laws that would rekindle the last remaining spark of hope, that their future would be relieved of some of the horrors of hunger and nakedness. . . . .[37]

The Commonweal armies demanded free transportation by railroad and, when refused, commandeered trains. Distances in the West were great, and the incentive was stronger there than elsewhere for lawless demonstrations. Many of the railroads affected were in bankruptcy, and receivers had been appointed by the federal courts. Judges met the situation promptly by issuing injunctions to protect such railroads against interference by disorderly elements; but, in attempting to carry out the court orders, the United States marshals encountered serious difficulties. The deputies were often halfhearted in performing their duty because of sympathy for the Commonwealers; and, in trying to enforce injunctions, the marshals found public sentiment in many communities arrayed against the government. Some of the industrial armies counted many hundreds of determined men, against whom the federal agents were powerless to take effective action. The marshals appealed to Richard Olney, attorney-general of the United States, who issued instructions that, if they could not enforce the court processes with deputies, they should inform President Cleveland of the situation and request military aid. Wherever possible they were urged to join with the federal judge and district attorney in making their representations for troops. The procedure proposed was followed, and regular soldiers were employed to put a stop to further violations of the injunctions.

In fourteen states, mostly west of the Mississippi River, the Department of Justice was called upon for aid, and wherever necessary the assistance of federal troops was promptly invoked.[38] The technique proved effective and was employed to advantage in the much greater crisis that was soon to follow. No longer did the central government need to depend so completely upon the state militia for the suppression of domestic disorders, since intervention by the federal government within a state was now much easier. The usual procedure of requisitioning for United States troops by the state legislature or governor was no longer necessary as a preliminary for federal intervention in certain spheres of activity. Under the guise of enforcing court processes, federal troops could be sent to protect railroads in receivership and thus keep open the channels of interstate commerce. Used sparingly in the Railroad Strike of 1877, the procedure was now utilized with great frequency. A different expedient was necessary to stop disorders on railroads not in federal receivership; and to meet this situation Commonwealers guilty of seizing trains on such roads were arrested by federal agents for "obstructing and retarding the passage of the mails."[39]

While the Coxeyites were on the march, the nation was faced by a serious bituminous coal strike. The panic of 1893 demoralized not only the coal market but also the wage scale for miners. Conditions became so intolerable that the United Mine Workers, with a treasury of only twenty-six hundred dollars and a membership of not more than twenty-four thousand, decided upon a general suspension of mining. Despite the meagerness of their resources and the apparent hopelessness of their cause, the members of this union refused to enter the pits on April 21 and were joined in their determined stand by the rank and file of miners throughout the country. The common plight of all miners, union and nonunion alike, infused in them a spirit of resistance.

The number of striking miners reached one hundred and eighty thousand, as the production of bituminous coal almost completely ceased. The miners struck in protest against wage slashes and for the prevention of further reductions that had been threatened.[40] In his official statement on the strike Governor Altgeld declared: "The mining population had found its condition getting steadily worse for a number of years until those who had worked hard all their lives and had been sober men found their families in rags and often without bread."[41] The strike lasted eight weeks, but for the miners it was a losing struggle. Conditions proved inauspicious for the workers; and public opinion, none too friendly at the outset, gradually turned against the strikers. This feeling may have been due to the threatened coal famine or to the press news which was largely antiunion. The mineowners, in a sense victims of conditions over which they had little control, proved adamant in most cases; and, although some adjustments were made, in general the end of the strike found the miners once more at the mercy of the operators.[42]

The sympathy which Governor Altgeld had for labor did not stand in the way of duty. Disorders accompanied the strike, but whenever an emergency arose in Illinois he met the situation promptly by ordering out the militia. Troops were rushed to at least eight different localities in the state during the strike, and without hesitation he ordered the arrest of any who violated the law.[43] He did not believe, however, that the civil or military arm of the government should be used for strikebreaking purposes. On one occasion he wired advice to a sheriff against having deputies used as private guards for coal operators[44] and on May 26 issued General Order No. 8 which forbade the employment of troops "as custodians or guards of private property." The function of soldiers, he announced, was to assist in preserving peace, quelling disturbances, and executing the laws; any person desiring to have his property guarded should do so at his own expense.[45] The governor was unalterably opposed to the practice of using the armed forces in the interest of one economic group against another, and on this matter the vested interests were left no illusions as to his policy in any future industrial crisis.

Equally significant in this strike was the attitude of Richard Olney as to the part which state troops should play in the enforcement of the judicial processes of federal courts. At Mount Olive, Illinois, for instance, the striking miners interfered with the shipment of coal on the Chicago, Peoria, and St. Louis Railroad, then in the hands of a receiver appointed by the United States district court. Injunctions were issued, but the marshal encountered difficulty in enforcing them and, upon inquiry, was advised by the attorney-general to seek first the assistance of civil authorities and then, should they prove inadequate, to apply to the governor for military aid. In carrying out these instructions the marshal was driven to the last alternative. Governor Altgeld responded with alacrity, and troops were ordered to Mount Olive.[46] This procedure was in sharp contrast to that followed during the Pullman Strike, when Olney preferred to ignore the availability of the militia and urged the marshals, upon failure to enforce injunctions, to apply at once to the President for federal troops.

The coal strike had barely subsided and the Commonweal movement had hardly taken its place among lost causes when a much greater crisis enveloped the nation. Originating in the town of Pullman, this struggle spread until it covered two-thirds of the United States. Labor and capital battled with a ferocity seldom equaled in the annals of labor warfare. The people seemed paralyzed with fear, while the lurid headlines and inflammatory stories of newspapers screamed forth the fearfulness of this battle between the classes and the masses. Not since the Civil War had the nation been treated to the spectacle of so many soldiers on the march.[47] Nearly all the forces of law and order, civil and military, were invoked. The strike ran its swift and terrible course, but not without leaving in its wake precedents, implications, and controversies which were destined to influence the course of capital-labor relations long after the hate engendered by that struggle had died away.

NOTES

1. *Public Opinion*, XVI (1894), 314.

2. Solon J. Buck, *The Agrarian Crusade* ("Chronicles of America Series," Vol. XLV), pp. 104–5.

3. *Striking for Life*, p. 297.

4. Allan Nevins, *The Emergence of Modern America, 1865–1878* ("History of Ameri-

can Life," Vol. VIII), pp. 319–20; *Sixth Annual Report of the Bureau of Statistics of Labor, 1875*, p. 503.

5. Nevins, *op. cit.*, pp. 321–22.

6. Samuel P. Orth, *The Armies of Labor* ("Chronicles of America Series," Vol. XL), p. 66.

7. Richard T. Ely, *The Labor Movement in America*, p. 340.

8. Nevins, *op. cit.*, pp. 69–70, 301.

9. Orth, *op. cit.*, pp. 28, 44–45; Nevins, *op. cit.*, p. 70.

10. Davis R. Dewey, *National Problems* ("American Nation," Vol. XXIV), pp. 49–50; Orth, *op. cit.*, 73–85.

11. Orth, *op. cit.*, pp. 87–98.

12. *American Federationist*, I (1894), 131–33.

13. Nevins, *op. cit.*, pp. 380–407.

14. *Ibid.*, pp. 34–40; Burton J. Hendrick, *The Age of Big Business* ("Chronicles of America Series," Vol. XXX), pp. 7–17.

15. Hendrick, *op. cit.*, pp. 19–57.

16. Nevins, *op. cit.*, pp. 179–81, 187.

17. A. C. Cole, *The Era of the Civil War* ("Centennial History of Illinois," Vol. III), pp. 405–16.

18. Hendrick, *op. cit.*, pp. 18–24.

19. Nevins, *op. cit.*, pp. 194–97.

20. Ida M. Tarbell, *The History of the Standard Oil Company*, II, 31 ff.

21. Nevins, *op. cit.*, pp. 380–86.

22. Edwin E. Sparks, *National Development* ("American Nation," Vol. XXIII), pp. 70–78.

23. Nevins, *op. cit.*, pp. 390–91.

24. *Ibid.*, pp. 391–92.

25. Sparks, *op. cit.*, pp. 78–79.

26. Dewey, *op. cit.*, pp. 43–44.

27. *Ibid.*, p. 45; Selig Perlman, *History of Trade Unionism in the United States*, p. 131.

28. Perlman, *op. cit.*, pp. 92–93; John P. Altgeld, *Live Questions*, pp. 399–400; Harry Barnard, *Eagle Forgotten: The Life of John Peter Altgeld*, pp. 234–35, 239–49.

29. Louis Adamic, *Dynamite*, pp. 104–5; Perlman, *op. cit.*, pp. 133–35.

30. Dewey, *op. cit.*, pp. 248–51.

31. *Op. cit.*, pp. 344–47.

32. *United States Strike Commission Report* (Senate Executive Doc. No. 7 [53d Cong., 3d sess.]), XXII, 11–12, 138.

33. Harry P. Robinson, "The Lesson of the Recent Strikes," *North American Review*, CLIX (1894), 195–201.

34. Dewey, *op. cit.*, pp. 266, 289; *Harper's Weekly*, XXXVIII (1894), 3.

35. *Report of the Bureau of Labor Statistics of the State of Illinois* (1902), pp. 488–89, 514.

36. Henry Jones Ford, *The Cleveland Era* ("Chronicles of America Series," Vol. XLIV), pp. 201–5.

37. *Railway Times*, June 15, 1894, p. 3 (address of Eugene V. Debs to the American Railway Union convention).

38. *Annual Report of the Attorney General of the United States for the year of 1894*, pp. xxx–xxxi; *Annual Report of the Secretary of War for the year of 1894*, I, 152–55.

39. Dillion and Pierce to Olney, May 24, 1894, Richard Olney Papers.

40. "Report of President McBride of the United Mine Workers," *American Federationist*, II (1895), 8–10.

41. "Governor's Message," *Journal of the Senate of the Thirty-ninth General Assembly of the State of Illinois* (1895), pp. 28–29.

42. *American Federationist*, II, 8–10.

43. *Biennial Report of the Adjutant General of Illinois to the Governor and Commander-in-Chief, 1893 and 1894*, pp. xi, xxxi.

44. Altgeld to C. L. Berry, June 11, 1894, Governor's Letter Books.

45. *Biennial Report of the Adjutant General of Illinois, 1893 and 1894*, pp. vii–viii.

46. *Ibid.*, pp. xii–xiii.

47. *Annual Report of the Secretary of War* . . . . *1894*, I, 4, 57.

CHAPTER II

THE PULLMAN PALACE CAR COMPANY

DURING the post–Civil War era—a period characterized by enormous industrial growth—George Pullman launched the Pullman Palace Car Company and in this industry achieved a success comparable to that of Cornelius Vanderbilt in railroads and Philip Armour in meat-packing. Pullman perceived the possibilities inherent in night railroad traveling and, like many entrepreneurs who were meeting popular needs, was able to establish a powerful monopoly.

In his lowly birth and humble background, George Mortimer Pullman was no different from other tycoons of this era. He was born in Brocton, New York, on March 3, 1831. His father, although a very intelligent mechanic, was unable to provide more than a bare living for the family of ten children. The education of George Pullman was limited to a few years at the village school, although later he acquired the habit of studying at night—a practice which he continued for many years.[1] When only fourteen years old he was obliged to secure employment in a small store at a salary of forty dollars per year. Three years later he moved to Albion, New York, where he joined his brother in the cabinet-making business. The knowledge gained from this trade proved indispensable in the palace-car industry which he later established.[2]

When Pullman found that cabinetmaking was none too profitable, he decided to abandon it for more remunerative work. The state of New York was interested in widening the Erie Canal and had advertised for bids on contracts to move back all warehouses and other structures resting on the old banks of the waterway. Pullman applied for a contract, which he secured and fulfilled with credit to himself.[3] At this time Chicago was engaged in the task of raising the level of the city approximately eight feet for the purpose of improving the drainage system. Impressed by the opportunities which this undertaking offered, Pullman went

19

to Chicago in 1855 and during the course of the next three years raised a number of large stone and brick structures. His capital soon reached twenty thousand dollars.[4]

Precisely at what time George Pullman became interested in sleeping cars cannot be determined, but it is probable that his curiosity and interest in this industry developed over a period of years. After 1855 he was constantly weighing the possibilities of improving the archaic type of sleeping car which then prevailed on the various railroads. His own experience in using the accommodations of these sleepers had not been very gratifying. While journeying on one occasion from Buffalo to Chicago in a sleeping car of the Lake Shore Railroad, Pullman found the facilities so uncomfortable that before morning he was obliged to take refuge in a seat at the end of the car. He could not understand why the superior sleeping accommodations of steamboats did not exist in railway travel.[5]

Despite the fact that the earliest sleeping car in the United States dated back to 1836, little improvement had been made in comfort or safety until George Pullman began to revolutionize the industry. The first type of sleeper comprised a passenger car crudely partitioned into berths; and the experiments subsequently conducted seemed to yield very little in the way of improved facilities. Coarse mattresses and pillows were furnished, but without bed linen and blankets. Ventilation was bad, while the constant jolting proved an even greater source of annoyance.[6] In the average car of the forties and fifties light was furnished by candles, heat by a coal or wood stove, and the berths were arranged in three tiers on only one side. The innovation of sheets and blankets was finally made, but the bedding was coarse and often soiled, thus contributing little to a restful night.[7] Transportation in general was making tremendous strides, but the sleeping-car industry lagged far behind.

George Pullman entered the sleeping-car business through his connections with Benjamin Field, who served in the state senate of New York during the years 1854–56. As a legislator Field labored in the interest of the Woodruff Sleeping Car Company, and as a reward received the right to run sleepers on two western roads, one of them being the Chicago and Alton. Becoming friends, Pullman and Field often discussed the future possibilities of the sleeping-car industry. While Pullman was raising buildings in Chicago, Field obtained some loans from him; and, as a result of this accommodation, it was arranged that together they would operate sleeping cars on the Alton Railroad. Subsequently, Pullman bought out the interest of his partner.[8]

It became the policy of George Pullman to employ men who possessed the requisite expertness and to impart to them with infinite care the ideas that were constantly evolving in his mind. He began by procuring two ordinary coaches, which under his personal supervision were transformed into sleeping cars. The remodeling was done without the aid of blueprints or plans, and all details were worked out as they presented themselves. In the fall of 1858 the cars were ready for service;[9] but for some reason they did not meet with the success which Pullman had anticipated. Restless and discouraged, he was later caught in the gold rush to Pike's Peak, where he remained for two or three years, returning to Chicago in 1864. With renewed interest he turned to the problem of perfecting a sleeping car which would represent a substantial improvement over anything that had yet been built.[10]

Before the Civil War ended George Pullman evolved a sleeper which completely revolutionized the industry. Without regard to cost it was constructed with numerous innovations and in a manner so elaborate as to mark a radical departure in the style of car to which night travelers were accustomed. Heretofore the cost of building a sleeper was seldom more than five thousand dollars, but in this single venture twenty thousand dollars were invested. Known as the "Pioneer," this epoch-making car could be converted into a day coach; and the bedding and mattress were left in the recess of the closed upper berth, instead of being stored at one end of the sleeper as in all former cars. In order to introduce the hinged upper berth, which was perhaps the greatest innovation of the many which characterized this new sleeper, the car was built one foot wider and two and one-half feet higher. Attention was given to beauty as well as convenience, and the car was luxuriously furnished and decorated.[11]

The daring of this venture was evidenced by the fact that the size of the car would not permit its immediate use, since it was too large for the bridge and station-platform dimensions, which were uniformly the same on most railroads. The costliness and size of the sleeper elicited many unfavorable comments from railroad executives, but, notwithstanding, the car speedily came into its own. In the spring of 1865 the Chicago and Alton Railroad hastily made the necessary alterations in all bridge and station obstructions in order to permit the use of this ornate car for the purpose of conveying the body of Abraham Lincoln from Chicago to Springfield. Not many months afterward the Michigan Central Railroad made similar changes in its railroad dimensions for the express purpose of allowing General Grant to enjoy the convenience of the "Pioneer" from Detroit to Galena during his trip home from the war. Eventually this car was put into regular service by the Chicago and Alton Railway.[12]

George Pullman built up his industry on the theory that greater safety and more comfort in traveling, in spite of additional charges to patrons, would result in the destruction of all competitors. The Pullman monopoly came to rest upon the superiority of its sleepers over all others; and the objections raised by railroads to the fifty-cent additional charge for a berth on the Pullman sleeper were met by the decided preference which patrons quickly developed for this type of car. Adhering steadfastly to his determination to produce the very best sleepers, George Pullman spent twenty-four thousand dollars on each of the four cars which followed the construction of the "Pioneer."[13] The success of the Pullman car was assured.

The construction of more sleepers followed rapidly, and by 1867 Pullman owned forty-eight such cars.[14] Individual enterprise, however, imposed serious limitations upon production; and in order to expand an industry whose possibilities seemed illimitable, more capital was necessary than George Pullman possessed. Consequently, he decided to incorporate, and on February 22, 1867, the Illinois State Legislature granted a charter for the creation of the Pullman Palace Car Company. This organization was privileged not only to purchase, manufacture, and sell railway cars but also to operate the cars or permit them to be operated in any way it chose. Permission was granted to the company to own such real estate as might be deemed necessary for the successful prosecution of its business,[15] but whether this provision permitted the corporation to build a town adjoining its works was a matter the Illinois Supreme Court had to decide some thirty years later.

Without delay the Pullman Corporation was organized and the building of sleeping cars pushed to the utmost. The growth of the company was featured by notable improvements in accommodations for the traveling public. In 1867 the "hotel" car, equipped with eating and sleeping facilities, was put into service; and subsequently the dining car, devoted entirely to restaurant purposes, was introduced. In 1875 the first parlor car was perfected. Innovation followed innovation.[16]

Expansion of the Pullman Palace Car Company was not without opposition, but at no time was its supremacy seriously contested. Steady growth and absorption of competitors marked its history. By 1889 it had acquired complete control over the Mann Boudoir Car Company and the Woodruff Sleeping Car Company, adding thereby fifteen thousand miles of road on which Pullman cars operated. The only remaining companies in the United States were the Monarch Sleeping Car Company, which operated exclusively in New England, and the Wagner Palace Car Company, which was supported by the Vanderbilt interests. Against the latter company George Pullman waged a long and bitter war, which involved famous cases of litigation based on alleged infringements of Pullman patents.[17] How completely the Pullman sleeping-car service dominated the field is evident by the fact that in 1894 it covered one hundred and twenty-five thousand miles, or three-fourths of the railway mileage of the United States.[18]

In England a fair measure of success was experienced in the introduction of Pullman cars. The Midland Railway Company, the most important road in England, decided to adopt Pullman sleepers in February, 1873, and on this occasion George Pullman journeyed to England and personally addressed the directors of the company. By 1879 Pullman cars were operated on three English and as many Scottish lines. The only other European country in which Pullman sleepers made any headway was Italy, where in 1875 the Pullman Company established a shop for the construction of cars to be used on the principal Italian lines.[19]

The growth of the Pullman Corporation was most clearly reflected in its capitalization, which amounted to $1,000,000 when the company was launched in 1867. This amount was gradually increased to meet expanding needs. In 1885 the capital stock was $15,900,000, while the assets represented over $28,000,000;[20] and within the next ten years the capitalization reached $36,000,000 and the assets more than $62,000,000.[21] One of the unique aspects of the financial structure was the large amount of undivided profits.

In 1879 the company was operating a manufacturing plant at Detroit and three repair shops at key points throughout the country, but these were no longer adequate. Because of an urgent need for much larger repair and production facilities, in 1880 the corporation decided to concentrate its major works in one locality. In addition to manufacturing palace cars for its own use, the company planned to make all kinds of railway cars for sale in the general market.[22]

A very necessary adjunct to the new shops was the town of Pullman, whose well-being depended upon the prosperity of the Pullman works. An increase in population paralleled an increase in employment; and, conversely, a reduction in the working force was followed by a decrease in the number of inhabitants. In 1885, five years after the establishment of the town, there were 8,500 residents and 2,700 workers on the pay rolls of the shops.[23] The high peak for the town was reached shortly before the panic of 1893 when the population touched 12,600. This year represented a boom period, during which no less than 5,500 individuals toiled in the Pullman works.[24] The depression, followed by the great strike of 1894, changed the situation completely; and both employment and population decreased, though not in exact proportion, until by 1895 there were only 8,000 inhabitants, with 3,500 laborers at work in the shops.[25] Subsequently employment increased in an amazingly rapid manner, but the town never was destined to recover its buoyancy.

The town of Pullman, including all the shops, did not constitute the greatest asset of the Pullman Corporation. In 1893 this property was valued at approximately $8,000,000, as compared with total company assets of $62,000,000. Approximately one-half of the wealth of the company was invested in palace cars, and most of the income was realized from the operation of these cars. In the fiscal year of 1893 the earnings of the corporation totaled $11,400,000, of which $9,200,000 represented revenue from palace cars, while the remainder consisted chiefly of income from patents and the manufacturing of cars. Perhaps the best indication that the town of Pullman did not represent the dominant interest of the corporation was the ratio which the number of employees in the town bore to the total number employed by the company. In 1893 the entire working force of the corporation comprised 14,500 employees, of whom only about one-third labored in the shops of the town of Pullman.[26]

The operation of palace cars was ingeniously managed. Dining, parlor, and sleeping cars were manufactured exclusively for use by the company, and the number of such cars produced annually fluctuated in accordance with business conditions. In 1893, a banner year, 314 were built, and the number of palace cars then owned by the company reached 2,573.[27] In permitting the cars to be used on any railroad, the Pullman Corporation required a written agreement, under the terms of which it received all net revenue derived from the sale of accommodations in the cars. Conductors, porters, cooks, and waiters were furnished by the Pullman Company. Previous to 1873 the railroads maintained the cars; but subsequently the Pullman Corporation repaired its own equipment with the understanding that in return for this service it would receive from the railroads a two-cent mileage fee for each ticket sold. Provisions in each contract controlled rigorously the prices charged for berths and other services, and depressions had no effect upon these rates. Not even the panic of 1893 affected in any way the charges prescribed for palace-car accommodations.[28]

Pullman rates were not always considered reasonable. In 1879 the committee on railroads in the lower house of the Illinois state legislature conducted an investigation of these rates for the purpose of determining the advisability of forcing a reduction. Nothing, however, came from the investigation.[29] United States Senator John Sherman expressed himself strongly in 1894 about Pullman charges: "I regard the Pullman Company and the Sugar Trust as the most outrageous monopolies of the day. They make enormous profits and give their patrons little or nothing in return in proportion."[30] Governor John Altgeld, in his annual message to the legislature of Illinois in January, 1895, referred to Pullman rates as "extortionate" and recommended the adoption of legislation establishing reasonable charges.[31] Significantly, neither the management of the Pullman Company nor the rates which it charged were subject in any way to control by the Interstate Commerce Commission, which held that such an enterprise could not be classified as a common carrier for the reason that it did not operate its own cars but had them hauled about by railroads.[32]

In the shops of the town 60 or 70 per cent of all construction work was normally in fulfilment of outside contracts. In such a typical year as 1891, 64 per cent of the employees in the shops were engaged in building cars for the general market, as compared with only 18 per cent employed in repair work and a similar percentage in the construction of palace cars.[33] In 1894, however, the car market was in a demoralized condition, and only a comparatively small percentage of employees was then at work erecting cars for outside purchasers. The manufacturing division was thus subject to a much greater variation in income and employment than the more stable and important division of car operation.

Both the operating and the manufacturing divisions were under the direct jurisdiction of a manager responsible to George Pullman. Functioning as a vital part of the operating division were the repair-shops which, although of considerable importance, never attained the status of a major division. The activities of all branches were co-ordinated in the general offices of the company at Chicago.[34]

The Pullman Corporation was organized along the most conservative lines. Ample guaranty that it would develop in a sound and efficient manner was to be found in the character of the board of directors who, with few exceptions, represented business leaders of Chicago. George Pullman, John Crerar, and Norman Williams, Jr., were listed in the charter of incorporation, and these members, together with Marshall Field, A. S. Sprague, J. W. Doane, and Henry C. Hulbert, served as directors for a long period of years.[35] The permanence of the board gave continuity to any program which George Pullman favored, and the directors did little more than confirm his recommendations. In October of each year the directors assembled to hear the annual report of George Pullman and to go through the formality of re-electing him to the presidency.

Financially the Pullman Corporation was among the soundest institutions in the United States. Its reputation was never tarnished by stock-watering or its standing jeopardized by debt. In order to meet any emergency, the company maintained large financial reserves, which in 1893 exceeded twenty-five million dollars. With such a surplus the organization was enabled to pass unperturbed through depressions and to finance large orders which railroads could not pay for outright. This ability gave the Pullman organization a distinct advantage over all competitors.[36] The financial strength of the company was reflected in the rating enjoyed by its stock, which in 1892 was quoted at two hundred dollars, or twice the par value.[37] Not even the crisis of 1894 caused the market quotation to sag below one hundred and fifty-two dollars per share.[38]

Dividends of the company were always substantial. Between 1867 and 1871 they ranged annually from $9\frac{1}{2}$ to 12 per cent and subsequently were reduced to 8 per cent. Irrespective of business fluctuations, quarterly dividends were never less than 2 per cent.[39] The panic of 1893 caused drastic wage reductions but did not diminish the regular distribution of profits. During the fiscal year of 1893, dividends aggregated $2,500,000 and wages $7,200,000; while the ensuing year witnessed an increase of $360,000 in the total amount of dividends, as contrasted with a reduction of $2,700,000 in the sum total of wages paid.[40]

In 1894 there were forty-two hundred shareholders in the company, of whom more than one-half were women and trustees of estates. The average holding was eighty-six shares.[41] There is no information available as to how much stock was concentrated in the hands of George Pullman, but it can be assumed that a controlling block fortified him in his dealings with the directors. Until his death in 1897, he retained undisputed control over the organization.

Toward labor the Pullman Company pursued a policy not unlike that of most corporations during this era. The working day in the Pullman shops fluctuated from ten to eleven hours, and in 1894 constituted ten and three-fourths hours.[42] Not until 1903 did the company institute the nine-hour day.[43] Wages were governed entirely by the condition of the labor market. A large proportion of the workers at Pullman were skilled and semiskilled and during prosperous times were paid fair wages. In the face of adverse business conditions wages underwent drastic readjustment.

A survey of the labor difficulties in Pullman prior to the great strike of 1894 reveals that outbursts of discontent were not uncommon among the employees. In measuring its strength against the Pullman Company, labor invariably sustained defeat. The corporation apparently hoped that, by assuming an unyielding attitude toward all demands, the workers could be brought to perceive the futility of strikes and to submit quietly to any rules or wage reductions it chose to make.

The first of the strikes to occur in Pullman took place in 1882 and involved one thousand employees. Since the town was still under construction, it was necessary for a large proportion of the men to travel daily from Chicago on the Illinois Central Railroad. The cost of transportation, twenty cents per worker, was assumed by the Pullman Company for several months; but, finding this rather burdensome, it refused to pay more than one-half of the fare for each man. Protesting against this arrangement, the men struck, but the attempt to organize a union failed, as did the primary purpose of the strike.[44]

In March, 1884, more than one hundred and fifty men in the freight-car department refused to work because of a wage slash which they claimed had so reduced their earnings that they could no longer support their families. Anxious as always to minimize its labor difficulties, the corporation announced that the trouble was of minor importance and was caused by a few men recognized as "chronic kickers." Moving swiftly, the company replaced most of the strikers with workers brought from Chicago.[45]

During the early part of October, 1885, the company ordered a general 10 per cent wage slash but in order to minimize the danger of a strike made the reduction effective in only a few departments at a time. Some of the men withdrew from the shops, but the strike which threatened never materialized. Winter was approaching, and this, together with the belief that a strike would lead to eviction from their homes, caused the workmen to accept the new wage scale with little more than a verbal protest.[46] This reduction may have served as an inducement for the workers to join the Knights of Labor.

In the spring of 1886 the estimated strength of this union in Pullman was fourteen hundred members. On May 1 a nationwide strike for an eight-hour day was launched, and with some hesitation the Pullman employees decided to join the movement and demand not only the shorter working day but also a 10 per cent increase in wages. When the demands were presented, George Pullman flatly refused to consider them and warned that labor would never be permitted to control the policy of his company.[47] Confident of victory, the workers struck. Within ten days, however, the shops were reopened under police protection. The unity of the strikers quickly dissolved, and the men returned to work under the old terms.[48] So thoroughly was this venture in unionism crushed that not until 1894 was any further attempt made to organize the employees.

Yet there were other strikes, among them being the Wood Carver's Strike of January, 1888. Unlike former disputes, this one was precipitated by the obnoxious authority exercised by the foreman over the men in the cabinet department. Demanding his removal, the wood-carvers withdrew from the shops. After giving the strikers a limited time to return to work under existing shop conditions, the Pullman Company ordered the men to stay out permanently.[49] Similar tactics were used to break a strike at the freight-car shops in January, 1891, and the men were directed to re-enter the shops within nine days or to be refused work forever. Defiantly, the strikers voted not to return; but long after the strike at least one of them obtained a job in the shops under an assumed name.[50]

The policies of the company, whether against unionism or in favor of the most conservative business procedure, were peculiarly those of George Pullman. It is not easy to characterize this man, whose conduct at times seemed puzzling and enigmatic. Pullman was primarily a hardheaded businessman, who possessed a remarkable memory and a complete grasp of details and who was able to control all branches of his corporation with a rigorous hand. Conscious of the need for capable assistants, he gathered into his organization a select group, which was trained in his methods and whose services were retained by high salaries.[51]

Having risen from poverty to pre-eminence by dint of hard labor and careful planning, he was inclined to expect the utmost from his subordinates. His temperament was far from genial, and for the most part he was brusque, unapproachable, and domineering. In his business relations with employees as well as with railroad executives, he proved unyielding and consistently refused to brook opposition to any plan or policy which he might devise.[52] John McLean, the company's surgeon in the town of Pullman, described George Pullman as an irascible individual, who for slight provocation would discharge employees.[53] Rev. William Carwardine, pastor of the First Methodist Episcopal Church of Pullman, portrayed him as a domineering lord, whose conduct toward his subordinates was most reprehensible.[54]

The reserve and taciturnity of George Pullman, together with other qualities which have been mentioned, made him very unpopular and left him few confidential friends. According to some of his closest acquaintances, he was misunderstood by the great majority of people, and his apparent coldness in reality cloaked a generous heart.[55] Pullman certainly had his human qualities and, like most capitalists of this period, was generous in personal benefactions, for he bequeathed one-sixth of his fortune of over seven

GEORGE M. PULLMAN

and a half million dollars to charitable organizations.[56] Although very dignified and seldom given to mirth, his pretentious home was the center of many gay social affairs. He was fond of good music, especially orchestral selections and old hymns, and in his home he installed an organ and occasionally invited an organist to play in the evenings. While a Universalist in religion, he was tolerant of all faiths. In 1867 he married Hattie Sanger, and from this union four children were born.[57]

George Pullman took virtually no part in the civic life of Chicago but, like Marshall Field and Philip Armour, preferred to hold himself aloof from the affairs of the city. The only public position which he ever held was that of treasurer of the Chicago Fire Relief Fund. In politics Pullman was more active and was well known in Washington as a staunch Republican who contributed generously to campaign funds.[58]

At times George Pullman was inclined to be vain and pompous. Several years before his death he received from the king of Italy a patent of nobility, which he took very seriously and carried rather ostentatiously.[59] The pride which Pullman took in the model town often bordered on vanity. Special excursions were made to the town, and with gusto he would conduct his guests on a tour of inspection through the most beautiful portions. It was doubtless because of the vanity which he displayed in the town that Jane Addams was disposed to call it a "show place."[60]

Necessity had compelled the Pullman Company to construct a town in conjunction with the new shops. The site selected for these works was a sparsely settled region on the prairie south of Chicago, and in order to accommodate the thousands of workers a town had to be established. In providing housing facilities George Pullman could have erected cheap, ugly frame structures and charged a nominal rent, or he could have permitted the haphazard construction of houses and tenements by landlords, workers, and speculators. In discussing the matter with the board of directors, Pullman seems to have been opposed at first by certain members who favored the construction of mere huts. To these members a lavish expenditure of money in establishing a model town represented a poor financial investment.[61] Pullman brushed aside all opposition and set himself resolutely to the task of building a beautiful town which would be exemplary in a period when living conditions for labor were notoriously bad.

To what extent the post–Civil War industrial strife influenced George Pullman in this venture is difficult to determine. He clearly realized that labor disputes militated against the well-being of industry and tended to injure the employer as much as the employee. It was apparent that discontent among workers was in part due to bad housing conditions. Pullman believed that attractive homes, beautiful parks, and other features essential to a well-planned community would lull the restless yearnings of the workers and give to his corporation a stability in labor conditions not hitherto known.[62] Not only would mechanics of high caliber be attracted to the town, but it was felt that there would be greater permanency in employment and less likelihood of labor disputes. The Pullman experiment was essentially a business proposition and not, as some writers have suggested, a venture in philanthropy. Charitableness of spirit in no wise prompted Pullman in building the town, nor did he make any pretensions of playing the part of a philanthropist. As a financial investment the model town was expected to earn at least 6 per cent on the entire cost.[63]

It cannot be definitely ascertained where the founder borrowed the ideas for his venture in paternalism. Concerning his motives there is ample material, but as to the origin of his ideas there is nothing but conjecture. Unfortunately, Pullman left virtually no correspondence from which one might hope to glean the answers to certain perplexing questions.

A book published in 1870 by Charles Reade entitled, *Put Yourself in His Place*, is alleged to have had considerable influence on the life of George Pullman.[64] The book is a dramatic study of social problems in England touching upon labor and capital. The story is laid in the manufacturing town of Hillsborough, where trade-unions were well organized, and where violent deeds were perpetrated by these unions in the enforcement of their demands. The hero of the novel was a skilled workman and inventor who came from London and, because he invented quicker processes, was subjected to a series of terrible persecutions by the cutlery unions. By dint of hard work and good fortune he eventually became a manufacturer, whose factory was a model and whose interest in the welfare of labor was genuine. When he introduced labor-saving devices, however, the unions turned against him with all their fury, finally blowing up his factory. The story is one to incite a feeling of hatred for labor unions. Whether or not the book served to promote a greater paternal interest on the part of Pullman in his employees cannot be affirmed.

Prior to the founding of the model town, there were in Europe three active paternalistic experiments: Saltaire, England; Guise, France; and Essen, Germany. It is not known to what extent, if at all, George Pullman borrowed from them, but he was doubtless familiar with their existence from the publicity which they received during the seventies and eighties. A few authors in describing the town of Pullman have compared it with certain of these European experiments, and one writer has even declared that George Pullman used Saltaire as a model for imitation and followed it very closely.[65] Certainly, the only foreign venture that bore resemblance to the town of Pullman was Saltaire; and the others, because of their great dissimilarity, may be excluded from further consideration. Saltaire shared so much in common with the town of Pullman that it is quite likely George Pullman scrutinized the English experiment before working out the blueprints of his own model town. He visited England in 1873, and on that occasion may have inspected Saltaire; but, in any event, literature on the experiment could have supplied him with the necessary data.

The founder of Saltaire, Sir Titus Salt, was a successful manufacturer of alpaca woolens. Rapid expansion in his business forced him to enlarge plant facilities, and in 1853 he constructed elaborate works on the banks of the Aire River, a few miles from Bradford.[66] He built an attractive village adjoining the factory to accommodate his employees. The homes were constructed of stone and surrounded with lovely lawns and flower beds, while the streets were paved and bordered with rows of trees. A fourteen-acre park was laid out, equipped with cricket and croquet grounds, bowling greens, and bathing facilities. Everything was designed with an eye to beauty, sanitation, and the comfort of the four thousand inhabitants.[67]

The paternalistic interest of Sir Titus Salt in his employees led him to provide fully for their spiritual and physical needs. A picturesque Congregational church was erected, designed in an Italian style of architecture. Schools were organized and instruction furnished at a small nominal charge to each child. The most significant structure—the Saltaire Club and Institute—was an educational and recreational center, for which a small membership fee was charged. The improvident and sick were cared for within the framework of the experiment. Almshouses were established with due regard to comfort and beauty, and a large infirmary was similarly provided to meet the needs of the community.[68] Co-operative stores were set up, the management of which was vested in a committee, half of whom were selected by Salt and the remainder by the employees.[69]

The entire village was controlled by Sir Titus Salt, who jealously retained ownership of all the homes and other buildings and who laid down whatever regulations were deemed necessary. Rentals were charged for the use of public buildings as well as dwellings, and fees were assessed for other accommodations. Salt doubtless expected a return on his investment, although he seemed more genuinely interested in the well-being of the inhabitants than did George Pullman. The founder of Saltaire was willing to sell lots upon which operatives could build their homes,[70] a course to which Pullman was unalterably opposed. Both industrialists placed great emphasis on aesthetic appearances and stressed the importance of physical and mental activity on the part of the employees.

Whatever may have been the source of inspiration for the town of Pullman, this experiment marked in the United States a new departure in the approach to the labor situation. The capitalists had been dealing labor blow for blow and had presented a front which in militancy and pugnacity was equaled only by that of the workers. George Pullman was as determined as his colleagues to dominate labor, but he believed more subtle means could be used. He was convinced that paternalism wisely administered would make labor more amenable to the interests of his corporation. The reasons for creating the model town were thus easy to discern; but the frustration of purpose which characterized the experiment as it ran its devious course is a story of more color and greater complexity.

NOTES

1. *Chicago Tribune*, October 20, 1897, p. 3 (obituary of Pullman).
2. Joseph Husband, *The Story of the Pullman Car*, pp. 24–25.
3. Walter R. Houghton, *Kings of Fortune*, pp. 213–14.
4. *Inter Ocean*, October 20, 1897, p. 2 (obituary of Pullman).
5. Houghton, *op. cit.*, p. 215; Horace Porter, "Railway Passenger Travel," *Scribner's Magazine*, IV (1888), 303.
6. Porter, *loc. cit.*
7. Husband, *op. cit.*, pp. 22–23.
8. *Inter Ocean*, October 20, 1897, p. 2.
9. Husband, *op. cit.*, pp. 28–32.
10. Houghton, *op. cit.*, p. 216.
11. Husband, *op. cit.*, pp. 32–34; *Inter Ocean*, October 20, 1897, p. 2.
12. Porter, *op. cit.*, p. 304.
13. *Pullman Journal*, January 7, 1893, p. 1 (reproduction of an article based upon an interview with George Pullman, *New York World*, December 23, 1892).
14. Husband, *op. cit.*, p. 47.
15. *Private Laws of the State of Illinois by the Twenty-fifth General Assembly* (1867), II, 337–38.
16. Porter, *op. cit.*, p. 305; Husband, *op. cit.*, pp. 52, 58.
17. Husband, *op. cit.*, pp. 53, 73–85.
18. *United States Strike Commission Report*, p. 611.
19. Husband, *op. cit.*, pp. 61–69.
20. "Annual Report of the Pullman Company," *Inter Ocean*, October 16, 1885, p. 3.
21. "Annual Report of the Pullman Company," *Pullman Journal*, October 21, 1893, p. 4.
22. *U.S. Strike Commission Report*, p. 529.
23. "Annual Report of the Pullman Company," *Inter Ocean*, October 16, 1885, p. 3.
24. "Annual Report of the Pullman Company," *Pullman Journal*, October 21, 1893, p. 4.
25. *Ibid.*, October 20, 1894, p. 4, and October 19, 1895, p. 4.
26. *Ibid.*, October 21, 1893, p. 4.
27. *Ibid.*
28. *U.S. Strike Commission Report*, pp. 33, 547–50, 624.
29. *Appleton's Annual Cyclopaedia* (1879), p. 485.

30. *New York Times*, July 1, 1894, p. 9.

31. "Governor's message," *Journal of the Senate of the Thirty-ninth General Assembly of the State of Illinois* (1895), p. 26.

32. *New York World*, July 11, 1894, p. 2.

33. *U.S. Strike Commission Report*, pp. 535, 572.

34. *Ibid.*, p. 531; John McLean, *One Hundred Years in Illinois*, pp. 233, 252–53.

35. "Annual Report of the Pullman Company," *Inter Ocean*, October 16, 1885, p. 3. The list of directors appearing in 1894 revealed the same members except for John Crerar, whose place had been taken by Henry Reed.

36. *U.S. Strike Commission Report*, p. 535.

37. *Pullman Journal*, January 7, 1893, p. 1.

38. *New York World*, July 11, 1894, p. 2.

39. *U.S. Strike Commission Report*, p. 535.

40. *Ibid.*, p. xxi.

41. *Ibid.*, pp. 541, 586.

42. *Pullman Journal*, April 21, 1894, p. 8.

43. *Calumet Record*, February 5, 1903, p. 1.

44. *Chicago Times*, February 16, 1882, p. 7; *Chicago Tribune*, February 15, 1882, p. 8, February 16, 1882, p. 10, and February 17, 1882, p. 8.

45. *Chicago Times*, March 5, 1884, p. 8, and March 6, 1884, p. 8; *Chicago Evening Journal*, March 6, 1884, p. 3, and March 7, 1884, p. 3.

46. *Chicago Times*, September 30, 1885, p. 6, October 3, 1885, p. 6, and October 7, 1885, p. 8.

47. Joseph Kirkland, *The Story of Chicago*, pp. 398–400; Charles H. Eaton, "Pullman: A Social Experiment," *Today*, II (1895), 8; *Chicago Times*, May 2, 1886, p. 6, and May 5, 1886, p. 3.

48. *Chicago Times*, May 5, 1886, p. 3, May 11, 1886, p. 2, May 14, 1886, p. 2, May 16, 1886, p. 6, and May 18, 1886, p. 8.

49. *Ibid.*, January 21, 1888, p. 2; *Chicago Herald*, January 9, 1888, p. 8.

50. *U.S. Strike Commission Report*, p. 441.

51. *Chicago Record*, October 20, 1897, p. 3 (obituary of Pullman); *U.S. Strike Commission Report*, p. 567.

52. *U.S. Strike Commission Report*, pp. xxxvii–xxxix; *Chicago Record*, October 20, 1897, p. 3.

53. *Op. cit.*, pp. 226–27.

54. *The Pullman Strike*, p. 47.

55. *Inter Ocean*, October 20, 1897, p. 2.

56. *The Last Will and Testament of George Pullman*, pp. 11–12 (reprint), Pullman Collection, Pullman Branch Library.

57. *Chicago Tribune*, October 20, 1897, p. 3.

58. *Ibid.*; William T. Stead, *If Christ Came to Chicago*, pp. 90, 113.

59. *Chicago Tribune*, October 20, 1897, p. 3.

60. Graham R. Taylor, *Satellite Cities*, p. 76, chap. iii being Jane Addams', "A Modern Lear."

61. *Ibid.*, pp. 72–73; *Pullman Journal*, November 3, 1894, p. 5.

62. George M. Pullman, *The Strike at Pullman*, pp. 1–2.

63. *U.S. Strike Commission Report*, pp. 529–30; *The Story of Pullman*, pp. 22–23 (a pamphlet distributed at the Pullman exhibit at the World's Columbian Exposition, Chicago, 1893).

64. Statement made by Mrs. Florence Pullman Lowden, eldest daughter of George Pullman, in an interview on September 29, 1934.

65. Thomas Grant, "Pullman and Its Lessons," *American Journal of Politics*, V (1894), 199.

66. Anonymous, "Sir Titus Salt," *Chamber's Journal*, LV (1878), 545–47.

67. Anonymous, "Saltaire and Its Founder," *Harper's Magazine*, XLIV (1872), 830–31, 833, 835.

68. *Ibid.*, pp. 831–35.

69. Anonymous, *Chamber's Journal*, p. 547; Charles Dickens, "A Yorkshire Colony," *All the Year Around*, XXV (1871), 186.

70. Dickens, *op. cit.*, pp. 186–87.

CHAPTER III

GROWTH OF THE MODEL TOWN

During the early part of 1880 the Pullman Company quietly purchased more than four thousand acres of prairie land, the bulk of which comprised a compact unit on the western shore of Lake Calumet, some twelve miles south of the business district of Chicago. As developments showed, the acquisition proved far in excess of any needs which the company ever experienced, not more than three hundred acres being required for the actual site of the model town. The purchase of such a vast area was partly in anticipation of needs which never materialized and partly for speculative purposes. In 1892 George Pullman estimated that this land, for which his company originally paid eight hundred thousand dollars, was then worth five million dollars.[1] As he perceived, the success of the experiment required that it be protected from objectionable surroundings, and this doubtless influenced him in the purchase of such a large acreage. On the most secluded portion the town was erected, being bounded on the east by a large expanse of water and in all other directions by a substantial belt of uninhabited Pullman property. In the surrounding country, not far distant, existed a few straggling settlements.

George Pullman was greatly impressed with the advantages of the Calumet site, among them being the fertility of the soil, the excellent nature of the topography, and the presence of vast clay deposits. Chicago was believed to be sufficiently far removed to permit the experiment to be conducted free of any "debasing" influences from that metropolis. Extremely important were the industrial and commercial factors. Chicago served as the transportation center of the Middle West, and virtually all railroads entering this city from the south and east passed through the Calumet region. No part of the Chicago area was more accessible to these lines than the district in which the model town was built.

The possibilities of water transportation, however, assumed exaggerated importance in the mind of George Pullman, who envisioned the day when the town would become a great inland port. He believed that Lake Calumet and the river into which it drained would be dredged and that boats from Lake Michigan would discharge ore and other cargoes at Pullman.[2] The extreme shallowness of Lake Calumet made dredging operations impracticable and caused the rosy predictions of George Pullman to become fantastic.

Solon Spencer Beman, a young New York architect, was the master-builder of the model town. Not until the late seventies did George Pullman become acquainted with him. Desirous at this time of establishing a beautiful residence at Elberon, New Jersey, Pullman engaged the services of Nathan F. Barrett, a noted landscape engineer, to lay out the grounds of his new estate. It was largely through the efforts of Barrett that his friend, Solon Beman, was induced to submit drawings for the proposed dwelling. George Pullman became impressed with the ability and personality of this young architect and later commissioned him to design the model town and serve as general supervisor of all construction work. Beman's primary interest was in architectural planning, and in that capacity he was of inestimable service to George Pullman. The task of landscaping the town was left largely to the discretion of Nathan Barrett.[3] Pullman not only employed numerous engineering and industrial experts but, because of his insatiate desire for fresh ideas, occasionally used the services of men who might be referred to as "educated idealists." Serving in an advisory capacity, they were as a rule retained only for a short time.[4]

Operations began in the spring of 1880. Thousands of laborers were employed, some of whom traveled daily from Chicago in special trains over the Illinois Central Railroad. A roughly constructed frame building called "Hotel de Grab" furnished meals. The approach of winter, which proved unusually severe in that year, slowed up construction; but progress was nevertheless quite rapid. Of first consideration were the shops, and work on them moved at maximum speed from the outset; but, simultaneously, excavations were made for sewer, water, and gas mains.[5] January, 1881, witnessed the moving into the town of the first permanent resident; April of that year saw the Pullman Car shops in operation; and the succeeding month beheld three hundred and fifty people housed in Pullman homes.[6] Gradually a town took shape, as public buildings, residences, paved streets, and parks were established; but not until 1884 was this undertaking brought to completion. From the prairie had risen a charming little city.

Although anxious to build a town of exemplary character, George Pullman was just as solicitous about making it pay substantial dividends. Construction costs were of primary importance, and materials were accordingly purchased in large quantities at the lowest figures. The Pullman Company hired its own workmen instead of contracting the building of the town and, in order to reduce expenses to the minimum, established its own carpentry shops and brickyards. Such products as sashes, doors, paneling, sills, and moldings were manufactured in wholesale fashion by Pullman employees. Slightly south of the town stood the brickyards, which employed a force of two hundred and fifty workman; and for manufacturing the millions of cream-colored bricks clay was dredged from the bottom of Lake Calumet. It was the low production cost of this material that proved a determining factor in building the city of brick.[7]

No problem was more uniquely solved than that of sewerage. The sanitary engineer had no difficulty in disposing of surface drainage, since it was merely a task of laying pipes that would insure a rapid gravity discharge of all surface water into Lake Calumet. In the disposal of sewage, however, a serious engineering obstacle arose because of the impracticability of using Lake Calumet as a receptacle, since it was shallow and drained only a small area. Sewage could have been pumped into Lake Michigan, but this would have necessitated the laying of six and one-half miles of pipes. Some form of land purification remained as the only alternative and, as this method was considered more expeditious, a sewage farm was established three miles south of the town.[8]

All sewage was carried by force of gravity into a large reservoir under the water tower, and from there it was immediately pumped to the model farm for distribution. The size of the farm grew as needs required, and by 1885 it approximated one hundred and seventy-five acres. All land was carefully underdrained with three- and four-inch farm tile laid in rows; and hydrants were conveniently located for the distribution of the sewage by means of hose. Organic matter was absorbed by the soil and growing vegetation, and the water was carried off through the drains to Lake Calumet. In dry seasons sewage was used more freely on growing crops than during wet periods, but ordinarily an acre of tiled land could dispose of sewage from one hundred people. In order to facilitate the rapid disposal of all sewage, whether in winter or in summer, fifteen filter beds surrounded by dirt walls and closely underlain with tile were created to care for sewage that could not be distributed in the regular way.[9]

In spite of the fact that many people questioned at the outset the practicability of the sewage farm, results justified the faith which George Pullman placed in it. The cost of the entire system of sewage disposal amounted to three hundred thousand dollars;[10] but, whatever portion of this sum may have been spent for the farm, the investment proved judicious. By 1882 the farm was self-supporting, and the following year it yielded 8 per cent on the investment.[11] Almost any crop could be produced on the irrigated, well-fertilized soil. Employing as many as fifty men, the sewage farm sold large quantities of vegetables not only in Pullman but also in Chicago.[12]

The problem of supplying the town with water occasioned some difficulty. During the first year or so the people were obliged to draw their drinking water from wells, because the water pumped into the homes from Lake Calumet was impure and scarcely suitable even for laundry purposes. In the fall of 1882, after considerable delay, the Pullman Company made arrangements with the village of Hyde Park for an adequate supply of good water which was drawn from Lake Michigan and pumped from the town of Hyde Park to Pullman, a distance of six miles. Fire hydrants were distributed throughout the town, but the company did not deem it essential to instal public drinking fountains. About the only use that water from Lake Calumet continued to serve was for industrial purposes. One of the most imposing structures in Pullman was the water tower; but its function in the distribution of water did not long remain of primary importance. Pressure from Hyde Park proved sufficient for ordinary household purposes, and the large reservoir of water in the tower served only in emergency.[13]

Because of the restless activity of George Pullman, his company embraced many fields of endeavor. On the shore of Lake Calumet was erected a plant for the generation of water gas, to be used in illuminating the shops, streets, and homes and for cooking purposes in the better dwellings.[14] Icehouses were built, and the men who labored during the summer in the brickyards worked in winter at the task of harvesting ice from Lake Calumet.[15] The need for lumber, primarily for shop purposes, necessitated the creation of a large lumber yard and immense kilns for drying lumber. Steam was piped from the boilers of the shops to heat the better homes and all public buildings. In proximity to the sewage farm the Pullman Company established a dairy farm, which was expanded as needs required. In 1890 there were 100 cows on the 420-acre farm, from which milk, butter, and cream were supplied to the inhabitants of Pullman. Like the model farm, it also proved a paying investment.[16]

In the construction of the streets, beauty and durability were combined. All thoroughfares, including the alleys, were macadamized, and the gutters were laid with cobblestones. The sidewalks were constructed mostly of heavy planks, although brick, gravel, and stone flagging were sometimes used. Stretching from the sidewalks to the homes, a distance of twenty feet or more, the ground was heavily sodded and usually terraced. The streets were spacious enough for all purposes, but this did not keep the front yards from presenting a somewhat cramped appearance.

Pullman had a predilection for inventors, as evidenced by the names given to the streets of the town; and among those honored in such fashion were Watt, Fulton, Stephenson, Morse, Whitney, Bessemer, and Ericson. The streets for the most part were laid out in monotonous regularity, crossing one another at right angles; but occasionally the architect had ingeniously set public buildings across streets in such manner as to break the regular line without inconveniencing traffic. An abundance of trees, mostly white elm, maple, and linden, bordered the streets and adorned the parks; and, in order to maintain a steady and inexpensive supply of shrubs and saplings, six acres of land on the shore of Lake Calumet were appropriated by the company for a nursery and greenhouses.[17]

With few exceptions the factories established in Pullman were carshops or subsidiary industries. The one absorbing the overwhelming proportion of laborers was the Pullman works, which covered an area of fifteen acres and comprised four mammoth brick buildings, each three stories in height. The remaining industries served an auxiliary purpose, being organized under the supervision or encouragement of George Pullman and in many cases controlled by the same group of stockholders that owned the Pullman Corporation. Among these enterprises were the paint factory, foundry, car-wheel works, screw factory, laundry, glass industry, and terra-cotta lumber plant. One of the few independently operated industries was the knitting mill. The industrial buildings, all owned by the Pullman Company, were designed as a harmonious part of the model town and were localized in either the northern or the extreme southern portion of Pullman.[18]

The most favorable view of Pullman could be obtained from the Illinois Central Railroad, which skirted the western edge of the town, and travelers entering or leaving Chicago by this road enjoyed an urban scene of beauty, with parks, public buildings, and homes spread out in panoramic fashion. Florence Boulevard, the most attractive and important thoroughfare in Pullman, separated the Pullman works from the major portion of the town. Just north of this boulevard and near the tracks was Lake Vista, back of which stretched the stately administration building of the Pullman shops; while to the south of this main thoroughfare and not far distant from the railroad were located the Illinois Central depot, the Florence Hotel, Arcade, livery stables, Casino, Pullman School, Green Stone Church, and Market Square. All were laid out with a view to symmetry and beauty. The architect showed foresight in building most of the imposing homes along

Florence Boulevard and on property facing Arcade Park—where they would be shown off to the greatest advantage. The loveliness of Pullman thus tended to be concentrated within a certain area, although the entire community presented a pleasing appearance.

Florence Hotel was fashioned in Queen Anne-style architecture and, like most of the public buildings, was constructed of brick, trimmed in light stone, and roofed with slate. Rising to a height of four stories, the hotel contained seventy rooms, including a large dining hall. The architect finished the first floor in cherry, decorated the entire building elaborately, and along the front and sides designed a roomy veranda measuring over two hundred and fifty feet in length.[19]

The most expensive and impressive of all public buildings was the Arcade, which housed most of the stores and all the offices in Pullman and which represented an investment to the company of three hundred and eighteen thousand dollars. Surrounded by paved streets and a spacious walk of stone flagging, it was easily accessible. Running lengthwise through the central portion of the structure was a wide passage, over which stretched a roof of glass. The first floor accommodated a restaurant, numerous merchandise stores, the Pullman Post Office, and the Pullman Loan and Savings Bank; and on the floor above were the theater, public library, barbershops, halls for civic and religious organizations, and offices for doctors, dentists, and town officials. Lodgerooms occupied the third floor.[20]

George Pullman favored an atmosphere of sumptuousness and grandeur for the theater and library. The latter, consisting of five rooms, was richly decorated and furnished with Wilton carpets and comfortable plush-covered chairs. Suspended from the ceiling were large gas chandeliers. In the main reading-room massive ornamental pillars supported the roof and stained-glass dome; and open, mahogany bookcases displayed the volumes of the library.[21] In the theater luxury was even more in evidence, and no expense was spared in making it one of the most attractive in the Middle West. Hughson Hawley, who painted scenery for the Madison Square Theater of New York City, was engaged to decorate the auditorium, design the drop curtain, and paint the

MAIN ADMINISTRATION BUILDING, HOTEL FLORENCE, THE ARCADE, LAKE VISTA

scenery sets. The auditorium was done in oriental style, and on each side were five boxes designed in Moresque fashion. The ceiling was frescoed with graceful figures, and in every detail there was said to be complete harmony in tone and color, the hues changing gradually from rich red and purple near the floor to delicate blue and olive in the dome. One thousand seats were installed, all upholstered in dark-red leather. From the central dome hung a huge bronze chandelier; but more striking was the drop curtain which portrayed an oriental scene on the shores of the Bosphorous. The stage was equipped with trap doors and all the then modern appliances.[22] In the opinion of the *Chicago Times* this theater rivaled "the most elegant theaters in the country in point of architectural beauty and artistic design."[23]

The only religious edifice in the model town was the Green Stone Church which, unlike other Pullman structures, was built of green serpentine rock quarried in New England. Gothic in style, the church was graced with a lofty steeple that sheltered a chime of bells. Built as an integral part of the edifice was the parsonage—which always rented as a separate unit. The auditorium was finished in highly polished oak and decorated artistically in neutral tints, the ceiling representing the firmament. Although intended to meet the religious needs of all Pullman inhabitants, the church had a seating capacity for only six hundred people.[24]

Tastefully but not so elaborately constructed were the other public buildings. In the midst of a spacious playground stood the Pullman School—a three-story structure which was abundantly lighted and, for its time, modern in every way. In complete harmony with the architectural pattern of the town was the Pullman stable, which housed the fire department and all horses in Pullman. The Casino was used partly as a repair-shop for the town but served also for social and religious purposes.[25] In the attempt to vary the monotonous regularity of streets, the architect laid out the Market Place at a street intersection and constructed the four corner dwellings of the Market Circle with an open arcade over the sidewalks. Supported by stone columns, the second story in each quarter projected over the circular sidewalk.

In the center of the Market Place was erected the Market House, where the meat and vegetable shops of Pullman were concentrated. On the second floor was a large hall designed for social gatherings.[26]

In the establishment of the town the greatest undertaking was obviously the homes, the construction of which the company carried on over a period of several years. In 1885 there were fourteen hundred tenements, while nine years later the number touched eighteen hundred; and all the dwellings, with the exception of sixty frame houses at the brickyards, were erected of brick with stone trimmings and roofed with slate. In order to economize, the company built the houses in blocks of two or more, except for a dozen of the very best dwellings, that stood detached.[27] In spite of the methods employed to diversify the skyline with various-shaped roofs, the architecture tended to become monotonous; but this uniformity was relieved somewhat by the beauty of trees and shrubbery and by the construction of the finest homes where they would contribute most to the appearance of the community.

Wide divergence existed in the character of Pullman homes. The brickyard dwellings, which George Pullman denied were a part of the town, consisted of small shanties without modern sewage facilities or other conveniences. In the most eastern part of Pullman, on Fulton Street, were located the great tenement blocks with a total of ten large buildings. Three stories tall and containing flats of two to four rooms, these buildings each accommodated from twelve to forty-eight families. Although modern, some of the facilities in these tenements were restricted: only one water faucet for each group of five families, and the same toilet for two or more families.[28] In sharp contrast to the Fulton Street flats were the spacious nine-room cottages in the vicinity of the Florence Hotel. Designed for highly salaried Pullman officials, they were steam heated and equipped with a large fireplace, a bathroom, numerous closets, a laundry, and large bay windows. The rooms were commodious and artistically decorated.[29]

In an era when comparatively little attention was paid to housing, George Pullman constructed decent homes; and, although the size and rental of these dwellings varied greatly, there were certain characteristics common to all. The brick houses had roomy, well-ventilated basements. Furnished with gas, water, and excellent sewage facilities and designed so as to have an abundance of fresh air and sunlight, these homes were clean and livable.[30] A typical cottage consisted of a two-story structure of five rooms furnished with a sink, water tap, toilet facilities, and ample closet and pantry space—the total cost of which was seventeen hundred dollars, including a charge of three hundred dollars for the lot. The company sodded the front lawn, inclosed the back yard with a high fence, and, toward the rear near the macadamized alley, built a coal-and-wood shed. No barns were permitted on any of the premises, the livery stables being deemed the proper place for horses.[31] Neat and attractive were the Pullman homes, giving the model town the appearance of a snug village inhabited by a contented people.

The beauty of Pullman was in large measure due to her parks and playgrounds, the most charming of which were Lake Vista and Arcade Park. Although the *Arcade Journal* declared in a burst of enthusiasm that the whole town was in reality a park, only thirty acres were actually devoted to park purposes.[32] Lake Vista, surrounded by green turf, flowers, and shrubbery, was considered one of the most scenic views in Pullman. In the creation of this miniature lake, which covered three acres, beauty and utility were combined: for in excavating the lake the dirt was used to raise the site of the carshops; and in supplying water for the lake the company utilized the overflow of the great Corliss engine which furnished power for the Pullman shops. At one end of the lake the architect designed an "ornamental rookery of granite," over which tumbled daily three hundred thousand gallons of water. Just south of Florence Hotel stretched Arcade Park, in the center of which stood a stone concert platform; and, although this garden spot was not very large, it contributed much to the picturesqueness of the town.[33]

Athletics and physical recreation were restricted to two parks: the Playground and Athletic Island, both of which played a vital part in the lives of the inhabitants. Comprising a ten-acre tract on the shore of Lake Calumet, the Playground was underdrained, sodded, and especially prepared for athletic games. More unique was the Athletic Island—a five-acre tract in Lake Calumet which was accessible to the mainland by means of a bridge. Such facilities as a grandstand, boathouses, and a small racecourse were established there. In building up the island out of clay from the bottom of the lake, the dredging machine created an excellent channel which served as a watercourse for boat-racing and ice-skating.[34]

When completed, the town cost eight million dollars.[35] This disbursement was not spent as most capitalists would have favored; they would have erected homes unrelieved by beauty and designed to meet the barest needs of industry. The uniqueness of Pullman elicited numerous comments; but on one point there was general agreement—that the physical features of the town were highly praiseworthy. One visitor to Pullman pictured his impression in the following vein: "I stepped from the cars. Beauty, grace and art met me on every hand. I had seen landscape gardening elsewhere. Here was also architectural gardening. Eye and taste were at once content and glad."[36] The *Inter Ocean* reflected the sentiment of many newspapers in 1885, when it described the model town with zestful appreciation: "It is famous already as one of the wonders of the west. Splendid provision has been made for the present comfort of its eight thousand residents, its four thousand workmen. . . . . More completely and on a larger scale than was probably ever before attempted, there is seen here a sympathetic blending of the useful and beautiful."[37]

In 1896 the town of Pullman was honored by the jury of the second International Hygienic and Pharmaceutical Exposition held at Prague, Bohemia. After weighing the merits of various outstanding towns, the committee adjudged Pullman to be the most perfect in the world and awarded to George Pullman two magnificent medals and a gorgeous diploma. The committee agreed that in the matter of homes, sanitation, water system, shops, public halls, churches, and parks the town of Pullman was without a peer.[38]

Health conditions were so excellent in Pullman that few communities could boast of a smaller death rate or show a better rec-

ARCADE PARK, GREEN STONE CHURCH

ord in the matter of epidemics. Although the town was highly industrialized, the average death rate from 1881 to 1895 ranged from 7 to 15 per thousand, as contrasted with a much higher rate for American cities, which in 1894 averaged 22.5 per thousand.[39] A report to the state of Illinois in 1885 disclosed that in the history of the town there had been no cases of cholera, no yellow fever or typhoid, only two cases of smallpox, and a few of diphtheria and scarlatina. Proportionately fewer physicians were needed in Pullman than elsewhere, there being in 1890 only six in the town, or 1 to every seventeen hundred and fifty inhabitants, as compared with an average throughout the nation of 1 to every five hundred people.[40]

The sanitary and aesthetic characteristics were by no means the only distinctive features of the model town; as special effort was made to balance manual toil with adequate recreational and educational opportunities. George Pullman was doubtless convinced that the contentment of laborers depended largely upon the profitable utilization of their leisure hours. A survey of the social aspects of the town leads to the conclusion that nothing was left undone to create what was conceived to be an ideal environment.

Every precaution was taken to eliminate all debasing influences. Saloons and brothels were strictly prohibited. The small bar permitted at the Florence Hotel was for guests only, and, by charging exorbitant prices, it effectively excluded all laborers. As far as can be determined, the prying eyes of the Pullman Company prevented prostitution from taking root in the model town; but, as guardian of the people's morals, there were certain matters over which the company had little control. Beer wagons, licensed by the village of Hyde Park, made frequent deliveries in Pullman; and in the near-by communities saloons were abundant. In spite of George Pullman's efforts, there was considerable drinking among the laborers, although little drunkenness;[41] but, in general, moral conditions were very satisfactory.

The Pullman Company deemed the environment of the town so wholesome that in 1893 it announced a superior type of laborer was being evolved in Pullman. Effusively the company averred:

During the eleven years the town has been in existence, the Pullman workingman has developed into a distinctive type—distinct in appearance, in tidiness of dress, in fact in all the external indications of self-respect. . . . . It is within the mark to say that a representative gathering of Pullman workmen would be quite forty per cent better in evidence of thrift and refinement and in all the outward indications of a wholesome habit of life, than would be a representative gathering of any corresponding group of workingmen which would be assembled elsewhere in the country.[42]

Exaggerated as this picture may have been, it cannot be denied that the environment had a salutary effect upon the laborer. In terms of thrift this was unquestionably true. Savings in the Pullman Bank increased from $84,000 to $600,000 during the ten years ending in 1893; and in July of that year there were over 2,200 deposits in the bank, each averaging $271.[43] By 1894 no less than 560 employees owned their homes in near-by communities.[44]

A large proportion of the people were foreign born—totaling 51 per cent in 1884 and increasing to 72 per cent by 1892. In that year the Scandinavian nationality constituted 23 per cent of the population, the British and German each 12 per cent, the Dutch 10 per cent, and the Irish 5 per cent.[45] The presence of a large foreign element was emphasized by the thousands of international money orders issued annually to Pullman workers. Large numbers of the inhabitants were unnaturalized. In 1887 there were eight hundred British subjects who had made no attempt to become American citizens[46]—a situation which explains why the number of Pullman voters in 1884 did not exceed twelve hundred in a population of eighty-five hundred.[47] There is no evidence, however, that the history of the experiment would have been materially different, even if all the inhabitants had been American-born or naturalized citizens.

The schools of Pullman accommodated a maximum of thirteen hundred students in 1888 and thereafter experienced a slowly declining enrolment. Every child was assured of an eighth-grade education, the only condition for admission being vaccination for smallpox. The school term consisted of two hundred days, which for the period was exceptionally long. A free kindergarten was opened in the Arcade to all children between the ages of four and six, and one session was held each day throughout the regular school term. It was the intention of the school board as early as 1884 to provide high-school studies whenever the demand arose, and eventually this program was realized in the evening school. Originally designed to teach elementary subjects, the school enlarged its curriculum in 1891 to include such courses as mechanical drawing, bookkeeping, and stenography.[48] The standards maintained by the Pullman schools can be gauged largely by the fact that the school-tax rate in the town was higher than in any of the other fourteen school districts in the village of Hyde Park.[49]

Adult education was fostered by the Pullman Library, which was dedicated with elaborate exercises in the spring of 1883. A special train was chartered to take a large number of prominent Chicago people to Pullman for the ceremony in the Arcade Theatre, where announcement was made of George Pullman's munificent gift of five thousand volumes to the library. Professor David Swing delivered the dedicatory address, which proved to be little more than a eulogistic characterization of the model town.[50] The library, however, was not without merit. Extreme care was exercised in the selection of books, with the result that the collection showed an excellent balance in the fields of biography, travel, history, poetry, art, religion, and science. From time to time additions were made to the original collection, swelling the total in 1895 to eighty-five hundred volumes. Among the seventy journals, magazines, and reviews subscribed to were many of the very best. The maintenance cost of the library was born by the Pullman Company; but periodicals and new books were purchased largely with library fees and the proceeds from benefit entertainments.[51]

A very useful function rendered by the library was in organizing study groups in history, drawing, art study, and art needlework. University extension courses were similarly sponsored for the study of science, philosophy, literature, and history—a course usually comprising a series of lectures delivered by a visiting professor.[52]

An important educational force was the *Arcade Journal*, issued from November, 1889, to April, 1892, and its successor, the *Pullman Journal*, published until 1898. Both were semiofficial organs of the Pullman Company issued weekly under the editorship of Duane Doty. The *Arcade Journal*, which circulated two thousand copies, had no subscription charge; but, shortly after the publication was renamed the *Pullman Journal*, it was improved upon, enlarged, and sold for two cents per copy or one dollar per year. Ably edited, the paper revealed a wide and varied interest in scientific and literary matters.

In surveying the religious situation of the model town new light is shed on the experiment. George Pullman had some definite ideas on the function and need for churches, but here as elsewhere his expectations were eventually shattered by reality. Provision existed for only one religious edifice, the Green Stone Church, which architecturally was the most beautiful structure in the community. Largely because of his determination to make this church adequate to the needs of all religious denominations, George Pullman stubbornly refused to permit the construction of any other church building in the town. Being a Universalist and hence rather tolerant on the subject of religious dogma, he looked upon the creation of a union church as an excellent move, designed to insure the payment of an extraordinarily heavy rental on the Green Stone edifice.[53]

George Pullman was reported to have said once that "when the [Green Stone] church was built it was not intended so much for the moral and spiritual welfare of the people as it was for the completion of the artistic effect of the scene."[54] After a careful survey of the model town in 1885, Professor Richard Ely declared there was a prevailing feeling among the men at Pullman that ". . . . the company cares nothing for our souls. They only want to get as much work as possible out of our bodies."[55] The *Chicago Herald* commented in 1885 on this very situation:

> Pullman has a church just as it has a market house. Both lend architectural variety to a pleasing prospect of brick. Formerly the church was the recipient of tithes. But at Pullman the tithes go to the company from the church on identically the same principles that the tenant of the Market pays for the use of the same. Religion is nothing to a corporation created for gain, except as a means of money getting. There is no waste at Pullman, even of sentiment. All is grist that comes to the mill. There are, it is said, eight thousand souls in

Pullman and for the gathering in and instruction of these in divine revelation just one church edifice is available, and that for the particular sect which has fiscal responsibility sufficient to assume payment of the rent.[56]

In the spring of 1881 the union church was organized, and meetings were held in the administration building of the car-shops. It was believed that the church could be held together through the ministry of liberal-minded clergymen, and Chicago pastors were invited to fill the pulpit for a short time, but dissension between various religious groups soon doomed the attempt to failure.[57] When John Waldron, a priest, sought permission in 1882 to purchase a site in the town for a Catholic church, George Pullman flatly refused, on the ground that it would be better for the various denominations to join together and rent the Green Stone Church.[58] How long Pullman persisted in his futile hopes cannot be ascertained, but his policy toward the churches was continued with slight change to the end of the experiment.

During the latter part of 1882 the Green Stone Church was completed and dedicated by Dr. James M. Pullman, a Universalist minister and a brother of George Pullman.[59] The annual rental of thirty-six hundred dollars for the church was so excessive that not until 1885, after the building had stood idle for several years and the rent had been reduced by two-thirds, did the Presbyterians lease it. For many years the parsonage, renting for sixty-five dollars monthly, remained vacant. With a membership of only two hundred people, mostly laborers, the Presbyterian sect soon discovered that the annual rental of twelve hundred dollars, together with the charges for steam heat and gas, proved unduly burdensome. Faced by a deficit of more than one thousand dollars in January, 1886, this denomination was compelled temporarily to give up the Green Stone Church and return for worship to the Market Hall, where services had originally been held. The debt was eventually liquidated with the aid of the presbytery, but not without the situation's evoking bitter criticism.[60] In discussing the matter before the presbytery, one of the ministers expressed himself rather sharply:

I preached once in the Pullman church, but by the help of God I will never preach there again. The word monopoly seems to be written in black letters over the pulpit and pews. It blazes forth from every window and seems to burn between the lines of the hymn book. I thought the organ groaned, "monopoly, monopoly" in all its lower tones.[61]

In 1893 there were at least fifteen religious denominations in Pullman, the largest of which were Catholic, Lutheran, Episcopalian, Methodist, and Presbyterian. Only ten of the religious groups were sufficiently strong to have ministers, but virtually all of them had to struggle for existence, and many were able to survive only with outside help. The congregations were predominantly laborers whose earnings were not large; but more significant, perhaps, was the rental policy of the Pullman Company. Prohibited from building in the town, the various denominations were compelled to worship in the Casino, Market Hall, Rock Island Depot, and various rooms in the Arcade, often stuffy and too small;[62] and the rent charged for such quarters was considered by many as oppressive. The Methodist Episcopal Church, for instance, conducted services in a large room of the Casino and was obliged to pay five hundred dollars annually for rent.[63] Whether because of the rental policy or because of some other factor, the tenure of most ministers at Pullman was short.

The unwillingness of George Pullman to alienate any land in the town for church sites was deeply resented. Refusing to worship in the town under existing conditions, the Catholics in 1882 erected a building outside the Pullman domain. In 1886 George Pullman receded somewhat from his earlier position and agreed to the construction of a Catholic church on Pullman land outside the town, and in 1892 accorded the same privileges to the Swedish Lutherans; but in both cases the leases for the sites were to expire in ninety-nine years.[64]

Shortly after the new foundation was laid for the Catholic edifice, a dispute arose over the terms of the lease, and the controversy degenerated into a personal feud between John Waldron, a zealous and popular priest, and George Pullman, who desired his removal from the parish. Out of the pulpit Waldron worked among his parishioners to the detriment of his enemy. The accusation that Pullman put "unscrupulous detectives" on the trail of the priest in order to ruin him is susceptible of serious doubt. So unbearable, however, did the situation become that Waldron finally resigned his pastorate rather than embarrass Archbishop Feeham; and in his last sermon, on January 21, 1887, the priest hurled anathemas at George Pullman and characterized him as a "capitalistic czar; a man who ruled, crushed and oppressed by the force of money."[65]

The need for a broad recreational program was not overlooked by those who helped shape the destiny of the model town. A large variety of social organizations and many different types of entertainment and sports were developed to meet a wide range of human interests.

The Arcade Theatre, which for many years delighted the theatergoing element in Pullman, was dedicated in January, 1883, and invitations for the occasion were sent to three hundred of George Pullman's social friends. Attired in full dress, they were conveyed from Chicago to the model town in new Pullman coaches and escorted from the train to the theater by a band. Among those assigned seats of honor on the stage were George Pullman, General P. H. Sheridan, Judge Lyman Trumbull, Marshall Field, John Crerar, and Professor David Swing.[66] While the ceremony was characterized by ostentation, it revealed the pride which George Pullman took in the new theater. Numerous plays and concerts were featured during a theatrical season which ordinarily opened in September and continued until June. Only high-quality plays were permitted, and during the history of the theater some of the best talent in the theatrical world performed there. Some of the entertainment was furnished by local organizations, such as the dramatic club and the Pullman minstrels.[67]

One of the most accomplished organizations was the Pullman Military Band, which attained a membership of eighty musicians, all recruited from the Pullman shops. Successful and popular, the band was seldom faced with financial stringency. Supported principally by the proceeds from musical entertainments given in the Arcade Theatre, the organization was able to present free weekly concerts in the Arcade Park during the summer months.[68] In 1890 the band won the Illinois state championship,[69] and a few years later took an extended tour through the South. While in Atlanta it was reviewed by the governors of Illinois and Georgia and proclaimed as "one of the completest military bands on the American Continent."[70]

The extent to which social life was emphasized is evident by the fact that in 1893 there were at least forty lodges, clubs and other social organizations in Pullman.[71] Ranking high among the social events of the year was the Annual Employees' Picnic held on Labor Day. In 1891 at least two thousand people attended, three trains being required to carry them to Pleasant Valley, Cedar Lake, where boating, yachting, dancing, and athletic games were enjoyed.[72]

In the field of athletics the model town was outstanding. Sports were fostered by the Pullman Athletic Association—an organization capitalized at ten thousand dollars and controlled by a board of directors who were predominantly Pullman officials. Utilizing the Athletic Island and Playground, the association promoted regattas, cycling contests, track meets, cricket matches, baseball games, and other types of physical competition. Each Memorial Day was the occasion for the Spring Games, in which all manner of track and field contests were held, the most spectacular event being the annual road race. Upward of four hundred cyclists participated for prizes totaling three thousand dollars, and as many as fifteen thousand spectators witnessed the finish of this race, which was run over a sixteen-mile course, stretching from the Leland Hotel in Chicago to Pullman.[73] The regattas on Lake Calumet were frequently of national importance, and some of the most famous scullers in the United States participated in races at which purses ranged as high as six thousand dollars.[74] During the winter months indoor athletic contests were held in the Market Hall, featuring wrestling, jumping, contortion acts, sword exercises, boxing, tug-of-war, and Indian-club swinging.[75]

With its many unique and attractive features, the town of Pullman became a source of interest to people from all over the world. Thousands of distinguished individuals inspected the town out of curiosity; but some scrutinized it for engineering reasons, and others examined it for a solution to industrial problems. Capitalists in particular were welcomed to Pullman; and in 1891 the town played host to a distinguished group of them, including Cornelius Vanderbilt and Chauncey M. Depew.[76] During the Columbian Exposition in Chicago in 1893 the model town was overrun by visitors, at least ten thousand of whom were foreigners.[77] Professors and students from universities were among those who journeyed to Pullman to examine its characteristics. The pride which George Pullman took in the model town was reflected in the hospitality shown to visitors. Groups of people whom he invited were often conveyed in his parlor car from Chicago to the town and, upon arriving, would be greeted at the station by Duane Doty and other high officials, and together they would make a tour of inspection. Doty, a charming conversationalist as well as a statistician, was ordinarily chief spokesman, and to his care all important groups were committed in the absence of George Pullman.[78] Pictured in rosy terms by this versatile individual, the experiment impressed many visitors as the beginning of a new era in industrialism.

The widespread interest in the Pullman experiment might suggest that it became a pattern for numerous other industrial communities; but few, if any, capitalists attempted to duplicate it, although many studied it carefully. Certain features may have been incorporated in other manufacturing towns; but the experiment, as it was created and operated, never was inaugurated elsewhere. Any false hopes capitalists may have entertained as to the success of the model town were dispelled by the Pullman Strike. Thereafter, the supporters of the town were placed on the defensive; and idealists no longer spoke of it as having a revolutionary effect on factory communities.

NOTES

1. *U.S. Strike Commission Report*, p. 529; *Pullman Journal*, January 7, 1893, p. 3.

2. *Pullman Journal*, January 7, 1893, p. 3; McLean, *op. cit.*, pp. 223 and 229.

3. Irving Pond, "Pullman—America's First Planned Independent Town," *Illinois Society of Architect's Monthly Bulletin*, June–July, 1934, pp. 6–8. Pond served as draughtsman for Beman in the building of the town.

4. McLean, *op. cit.*, pp. 232–33.

5. A. T. Andreas, *History of Cook County, Illinois*, p. 611.

6. *Chicago Tribune*, August 14, 1882, p. 6; Pond, *op. cit.*, p. 7.

7. Andreas, *op. cit.*, p. 611; Anonymous, "The Arcadian City of Pullman," *Agricultural Review*, III (1883), 86.

8. Oscar C. De Wolf, *Pullman from a State Medicine Point of View*, pp. 8, 11–12 (reprinted from the *American Public Health Association Proceedings*, IX [1884], 290 ff.

9. Carroll D. Wright *et al.*, "An Attractive Industrial Experiment," *Massachusetts Labor Report* (1885), Part I, pp. 4–6; Mrs. Duane Doty, *The Town of Pullman*, pp. 165–67.

10. Richard T. Ely, "Pullman: A Social Study," *Harper's Monthly*, LXX (1885), 462.

11. *Chicago Times*, August 6, 1882, p. 6, and April 25, 1885, p. 8.

12. De Wolf, *op. cit.*, p. 12.

13. "Report to the State of Illinois on the Status of the Town of Pullman, 1885," Pullman Collection, Pullman Branch Library, pp. 6–7; *Chicago Times*, September 16, 1882, p. 6.

14. *Chicago Tribune*, August 14, 1882, p. 6; undated newspaper clipping (approximate date, February, 1891), Pullman Collection, Pullman Branch Library.

15. Ely, *op. cit.*, p. 455; *Pullman Journal*, February 1, 1896, p. 13.

16. *Arcade Journal*, December 7, 1889, p. 5, and October 11, 1890, p. 1; Mrs. Doty, *op. cit.*, pp. 162–63.

17. "Report to the State of Illinois," pp. 10–11; undated newspaper clipping, "Pullman—Its Streets and Pavements" (approximate date, December, 1890), Pullman Collection, Pullman Branch Library.

18. De Wolf, *op. cit.*, p. 6; Mrs. Doty, *op. cit.*, pp. 20, 52, 87, 111–12.

19. Mrs. Doty, *op. cit.*, pp. 108–9; Ely, *op. cit.*, p. 459.

20. Ely, *op. cit.*, p. 458; Mrs. Doty, *op. cit.*, pp. 8–10; Duane Doty, "The Arcade at Pullman" (1883), p. 1, Pullman Collection, John Crerar Library.

21. Ely, *op. cit.*, pp. 458–59; Bertha S. Ludlum, "History of the Pullman Library," p. 2, Pullman Collection, Pullman Branch Library.

22. Duane Doty, "The Arcade Theatre" (1883), pp. 1, 9–11, Pullman Collection, John Crerar Library; Mrs. Doty, *op. cit.*, pp. 14–15.

23. August 6, 1882, p. 5.

24. Mrs. Doty, *op. cit.*, pp. 48–49; De Wolf, *op. cit.*, p. 7; Andreas, *op. cit.*, pp. 611–12.

25. Andreas, *op. cit.*, p. 620; "Report to the State of Illinois," p. 44; Mrs. Doty, *op. cit.*, p. 33.

26. Duane Doty, "The Market of Pullman" (1883), pp. 1–3, Pullman Collection, John Crerar Library; Ely, *op. cit.*, p. 458.

27. *U.S. Strike Commission Report*, p. 507; "Report to the State of Illinois," p. 13.

28. Duane Doty, "Homes of Operatives" (approximate date of newspaper clipping, 1891), Pullman Collection, Pullman Branch Library.

29. *Pullman Journal*, November 5, 1892, p. 1.

30. "Report to the State of Illinois," pp. 13–14.

31. Ely, *op. cit.*, pp. 458 and 461; Duane Doty, "Homes of Operatives."

32. *Arcade Journal*, June 14, 1890, p. 1.

33. *Ibid.*, December 7, 1889, p. 5; De Wolf, *op. cit.*, p. 6.

34. Mrs. Doty, *op. cit.*, pp. 109–10; *Arcade Journal*, June 14, 1890, p. 1, and June 6, 1891, p. 1; Andreas, *op. cit.*, p. 621.

35. Ely, *op. cit.*, p. 461.

36. *The Pride of Pullman*, p. 3 (reprint of an article from the *Inter Ocean*, January 10, 1893).

37. January 17, 1885, p. 12.

38. *Pullman Journal*, February 6, 1897, p. 5, and June 19, 1897, p. 5.

39. Eaton, *Today*, II, 4; De Wolf, *op. cit.*, p. 12.

40. "Report to the State of Illinois," p. 29; *U.S. Strike Commission Report*, p. 489.

41. *U.S. Strike Commission Report*, pp. 431, 463, 483; "Report to the State of Illinois," pp. 24–25.

42. *The Story of Pullman*, pp. 23–24.

43. *Pullman Journal*, October 20, 1894, p. 8.

44. Pullman, *op. cit.*, p. 21.

45. *Pullman Journal*, February 25, 1893, p. 4, and November 9, 1895, p. 4; Wright *et al.*, *op. cit.*, p. 9.

46. *Chicago Herald*, October 7, 1887, p. 3.

47. Wright *et al*, *op. cit.*, p. 10.

48. Andreas, *op. cit.*, pp. 620–21; *Arcade Journal*, August 30, 1890, p. 1; *Pullman Journal*, October 19, 1895, p. 4; Mrs. Doty, *op. cit.*, p. 70.

49. *Annual Report of the President and Village Officers of the Village of Hyde Park* (1886), p. 45.

50. *Inter Ocean*, April 12, 1883, p. 5.

51. *Pullman Journal*, August 10, 1895, p. 4; Ely, *op. cit.*, p. 458; Ludlum, *op. cit.*, p. 3.

52. Ludlum, *loc. cit.; Arcade Journal*, September 26, 1891, p. 1; *Pullman Journal*, October 8, 1892, p. 4.

53. John Waldron, "History of the Parish of the Holy Rosary Church" (1883), p. 1, archives of the church, Roseland, Chicago; Carwardine, *op. cit.*, p. 20.

54. Carwardine, *loc. cit.*

55. *Op. cit.*, p. 464.

56. February 4, 1885, p. 2.

57. Mrs. Doty, *op. cit.*, pp. 46–47; *Pullman Journal*, December 28, 1895, p. 4.

58. Waldron, *op. cit.*, p. 1.

59. McLean, *op. cit.*, pp. 235–36.

60. *Chicago Herald*, January 13, 1886, p. 2, and February 5, 1886, p. 2.

61. *Ibid.*, January 13, 1886, p. 2.

62. *Ibid.*, February 7, 1886, p. 2; Wright *et al.*, *op. cit.*, p. 10; Mrs. Doty, *op. cit.*, pp. 46–47; Andreas, *op. cit.*, p. 612.

63. Carwardine, *op. cit.*, p. 22.

64. *Ibid.*, p. 608; Waldron, *op. cit.*, p. 1; *U.S. Strike Commission Report*, p. 451; *Pullman Journal*, May 20, 1893, p. 8.

65. *Chicago Daily News*, February 11, 1887, p. 1; *Chicago Herald*, February 12, 1887, p. 8.

66. *The Pride of Pullman*, pp. 1–6; *Chicago Tribune*, January 10, 1883, p. 6.

67. *Arcade Journal*, December 17, 1889, p. 4; *Pullman Journal*, March 25, 1893, p. 9, and February 9, 1895, p. 8; McLean, *op. cit.*, p. 243.

68. McLean, *op. cit.*, p. 249; *Arcade Journal*, December 28, 1889, p. 5, and December 13, 1890, p. 1.

69. *Arcade Journal*, October 4, 1890, p. 5.

70. *Pullman Journal*, November 23, 1895, p. 5.

71. Mrs. Doty, *op. cit.*, p. 161; *Hyde Park Directory* (1887), pp. 44, 49.

72. *Arcade Journal*, September 12, 1891, p. 1.

73. Andreas, *op. cit.*, p. 621; *Chicago Times*, January 30, 1883, p. 6; Mrs. Doty, *op. cit.*, pp. 25, 109–10; *Pullman Journal*, May 6, 1893, p. 9.

74. *Inter Ocean*, June 23, 1883, p. 3.

75. *Arcade Journal*, October 4, 1890, p. 5, March 8, 1890, p. 1, and March 15, 1890, p. 4; Mrs. Doty, *op. cit.*, p. 25.

76. *Arcade Journal*, December 5, 1891, p. 5.

77. "Visitor's Register for the Town of Pullman," Pullman Collection, Pullman Branch Library.

78. Carwardine, *op. cit.*, p. 19; *Arcade Journal*, December 5, 1891, p. 5.

CHAPTER IV

PATERNALISM

GEORGE PULLMAN was never perplexed over the question of what pattern the management and control of the model town should follow. Having established and operated his corporation with an iron hand, he had boundless faith in the techniques of arbitrary administration; and it would, indeed, have been contrary to his principles had the inhabitants been permitted to share in the determination of policies affecting the town. The whole enterprise rested upon a commercial basis, and this necessitated, in the judgment of Pullman, a firm and business-like control. In order to safeguard the town from corrupting influences and preserve it as an object of beauty, he felt that the discerning and watchful eye of the corporation should see that the experiment did not deviate from its prearranged course.[1]

Paradoxical as it may seem, the town of Pullman was not a political entity. It was called a town only in a popular sense, as it belonged politically to the village of Hyde Park—a corporation stretching south from the city limits of Chicago thirteen miles and encompassing an area of forty-eight square miles. Territorially, Hyde Park claimed the distinction of being the largest village in the world, but the population was scattered in more than twenty distinct settlements and totaled in 1884 only forty-five thousand people.[2] Although each locality had its own churches, schools, and business district, the governmental functions for the entire region were exercised by an executive board of six trustees, which convened regularly in the town of Hyde Park, six miles north of Pullman. Every year one-half of the trustees were elected, the term of office being two years. Pullman and Kensington, which together constituted one of the five sharply defined political divisions in the village, elected one trustee and sometimes two— South Chicago alternating with this division in the choice of one of the trustees.[3]

Even though the model town was a part of this large political organization, George Pullman exercised over the town a control virtually absolute. Only in such matters as police, taxes, and wholesale water rates did the village government exert any control; and even here the trustees were restricted by the tremendous influence which George Pullman wielded in the affairs of Hyde Park. The great wealth he represented gave him considerable prestige; and, by exerting pressure in the elections, he experienced no great difficulty in adequately protecting the interests of the town. His untrammeled control was also due to the character of the town, in which none of the land was subdivided and all property, including buildings and improvements, were owned by the Pullman Corporation. By assuming from the start full control over municipal functions, the company was able to render unnecessary the establishment of such services by the village government.[4]

The model town and the Pullman shops were controlled by different agencies, both of which were responsible to the Pullman Corporation. Direct management of the town was lodged in the hands of an official known as the town agent, whose appointment and tenure of office rested with George Pullman. Essentially an executive, the town agent was commissioned to operate the experiment in a business-like manner and co-ordinate the various departments of the town by efficient and economical methods. Among them were the hotel, stables, maintenance of streets, dairy farm, nursery and greenhouse, gasworks, dwelling and operation, sewage farm, and fire department. Over each of these was a head responsible to the town agent, who maintained offices in the Arcade.[5]

During the period covered by the experiment, 1880–1907, there were six different town agents, whose tenure of office averaged about four years, although the shortest term lasted not more than one and a half years. Without exception, all these agents were men of training and in some cases of broad education and wide business experience;[6] but two in particular—Edward Henricks and Duane Doty—merit special consideration. The former was a graduate of the United States Naval Academy, but thoroughly trained in industrial matters. Employed in Pullman as chief clerk in 1880, Henricks was promoted to town agent in 1883 and performed the duties of that office until 1888, when he was transferred to the superintendency of the Pullman brickyards. During part of his incumbency as town agent, he functioned also in the capacity of village clerk of Hyde Park,[7] thus representing the interests of George Pullman in a double sense.

Most distinguished of all town executives was Duane Doty, who occupied a unique position in the model town and who labored with almost fanatical devotion in the interest of the experiment from its inception until his death in 1902. His training prepared him admirably for the many duties which he discharged as engineer, town agent, statistician, and editor. After graduating from the state university at Ann Arbor, he served in the Union army as officer and war correspondent and immediately after the war as assistant editor of the *Detroit Free Press*. During the next fifteen years he was city superintendent of public schools, first in Detroit and later in Chicago. In 1880 he entered the Pullman service as town agent, working in this capacity until 1883 and again from 1901 until his death. As the first executive of the town and subsequently as its civil engineer and statistician, he evolved a complete system of rentals for the town. He was given the editorship of the *Pullman Journal* and throughout the history of this paper guided its destiny. Extremely versatile and thoroughly steeped in all vital statistics and information pertaining to the inner workings of the model town, Duane Doty proved indispensable to George Pullman and was largely responsible for what success the experiment enjoyed.[8]

In the management of the town democracy was conspicuously absent, since all town officials were appointed by the Pullman Corporation except the members of the school board who, although elective, were still in the employ of the company and hence subject to the influence of George Pullman. Nor was this all, as the corporation endeavored to exercise control over the daily lives of the inhabitants. The *Pullman Journal*, at times subtly and then more openly, attempted to guide the thinking of the people. Without reservation, it supported all policies of George

Pullman and published nothing that would reflect on the merits of paternalism. A more flagrant type of control involved the influencing of voting, specific cases of which will be examined elsewhere. Even more striking was the policy of the company toward freedom of speech and action. Labor unions were anathema to George Pullman, and he vigorously combated their existence with all the weapons at his disposal.[9]

Labor agitators and radical speakers were barred from the town by the simple expedient of denying to them the right to rent or use public halls. This practice was illustrated in the case of a lecturer who in March, 1886, applied for the use of the Arcade Theatre. Rejecting his application, the Pullman authorities agreed to substitute Market Hall; but, after the meeting had been advertised, they decided that it was inadvisable to permit the address because it would touch on labor problems and notified the speaker that overlooked previous engagements would prevent his using the hall. With a feeling of outraged justice, he demanded an explanation of George Pullman, who declared that in his opinion any discourse on the labor question at that time was neither necessary nor politic.[10]

It is not possible to affirm to what extent, if any, the inhabitants were watched for liberal tendencies. Richard T. Ely, in his searching investigation of the experiment, complained of having trouble in persuading the inhabitants to talk because "the men believe they are watched by the 'company's spotter,' and to let one of them know that information was desired about Pullman for publication was to close his lips to the honest expression of opinion."[11] John Gibbons, later a circuit-court judge in Chicago, tended to verify Ely's findings by the following assertion: "The laborers in Pullman believe that 'spotters'—paid eavesdroppers of the company—mingle with them to catch and report to their masters any sign or word expressive of disapproval or criticism of the authorities."[12] In the judgment of Rev. William Carwardine, a system of espionage originated prior to the Pullman Strike, by which a weekly report was made to headquarters concerning what the inhabitants were doing and what they were discussing in the public buildings and elsewhere throughout the town.[13]

The very nature of this and other methods of control, often insidiously employed, makes it very difficult to appraise them with accuracy or fit them into an integrated picture. The obvious lack of freedom and democracy, however, was apparent to candid observers of the experiment and prompted the *New York Sun* in 1885 to declare:

> The people of Pullman are not happy and grumble at their situation even more than the inhabitants of towns not model are accustomed to do. They say that all this perfection of order costs them too much in money and imposes upon them an intolerable constraint. . . . . They want to run the municipal government themselves, according to the ordinary American fashion. They secretly rebel because the Pullman Company continues its watch and authority over them after working hours. They declare they are bound hand and foot by a philanthropic monopoly.[14]

In purchasing four thousand acres of land in the Calumet region, George Pullman realized that such a large acquisition could not legally be held by the Pullman Palace Car Company, which, under the terms of the charter, was permitted to acquire only as much property as the successful prosecution of its business required. Consequently, a separate company known as the Pullman Land Association was organized for the purpose of acquiring and holding this land. Eventually, out of its earnings, the Pullman Car Company purchased all the shares in the Pullman Land Association; and, although the two enterprises were thus owned and controlled by the same interests, the fiction of their remaining separate and distinct entities was scrupulously observed. Perplexed as to how many acres the Pullman Car Company could lawfully hold, George Pullman was advised by eminent counsel that five hundred acres would represent a fair interpretation of the charter; and this amount of land was accordingly transferred by the Pullman Land Association to the Pullman Palace Car Company. Largely within this tract was built the town of Pullman; and all factories, public buildings, and dwellings were owned by the Pullman Car Company, except a few homes in the northern part of the town which rested on property held by the Pullman Land Association.[15]

It was the policy of the company not to sell any property in

Pullman, although the original plans seem to have included the possibility of selling sites for homes in proximity to the town. In 1885 George Pullman revealed that such plans were being perfected,[16] and in 1894 Duane Doty acknowledged that it had been originally intended to project the streets and improvements of Pullman into adjacent land and give the employees an opportunity to build.[17] This program, however, never materialized, nor does the evidence show that Pullman considered it very seriously for any length of time.

In his judgment there were many reasons why individual homeownership should not be permitted in the model town. Pullman property was constantly being enhanced in valuation, and it would have been poor business to sell land on a rapidly rising market. To arrange for the sale of sites, it would have been necessary to subdivide the acre property—a move to which George Pullman was unalterably opposed. Most important, perhaps, was the realization that a unified and purposeful control over the town would be destroyed and the course of the experiment drastically altered if portions of the town were lost to company ownership. A broad belt of uninhabited property had been established around Pullman primarily to preserve the integrity of the town by excluding all baneful influences; and this advantage, in the opinion of George Pullman, would be nullified and the success of the experiment seriously jeopardized by permitting homeownership.[18] As early as 1881 he announced: "We will not sell an acre under any circumstances, and we will only lease to parties whom we are satisfied will conform with our ideas in developing the place."[19]

During normal times the Pullman Company did nothing to discourage homeownership in surrounding towns; and, indeed, many Pullman employees purchased property in the near-by communities of Kensington, Riverdale, Gano, and Roseland.[20] When work was plentiful and Pullman dwellings could easily be rented, it made no difference to the company where the workers resided. Prior to the panic of 1893 few tenements in the model town remained vacant, and for the better homes there was usually a waiting list.[21] During the ensuing depression, however, the company was faced by diminishing revenue from rentals and accordingly pursued a policy of discrimination against non-Pullman renters.[22]

George Pullman was convinced that in order to make the experiment a permanent success it would have to be self-supporting, and from the outset he expected a 6 per cent return on the cost of the town. In spite of the greatest economy in the construction and operation of the town, this amount was never realized. For several years the investment yielded a net revenue of $4\frac{1}{2}$ per cent, but in 1892 and 1893 additional taxes and heavy repairs reduced the earnings to 3.82 per cent.[23]

From the utilities of gas and water the Pullman Company hoped to realize substantial profits; but the somewhat contradictory evidence makes it impossible to determine the nature of these earnings. Fair dividends must have been realized, to judge by the fact that gas sold for $2.25 per thousand cubic feet, as compared with the Chicago rate of $1.25.[24] To many people the Pullman rates for this service seemed excessive, if not extortionate. Normally, a large proportion of wage-earners in Pullman used gas; but so burdensome did the charges become during the depression of 1893 that most of the inhabitants were forced to surrender this convenience. The one hundred and twenty-two laborers who could still afford it in 1894 paid an average monthly assessment of $1.67.[25]

Water rates were fixed by the Pullman Company at 71 cents per month for each tenant; and, regardless of how much or how little was used, the rate never varied. Until 1894 the only water meters in the town were those registering the volume of water which flowed into Pullman mains from the town of Hyde Park; and it was therefore impossible to determine what portion was consumed by the tenants and how much was used in the public buildings, the shops, and for city purposes. It does not appear, despite protests, that charges for water were unreasonable or greatly out of line with those in the village of Hyde Park. Wholesale water rates for the town of Pullman averaged 4 cents per thousand gallons between 1886 and 1894 and then were increased to almost 7 cents per thousand gallons.[26] It was alleged that the

Pullman Corporation realized a profit of 150 per cent on water,[27] but this charge was emphatically denied. In a carefully prepared statement the company attempted to demonstrate that between 1889 and 1893 it earned a net monthly profit of only $30 on all water sold to tenants and actually sustained a loss following the inauguration of the new wholesale water rates of 1894.[28]

In devising the schedule for rents, Duane Doty considered not only the original and maintenance cost of property but also the expenses incurred in all such improvements as sewers, water and gas piping, pavements, sidewalks, parks, lawns, and street lights. Everything, except the cost of the Pullman shops, served as a basis for calculating rent; and by spreading the expense of municipal improvements over every block on a basis of front feet, each dwelling and public building bore its share of the general costs.[29] Excluding sanitary and aesthetic features, Pullman rents averaged 20–25 per cent higher than rents in Chicago or surrounding communities. Rentals for the eighteen hundred dwellings of Pullman ranged from $4.00 monthly for a two-room tenement in a second-story flat to $77.25 per month for the most exclusive house. The majority of tenements averaged in rent $10.00 per month. Five-room cottages were available for $16.00, but any dwelling which leased for less than this amount was a tenement in a building with two or more flats. The 6 per cent profit basis was not applied to the frame dwellings in the brickyards which, renting monthly for $8.00 each, yielded dividends of 40 per cent on the investment.[30]

Rentals for public buildings, stores, and offices seem extraordinarily high. Each of the sixteen stalls in the market building rented for $40 monthly, while the hall on the second floor was scheduled to yield $320 per year. The total annual income expected from this structure was thus $8,000, or 19 per cent on the investment.[31] In the Arcade, each store paid an annual rental of from $1,600 to $1,800; the United States Post Office, $1,600; the Pullman Loan and Savings Bank, $1,800; and offices, approximately $300. The theater was expected to return an annual rental of $4,000, and the gymnasium $1,800.[32] So high did rents range that it was difficult for the Pullman storekeepers to compete with the merchants in Kensington and Roseland,[33] but this condition did not seem to disturb the Pullman Company much. In renting stores the town agent originally planned to maintain a rigid balance among the different types of business establishments. By such a policy he felt that business conditions would be healthier than under a policy of haphazard leasing. There may have been some need for this, judging by the flood of applications received by Doty for the twenty-eight stores in the Arcade, when this structure was first made ready for occupancy.[34] To what extent and for how long the authorities pursued this program cannot be ascertained, but eventually it was abandoned. The general character of the rules governing the renting of stores, however, remained unchanged during the entire experiment. The sale of intoxicating beverages was prohibited except in the Florence Hotel, where a small bar existed for the convenience of guests only. All retail enterprises were confined to two buildings: the Market House, which accommodated the vegetable and meat markets,[35] and the Arcade, which housed all other stores. A high standard of cleanliness was enforced by an inspector who visited the market daily.[36]

The renting of all dwellings and stores was under the jurisdiction of the town agent, who required that every tenant sign a lengthy lease. Each renter agreed to keep his tenement clean and tidy and, upon the expiration of the lease, to leave it orderly and in complete repair or to pay the company to put it in such condition. Nothing was to be stored on the premise which would increase the hazards of fire, nor was the renter permitted to post signs, drive tacks or nails, or in any way to alter the property without the written consent of the authorities. No part of a dwelling could be sublet without permission, and the company reserved the right at any time to enter the premise for the purpose of inspection. The tenant could be made to pay for all repairs, whether due to carelessness, ordinary wear, or simply a desire on the part of the company to improve the dwelling.[37] In practice, however, this particular clause was greatly softened;[38] and, as far as can be determined, no renter was ever charged for repairs except those due to gross carelessness or malicious breakage.

One of the most interesting features of the lease was the "ten-day clause," by virtue of which a lease could be voided within ten days by either party. Following the expiration of the ten-day notice, required to be in writing, the tenement had to be vacated immediately, even though advance payment of rent had been made.[39] The reason for this provision was to eliminate quickly and without recourse to lawsuits any tenant who should prove obnoxious to the Pullman authorities. When asked by Graham Taylor in 1893 what means the Pullman Company took to ally the inhabitants with its policies, George Pullman explained tersely that a clause in each lease enabled the company on short notice to get rid of undesirable renters.[40] This provision, however, was seldom invoked by the authorities, and comparatively few tenants were ejected from the town;[41] but the potential effectiveness of the clause served as a powerful threat to keep the Pullman inhabitants from criticizing or opposing the policies of the company.

In signing the lease the renter agreed to observe all rules which the company might choose to make concerning the dwellings; and the completeness of these regulations, no less mandatory than the terms of the lease, left little to be desired from the standpoint of rigid paternalistic control. The grounds surrounding the dwelling could not be dug or planted without permission, nor was mechanical work, calcimining, or painting allowed on any premise without official consent. The keeping of pigs and chickens was strictly prohibited because of their offensive odor. The following clause, quoted only in part, indicated how minutely framed were the restrictions:

Tenants should always enter or leave the building quietly; always avoid entering the halls with muddy feet; never permit hammering, pounding or splitting of wood upon the floors or in the cellars, or anything which disturbs and annoys those occupying neighboring rooms; avoid the use of musical instruments after bed time; avoid all loud noises or boisterous conduct that might annoy others or disturb the sick and weary; avoid loitering in the stairways; avoid smoking in the cellars; always fill and trim lamps in the forenoon; . . . . always leave some ashes in the bottom of the stove. . . . .[42]

From the enforced orderliness and cleanliness the tenants naturally derived benefits, but the restrictions represented an irritating infringement upon the personal rights of the inhabitants.

Every means was utilized to assure the prompt collection of rent. Under the terms of the lease, the company was authorized and for a number of years followed the practice of subtracting in advance from each pay check, issued semimonthly, the water charges and rent. In case the laborer fell behind in rent payments because of illness or unemployment, upon returning to work he suffered an additional deduction from each check until all delinquent rent was paid.[43] This procedure was rendered illegal in 1891 when the Illinois state legislature passed the Truck Law forbidding the practice of making such deductions and requiring that wages be paid in full.[44] The system of collection was accordingly revised, and each employee thereafter received two checks, one covering the amount of the rent and the other the balance of wages. Accompanying the paymaster was the rent collector, who urged each tenant to indorse and surrender the check for rent without delay.[45]

The Pullman Loan and Savings Bank functioned as collector of rent. During the depression of 1893, drastic reduction in wages made it difficult for the wage-earners to meet their rental payments, and many became delinquent. In order to facilitate collections the paymaster was ordered to send both checks to the bank; and, when the employee called for his checks, he was strongly urged to apply on his rent the largest amount possible, often more than his meager earnings would permit. Should the tenant prove obdurate, he was reminded that failure to pay rent would force the bank to recommend eviction; and the fear of discharge as well as eviction served to stimulate rent payments. Usually the bank held the rent bills several months before returning them to the officials of the company, who as a matter of policy found it advisable to use eviction sparingly and wherever possible to apply less obnoxious means to persuade hopelessly delinquent renters to leave the town.[46]

In the management of the town little was left to the initiative of the inhabitants. The company provided garbage receptacles and removed daily at its own expense all rubbish, ashes, and garbage. In the public buildings janitors kept the halls and rooms faultlessly clean. During the summer the company was active in keeping the streets, parks, and front lawns sprinkled and free of paper and other refuse.[47] Front lawns were mowed at company expense, and every house was maintained in excellent condition by the repair department.[48] About all that remained for the inhabitants was to plant a few flowers and to preserve a clean and tidy appearance within the dwelling. In encouraging this the Pullman authorities occasionally would acknowledge by a note of thanks or a gift of plants from the greenhouse the special interest taken by some of the tenants in keeping their homes attractive.[49] The cost of the sanitary and aesthetic program was classified by the company under general expense and charged to the inhabitants in higher rents.

Complete in most respects, the model town was without a hospital, cemetery, almshouse, orphange, jail, or system of public charity; and the only one of these which the Pullman Company ever seriously considered establishing was a hospital. The others were not deemed essential in the type of experiment which George Pullman conducted. Indeed, he would have considered most of them a reflection upon the town, the success of which demanded industrious, self-sustaining, and law-abiding inhabitants. The need for a jail was nonexistent as arrests were rarely made, and, in case confinement was necessary, the Hyde Park jail was adequate.[50] Paupers, orphans, and the aged poor had no place in the town, and an individual who lost his job and could no longer pay rent was ordinarily expected to leave. The creation of relief organizations was never encouraged by Pullman officials. For many years the problem of relief was of slight importance, and the little charity required was handled principally by the ladies' aid society; but during the depression of 1893 the nonexistence of a public system of relief was keenly felt. Widespread poverty at this time necessitated a vast amount of public assistance, none of which was supplied by the Pullman Company.[51]

Medical aid was furnished by the company without charge to injured employees. In 1884 the office of company surgeon was created at Pullman and given to John McLean, a resident physician of the town, who was assigned the duty of attending any injury sustained by employees or visitors. Most cases were cared for in his surgical laboratory, located near the Pullman shops; but whenever in his judgment it seemed necessary the patient was sent to a Chicago hospital and all expenses were borne by the company.

In case of injuries to employees the Pullman Company safeguarded its interests from the danger of liability suits. Every injured employee was compelled to sign a statement prepared by the company physician stating the time, cause, and nature of the injury and what disposition was made in the case. Immediately following an accident, Dr. McLean was required to make a report to the manager of the Pullman shops and the head of the department in which the man was disabled. Complete data were then assembled from witnesses concerning the accident, and in case there was prospect of damages McLean notified the company immediately. He always advised injured men to settle and was prepared to testify for the company in case of litigation.[52] Rev. Carwardine declared boldly that the company gave damages only under compulsion and was notorious in the practice of evading claims.[53] Certainly the entire system was admirably conceived to protect the corporation from lawsuits and to effect a quick settlement of claims for damages upon terms offered by the company; and, whether because of the precautions or not, the number of cases involving lawsuits for personal damages was comparatively small.[54]

Morris L. Wickman, pastor of the Pullman Swedish Methodist Church, testified in 1894 before the United States Strike Commission that the policy of the Pullman Corporation toward its injured employees was not based upon principles of humanity. In proof of this, he disclosed the case of a member in his church, who suffered a serious injury in the Pullman shops while holding a riveting stake, a piece of which chipped off and struck him in the hand, severing a tendon and crushing a bone. Despite medical aid rendered by Dr. McLean, complications set in, and without delay Rev. Wickman rushed the patient to a Chicago hospital where an operation was performed. For days the man's life hung in the balance, but finally he recovered after nine weeks in the hospital. When Wickman went to the Pullman officials to see what could be done in behalf of his parishioner, he was confronted with a statement signed by the company physician and foreman of the shops pronouncing the accident "unavoidable." General-Manager Brown explained that, although the case was very sad and he personally felt sympathy for the man, there was nothing that he, as agent of the company, could do about it. The victim of this accident received no disability allowance and had to finance his hospital bills and upon returning to work suffered a reduction in wages because he could no longer perform the work he had done before.[55]

During the first few years of the Pullman experiment, employees temporarily injured were paid full wages except in the case of carelessness when only one dollar a day was allowed; but after 1886 the practice of paying any wages to injured employees was discontinued on the theory that under the old system a man could easily take advantage of the company.[56] In refusing to give employees security against the hazards of life, the Pullman Company differed in no way from other corporations of the period.

Undemocratic as were most of the public institutions of Pullman, they were, nevertheless, administered with efficiency and economy. None was more illustrative of this fact than the Pullman Fire Department. Owned by the Pullman Corporation, this organization was equipped with the most modern fire-fighting appliances, housed in the Pullman Stables, and operated by a fire marshal and twenty-five volunteers.[57] So smoothly and effectively did it function that arrangements were made in 1886 for its use to combat fires in the near-by communities of Gano, Roseland, and Kensington. In return for this service and without disturbing George Pullman's control over the agency, the village of Hyde Park reimbursed the Pullman Company to the extent of seventy-two hundred dollars and further agreed to finance the operating expenses of the department.[58]

In 1882 the library was incorporated, with George Pullman serving as president of the board.[59] Although public, this institution was not free—adults being annually assessed three dollars and children one dollar for the privilege of using its facilities. The charge was justified on the grounds that if the library were free the workers would neither appreciate nor develop any interest in it.[60] The fee served to restrict greatly the usefulness of the library, which, prior to the Pullman Strike, never possessed a membership of more than two hundred and fifty persons. Even so, the circulation of books increased fivefold during the ten-year period ending in 1894, thus giving support to the assertion that for every subscriber there were no less than five readers.[61] It was alleged that the extreme luxuriousness of the reading-rooms further discouraged membership among workers who were unaccustomed to an atmosphere of such grandeur.[62] In commenting upon the paucity of membership, the Strike Commission advanced a further reason: "It is possible that the air of business strictly maintained there, as elsewhere, and their exclusion from any part of its management prevented more universal and grateful acceptance of its advantages by employees. Men as a rule, even when employees, prefer independence to paternalism in such matters."[63]

The Pullman schools seemed to possess the attributes of democracy since the choice of the board of directors was determined in an annual election by the voters of the town. In practice, however, Pullman officials were usually chosen. The company surgeon was president of the school board from 1883 to 1889, and among others who served as directors were the town agent and the chief clerk of the manager's office.[64] Although the board as constituted was amenable to the wishes of George Pullman, it strongly resented interference from any source outside of the town. On one occasion, the Cook County superintendent of schools demanded the removal of Daniel Martin, principal of the Pullman Schools, because, as was charged, his methods were too old fashioned. The superintendent insisted upon the right to choose Martin's successor. Nettled by these demands, John McLean replied that Martin was very satisfactory and, whenever a change in school administration was deemed necessary, the school board of Pullman was competent to handle the matter.[65]

The hotel, theater, and bank were operated by the Pullman Company as business enterprises, just as were the iceworks, dairy farm, brickyards, gas plant, and sewage farm. Over each was placed a business executive, usually known as a superintendent. In order to maintain in the hotel a "prescribed standard of excellence," the company refused to relax in the slightest degree its rigid control in the management of this institution. It was here that George Pullman entertained his guests while in the town, and he was thus anxious that the hotel should rank among the most popular in the Calumet region.[66] His interest in preserving the beauty of the Arcade Theatre was just as great, and whenever necessary the auditorium was completely redecorated. A very close censorship controlled the type of lectures and plays that were given. Although the theatrical performances were of a high appeal, the admission charges, ranging from 35 to 75 cents, proved too much for many workers.[67]

The Pullman Loan and Savings Bank was chartered in 1883 at a capitalization of $100,000. George Pullman served as president from its origin until his death and was thus able to direct the policies of the bank in accordance with the best interests of the Pullman Corporation. Financially successful, the bank paid 6 per cent dividends on its stock. Large commercial sums for pay-roll purposes were kept on deposit here by the Pullman Company. The bank functioned as collector of rent and other debts due the company and served also as a depository for the savings of the workers.[68] This latter service ranked high in the mind of George Pullman, who took the greatest pride in the evidence of thrift among the inhabitants.[69]

In maintaining control over the model town and protecting the interests of his corporation, George Pullman found it necessary to wield considerable interest in local politics. In doing so, he did not hesitate to employ political techniques that were distinctly undemocratic.

The village of Hyde Park, of which the model town comprised only a small part, experienced a phenomenal increase in population between 1880 and 1889. In meeting the problems attendant upon this growth, the village government proved to be very unwieldy. The northern part of Hyde Park was largely residential, whereas the southern portion was industrial; and this divergency in interests imposed a double burden upon the six trustees, who, living in various parts of the village, ordinarily met in session once every week. So loosely organized was the village system that responsible government on the part of the trustees seemed at times almost fictitious. As the system operated, it was comparatively easy for the large industrialists of Hyde Park to manipulate the choice of trustees and exert a real influence in the affairs of the village.[70] Demand for revision in the character of this government was made as early as 1882; but, because of opposition from the powerful interests, the old system was not broken down until 1889.

George Pullman was unsympathetic toward those who advocated any change, since under the loose type of village organization he was able to conduct his experiment without molestation. It was his policy from the outset to maintain representation in the village government. The first Pullman official to serve on the board of trustees was elected in 1881; and from then until Hyde Park was absorbed by Chicago there was Pullman representation either on this board or in one or more of the important administrative positions in the village.[71] By supporting various successful candidates, George Pullman managed to exercise considerable influence over other trustees and administrative officeholders.

His prestige in Hyde Park became quite apparent when he negotiated in 1881 for water rights. He issued a warning to the village that, if the terms were not satisfactory, the town of Pullman would erect its own waterworks on the shore of Lake Michigan. The trustees acceded to terms suitable to Pullman.[72] In 1885 he won a small reduction in the water rates and in the following year secured a further reduction of 20 per cent. The significance of this new rate, which amounted to 4 cents per thousand gallons, can be appreciated when it is observed that the general meter rate in Hyde Park to large water consumers was 10 cents per thousand gallons.[73]

Nothing interested Pullman more than the question of taxation, and on various occasions he used his influence to scale down tax assessments. The property of the town, including factories, homes and public buildings, was assessed in 1882 at $550,000. Convinced that this was excessive, George Pullman protested to the board of equalization, of which Edward Henricks, as village clerk, was a member. Pullman held that manufacturing enterprises should be taxed lightly in order to attract more of them to Hyde Park. He further explained that, since all of the public improvements in Pullman were financed by his company and not by the village government, taxes on the town should represent the minimum. The assessment was accordingly reduced to $200,-000.[74]

In 1883 George Pullman joined in the formation of a new political organization known as the Taxpayer's party. Among those who labored in its behalf were such Pullman officials as Edward Henricks and John Hopkins. In opposition was the Citizens' ticket, controlled by J. T. Torrence, a politician, who openly accused Pullman of seeking to dominate the village government so as to promote the interests of the Pullman Corporation. The election in 1883 and 1884 witnessed a complete victory for the Taxpayer's party.[75]

The political campaign of 1885 involved the issue of Pullman taxes and was especially bitter. A realignment of political forces caused George Pullman to abandon his support of the Taxpayer's party in favor of the Republican party, which was gathering strength in the local politics of the village. As a part of their strategy the Taxpayer's faction hammered on the low Pullman property assessment and stressed the identity of interest between George Pullman and the Republican ticket. A circular was printed showing a map of a large part of the nonindustrial portion of the model town, including all the public buildings and five hundred and thirty-one dwelling-houses, all of which was assessed in 1884 at only $32,000 and taxed for $2,773. In contrast was cited a typical residential block in Hyde Park which contained only twenty-two houses, and, although valued at less than one-sixth of the Pullman property shown on the chart, actually paid $159 more in taxes. The circular explained that the industries of the model town were excluded from the analysis because of the prevailing conception that public policy required low taxes on factories in order to induce others to move to Hyde Park; but such an argument, emphasized the document, could not be used to justify the absurdly low taxes paid by the Pullman Company on the residential part of the town.[76] George Pullman branded this circular as misleading, averring that in return for the taxes paid to Hyde Park all that the model town received was the services of one policeman and a connection with the waterworks of the village. He intimated that, instead of carrying too small a tax burden, his company was paying more taxes than conditions warranted.[77]

The party supported by George Pullman won control of the board of trustees but lost a majority of seats on the board of review, including the post of assessor.[78] In the matter of taxes, Pullman was forced to assume the defensive. When the assessment on the residential portion of the model town was boosted from $35,000 to $214,000, he protested, stressing the experimental character of the town and the fact that all land there was held as acre property and was no more expensive to Hyde Park than any other acre property. A substantial reduction in the assessment was finally secured.[79]

Because elections in the model town seldom went against the wishes of George Pullman, the question of political pressure is raised. The evidence indicates that, when circumstances required, Pullman did not hesitate to influence voting. In the Hyde Park election of 1887 the Pullman Company was accused of resorting to intimidation in order to marshal the Pullman vote against the labor ticket. The town was the largest labor district in the village, and yet the Republican party carried it by a landslide. Wagons belonging to the Pullman Company conveyed large numbers to the polls; and the head timekeeper and the chief accountant of the Pullman shops were among those charged with peddling tickets for the Republican party and standing near the polls in order to observe how the men voted.[80] The *Chicago Herald* demanded an investigation of the election methods used on this occasion by the Pullman Company.[81] Again in 1889 it was charged that the foremen in the Pullman shops were instructed to influence the workers in behalf of the Pullman ticket, and in proof of this the names of several shop bosses were cited as having applied pressure.[82]

George Pullman refused to brook any sort of political opposition in the model town. In the early life of John P. Hopkins can be observed the struggle of a man who became a political force in the town but who was tolerated only as long as he did not seek to thwart any aims of Pullman. Entering the employ of the Pullman Corporation in 1880 at the age of twenty-two, Hopkins was elevated by a series of rapid promotions from a laborer's job in the lumberyards to paymaster of the Pullman works. He knew virtually all the men in the shops—a fact which contributed immeasurably to his popularity and influence as a politician.[83] With the encouragement and support of George Pullman, Hopkins decided in 1886 to form a partnership with Frederick Secord and establish the Arcade Trading Company—a retail merchandise organization which leased four stores in the Arcade and was capitalized at $10,000. Anxious to have the enterprise succeed, Pullman agreed at the outset that a portion of the regular rental, over $100 monthly for each store, would be secretly remitted.[84] Under such an agreement, the company was formed; and, still retaining his position as paymaster, Hopkins seemed well intrenched in the town of Pullman.

Although affiliated with the Democratic party, John Hopkins was content for several years to support the policies of George Pullman; but eventually he began to assert himself in a very objectionable manner. Always sympathetic with the employees, he supported them on one occasion during some labor difficulties and was immediately discharged as paymaster. Because of his extraordinary ability, he was subsequently re-employed, but his zeal to pursue an independent course was in no wise diminished.[85] Working quietly among the men, he became so influential that in the national election of 1888 he carried the model town for Cleveland, notwithstanding a vigorously conducted Republican campaign supported by Pullman. This type of rebellion proved intolerable, and without ceremony Hopkins was discharged from the employment of the corporation.[86] In the Hyde Park election of 1889, he opposed George Pullman politically; and in the campaign to annex Hyde Park to Chicago he served on the executive committee that favored this course.[87] The enmity between Pullman and Hopkins, following these political battles, did not abate and subsequently became a stumbling block for Hopkins who, as mayor of Chicago, tried to arbitrate the Pullman Strike. In retaliation for the recalcitrance of Hopkins, the rental of the stores of the Arcade Trading Corporation was advanced to the point where Hopkins and Secord were compelled to leave the town and establish their firm in Kensington. Charging the Pullman Company with bad faith, John Hopkins alleged that, contrary to the original agreement, his enterprise was denied a remittance of any part of the rental during occupancy in the Arcade. The amount which should have been refunded, he averred, was the equivalent of an overcharge of rent and totaled $10,000. In 1891 suit was filed against the Pullman Corporation for this sum, and the plaintiff was awarded $5,500 by the circuit court; but seven years later this decision was reversed by the appellate court on the grounds that a "proposition made to individuals on the condition precedent that they will form a corporation cannot be regarded as a proposition to the yet unborn corporation."[88]

It was the firm conviction of George Pullman that the absorption of Hyde Park by Chicago would endanger the success of the experiment. The need for reorganizing the antiquated village government, however, was incontrovertible, and the course which appeared most logical was annexation to Chicago. The struggle waged by Pullman against this solution furnishes an excellent insight into the question of political control.

Agitation for a change in the status of the village government grew increasingly strong after 1885 and in 1887 reached such proportions that it was decided a vote should be taken on the question of annexation. Convinced that public opinion would support the proposition, George Pullman determined that the most expedient course would be not to fight the general issue but to get the model town and the surrounding communities of Kensington, Roseland, and Riverdale exempted from the territory involved in the movement for annexation. In this strategy he was successful, and one-fourth of the village was excluded from the proposition submitted to the voters.[89] Although the vote was rather light, the issue carried; but the legality of the procedure was immediately questioned and, when tested in the courts, held invalid. The law governing the annexation proceedings was held unconstitutional by the Illinois supreme court, and the government of Hyde Park ordered restored to its former status.[90]

In the spring of 1889 the way for annexation was paved by the passage of a new state law which met the objections of the supreme court. The question was resubmitted to the people of Hyde Park; but this time the entire village was involved in the proposal, and so George Pullman opposed the issue. With consummate skill he engineered the antiannexation campaign in which large sums of money were spent and numerous meetings held in Pullman and throughout the village of Hyde Park.[91] Even from the pulpit of the Green Stone Presbyterian Church the battle was waged by Rev. E. C. Oggel, who on May 13 preached an antiannexation sermon, using as his text the following passage from Isaiah: "Woe unto them that join house to house, that lay field to field until there be no place; that they may be placed alone in the midst of the earth."[92]

Tremendous pressure was doubtless applied on the Pullman employees, since in all of the village only one locality besides the model town was carried by the antiannexationists. In the Pullman district a majority of eight hundred and forty three votes was rolled up against the proposition.[93] It was openly charged that coercion was used in securing this vote and that several men were discharged for signing petitions in favor of annexation or for refusing to sign antiannexation petitions. John Hopkins characterized the action of the Pullman officials during the election as "the biggest outrage on American freedom ever perpetrated." Employees were bulldozed, he affirmed, and threatened with dismissal if they voted for annexation and on election day were supplied with tickets by Pullman bosses and allowed to leave the shops in squads of four. The mandate of the election commission—that electioneers remain ten feet from the polls—was claimed by Hopkins to have been flagrantly violated.[94]

The annexationists were admirably organized for the contest and ably assisted by the Chicago newspapers. So effective was their campaign that they won by over two thousand votes.[95] In spite of many gloomy forecasts, the absorption of Hyde Park did not greatly disturb Pullman's position in the model town. Schools, taxes, fire protection, and wholesale water rates were now subject to control by Chicago, though the actual administration of these did not change greatly.[96] Although the school board was abolished, Daniel Martin was retained as principal, and the general system was subjected to no important revision.[97] As a part of the Thirty-fourth Ward of Chicago, the town of Pullman remained fundamentally the same as before annexation.

Not even in the matter of taxes did the Pullman interests suffer, and from every indication less concern was shown by George Pullman about local assessments than when the village government existed. In 1894 the mayor of Chicago, John Hopkins, complained that the entire town of Pullman paid annually no more than fifteen thousand dollars in taxes—a rate even below that on unimproved property in the vicinity of Pullman. The assessment of the town was based on acre-property and primarily for this reason was substantially lower than on other city property. Protesting against the situation, Hopkins averred: "I have known of the manner by which Pullman has escaped equitable taxation for years. It affords one of the most glaring illustrations of corporation tax dodging in Chicago." The mayor explained that not until the streets of the town were declared open by the city of Chicago and the land assessed by the block, would the Pullman Company be obliged to shoulder its just share of the tax burden; and this, he did not believe, could be legally done until twenty years had expired from the time the town was laid out.[98]

Annexation did not destroy the interest of George Pullman in local politics. As in the Hyde Park board of trustees, so in the Chicago city council, Pullman felt the need of representation; and the aldermanic contests of the Thirty-fourth Ward revealed the same type of political pressure on Pullman employees as during the earlier contests for village trustees. In the election of 1890, for instance, George Pullman was anxious that Dr. James Chasey, town agent of Pullman, should become an alderman. Following the customary practice, officials of the shops campaigned in behalf of Pullman's choice, resorting to means that seemed to in-

volve intimidation. The tactics of two officials—General Superintendent H. H. Sessions and General Manager G. F. Brown—
resulted in a scandal, which was ultimately aired before the
Board of Election Commissioners. In canvassing for votes these
officials were alleged to have threatened any who should vote
against Chasey. Three employees were actually discharged, presumably for supporting the other candidate, although the company denied that this was the reason. Election tickets were
printed upon paper of a distinctive color and distributed in the
shops by foremen, some of whom stood near the polls on election
day.[99] The efforts of the Pullman Company were not without
success, as both Chasey and his Republican colleague were
chosen.[100]

Not always was George Pullman successful in marshaling the
vote of the inhabitants. On the eve of the presidential election of
1888, the Republicans held an impressive rally in the Arcade
Theatre attended by Pullman and other officials of the company.
Despite this and other attempts to influence the voters, a majority in the town supported Grover Cleveland.[101] In the campaign of 1892 George Pullman was extremely anxious to have
Cleveland defeated and made a very indiscreet and impulsive
speech to his employees, declaring that, in case they did not sustain tariff protection and vote the Republican ticket, he would
not be accountable for their folly. The character of his remarks was
alleged to have been responsible for the tremendous majority which
the Democratic presidential nominee received in the town.[102]

Before concluding the discussion on paternalism, a few of the
comments made by writers on the Pullman experiment should be
examined. When the town was in its heyday, numerous articles
and editorials were written, some eulogizing the experiment,
others commenting adversely. Not until after the Pullman Strike,
when the defects of the town were thrown into relief, did the
writers become almost uniformly convinced that the experiment
was fundamentally unsound.

Few writers were more enthusiastic about the future of the
town than Oscar C. De Wolf, commissioner of health for Chicago. Writing largely from the medical point of view, he alluded

in 1884 to the great need in most communities for sanitation. While acknowledging that paternalism was resented by many people, he nevertheless justified it as a means of educating the laboring classes to the value of civic sanitation.[103] No less favorable was the report of the commissioners of the Bureau of Labor Statistics in 1885, which commended George Pullman on the grounds that the social, moral, and sanitary influences of his town made possible a more abundant life for the employees. Recognizing that eventually it would be wise for the Pullman Company to share with the workers some of its profits, the report proclaimed that the experiment should be held up for emulation by other employers.[104]

No Chicago newspaper was more outspoken in support of the model town than the *Inter Ocean*, which stressed the benefits that accrued to labor from the improved living conditions of Pullman. Convinced that the experiment should be duplicated elsewhere, the editor explained that the "idea that capital will be the gainer by placing within reach of the laborer most of the comforts that money can bring, and a recognition that these comforts are rightfully due the laborer, are steps far in advance in practical philosophy and enduring philanthropy; they are steps that mark an era in the history of labor."[105]

John Gibbons, a Chicago lawyer and later circuit judge of Illinois, wrote feelingly in condemnation of the venture. While granting that the Pullman Company had provided for the material comforts of the inhabitants, he protested that the undesirable features of the experiment militated overwhelmingly against the success of the enterprise. The complete lack of democracy, Gibbons affirmed, was one of the most serious defects as "every municipal act is the act of a corporation." In his opinion, pleasant surroundings were created for the employees primarily to prevent any "stirring impulse within for social, moral or mental growth that might breed discontent." After surveying all implications, he concluded that the arbitrary methods of control employed by the company tended to destroy individuality, stifle initiative, crush civic pride, and deny to the inhabitants practical training in citizenship.[106]

The study which Richard T. Ely made of the experiment in 1885 convinced him that the most dangerous aspect was monarchical control and its deadening effect on morale. He explained: "It is especially to be desired that means should be discovered to awaken in the residents an interest and a pride in Pullman. It is now thought a praiseworthy thing 'to beat the company' which phrase in itself points to something radically wrong." He protested that the experiment should not be dependent upon the life of a certain individual but, instead, should rest upon a co-operative basis and that it was dangerous to place in the hands of capitalists, however well-meaning, so much power over the lives of employees. He professed:

In looking over all the facts of the case, the conclusion is unavoidable that the idea of Pullman is un-American. It is a nearer approach than anything the writer has seen to what appears to be the ideal of the Great German Chancellor. It is not the American ideal. It is benevolent well-wishing feudalism, which desires the happiness of the people, but in such a way as to please the authorities.[107]

The absence of democracy was obviously a basic weakness, and the development of civic pride was difficult under the existing political conditions. Had a free, unhampered society been established, privileged to work out the solution of its own political and social problems, the history of the model town would have taken another and perhaps more successful course. The town of Pullman was literally forced into a political strait jacket which contributed immeasurably to its final destruction.

NOTES

1. *U.S. Strike Commission Report*, pp. 529–30.
2. Andreas, *op. cit.*, pp. 516, 521; *Annual Report . . . . of the Village of Hyde Park* (1882), pp. 1–2.
3. *Annual Report . . . . of the Village of Hyde Park* (1882), pp. 41, 70; *Chicago Times*, March 3, 1883, p. 6.
4. Ely, *op. cit.*, p. 461; "Report to the State of Illinois," p. 24; *Chicago Evening Journal*, July 10, 1885, p. 3.
5. "Town of Pullman Pay Rolls, March 15, 1886, to March 31, 1887," pp. 1–19; McLean, *op. cit.*, pp. 252–54.
6. McLean, *op. cit.*, pp. 253–54; *Pullman Journal*, May 7, 1902, p. 4; Andreas, *op. cit.*, p. 625.
7. Andreas, *op. cit.*, p. 626; *Hyde Park Directory* (1888), pp. 565, 579; *Annual Report . . . . of the Village of Hyde Park* (1883), p. 7; *Chicago Times*, April 2, 1884, p. 8.

8. Andreas, *op. cit.*, pp. 625–26; *Calumet Record*, November 20, 1902, p. 1.

9. *U. S. Strike Commission Report*, pp. xxvii, 453–54, 562.

10. *Chicago Herald*, April 2, 1886, p. 4.

11. *Op. cit.*, p. 464.

12. *Tenure and Toil*, p. 188.

13. Carwardine, *op. cit.*, p. 51.

14. *Chicago Herald*, October 12, 1885, p. 2 (reprint of an editorial, *New York Sun*, October 11, 1885).

15. *U.S. Strike Commission Report*, pp. 539–42.

16. "Annual Report of the Pullman Company," *Inter Ocean*, October 16, 1885, p. 3.

17. *U.S. Strike Commission Report*, p. 504.

18. *Ibid.*, pp. 503–5, 529–30, 542; *Pullman Journal*, January 7, 1893, p. 3.

19. *Chicago Tribune*, August 16, 1881, p. 8.

20. Pullman, *op. cit.*, p. 21.

21. "Annual Report of the Pullman Company," *Pullman Journal*, October 21, 1893, p. 4; *U.S. Strike Commission Report*, pp. 499, 503.

22. *U.S. Strike Commission Report*, pp. xxxv–xxxvi, 426, 461.

23. *Ibid.*, p. 530.

24. Carwardine, *op. cit.*, p. 98; "Report to the State of Illinois," p. 15.

25. *U.S. Strike Commission Report*, p. 601.

26. *Annual Report . . . . of the Village of Hyde Park* (1886), p. 90; Pullman, *op. cit.*, p. 23.

27. Carwardine, *op. cit.*, p. 98; William T. Stead, "How Pullman Was Built," *Socialist Economist*, VII (1894), 86.

28. *U.S. Strike Commission Report*, p. 601.

29. *Ibid.*, pp. 495–501; Duane Doty, "The Arcade at Pullman" (1883), pp. 1–9.

30. *U.S. Strike Commission Report*, pp. xxxv, 495–501, 506–7.

31. Duane Doty, "The Market of Pullman" (1883), pp. 1–3.

32. Duane Doty, "The Arcade at Pullman," pp. 5–9; *U.S. Strike Commission Report*, p. 525.

33. *Chicago Tribune*, September 21, 1888, p. 9. A few years before the panic of 1893 there was a reduction in some of the Arcade rentals (*U.S. Strike Commission Report*, p. 478).

34. *U.S. Strike Commission Report*, p. 534; *Inter Ocean*, December 27, 1881, p. 3.

35. An exception was made in the case of one small meat market which was permitted at the extreme southern end of the town ("Report to the State of Illinois," p. 18).

36. *Ibid.*, pp. 18, 25; *U.S. Strike Commission Report*, p. 431.

37. *U.S. Strike Commission Report*, pp. 531–33 (reprint of a copy of the lease).

38. *Ibid.*, pp. 636–37.

39. *Ibid.*, pp. 532–33.

40. Graham R. Taylor, *Pioneering on Social Frontiers*, p. 115.

41. *U.S. Strike Commission Report*, p. 534; Eaton, *Today*, II, 7.

42. *Chicago Herald*, February 7, 1886, p. 2 (reprint of some of the rules governing Pullman tenants).

43. "Pay Rolls of the Pullman Company, 1-B, Oct., 1882, to Jan., 1883," p. 40; *U.S. Strike Commission Report*, pp. 515, 533.

44. *Revised Statutes of the State of Illinois* (1898), 1530*a*–1530*b*.
45. *U.S. Strike Commission Report*, pp. 515–17.
46. *Ibid.*, pp. xxxvi, 509, 515–17, 520–22.
47. "Report to the State of Illinois," pp. 16–19, 27, 38.
48. *Calumet Record*, June 13, 1901, p. 9, and November 14, 1907, p. 5.
49. Ely, *op. cit.*, p. 462.
50. "Report to the State of Illinois," p. 2.
51. Carwardine, *op. cit.*, pp. 41–44; *U.S. Strike Commission Report*, pp. 639–40.
52. *U.S. Strike Commission Report*, pp. 483–84, 487, 591; McLean, *op. cit.*, pp. 217–18, 262–63.
53. *Op. cit.*, p. 112.
54. McLean, *op. cit.*, p. 487; *U.S. Strike Commission Report*, p. xxii.
55. *U.S. Strike Commission Report*, pp. 464–65.
56. *Ibid.*, p. 488; Ely, *op. cit.*, p. 462.
57. Andreas, *op. cit.*, p. 620; "Report to the State of Illinois," pp. 24–25.
58. *Annual Report . . . . of the Village of Hyde Park* (1887), p. 18.
59. "Charter of Incorporation for the Pullman Public Library, October 14, 1882," Pullman Collection, Pullman Branch Library.
60. Ludlum, *op. cit.*, p. 2; Pullman, *op. cit.*, p. 23.
61. *U.S. Strike Commission Report*, pp. xxi–xxii; *Pullman Journal*, August 10, 1895, p. 4.
62. Carwardine, *op. cit.*, p. 18.
63. *U.S. Strike Commission Report*, p. xxii.
64. Andreas, *op. cit.*, p. 621; McLean, *op. cit.*, pp. 239–43; Ely, *op. cit.*, p. 461.
65. McLean, *op. cit.*, p. 259.
66. Mrs. Doty, *op. cit.*, pp. 108–9; McLean, *op. cit.*, p. 227.
67. McLean, *op. cit.*, p. 243; Ely, *op. cit.*, p. 458; *Pullman Journal*, January 7, 1893, p. 4, and October 6, 1894, p. 8.
68. *U.S. Strike Commission Report*, pp. 508–10, 514.
69. McLean, *op. cit.*, p. 285; *Pullman Journal*, October 20, 1894, p. 8.
70. *Report . . . . of the Village of Hyde Park* (1882), pp. 10–11; *Municipal Code of the Village of Hyde Park Together with General Laws* (1887), p. 94.
71. Andreas, *op. cit.*, pp. 516, 627; *Chicago Times*, April 2, 1884, p. 8, and May 10, 1885, p. 19; *Annual Report . . . . of the Village of Hyde Park* (1886), p. 7, and (1889), p. 3.
72. *Annual Report . . . . of the Village of Hyde Park* (1882), p. 27; *Chicago Times*, September 16, 1882, p. 6.
73. *Annual Report . . . . of the Village of Hyde Park* (1886), p. 90.
74. *Chicago Tribune*, August 22, 1882, p. 3, and August 25, 1882, p. 6.
75. *Ibid.*, February 13, 1883, p. 7, and March 27, 1883, p. 2; *Chicago Times*, April 4, 1883, p. 3.
76. *Is This Equal Taxation?* (a campaign document published by the Taxpayers' party in Hyde Park, 1885).
77. *Chicago Times*, April 7, 1885, p. 8.
78. *Chicago Tribune*, April 8, 1885, p. 3, and April 10, 1885, p. 8.
79. *Chicago Times*, July 12, 1885, p. 17; *Chicago Herald*, June 25, 1885, p. 3.
80. *Chicago Herald*, April 6, 1887, p. 1.
81. *Ibid.*, April 10, 1887, p. 4.

82. *Ibid.*, March 31, 1889, p. 11; *Chicago Times*, April 3, 1889, p. 1.

83. *Chicago Times*, April 21, 1889, p. 1; Stead, *If Christ Came to Chicago*, p. 293.

84. *Chicago Herald*, February 4, 1886, p. 1; *Chicago Times*, April 21, 1889, p. 1.

85. Stead, *If Christ Came to Chicago*, pp. 294–95.

86. Taylor, *Satellite Cities*, p. 62; *Chicago Times*, November 7, 1888, p. 1.

87. *Chicago Times*, April 4, 1889, p. 4, and May 12, 1889, p. 1.

88. *Chicago Tribune*, January 11, 1898, p. 10; *Chicago Evening Post*, January 10, 1898, p. 2.

89. *Chicago Herald*, October 20, 1887, p. 6, and October 22, 1887, p. 4.

90. *Annual Report* . . . . *of the Village of Hyde Park* (1888), pp. 32–36.

91. *Chicago Times*, April 27, 1889, p. 9, May 24, 1889, p. 5, and June 29, 1889, p. 2.

92. *Ibid.*, May 13, 1889, p. 1.

93. *Ibid.*, June 30, 1889, p. 2.

94. *Chicago Herald*, May 14, 1889, p. 3, and June 30, 1889, p. 10.

95. *Ibid.*, March 31, 1889, p. 11; *Chicago Times*, May 12, 1889, p. 1, and June 27, 1889, p. 2; *Inter Ocean*, June 30, 1889, p. 15.

96. Carwardine, *op. cit.*, p. 99; *Chicago Times*, June 30, 1889, p. 2.

97. *Arcade Journal*, August 30, 1890, p. 1; *Calumet Record*, September 26, 1907, p. 1.

98. *Chicago Times*, June 20, 1894, pp. 1, 4.

99. *Ibid.*, May 1, 1890, p. 1, and May 7, 1890, p. 2; *Chicago Tribune*, May 3, 1890, p. 1.

100. *Chicago Tribune*, April 2, 1890, p. 2.

101. *Chicago Times*, November 6, 1888, p. 2; *Inter Ocean*, November 14, 1888, p. 7.

102. Grant, *op. cit.*, p. 194.

103. *Op. cit.*, pp. 3–4.

104. Wright *et al.*, *op. cit.*, pp. 25–26.

105. November 8, 1884, p. 12.

106. *Op. cit.*, pp. 184–91.

107. Ely, *op. cit.*, pp. 465–66.

CHAPTER V

ORIGIN OF THE PULLMAN STRIKE

EW people prior to 1894 realized that the Pullman experiment harbored tragic weaknesses. Underneath the apparent calm and contentment of the Pullman citizenry existed basic grievances, which helped to condition the psychology of labor on the eve of the great strike. For many years the underlying causes for discontent had to a large degree remained dormant in the model town, finding expression only in sporadic instances; but in the face of starvation wages, ushered in by the panic of 1893, all grievances were fused into a spirit of violent resistance against a corporation which the employees had come to distrust, fear, and hate. The grievances thus became cumulative, some of which related to the operation of the model town and others of which involved the policy of the company toward labor.

Paternalism—the very basis of the Pullman experiment—was a source of constant annoyance to the inhabitants. The lack of freedom, the persistent surveillance of the Pullman officials, and the numerous restrictions imposed upon the tenants served to develop a feeling of antagonism toward the Pullman Company. The absence of democracy in almost every phase of the experiment could not have been welcomed by the Pullman employees, whose sense of independence was as keen as that of any labor group. Irving Pond, a collaborator in the building of Pullman and an ardent supporter of the experiment, acknowledged years afterward that there had developed among the Pullman inhabitants by 1894 a feeling that the town was anachronistic and represented some form of medieval barony.[1] An investigation of conditions at Pullman in 1888 convinced the *Chicago Tribune* that the advantages existing in the communities surrounding the model town were only partially enjoyed in the "pent-up Utopia across the Pullman line." The paper observed:

There are variety and freedom on the outside. There are monotony and surveillance on the inside. None of the "superior," or "scientific" advantages of the model city will compensate for the restrictions on the freedom of the workmen, the denial of opportunities of ownership, the heedless and vexatious parade of authority, and the sense of injustice arising from the well founded belief that the charges of the company for rent, heat, gas, water, etc. are excessive—if not extortionate. . . . . Pullman may appear to be all glitter and glow, all gladness and glory to the casual visitor, but there is the deep, dark background of discontent which it would be idle to deny.[2]

Among the major causes for dissatisfaction was the refusal of the corporation to give the inhabitants the right to own property in Pullman. The company seemed to have been cognizant of the need to eliminate this source of discontent, but nothing was ever done about it for fear that homeownership would endanger the successful continuance of the experiment. Against the natural yearnings of the employees, the position of the company carried no conviction; and, with unfailing persistency, the inhabitants continued to make requests for the privilege of purchasing sites and building homes in Pullman.[3] The United States Strike Commission held that the policy of the company in this matter not only served to intensify differences during the great strike but was responsible for the absence among the inhabitants of any "local attachment or any interested responsibility in the town, its business, tenements, or surroundings."[4]

The desire for homeownership was satisfied to some extent in near-by communities where, on the eve of the strike, 17 per cent of the employees owned their homes.[5] Non-Pullman residents, however, were obliged to cross a broad strip of open, uninhabited prairie, as wide as one and a half miles, in order to reach the Pullman shops; and this inconvenience doubtless caused many employees to remain in the model town. The fear of discrimination during slack periods obviously deterred many workers from living outside of Pullman whether as homeowners or as renters.

Gas and water charges and the library fee to a lesser extent contributed to the general feeling of antagonism toward the Pullman Company. Judging by the small number of inhabitants who paid the three-dollar annual library fee, not many took very seriously the declaration of the Pullman Company that this charge was made "not for profit, but to give subscribers a sense of ownership."[6] Whatever may have been the actual facts relative to the profits enjoyed by the company in the sale of gas and water, it was widely believed that the charges for these utilities were exorbitant.

Few matters rankled in the minds of the Pullman inhabitants as much as the question of rentals which, throughout the strike, gained recognition as a grievance of the first order. The level of rents, which has been analyzed elsewhere, was extraordinarily high in comparison with the rents charged in Kensington, Gano, and Roseland. One influential real estate agent, who operated extensively in these communities, affirmed that houses with similar conditions to those renting for $17 in Pullman could be leased for $10 in neighboring towns.[7] Not only he but others declared that rent in Pullman was approximately 33 per cent higher than elsewhere.[8] The Strike Commission, after sifting a tremendous amount of evidence, concluded that rents in Pullman were from 20 to 25 per cent higher than elsewhere in Chicago for similar accommodations, excluding sanitary and aesthetic characteristics. In justification of its rental policy, the Pullman Company stressed the superior hygienic and aesthetic features of its homes; but these modern aspects, as the Strike Commission pointed out, possessed little value when bread was lacking. Indeed, in 1894 conditions had reached the stage where better homes had lost their meaning to a people struggling desperately to eke out a bare subsistence. The Pullman Corporation preferred to ignore all this, contending that since rentals yielded less than 4 per cent on the investment they were, if anything, too low.[9]

During the panic of 1893 the Pullman Company as paymaster reduced wages sharply, while as landlord it refused to make any adjustment in the charges for rent. Exercising freely the right to employ in the labor markets as cheaply as possible, the corporation would not recognize that the same conditions which depressed wages should force down rentals. In defense of this position, George Pullman explained that the employment of laborers and the renting of dwellings were in no way tied together.[10] The claim that dissatisfied Pullman tenants were free to take residence elsewhere was hardly tenable. Rev. Morris L. Wickman, pastor of the Pullman Swedish Methodist Church, was among those who testified before the Strike Commission to the practice of pressure being applied on non-Pullman tenants. He declared that in the fall of 1893 the foremen of the Pullman shops ordered the men who lived in neighboring towns to move into Pullman if they wished to retain their positions. As Wickman explained, highly skilled workers were not so much affected by this ruling; but several laborers, with whom he was personally acquainted, were compelled to transfer their residence from Kensington to Pullman.[11] Although the amount of this pressure cannot be accurately gauged, it should be observed that, whereas before the depression only one-half of the employees were inhabitants of the model town, more than two-thirds were Pullman residents by April, 1894.[12]

The rent proved an intolerable burden on the underpaid workers. In spite of all the company could do, the arrearage in rent mounted rapidly, reaching seventy thousand dollars at the time of the strike and finally touching one hundred thousand dollars.[13] In view of such general delinquency, the Pullman officials could not very satisfactorily resort to eviction; nor was this necessary, as most of the unemployed sooner or later made their exit from the town.[14] The rental situation forced large numbers of tenants to sublet rooms, with the result that more than eleven hundred Pullman employees were lodgers in 1894—a fact which explained the overcrowded condition in many homes, while numerous dwellings stood vacant. As the strike drew to a close, the tragic story was most impressively revealed by the 33 per cent of unoccupied tenements in a town that had been characteristically busy, prosperous, and free of distress.[15]

It was through no fault of the Pullman Company that the arrearage in rent reached such startling proportions, since everything possible was done to collect rent. Under the drastic wage slashes and the irregular working conditions of 1894 the earnings of many laborers were so small that every bit was needed for the purchase of food and clothing. The Pullman bank, in the capacity of rent collector, was inclined to ignore this situation.

Tenants were told that the Pullman Company expected the payment of rent the same as any landlord and that, in case the renter refused to pay, the proper authorities would be notified and eviction recommended.[16] Regardless of this pressure, hundreds of men during the dark days of that depression were unable to apply more than the scantiest amount on their rent bills.

In the winter of 1893 and 1894 pathetic scenes were enacted at the bank. Some witnesses testified before the Strike Commission —and this was not refuted by the company—that at times employees received for work done in a period of two weeks from 4 cents to $1.00 over and above their rent.[17] Rev. Carwardine affirmed that many laborers, after paying their rent, had from $1.00 to $6.00 left on which to support their families for two weeks. Among the cases he cited was that of a skilled mechanic whose semimonthly pay check on one occasion totaled only $9.07, all but 7 cents of which was taken by the bank for rent.[18] In describing his experience, Thomas W. Heathcoate, a skilled employee, revealed how harshly the system of rent collection tended to operate:

> If I only had nine dollars coming to me, or any other amount, the rent would be taken out of my pay; that is, the rent check would be left at the bank, and I would have to leave my work in the shop, go over to the bank and have an argument there for a few minutes to get the gentlemen to let me have money to live on, and sometimes I would get it and sometimes not. I have seen men with families of eight or nine children to support crying there because they got only three or four cents after paying their rent; I have seen them stand by the window and cry for money enough to enable them to keep their families; I have been insulted at that window time and time again by the clerk when I tried to get enough to support my family, even after working every day and overtime. . . . .[19]

Resentment among the employees was further aggravated by conditions in the shops. The policy which the company pursued toward labor was rarely tempered with the spirit of conciliation. So effectively did the officials of the corporation resist unionization that prior to 1894 organized labor could gain no foothold in Pullman. It made little difference how much justice sustained the cause of the workers, since the company would never submit any issue to arbitration and would proceed to lay down whatever terms and regulations were believed best to serve its interests.

Much of the ill will was attributed to such shop abuses as black-listing, arbitrary dismissal of laborers, nepotism, favoritism, and tyranny on the part of the foremen. How serious these really were cannot be ascertained, although some Pullman employees, in testifying before the Strike Commission, attached much importance to them. Some witnesses charged that the foremen were unfair, capricious, and often abusive to the employees and that men were hired and discharged, not on a basis of merit, but according to favoritism. It was further averred that the workers were required to experiment occasionally with new and different materials and paints; and, if anything went wrong, they were obliged to make it right without pay for the time lost.[20] There is reason to believe that these complaints were less serious than alleged and that they were due in part to the more stringent shop rules to which the company resorted in seeking to repress the growing discontent. But, whatever may have been the actual situation, it was apparent that no system existed by which the complaints of employees could be registered and investigated impartially.

Most hated of all shop abuses was blacklisting. In December, 1893, for instance, a strike by the steamfitters caused the corporation to prepare a blacklist of forty-one names. Signed by the manager of the Pullman shops, the order served notice on all foremen: "In connection with the recent trouble we have had with steam fitters, both in the construction and repair department, I give below the names of the men who have left our employ, and I hereby instruct that none of these men be employed in these works." According to some witnesses, this blacklist was even sent to various railroad companies.[21] Jane Addams related in *Twenty Years at Hull House* the case of a Pullman worker who, as leader during the Pullman Strike, was so thoroughly blacklisted that three years afterward he was unable to get work. Once under an assumed name he obtained a job in the repair shops of a streetcar company, but as soon as his identity became known he was peremptorily discharged.[22]

The principal cause of the strike of 1894 was a radical reduction of wages fostered by a depression in business conditions.

During the fiscal year ending July 31, 1893, the Pullman Company experienced a period of exceptional prosperity, earning total profits of over $6,500,000 and employing 5,500 men in the shops at Pullman.[23] Unexpectedly, in the late summer of 1893, business slumped tremendously. In the construction division, where cars were manufactured for the general market, the blow fell heaviest. Here most of the workers were employed, and here the corporation suffered losses. Orders for cars were canceled, and pending contracts failed to materialize, with the result that by November 1 there were less than 1,100 employees at work in the Pullman shops. The Detroit branch of the corporation, normally employing about 800 men, was closed so that its contract and repair business could be concentrated at Pullman. Every department witnessed the most rigid retrenchment.[24]

In August, 1893, the company was not invited to bid on a single contract; in September it was offered the opportunity to make six bids, all of which were rejected; and in October, by reducing its bids, the corporation managed to win seven contracts which netted an aggregate profit of slightly over $1,100. Two alternatives remained open to George Pullman: either close the construction division completely or meet competition by submitting bids for less than the cost of production. The latter course seemed preferable, and prices for the construction of passenger cars, baggage cars, refrigerator cars, streetcars, and boxcars were reduced an average of almost 25 per cent. During the seven and one-half months prior to the strike, the company, by virtue of this drastic policy, managed to secure forty-four contracts, aggregating almost $1,500,000 worth of business, but lost thirty-nine other contracts, representing an amount almost as large. In meeting competition, the Pullman Corporation was thus able to keep the construction shops operating; and because of this and other adjustments, the working force in the Pullman shops by April, 1894, had increased to almost 3,300 employees.[25]

Regardless of financial losses, George Pullman was anxious to keep the shops open—an action which he interpreted as a generous move designed solely to benefit the workers.[26] The Strike Commission, however, preferred to attribute this policy to business expediency. In their judgment the evidence seemed fairly conclusive that the Pullman Company

sought to keep running mainly for its own benefits as a manufacturer, that its plant might not rust, that its competitors might not invade its territory, that it might keep its cars in repair, that it might be ready for resumption when business revived with a live plant and competent help, and that its revenue from its tenements might continue.[27]

In the operating division, to which the repair department belonged, the effect of the depression was not serious. In comparison with the 1893 fiscal year, that of 1894 showed only a 7 per cent decrease in the number of palace-car passengers and revealed the earnings from this source to be $8,762,000, or only $438,000 less than in 1893. The revenue from the operating division in 1894 was sufficient to have absorbed all losses sustained in the construction department, to have permitted the payment of regular dividends, and in addition to have left a tidy surplus of over $2,000,000.[28] It was the contention of George Pullman, however, that the operating division was distinct from the car-building division and that the profits of one should not, as a matter of business, be used to cushion the losses incurred in the other.

Adhering to a philosophy of business that was extremely hard and realistic, George Pullman could understand only one way to meet the situation in the profit-losing division and that was to slash wages to the minimum. Reducing pay in one department to the exclusion of another was deemed inexpedient, and so it was decided that irrespective of departments none of the workers would be exempted from the new and drastic wage policy. Thus the repair division, which continued to show profits, was in no way spared. Although normally two-thirds of the employees at Pullman were engaged in the construction of cars for the outside market, the depression had crippled this department so badly that previous to the strike only a minority of employees, estimated by some to be less than 20 per cent, were engaged in this type of work.[29] Nevertheless, it was this department that determined the wage scale for all Pullman workers. In probing the matter the Strike Commission discovered that the reduction in the repair department was part of a plan to slash wages in every department to the lowest possible level to be reached in the department affected most seriously by business conditions. In the opinion of the commissioners such a policy could not be defended as fair or just.[30]

In operating the construction shops at a deficit, George Pullman contended that both the company and the workers should shoulder the loss equally. In his opinion, wages differed in no way from other commodity prices and should likewise be subject to the inexorable law of supply and demand. Paying wages above the market price, he believed, would be the same as sharing with labor the profits of the company, and this the corporation could never do, since profits were subject to division only among the shareholders.[31] In distributing the losses sustained in the construction of cars, from September 18, 1893, to May 1, 1894, the company absorbed fifty-two thousand dollars and, by reducing wages, forced labor to assume over sixty thousand dollars. The materials utilized in this contract work represented more than 75 per cent of the total costs; and, since the cost of labor counted for less than one-fourth, it was evident that the employees were obliged to absorb the greater proportion of the losses.[32] A more equitable division, according to the Strike Commission, would have been three-fourths for the company and the balance for labor.[33]

Reduction in wages was realized in two ways: by scaling down contract and piece-work rates and by reducing proportionately the wages of those paid by the hour. A majority of the men were normally paid by the former method, and the rates, so the company explained, were based upon what a competent worker could accomplish in a day; but the employees held that during 1893–94 the rates were, instead, determined by what experts could do. The reduction in wages throughout the shops averaged about 25 per cent[34] but was considerably higher in the case of many workers. There was little evidence that the company attempted in any way to equalize the pay slashes, and this furnished additional cause for dissatisfaction. Those who suffered least as a group were the painters, whose reduction in pay averaged 17½ per cent; and those who suffered most were the freight-car builders, whose loss in earnings represented 41 per cent. The average daily earnings of this group declined from $2.61 to $1.54 between April, 1893, and April, 1894; but for all categories of journeymen mechanics, according to statistics of the company, the decline in the average daily earnings during this period was from $2.63 to $2.03.[35]

A few specific cases will illustrate even more clearly the scope of the reduction. Thomas W. Heathcoate, an inside finisher, averaged in May, 1893, 30 cents per hour doing contract or piece work, but only 20½ cents in April, 1894. More serious was the case of Robert W. Coombs, car-builder, whose rate of pay during this period declined 37½ per cent; and almost as unfortunate was Jennie Curtis, seamstress, whose earnings fell from 17 cents per hour to 11 cents—a reduction of 35 per cent. The skilled mechanics, who comprised 60 per cent of the workers at the time of the strike, were affected more seriously by the new wage schedules than any other group, owing perhaps to the fact that their earnings were larger and hence more vulnerable to a policy of wage slashing. Figures of company origin indicate that ordinary laborers and semiskilled workers were reduced only 11½ per cent, but, even so, their average daily earnings in April, 1894, did not exceed $1.48.

The situation was further aggravated by scarcity of work, which caused the company to adopt a policy of staggering employment wherever possible. With reference to the above three workers: Heathcoate, for instance, averaged weekly during October, 1893, 28½ hours of work and $6.73 in wages; Coombs in the same month averaged per week only 10 hours of work and $1.85 in wages; and, although Jennie Curtis was supplied regularly with work, her rate of pay was so low that in March, 1894, she averaged $6.23 weekly. During April, the month prior to the strike, the average daily earnings of these employees were: Heathcoate, $1.51; Coombs, 36 cents; and Curtis, 88 cents.[36] Others fared somewhat better, but too many received a mere pittance because of successive wage reductions and the inability of the shops to supply work to the employees for all or even a major part of the full 10¾-hour day. With earnings so low it was impos-

sible for many of the workers to pay rent and purchase even the
barest essentials of life. The winter of 1893–94 was crowded with
tragedy for many Pullman toilers, some of whom were unable to
secure any work in the shops. Spring brought little relief and not
much more hope.

Interestingly enough, the salaries of all Pullman officials, superintendents, and foremen were not reduced at all. In defending
this policy George Pullman pointed out that it was necessary to
leave the pay in the higher brackets untouched in order to keep
the official force intact and prevent resignations. As an explanation for not reducing his own salary, he said that such a reduction
would have only an infinitesimal effect on the cost of a car.[37] In
commenting on the inequality of Pullman's wage and salary policy, the Strike Commission took the position that a reduction in
salaries "would not have been so severely felt, would have
showed good faith, would have relieved the harshness of the situation and would have evinced genuine sympathy with labor in
the disasters of the times."[38]

To an impartial observer the financial strength of the Pullman
Company was in strange contrast to the pitiful plight of its employees. In 1893 the company possessed assets worth $62,000,-
000, of which $26,000,000 represented undivided profits. After
the dividends of 8 per cent were paid in that year, a surplus of
$4,000,000 remained from the profits of the year—an amount
sufficient to have declared additional dividends of 10 per cent.
Pullman stock, never watered, was quoted in April, 1893, at 106
per cent above par and throughout the most disturbing phases of
the strike at never less than 50 per cent above par. In spite of the
losses sustained in the construction department, the earnings of
the corporation in the 1894 fiscal year were such as to warrant the
regular 8 per cent dividends, which totaled $2,880,000, and in
addition to yield a surplus of $2,320,000. Out of its earnings in
that depression year, the company could have paid a total of 14
per cent on its stock.[39] Had the Pullman Corporation dipped but
lightly into the $4,000,000 surplus of 1893 or had been willing to
accept a somewhat smaller surplus for 1894, there would have
been no need for the drastic wage reduction.

Vastly different from the Pullman Corporation was the plight of the underpaid employees. The statement of the company at the world's Columbian Exposition of 1893—that the inhabitants of the model town were 40 per cent better off than the men in ordinary manufacturing towns—was no longer tenable. In the face of starvation wages, living standards in Pullman declined sharply. Savings accumulated over a period of years were in many cases quickly exhausted. During the boom months of 1893, 50 per cent of the Pullman workers had bank deposits, one-half of whom possessed less than $100 and five-sixths less than $500.[40] Such reserves proved far too small as the weeks of reduced earnings and empty pay envelopes stretched into months.

The Pullman employees thus did not enter the strike with well-filled larders or with sufficient resources to sustain them as they battled for redress of their grievances. It was rather as despairing, penniless, and desperate workers that they hurled the gauntlet at the feet of one of the most powerful corporations of the age. The plight of the Pullman inhabitants can be envisaged from the following appeal made to the citizens of Chicago during the early stages of the strike:

The people of Pullman are destitute and starving. Over five thousand human beings are in dire necessity, and appeal to the liberal minded people of Chicago for help. Their unfortunate condition is due to no fault of theirs. They have been noted for their thrift, sobriety, and industry. The fault lies in the hard times and a hard taskmaster. . . . . They have struck against a slavery worse than that of the negroes of the South. They, at least, were well fed and well cared for, while the white slaves of Pullman, worked they ever so willingly, could not earn enough to clothe and feed themselves decently—hardly enough to keep body and soul together. Now that they have struck for a living wage, for a fair day's pay, for a fair day's work, they find themselves penniless, with gaunt famine and despair staring them in the face. . . . . Help them as you wish to be helped in the hour of affliction. Their cause is the cause of humanity. Their struggle is the struggle of honest industry against corporate greed.[41]

Within the model town there developed two factions: one, small but influential, which supported George Pullman; the other, large but poverty-stricken, which resisted his policies. Belonging to the former group were the Pullman officials, who during the strike assembled frequently at the Florence Hotel and who wore as their insignia a miniature American flag. The discontented laborers, comprising the opposing faction, adopted the white ribbon as their symbol.[42] Rev. E. Christian Oggel, pastor of the Green Stone Church, reflected the viewpoint entertained by the Pullman supporters; while Rev. William Carwardine, pastor of the Pullman Methodist Church, championed the cause of the toilers.

Less than three weeks before the Pullman employees struck, Rev. E. C. Oggel preached to his congregation on "George M. Pullman, his services to his age, his country, and humanity." Using as his text: "Thou hast made him a little lower than the angels and hast crowned him with glory and honor," Oggel traced carefully the rise of Pullman from poverty, emphasizing his persevering industry and executive ingenuity. The Pullman experiment was referred to as a venture in "contemplated beauty and harmony, health, comfort and contentment." Declared the minister:

Surely it would seem as if Mr. Pullman has done his part. It is not for me to say what "If Christ came to Chicago" He would say to the founder of the town, but one would think that He who said, "To every man his work," and who required of men to use their God given talents would not undertake to say that Mr. Pullman has buried his in a napkin. . . . . There is wealth that is material and it is his today, having come to him as fragrance comes from a flower; and then another wealth is his also—soul wealth and that man is truly rich who has the noblest ideas and the highest aspirations.[43]

Cast in a different mold was the sermon preached by Rev. William Carwardine to his congregation shortly after the commencement of the strike. In characterizing George Pullman, Carwardine belittled the remarks of Rev. Oggel by declaring: "I have nothing to say of him that savors of fulsome eulogy or nauseating praise. I will not speak of him as a philanthropist, for I have neither seen nor heard of any evidence of this. I will not speak of his services to his country, as history is silent thereon." Why, inquired the minister, did George Pullman refuse to render adequate assistance to his employees during the past winter when wages were at their lowest level and many families were in want? Instead of recognizing the existence of destitution and meeting the situation, why did he pretend there was none? If this man has our interest at heart, asked the clergyman, why does he not

bring himself into a little closer contact with the public life of our town, cheer his employees with his fatherly presence and allow the calloused hand of labor occasionally to grasp the gentle hand of the man who professes to be so interested in our welfare? Never until George Pullman can give a satisfactory answer to this question will I account him a benefactor to his race, a lover of his kind, a philanthropist, or one who has done anything for posterity which will cause mankind when his dust slumbers beneath the sod, to rise up and call his name blessed. . . . . To the casual visitor it [the Pullman system] is a veritable paradise; but it is a hollow mockery, a sham, an institution girdled with red tape, and as a solution of the labor problem most unsatisfactory.[44]

Fully convinced that their grievances could not be redressed except through united effort, the employees began to organize during the early part of April, 1894. Throughout the winter months dissatisfaction had multiplied and with it a growing determination to take some action in the spring. On the horizon loomed a new labor organization, the American Railway Union. With a rapidly expanding membership and a very promising future, it offered a tremendous appeal to the restless Pullman employees, who were encouraged to join. Since all union activity in the model town was forbidden, recruiting was done at Grand Crossing and Kensington; and so successful was the unionization drive that ultimately nineteen local unions were founded with a total membership of four thousand men.[45]

Fortified by a feeling of solidarity, the Pullman workers decided to demand certain concessions from the Pullman Corporation. Aware that general conditions were inauspicious for a strike, the American Railway Union strongly advised against the employment of this weapon;[46] but the Pullman employees were in no mood to heed such counsel. They had been in a state of discontent for several months and were now prepared to enforce their demands for reduction in rent, an investigation and correction of shop abuses, and the restoration of wages to the pre-depression level. The workers selected a grievance committee of forty-six members, headed by Thomas W. Heathcoate; and on

May 7 this group called on the second vice-president of the Pullman Corporation, Thomas H. Wickes, to whom their demands
were presented. As spokesman, Heathcoate explained that it was
imperative that the old wage level be restored or a reduction in
rent be made and the rates of pay increased sufficiently so the
workers could meet their rental payments and support their families. It was agreed that on May 9 they would return for a further
conference and present a written statement of their grievances.[47]

In the second conference George Pullman participated and,
using a carefully prepared statement, declared that business conditions did not warrant any increase in the present wage scale.
He professed great interest in the welfare of the employees, alluding to the fact that for their benefit the shops were kept open in
spite of losses. It would be impossible, he explained, to secure orders for work at prices based upon the wages demanded. As proof
that losses were being sustained in the construction department,
Pullman offered to allow a small committee of workers to inspect
the books and contracts relative to this phase of the company's
business. As to rent, he categorically refused to make any revision, on the grounds that it had nothing to do with wages and
that the income from this source was no more than reasonable.
The only request which Pullman showed any willingness to grant
was in regard to the investigation of shop complaints.[48]

In the capacity of observer, George W. Howard, vice-president
of the American Railway Union, attended this as well as the
previous conference. Here his role by necessity was passive; but
he did seek assurance, which was readily granted by Wickes, that
membership on the grievance committee would not prove prejudicial to the status of these men in the shops.[49]

The brusque and uncompromising attitude of George Pullman
increased the determination of the workers to strike. All hope
that their grievances would be harmoniously adjusted seemed
completely shattered, and the only remaining alternative appeared to be self-help. The plea that the shops were kept open in
their behalf was received cynically by men who had seen little
evidence of paternal love on the part of George Pullman. As for
the invitation to inspect the books of the company, the employees

were disposed to ignore this, because they had no confidence in books believed to be specially prepared for the occasion.[50] Quarterly dividends had in no wise been suspended or reduced, and this rankled in the minds of the workers who grew increasingly suspicious of the claim that the company was losing money in the shops. Slashing wages in all departments because of losses proclaimed in one seemed incongruous, as did the refusal to scale down the rentals. In the opinion of Heathcoate and others, including the Strike Commissioners, the difficulties would probably have been averted had the rent been reduced in proportion to wages.[51] Although officials of the company launched an investigation of shop complaints on the morning of May 10, the workers, in their agitated mood, were not impressed and preferred to consider the whole thing a sham.[52] They were now eager to abandon further negotiation and to try other means for the redress of their grievances.

NOTES

1. *Op. cit.*, p. 8.
2. September 21, 1888, p. 9.
3. *U.S. Strike Commission Report*, p. 504.
4. *Ibid.*, pp. xxii–xxiii.
5. Pullman, *op. cit.*, p. 21.
6. *Ibid.*, p. 23; *U.S. Strike Commission Report*, pp. xxi–xxii.
7. *U.S. Strike Commission Report*, pp. 466–67.
8. *Ibid.*, pp. 462, 492–93.
9. *Ibid.*, pp. xxxv, 530, 564.
10. *Op. cit.*, p. 28.
11. *U.S. Strike Commission Report*, pp. 462–64.
12. *Ibid.*, p. 598; "Annual Report of the Pullman Company," *Pullman Journal*, October 21, 1893, p. 4.
13. *U.S. Strike Commission Report*, pp. xxxvi, 611.
14. "Annual Report of the Pullman Company," *Pullman Journal*, October 20, 1894, p. 4.
15. *U.S. Strike Commission Report*, pp. 507, 598.
16. *Ibid.*, pp. 515–17, 520–22.
17. *Ibid.*, p. xxxiv.
18. Carwardine, *op. cit.*, p. 69.
19. *U.S. Strike Commission Report*, p. 426.
20. *Ibid.*, pp. xxxvi, 436–37, 440; *Chicago Times*, May 13, 1894, p. 1.
21. *U.S. Strike Commission Report*, pp. 421, 453.
22. P. 218.
23. "Annual Report of the Pullman Company," *Pullman Journal*, October 21, 1893, p. 4.

24. *U.S. Strike Commission Report*, pp. xxxii, 536, 571–73.
25. *Ibid.*, pp. 536, 572–73, 577, 592.
26. Pullman, *op. cit.*, p. 26.
27. *U.S. Strike Commission Report*, p. xxxv.
28. "Annual Statement of the Pullman Company, 1893 and 1894," "Annual Reports of the Pullman Palace Car Company, 1883–1921."
29. *U.S. Strike Commission Report*, pp. 423–24, 458, 472, 554–57.
30. *Ibid.*, p. xxxiv.
31. *Ibid.*, pp. 557, 565.
32. *Ibid.*, pp. xxxii, 603–4.
33. *Ibid.*, p. xxxii.
34. *Ibid.*, p. xxxiii.
35. *Ibid.*, pp. 592, 593.
36. *Ibid.*, pp. 593, 596.
37. *Ibid.*, p. 567.
38. *Ibid.*, p. xxxiv.
39. "Annual Statement of the Pullman Company, 1893 and 1894," "Annual Reports of the Pullman Palace Car Company, 1883–1921"; *New York World*, July 11, 1894, p. 2.
40. *U.S. Strike Commission Report*, pp. xxii, 510–11.
41. William T. Stead, *Chicago Today*, p. 178 (reprint of appeal made to the citizens of Chicago on May 28, 1894).
42. Carwardine, *op. cit.*, p. 45.
43. *Pullman Journal*, May 5, 1894, p. 5.
44. Stead, *Chicago Today*, pp. 125–26 (quotation from sermon of Rev. Carwardine on May 21, 1894); Carwardine, *op. cit.*, pp. 27–29.
45. *U.S. Strike Commission Report*, pp. xxiii, xxvii, 6–7, 417.
46. *Ibid.*, pp. xxvii, 7, 79, 433.
47. *Ibid.*, pp. xxxvii, 417, 419, 423, 432.
48. *Ibid.*, pp. xxxvii, 538, 579–80, 584, 586, 611.
49. *Ibid.*, pp. 7, 586.
50. *Ibid.*, p. 425.
51. *Ibid.*, pp. xxxvii, 424, 445–46.
52. *Ibid.*, p. 598; Carwardine, *op. cit.*, p. 36.

CHAPTER VI

THE AMERICAN RAILWAY UNION AND THE GENERAL MANAGERS' ASSOCIATION

THE founder of the American Railway Union was Eugene Victor Debs, whose consuming passion in life was to champion the cause of labor and to wage an untiring struggle in behalf of social justice. Few men possessed more courage or determination than this leader, and none was actuated by a higher sense of idealism. If the causes for which he battled proved to be lost causes, it was not due to a lack of fortitude or resourcefulness on his part but rather to the times, which made the odds against him fearfully great. In a life featured by tempestuous and stormy incidents, no period was more dramatic or adventuresome than the Pullman Strike. Here as elsewhere he displayed the qualities which endeared him to those who knew him best. In tribute to this individual, Clarence Darrow wrote:

There may have lived some time, somewhere, a kindlier, gentler, more generous man than Eugene Debs, but I have never known him. Nor have I ever read or heard of another. . . . . He was not only all that I have said, but he was the bravest man that I ever knew. He never felt fear. He had the courage of the babe who had no conception of the world or its meaning.[1]

Eugene Debs was born of French parentage on November 5, 1855, at Terre Haute, Indiana. He attended the public schools in that city and subsequently took a short business course in a commercial college; but his intellectual advancement was due primarily to his voracious appetite for good books and magazines. In 1870, at the age of fourteen years, he obtained railroad employment, serving first as car-cleaner, then as car-painter, and finally as locomotive fireman. In 1874 Debs left this service and subsequently accepted a clerkship in a grocery firm and a few years later was elected city clerk of Terre Haute—a position to which he was annually chosen for a period of four years. His political ambitions, although short lived, carried him in 1884 to a term in the Indiana legislature, after which he was so disgusted with politics that he abandoned further interest in public office. For many years previously he had been associated with labor-union activity, and to this field he now turned his full attention. When the Brotherhood of Locomotive Firemen was organized at Terre Haute, Debs joined as a charter member; and so effectively did he serve this union that in 1878 he was chosen associate editor of their journal, the *Locomotive Firemen's Magazine*. Two years later he was made editor and manager of this publication and also grand secretary and treasurer of their union. Until his resignation from these offices about thirteen years later, Debs was re-elected by successive conventions of the union and during his incumbency immeasurably strengthened the financial status of the organization and increased the circulation of the journal from fifteen hundred to thirty-seven thousand copies per month.[2] His extreme success and popularity, however, did not blind him to what he considered the obsoleteness and inadequacy of this as well as of the other railroad brotherhoods.

The various railroad unions were seeking to promote their own ends, irrespective of the best interest of all and often to the disadvantage of one another. Instead of a spirit of unity and co-operation among the brotherhoods, there was a feeling of mutual jealousy and rivalry. This condition proved extremely auspicious for the railroad corporations, which could deal with each brotherhood separately and in a labor dispute could combat the aggrieved union without any great danger of the others rallying to its support. Nor was this the whole picture, since the brotherhoods represented only a small fraction of all railroad employees. The great mass of those who toiled as unskilled and semiskilled workers remained unorganized, and even among the firemen, conductors, engineers, and trainmen many were nonunion.[3] In sharp contrast to this disorganization and disunity were the powerful railroad companies which had learned from experience the value of co-operation. All railroads having terminals in Chicago had formed the General Managers' Association, which, in labor policies and other matters of common concern, pursued a policy of one for all and all for one.

As Debs surveyed the situation, he was impressed with the need for a new order of affairs among railway toilers. Complete unity, in his judgment, could be realized only through one great union, to which all railroad workers, skilled and unskilled, would be admitted. Under such a banner they would no longer be divided and conquered but could defend their rights with dignity and assurance.[4] Before the Cincinnati convention of the Brotherhood of Locomotive Firemen in 1892 Eugene Debs explained the need for such a union and revealed a strong desire to establish it. In order to be free for this work, he tendered his resignation as grand secretary and treasurer; but the delegates, grateful for his services, rejected it and voted him two thousand dollars for a trip to Europe. This he declined, and no amount of entreaties could swerve him from his decision. He agreed, however, to retain for a time the editorship of their journal.[5] In justifying before the convention his venture into a new and untried field of union activity, he declared:

I do this because it pleases me, and there is nothing I would not do, so far as human effort goes, to advance any movement designed to reach and rescue perishing humanity. I have a heart for others and that is why I am in this work. When I see suffering about me, I myself suffer, and so when I put forth my efforts to relieve others, I am simply working for myself. I do not consider that I have made any sacrifice whatever; no man does, unless he violates his conscience.[6]

When the American Railway Union was launched, Eugene Debs was thirty-eight years of age. Over six feet in height, he carried himself erectly. Though he was afflicted with considerable baldness and obliged to wear glasses, his appearance in general was prepossessing and his clean-shaven face radiated strength of character. Endowed with a habitually serious expression, he was nevertheless gifted with a keen sense of humor and in conversation became extremely animated. He was an able, forceful, and eloquent speaker, and his charming personality inspired absolute confidence among his followers. Few men were more devoted to their families than Eugene Debs, who spent most of his evenings at home, having no outside pleasures. His affection for his parents was revealed during the Pullman Strike when, despite crushing responsibilities, he always found time to wire or write to them daily. He did not attend church and was a great admirer of Colonel Robert Ingersoll.[7]

The American Railway Union was founded in the city of Chicago on June 20, 1893, by Eugene Debs and others who had been invited to participate in the movement. Membership was open to all white employees who served the railroads in any capacity, except superintendents and other high officials. Even coal-miners, longshoremen, and car-builders, if in the employ of a railroad, were invited to join. Because the Pullman Corporation owned and operated a few miles of railroad, its employees were eligible. The admission of workers having such a remote relationship to railroading was perhaps a source of weakness and, in the opinion of some, most unfortunate.[8]

In working out the constitution for the union, it was deemed advisable to make the government as democratic as possible. Ten or more workers could establish a local union by petitioning the directors of the national organization for a charter. Former railroad workers were admitted as members by a two-thirds vote of the local union, while all others who were eligible required only a majority vote. Any member who engaged directly or indirectly in the sale of intoxicating liquor was subject to immediate dismissal. The only membership fee regularly demanded by the general union was an annual assessment of one dollar, to be transmitted to the headquarters in Chicago. District conventions were to be held annually in each state and territory, and a national convention was to be convened quadrennially in Chicago. The latter assembly elected the executive board, which comprised nine directors and which met at least four times annually. This group directed the affairs of the union, supervised and participated in organizational work, and, whenever the occasion demanded, could call a special convention of the general union. The president, vice-president, and secretary were chosen annually by the executive board to whom they were directly responsible. In such a framework, the president could not very easily usurp power or impose his will dictatorially upon the organization.[9]

EUGENE V. DEBS

Realizing that strikes were equally disastrous to the employees and the employers, the American Railway Union in its statement of principles expressed the belief that, by being reasonable and fair in all demands and honorable in all relations, it would be possible to adjust differences without recourse to lockouts, strikes, blacklists, and boycotts. The machinery of the union was carefully geared to settle grievances in a harmonious fashion. Each local union elected a board of mediation, to which grievances could be referred for adjustment. In case of failure, the matter would then be presented to the general board of mediation, comprising the chairmen of all the local boards of mediation on a given railroad. Failure here would cause the grievance to be brought to the attention of the president of the union who, through the directors, would further try to seek a conciliatory solution. In the event that all other methods failed, the various local unions on the railroad involved in the dispute would vote on the advisability of calling a strike, and such action could be taken if a majority decided favorably. The general union thus had no authority to call a strike on any railroad unless the local unions on that line favored such a course. Only in matters of general concern did the whole organization operate as one.[10]

The maintenance of a living-wage scale and satisfactory working conditions, although highly important, was only one phase in a program designed to promote the general welfare of all members. Various departments, under the direction of appointive committees, were to be created. The department of legislation and co-operation, for instance, was to campaign and lobby for laws in behalf of the eight-hour day, safety appliances for trains, restriction of Sunday work, the employers' liability law, and the right of the laborers to be heard in the courts whenever they had claims to be adjudicated. Among other services which the union hoped to render was life and disability insurance at the lowest possible cost compatible with sound business principles. Unemployed members were privileged to register in the employment department, which would assist them in finding work. All members were to be educated in the policies and measures best calculated to promote their well-being. Lecturers were to discuss such matters as wages, strikes, and employer-employee relations; but more effective in influencing thought were such projected organs as a daily newspaper and a monthly magazine.[11]

These and other objectives were included in the scope of the American Railway Union's program; but, owing to the stormy and short-lived career of the organization, most of its ambitious plans and aims were never translated into reality. In 1894 the union launched a semimonthly newspaper, the *Railway Times.* Edited by L. W. Rogers, it contained four pages, for which there was an annual subscription charge of one dollar. After the Pullman Strike, this publication declined with the union and was finally superseded in July, 1897, by the *Social Democrat.*[12]

Selected for the major offices of the union were Eugene Debs as president, George W. Howard as vice-president, and Sylvester Keliher as secretary. Pursuing the most rigorous economy, Debs set the pattern by accepting a salary of only nine hundred dollars per year. Although the convention of 1894 raised it to three thousand dollars, there is no evidence that he benefited from the increase, since the union was soon impoverished by the great strike. During the last two years of the existence of this organization, Eugene Debs drew no salary at all; and, in order to help liquidate the forty-thousand-dollar indebtedness of the union, he wrote and made lecture tours. Owing largely to his efforts, there remained no unpaid obligations.[13]

The seal of the American Railway Union featured a hand firmly clasping a torch, symbolizing the enlightenment and hope which the new order expected to inaugurate for labor. Every effort was made to avoid antagonizing the brotherhoods, whose members were informed that they could join the new organization without being obliged to abandon membership in any other union. The brotherhoods, however, realized the implications of the movement and were unable to view it in any other light than as a menace and danger to their security. Their policy immediately became one of nonco-operation, if not downright hostility. Although some recruits came from these older orders, the majority were from the ranks of unorganized labor.[14] The membership drive received extraordinary impetus from the victory enjoyed by the union in a strike on the Great Northern Railroad during the early spring of 1894, and within a year from the date of origin the union boasted of one hundred and fifty thousand members. The American Railway Union was barely ten months old when it engaged in its first struggle. The depression had caused wage slashes on numerous railroads, but on the Great Northern the reductions had been particularly drastic. A circular was issued to members of the union showing that the schedule of wages on this road was lower than that paid on any other Pacific transcontinental line. It is doubtful whether the union at this time had enrolled more than a minority of men on the Great Northern Railroad. When a demand was presented in April for an upward revision of wages and an adjustment of certain other grievances, James Hill seemed unwilling to make any concessions; and, to aggravate the situation, it was rumored that men from the East would be brought in to fill the places of the American Railway Union members. Without delay a strike was ordered, and the employees, displaying unexpected unity, struck in overwhelming numbers. Members of the brotherhoods as well as unorganized workers responded, and so effectively was the railroad paralyzed that no freight moved and no wheels turned except those of mail trains, which were allowed to proceed as usual.

Membership in the American Railway Union was increased by thousands under the astute leadership of Debs and Howard, who personally addressed large gatherings of strikers. Every precaution was utilized by the union to prevent rowdyism and lawlessness, and throughout the strike the men maintained such superb discipline that no blood was shed or any overt act committed. The strike lasted only eighteen days and was settled by arbitration. Hill and Debs agreed to submit the dispute to a group of fourteen representative businessmen of St. Paul and Minneapolis, the chairmanship of which was intrusted to Charles Pillsbury. In almost every respect the award was a smashing victory for labor, and the monthly wages on the Great Northern were increased by a total of $146,000.[15] This victory proved to be a source of profound satisfaction to Eugene Debs, who in a speech at Terre Haute declared:

> My glory, my friends, consists in the gladness which I know will be brought into the little cottage homes of the humble trackmen among the hills in the West. I can almost see the looks of gratitude on the faces of these men's wives and little children. In all my life I have never felt so highly honored as I did when leaving St. Paul on my way home. As our train pulled out of the yards the tokens of esteem, which I prize far more highly than all others, was in seeing the old trackmen, men whose frames were bent with years of grinding toil, who received the pittance of from eighty cents to one dollar a day, leaning on their shovels and lifting their hats to me in appreciation of my humble assistance in a cause which they believed had resulted in a betterment of their miserable existence.[16]

The American Railway Union had indeed made a splendid beginning; but it lacked the experience, prestige, and financial backing which made the General Managers' Association so formidable. Founded in 1886, the association had had a feeble existence for several years and in 1889 had lapsed into complete dormancy. In January, 1892, it was revived, and thereafter it functioned with exceptional vigor. All railroads having terminals in Chicago were eligible to membership. The association in 1894 comprised twenty-four lines, representing 41,000 miles of railroad, $818,000,000 in capital stock, and an aggregate of 221,000 workers. The combined net earnings of these systems exceeded $100,000,000 in the 1894 fiscal year. Many of the members might be classified as giants in the railroad world. Among them were the Atchison, Topeka, and Santa Fe; the Baltimore and Ohio; the Chicago and Northwestern; the Chicago, Burlington, and Quincy; the Chicago, Milwaukee, and St. Paul; the Chicago, Rock Island, and Pacific; the Chicago and Northern Pacific; the Illinois Central; the Chicago and Erie; and the New York, Chicago, and St. Louis. Membership did not necessarily mean that all the trackage of a railroad was subject to the policies of the association. The amount depended entirely on how much a road desired to put in, the Santa Fe, for instance, preferring to exclude the more western portion of her system from the jurisdiction of the association. Although the organization was voluntary and unincorporated,[17] it nevertheless was closely knit and prepared to serve its members smoothly and efficiently both in normal times and during a crisis.

The constitution of this association was unique in its brevity, containing only the barest outline of the structural character of the organization. The purpose of the association was for the "consideration of problems of management arising from the operation of railroads terminating or centering in Chicago." Only the general managers, assistant general managers, and general superintendents were privileged to represent their respective railroads as members in the association. Meetings were to be held regularly every two months, but in case of emergency special sessions could be called. Each year the following officers were elected: chairman, secretary, and an executive committee of five members. To this executive board was intrusted control over matters not considered in the regular meetings, but all members were to be fully informed of every action taken, and they could thus demand a special meeting whenever the occasion warranted. Expenses entailed in the operation of the association were to be apportioned among all members.[18] From the constitution little light is shed on the real nature of the General Managers' Association, and only from its practical workings can its true purpose be envisaged.

Matters of common interest received the full attention of the association. A uniform policy was evolved for all railroads in the Chicago area toward such matters as car service, weights of livestock, loading and unloading of cars, and the schedule of rates for freight and switching. Labor contended that the primary purpose of the association was to determine wage schedules; but this was hardly true, since other problems, equally important, were handled by the organization. But certainly no subject was more vital than wages, even though the association, during its active life, was not faced by many wage controversies. The general managers fully recognized the need for approximate uniformity in wages and a unified policy toward labor.[19]

It was not until the threatened strike of the switchmen in the spring of 1893 that the General Managers' Association revealed the potentialities for united resistance against labor. On March 6 the Switchmen's Mutual Aid Association of North America presented to the managing officials of the various railroads in the Chicago area a demand for an upward revision of wages. These lines maintained for switchmen the same rate of pay, known as the "Chicago scale," and for this reason the request for an increase was made simultaneously to all the railroads in this region.[20] Anticipating the demand, the General Managers' Association held a special meeting on February 27 at its headquarters in the Rookery Building, Chicago. The situation was carefully surveyed, and it was decided that in the event of trouble the best strategy would be to take action through two small but effective committees, each comprising five members to be appointed by Everett St. John, chairman of the association. The first, known as Committee No. 1, was assigned the duty of securing, whenever the occasion demanded, the services of as many switchmen as were needed and bringing them to Chicago for replacement of strikers. The expenses incurred in this service were to be assessed to the roads in proportion to the number of switchmen they employed.

Committee No. 2, as the second group was officially labeled, was required to ascertain the schedule of wage rates and rules effective on all railroads in the association. Each road agreed to submit to this committee for consideration any demand made by labor for a revision in wages or regulations and to make no change not sanctioned by the committee without first notifying the chairman, provided that the committee would take action within five days.[21] This machinery had barely been established when, as expected, the switchmen served notice for a raise in wages, and without delay the demand was immediately referred by the association to Committee No. 2. At the special meeting of the organization on March 9 the committee advised that the request be rejected and no revision in the wage schedule made. The association accepted the report and accordingly notified the switchmen's union to that effect.

As the situation pointed toward a strike, Committee No. 1 was instructed to proceed to its assigned work. Agencies were established in the East, and men were enrolled in almost twenty different cities. A careful record of each application was made, and several thousand men thus became available for immediate employment, some of whom were transferred to Chicago and quartered there. On March 9 it was further decided by a unanimous vote of the general managers that, if the switchmen concentrated their efforts against certain railroads, the loss in revenue and increased expenses sustained by these roads would be borne by all members in "such proportion as may be assessed." As a final precaution, the association provided for the creation of Committee No. 3, to be composed of five members, all residents of Chicago, who could arrange to be in session continuously during a labor crisis. This group was charged with the duty of co-operating with the county and city officials and taking any action in their judgment deemed necessary to facilitate the speedy termination of any labor trouble.[22]

With every breach in its defenses closed and functioning as a harmonious unit, the General Managers' Association awaited the decision of the switchmen's union. Aware of the fearful odds, the switchmen decided on March 12 that conditions for a strike were inopportune and accordingly agreed to abandon their demands and accept the old schedules.[23] The machinery created for this emergency was not discarded but held in readiness for any future difficulties that might arise.

On March 22, 1893, the general-baggage agents of the Lake Shore and Michigan Southern Railroad applied for an increase in wages. Instead of handling the matter alone, the road promptly referred it to Committee No. 2, which approved an increase for baggage masters but not for any other class of baggage agents.[24] To ignore the recommendation of such a committee was deemed unwise and impolitic, nor was it likely that any road would do this, since the machinery of the association was geared to induce compliance. Thus a question of wages on any line became a matter for the entire association, and by virtue of this procedure the position of each member was strengthened immeasurably.

Seeking to foster even greater solidarity, the General Managers' Association appointed a committee in May, 1893, to report at its next regular meeting "as to what liability the organization should assume in connection with future emergencies that may arise." At the July meeting the committee rendered a report, which found ready acceptance. It was decided that if a road, involved in a dispute over wages or regulations, should abide by the recommendations of Committee No. 2, the matter immediately would become an affair of the association. In the event of trouble the entire weight of the organization would be thrown into the struggle, and all committees would function in behalf of the road assailed.[25]

Railroad officials in general shared the belief that the diversity in wage rates among the different roads for the same class of work promoted unrest among the employees and furnished a strong bargaining point to those employed on systems paying less than the highest wages. To eliminate this cause of trouble, it was strongly advocated that the various wage schedules be adjusted wherever possible so as to make them relatively uniform. In order to facilitate this, the General Managers' Association assembled in 1886 data on the wage schedules for each branch of service on all systems having terminals in Chicago. As changes occurred, an attempt was made to keep the members informed, but this was not always done.[26] In November, 1893, the association prepared a new and exhaustive classification of wage rates and grouped them geographically into three broad divisions: eastern, southern, and western. The schedules filled six volumes, covering minutely all classes of employees such as engineers, firemen, breakmen, switchmen, conductors, section men, clerks, and baggagemen. Each member of the association received one set of books for use as a guide in equalizing wages. Reductions in pay were subsequently made here and there on various roads in order to bring their scale of wages more in line with the average. The compilation of these rates was not available to railroads outside the association, but the action taken to standardize wage schedules on member-roads exerted considerable influence on other competing systems.[27]

In January, 1894, Committee No. 2 was instructed to determine the fair average of wages paid by the railroads of the association in the different sections of the United States for each class of yard and train employees. In rendering its report at the special meeting in February, the committee submitted, as requested, a statement of the average rates then paid on all lines but, in addition, proposed a new and greatly reduced schedule of rates for the eastern, western, and southern lines. It was suggested, for instance, that switchmen, switching engineers, and firemen in Chicago and wherever similar rates prevailed should receive the same rates of pay based upon twelve rather than ten hours of work. In numerous other classes of work the committee advocated sweeping reductions in wages or the lengthening of the working day. A lengthy discussion of the report followed, and it was finally decided to refer the entire matter of uniform regulations and average wages to an enlarged committee of ten, consisting of Committee No. 2 and five additional members.[28] The report of this new committee, presented to the association in March, was extremely detailed but in most cases did not favor reductions as drastic as those previously recommended. After a prolonged discussion, the members decided to take no action as an organization,[29] presumably because such a course was considered dangerous and impolitic. The table of recommended rules and rates was, nevertheless, made available to all members and doubtless served as a guide in such matters and was subsequently reflected in the downward revision of wages on certain railroads.

There was some discussion of enlarging the General Managers' Association. On August 31, 1893, a resolution was made favoring a mighty combination of all general managers in the nation and the appointment of a committee for the purpose of taking steps toward the realization of this plan. The resolution stressed the advantage in having wages equalized on all lines for the same class of work.[30] Nothing came of this suggestion, apparently because it was too ambitious and included too many competing systems.

Against the unity and resourcefulness of the General Managers' Association, labor experienced real difficulty in seeking redress of grievances. In pressing for the settlement of a dispute, the employees of a railroad were pitted against the united front of twenty-four powerful corporations. In view of the strikebreaking machinery of the association, geared for immediate action, the laborers, whether unionized or not, were obviously at a great disadvantage. It was this situation, more than any other, that determined Eugene Debs to unite all classes of railroad workers into a mammoth organization comparable in bargaining power to the General Managers' Association.

In seeking to regulate rates for services and wages, the association in all probability overreached the bounds of legality. In so far as it endeavored to eliminate competition by rate agreements, this organization certainly had no standing in the eyes of the law. After probing the workings and accomplishments of the association in 1894, the United States Strike Commission denounced it as illegal, dangerous to the public welfare, and wholly unjustifiable.

The commission questions whether any legal authority, statutory or otherwise, can be found to justify some of the features of the association which have come to light in this investigation. If we regard its practical workings . . . . the General Managers' Association has no more standing in law than the old Trunk Line Pool. It cannot incorporate, because charters do not authorize roads to form corporations or associations to fix rates for services and wages, nor force their acceptance, nor to battle with strikers. . . . . The association is an illustration of the persistent and shrewdly devised plans of corporations to overreach their limitations and to usurp indirectly powers and rights not contemplated in their charters and not obtainable from the people or their legislators. . . . . At least, so long as railroads are thus permitted to combine to fix wages and for their joint protection, it would be rank injustice to deny the right of all labor upon railroads to unite for similar purposes.[31]

NOTES

1. *The Story of My Life*, pp. 68–69.

2. Eugene V. Debs, *Debs: His Life, Writings, and Speeches*, p. 6; *Locomotive Firemen's Magazine*, XVIII (1894), 1078; *New York World*, July 12, 1894, p. 3. Unfortunately, no trace can be found of the Debs papers.

3. *U.S. Strike Commission Report*, pp. 12–14.

4. *Ibid.*, pp. 138, 160.

5. *Locomotive Firemen's Magazine*, XVIII (1894), 1078; *Debs: His Life, Writings, and Speeches*, pp. 6–7.

6. *Ibid.*, p. 7.

7. *New York World*, July 12, 1894, p. 3.

8. *U.S. Strike Commission Report*, pp. xxiii, 14–16; *Chicago Times*, February 7, 1895, p. 9; Grover Cleveland, "The Government in the Chicago Strike of 1894," *McClure's Magazine*, XXIII (1904), 229.

9. "Constitution of the American Railway Union," *U.S. Strike Commission Report*, pp. 52–57.

10. *Ibid.*, pp. xxiv, 27, 57.

11. *Ibid.*, pp. xxiii, 53–54.

12. *Railway Times*, 1894–97, John Crerar Library.

13. *Debs: His Life, Writings, and Speeches*, pp. 7, 21; *Railway Times*, July 15, 1894, p. 1.

14. *U.S. Strike Commission Report*, pp. xxiii, 11–12, 209–10.

15. *Railroad Trainmen's Journal*, XI (1894), 389–91, 485–86; *U.S. Strike Commission Report*, pp. 134–35; *Debs: His Life, Writings, and Speeches*, pp. 7–10.

16. *Debs: His Life, Writings, and Speeches*, p. 11.

17. *U.S. Strike Commission Report*, pp. 241 and 242.

18. "Constitution of the General Managers' Association," *Proceedings of the General Managers' Association of Chicago, 1894*, pp. 5–7.

19. *U.S. Strike Commission Report*, pp. xxix, xxx–xxxi, 132, 242.

20. *Proceedings of the General Managers' Association* (March 8, 1893), pp. 14–19.

21. *Ibid.* (February 27, 1893), pp. 10–12.

22. *Ibid.* (March 9, 1893), pp. 21–22, and (March 16, 1893), pp. 25–27; *U.S. Strike Commission Report*, pp. 245–46.

23. *Proceedings of the General Managers' Association* (March 16, 1893), p. 26.

24. *U.S. Strike Commission Report*, p. 249.

25. *Proceedings of the General Managers' Association* (July 20, 1893), pp. 4–5.

26. *U.S. Strike Commission Report*, pp. 246–47.

27. *Ibid.*, pp. xxx, 10–11, 247–48, 252, and 263.

28. *Proceedings of the General Managers' Association* . . . . *1894*, pp. 22–26.

29. *Ibid.*, pp. 47–52; *U.S. Strike Commission Report*, pp. 264–67.

30. David Karsner, *Debs: His Authorized Life and Letters from Woodstock Prison to Atlanta*, p. 143; *Chicago Times*, February 6, 1895, p. 9.

31. *U.S. Strike Commission Report*, pp. xxx–xxxi.

CHAPTER VII

THE STORM BREAKS

THE refusal of George Pullman to make concessions caused his employees to take matters into their own hands. Incidents arose which heightened feeling and hastened action. On May 10 three members of the grievance committee were discharged, allegedly in violation of the pledge made by Wickes on the preceding day. It was rumored that these men were dismissed by a superintendent in retaliation for being criticized by them in their conference with George Pullman. The corporation emphatically denied this, averring that they were laid off with others because of slack work and for no other reason.[1] In all probability the contention of the company was correct; and certainly this action was not taken with the knowledge or consent of either Pullman or Wickes. Notwithstanding, the employees impulsively rejected this explanation and characterized the affair as an act of bad faith. Occurring, as it did, in an already tense atmosphere, the incident had an electrical effect upon the employees.[2]

In an all-night session at Turner Hall in Kensington on May 10 the grievance committee deliberated on the advisability of calling a strike. In attendance were the vice-president and the general secretary of the American Railway Union, who, acting upon the advice of Eugene Debs, strongly advised against resorting to such extreme measures at this juncture. They urged delay, at least until the investigation of shop abuses was completed. Despite this advice, the committee on the third ballot voted unanimously to call a strike but decided not to set a date until the matter had been referred back to the local unions for ratification—a course hardly necessary, since the committee had already been empowered to take final action.[3]

The men went to work as usual on the morning of May 11 but very soon were galvanized into action by a rumor which quickly spread over the shops. It was reported that the officials of the company had gained information as to what had transpired at the all-night meeting in Kensington, and had decided to close the Pullman works at noon. Without verifying the rumor, which was groundless, the committee immediately called the men out of the shops in order to establish the status of a strike instead of a lockout. Almost simultaneously, the men laid down their tools and left their work benches. By noon approximately three thousand employees had withdrawn for the purpose of seeking through resistance some recognition and amelioration of their unhappy plight; while only three hundred men, mostly clerks, foremen, and unskilled laborers, remained at work. In the evening the Pullman officials posted on the entrance gate of the plant this information: "The works are closed until further notice."[4] In this fashion the company accepted the challenge to its right to employ labor on whatever terms or conditions that corporate interests might dictate.

A central strike committee, composed of members elected from the local unions, was quickly formed for the purpose of directing affairs. The chairmanship was conferred upon Thomas Heathcoate, who, possessing the respect and confidence of all, was thus honored a second time. It was decided that daily meetings of the strikers would be held at Turner Hall, open to everybody, at which time reports from the various committees would be heard and matters of policy determined. The strikers did not enter into the struggle with light hearts, and no one was more apprehensive about the outcome than Heathcoate, who urged the men to keep away from the Pullman works and conduct themselves like gentlemen and law-abiding citizens. Underscoring this advice, the vice-president of the American Railway Union warned the men in an address on May 11 to abstain from all disturbance and intoxicating beverages and not to congregate on street corners.[5] As precaution against violence, three hundred strikers were immediately thrown around the Pullman works for the announced purpose of guarding the property against hoodlums, and this protection was furnished night and day until July 6, when the union was relieved of this duty by the military. The Pullman Company characterized this activity as picketing, but the Strike Commission held that, in view of the "forbearance and conduct" of these men, the real reason was the protection of Pullman property.[6]

Upon being notified of the strike, Eugene Debs hastened to the town of Pullman in order to investigate the situation personally. From a standpoint of strategy, he realized that the strike was a great misfortune, since the times were highly unfavorable for such action. He examined the facts critically and interviewed many workers about their grievances. If he had entertained any misgivings about the justice of their cause, such doubts were quickly dissipated. He found the wages well below the subsistence level and the employees becoming more deeply involved in debt to the company. This he considered a shocking and dangerous trend, which, as he believed, was delivering the workers into the clutches of the corporation. He observed that expenses in the town remained largely at the predepression level, whereas the wage scale had been reduced sharply—all of which aroused the fighting spirit of this labor leader.[7] On May 16, in an address to the Pullman strikers, Debs gave expression to his feelings in a bitter tirade against George Pullman:

I believe a rich plunderer like Pullman is a greater felon than a poor thief, and it has become no small part of the duty of this organization to strip the mask of hypocrisy from the pretended philanthropist and show him to the world as an oppressor of labor. One of the general officers of the company said today that you could not hold out against the Pullman Company more than ten days longer. If it is a fact that after working for George M. Pullman for years you appear two weeks after your work stops, ragged and hungry, it only emphasizes the charge I made before this community, and Pullman stands before you as a self confessed robber. . . . . The paternalism of Pullman is the same as the interest of a slave holder in his human chattels. You are striking to avert slavery and degradation.[8]

The complete sympathy of Eugene Debs and other high officials of the American Railway Union for the embattled laborers of Pullman was heartening; but of more immediate concern to these strikers was the task of securing the necessities of life for themselves and their families. Their union, newly organized, possessed no treasury from which the members could draw benefits as the payless weeks slipped by. A relief committee, organized by the strikers, performed the prodigious task of soliciting money and supplies, and distributing them among the needy families.

In response to the plea for help, supplies poured into Kensington—the headquarters of the relief committee. The Secord-Hopkins firm furnished the use of a room for the care of the sick, and in addition contributed twenty-five thousand pounds of meat and as many pounds of flour. Physicians in Pullman donated their services, for which there was the greatest need because of the large amount of sickness from malnutrition. Labor in Chicago rallied magnificently and on May 27 held a mass meeting, attended by representatives of the various trade-unions, for the purpose of devising means of raising money. The generosity not only of labor but of other sympathetic groups proved more or less adequate in meeting the elementary needs of the Pullman inhabitants. As their slender resources dwindled, the burden of relief grew heavier and heavier, and by the middle of July the relief roll counted twenty-seven hundred families. By that time fifteen thousand dollars had been contributed, exclusive of provisions.[9] In hoping for a quick collapse of the strike, the Pullman Corporation did not reckon with the deep sympathy shared by countless thousands in the cause represented by striking labor in Pullman.

Public sentiment seemed to be largely in accord with the Pullman workers, whose cause, while tragic and hopeless, possessed popular appeal.[10] Against the financial might and staying power of the Pullman Corporation, the cause of the workers from the very beginning was a lost one. The press of Chicago perceived this and from the very outset pronounced the strike a stupid blunder. The *Chicago Record* referred to it as "a grave mistake at a time when mistakes are dear and dangerous." In another editorial this same newspaper deplored the struggle: "They struck at a time when the company was well able to stand an interruption of its operations and precisely at the time when to strike is to share bitterly with others in the industrial depression. It is not themselves alone they have to consider. Their wives and their children are, of course, the first objects of their care."[11] The *Chicago Tribune* held that in quitting work the Pullman employees listened to bad advisers.[12] In stronger language the *Chicago Evening Journal* accused the men who encouraged the strike with being "almost criminal in their disregard of the consequences."[13]

The *Chicago Times* stood almost alone among the larger publications in defending the course pursued by the Pullman workers. The editor explained that the situation in the model town was "most deplorable" and that the workers suffered "the evils of the competitive system without enjoying any of its benefits." Sympathy for the cause of the strikers did not make this newspaper any the less realistic and, like other organs of expression, it was not very sanguine about the prospects of a labor victory.[14]

Did the Pullman strikers realize the insuperable odds against which they battled? Did they enter the struggle with hope or from a feeling of desperation fed by months of privation and sharpened by numerous grievances? The answer to these questions may be gleaned in part from the comments made in an interview, early in the strike, by Thomas Heathcoate, who declared: "We do not expect the company to concede our demands. We do not know what the outcome will be, and in fact we do not care much. We do know we are working for less wages than will maintain ourselves and families in the necessaries of life, and on that proposition we absolutely refuse to work any longer."[15] Despite the gloomy note of these sentiments, there is every reason to believe, judging by the conduct of the strikers themselves, that they were not without hope as they fought on, looking to the powerful American Railway Union for help in fighting their battle.

The strike had been in progress for a month when the American Railway Union held its first quadrennial convention. More than four hundred delegates, representing four hundred and sixty-five local unions and one hundred and fifty thousand members, assembled at Uhlich's Hall in Chicago on June 12, and for almost two weeks the convention remained in session. The public and press were privileged to attend every meeting except one which was devoted strictly to financial affairs. As presiding officer, Eugene Debs did everything possible to foster a full and free discussion on all matters of vital interest.[16]

In his address at the opening of the convention Debs painted in glowing terms the mission which their organization was to fulfil. He protested that the movement bore no enmity toward the brotherhoods but was merely seeking to unite all railroad workers, including those who had been "left out in the cold to endure the pitiless storms of corporate power." With fervor he proclaimed:

The forces of labor must unite. The dividing lines must grow dimmer day by day until they become imperceptible, and then labor's hosts, marshalled under one conquering banner, shall march together, vote together and fight together, until working men shall receive and enjoy all the fruits of their toil. Then will our country be truly and grandly free, and its institutions as secure and enduring as the eternal mountains. . . . . Such an army would be impregnable. No corporation would assail it. The reign of justice would be inaugurated. The strike would be remanded to the relic chamber of the past. An era of good will and peace would dawn.[17]

While looking into the future, Debs did not ignore the realities of the present. The depression had left the industrial life of the nation prostrate and demoralized, and in view of this he warned the convention to proceed cautiously and to exercise forbearance in matters that under normal conditions would justify intervention by the union. Revealing deep sympathy for the coal miners, who had failed to ameliorate their condition, he expressed the hope that the American Railway Union would some day be able to co-operate with them when they fought for honest wages. The plight of the Commonwealers elicited further sympathy from Debs, who criticized the government for its harsh policy toward these "victims of a greedy and heartless capitalism." Relative to the Pullman Strike, he suggested no course of action but expressed the belief that the matter would occupy the attention of the convention. This strike, he affirmed, was a "terrible illustration of corporate greed and pharisaical fraud which for years has prevailed in this country, and which has created conditions in the presence of which the stoutest hearts take alarm."[18]

The convention during the course of its deliberations disposed of routine matters, selected important committees, and elected the executive board. It was the Pullman Strike, however, that proved to be of dominant interest. Many of the delegates had visited the model town and were deeply stirred by the plight of the inhabitants. On June 15 the convention voted to go into a committee of the whole to consider the Pullman situation, and on this occasion a lengthy report was submitted by a committee of Pullman strikers.[19] Buttressed by countless factual citations, the statement was ingeniously prepared to arouse the fighting spirit of the delegates. The picture painted was indeed a dark one. It was charged that the Pullman employees had suffered five successive reductions in wages, representing a total slash of 30–70 per cent, but that the dividends of the corporation had in no way been disturbed. Rentals in Pullman were claimed to be almost twice as high as in Roseland. Although rents were badly in arrears, there had been no evictions. This was attributed to pubic opinion and to a desire on the part of George Pullman to starve out the workers, smash all unionism, and upon the resumption of production to deduct from the "miserable" wages of the employees the last dollar they owed his company.

Reference was made to what was considered the extortionate assessments for water and gas. It was alleged that from rentals, utilities, and other sources, the company was able to recover most of the money paid out in wages. Homeownership in the town was denied to workers. When these and other grievances were presented to George Pullman, he would refuse to take any action and would tell them they were all his "children." The report emphasized that only in desperation and with no alternative did the workers resort to a strike; and, were it not for the charitable people of Chicago, the Pullman inhabitants would now be starving.[20]

We struck because we were without hope. We joined the American Railway Union because it gave us a glimmer of hope. . . . . We have learned that there is a balm for all our troubles, and that the box containing it is in your hands today only awaiting opening to disseminate its sweet savor of hope. . . . . We will make you proud of us, brothers, if you will give us the hand we need. Help us make our country better and more wholesome. Pull us out of our slough of despond. Teach arrogant grinders of the faces of the poor that there is still a God of Israel, and if need be a Jehovah—a God of battles. Do this, and on that last great day you will stand, as we hope to stand, before the great white throne "like gentlemen unafraid."[21]

Other representatives from the town of Pullman testified before the assembled delegates as to the plight of the workers and the "justice" of their cause. Among them was the seamstress, Jennie Curtis, who endeavored to show that the wage reductions had been so terrific that neither she nor her associates were able to support themselves. In relating the story of her own tragic experience, Miss Curtis divulged that, following the death of her father, who had worked thirteen years for the Pullman Corporation, she was required to assume full responsibility for all back rent which he owed the company. She explained that frequently her semimonthly pay check was only nine or ten dollars, of which seven dollars were required for board, the balance being turned over to the Pullman Company toward the payment of the sixty-dollar arrearage for rent. Fifteen dollars, she acknowledged, remained to be paid. "We ask you," she pleaded, "to come along with us because we are not just fighting for ourselves, but for decent conditions for workers everywhere." Rev. William Carwardine added his voice to the weight of evidence in behalf of the Pullman inhabitants who, he said, were on the verge of starvation.[22]

The convention was stirred deeply and convinced of the need for action. It was proposed that a boycott be declared on Pullman cars, but the delegates preferred to exhaust first all peaceful means in adjusting the difficulties. A committee of twelve was selected, six of whom were delegates from the town of Pullman, to call on the Pullman Company and see whether or not the issues could be submitted to arbitration. In the afternoon of the same day, June 15, the committee was received by the second vice-president of the company, Thomas H. Wickes, who flatly refused to entertain any proposition from the American Railway Union. He was asked if the company would arbitrate, and to this he replied: "We have nothing to arbitrate." In answer to an inquiry as to whether he would treat with the employees, Wickes explained he would on condition that they came as individuals and not as representatives of a union.[23]

The convention was anxious to explore every possibility for an amicable solution and so advised the Pullman delegation to appoint a special committee to call on the Pullman Corporation. Six Pullman workers were accordingly sent to confer with Wickes. When questioned, however, about an increase in wages, he announced that the policy of the company in this matter remained the same as when the grievance committee first called on George Pullman. Arbitration was suggested, but this was emphatically rejected. Wickes asserted that in his judgment they had no right, as former employees, even to ask him to consider the demand for a raise in wages since they "stood in the same position as the man on the sidewalk."[24]

The convention now turned to the consideration of what further steps should be taken. The donation of fifteen hundred dollars by Mayor John P. Hopkins to the Pullman relief fund caused the delegates at this juncture to adopt a resolution of appreciation. The need for relief among the Pullman workers, however, was beginning to assume serious proportions; and, when this was brought to the attention of the convention, it voted two thousand dollars from the general fund for this purpose and in addition moved that a weekly assessment of ten cents be levied on every member for the same purpose until otherwise ordered by the executive board.[25]

More important was the question of what strategy could most effectively be employed against the Pullman Corporation. On June 22 the special committee, which had been appointed to recommend a plan of action, proposed that, unless the Pullman Company agreed to adjust the grievances by noon on June 26, the members of the American Railway Union would refuse to handle Pullman palace cars and the employees in the Pullman shops at St. Louis, Missouri, and Ludlow, Kentucky, would be called out on a strike. The advisability of a boycott had already been discussed by the convention. Such a policy seemed too drastic to Vice-President Howard, who advised that closing the Pullman shops at St. Louis and Ludlow would be sufficient to secure the desired results. These shops he had helped to organize, and he believed that the cessation of work there would hopelessly cripple the Pullman Corporation. Eugene Debs was willing to defer to the judgment of the convention, although urging the most careful consideration on the part of all. The delegates, however, were in no mood to temporize further or resort to half-measures. In their judgment the policy of the Pullman Company was intolerable and offensive in the extreme, and nothing less than the most positive action would suffice to redress the wrongs suffered by the Pullman workers. On June 21 or earlier the delegates had wired their local unions for instructions, and on the twenty-second were prepared to accept enthusiastically and without a dissenting vote the strategy proposed by the committee. Three members were immediately sent to notify the Pullman Company of the convention's decision. Wickes informed the group that his company would neither submit anything to arbitration nor have any dealings with representatives of their union. Informed of this, the convention decided with complete unanimity to make the boycott effective as planned on the twenty-sixth unless the company should change its mind.[26] With all business disposed of, the delegates voted to adjourn *sine die* on June 23.

The boycott was designed to cut off the major source of revenue of the Pullman Company and thus compel it to assume a more conciliatory attitude toward the demands of labor. Recognition of the union was not an issue.[27] For six weeks the Pullman workers had been on a strike, but their grievances were no nearer adjustment than at the outbreak of the trouble. Entrenched behind its millions, the Pullman Corporation was patiently waiting until the strike should collapse and then, on its own terms, resume production with nonunion labor. It was apparent that this eventuality would weaken the cause of labor and reflect discredit on the rapidly expanding American Railway Union. Since the Pullman Strike could not be adjusted locally, the convention was disposed to consider it a matter of general concern which could be solved only with the full weight and power of the entire union.

Times were hard, and drastic action was admittedly inauspicious. The railroad workers, however, had grievances of their own which made them restless and more willing to espouse the cause of the Pullman workers. Beginning in September, 1893, the railroads throughout the country systematically reduced wages; but, in order not to arouse the united resistance of the workers, they made the reductions gradually, no two roads doing so at the same time. Those who apparently suffered most were the trackmen and common laborers.[28] Among other alleged grievances were blacklisting, long hours, arbitrary treatment, interference with seniority rights, and discrimination against prominent members of the American Railway Union.[29] Many of the complaints were of a purely local character, but they helped to influence the sentiment of labor at this critical juncture.

Extremely apprehensive about their own plight, it was thus relatively easy for the railroad workers to develop a sympathetic understanding of the wrongs endured by the Pullman employees. But it was not just a bond of sympathy that united them; it was the growing conviction that they were all at the mercy of the vested interests which had drawn together by virtue of business relations and a common policy toward labor. In the operation of palace cars the Pullman Company was fully protected by rigid contracts with virtually all members of the General Managers' Association. The unconcealed hostility of this association toward the American Railway Union was shared by the Pullman Corporation. It was the policy of the railroads to withhold from this union the courtesies extended to the brotherhoods, such as free transportation for the officers.[30]

The rank and file of the American Railway Union were thus willing to champion a cause which possessed implications vital to the concern of all. It should be observed, however, that had it not been for the Pullman difficulty, no action would have been taken at this time by the convention against corporate injustices. The men would doubtless have awaited a more favorable opportunity to adjust their differences and would then most likely have resorted to local action on their particular road without any attempt to extend the struggle to other railroads. This characterized the Great Northern Strike, and it was hoped that such procedure would be the pattern for all succeeding strikes under the aegis of the American Railway Union.

Although the boycott was not directed against the railroads, it was inevitable that they would be involved. It was the policy of the General Managers' Association to ignore all communications from the American Railway Union—a fact which explains why the convention did not formally notify the general managers of the proposed boycott. The serving of formal notice was left to the representatives of the local unions on each road; but in the press public notice was given to all parties concerned,[31] and through this same medium the General Managers' Association on June 26 replied by announcing its determination to resist the boycott to the utmost.[32] The Pullman Company had found a powerful ally, but this did not cause the American Railway Union to pause in its determined course or to revise its declared policies.

From the outset the union officials realized that the railroads would not submit quietly to the policy of sidetracking Pullman sleepers. On June 22 Eugene Debs revealed to the convention precisely what might be expected from the railroads and how to cope with the situation. In executing the boycott, he declared, car inspectors should refuse to inspect Pullman cars, switchmen should refrain from switching them onto trains, and engineers and brakemen should not haul them. He pointed out that trouble would most likely begin with the switchmen who, upon refusing to switch Pullman sleepers, would doubtless be discharged. If anybody were employed to take their place, then it would be necessary for every member of the union on that railroad to stop work immediately. In this way the railroad system would be completely tied up—an action which he did not believe would involve the Interstate Commerce Law. Debs explained that the boycott would be invoked against the Pullman cars wherever the union was strong enough to take action and that the greatest membership of the organization existed in the western and north-western part of the United States.[33]

Throughout the strike the headquarters for the American Railway Union remained at Uhlich's Hall in Chicago, where orders were issued and the strategy of the boycott was directed. On June 26, as scheduled, the boycott became operative, although it was not immediately effective. Some of the railroads, in attempting to circumvent this action, resorted to precautions. The Illinois Central, for instance, ordered its passenger trains made up in advance of the dead line and had the cars padlocked to one another and the couplings sealed. Each train was supplied with one or two sleepers and for protection carried a guard of ten special officers. Noon came and passed, but there was no evidence of any response on this road to the orders of the union. Several trains departed without any overt acts; and at nine o'clock in the evening George Pullman and some officials of the railroad visited the Twelfth Street station to witness the departure of the "Diamond Special" for St. Louis and to observe how "ineffective" was the action undertaken by the American Railway Union. The train left promptly, pulling several Pullman cars; but shortly after its departure the switchmen refused to switch Pullman cars and were forced to quit work. The day shift followed the same course, and with surprising rapidity the cessation of work spread among other departments until at least thirty-five hundred men had joined the strike, thus demoralizing transportation on the Illinois Central Railroad.[34] All categories of workers were urged to strike, whether members of the American Railway Union or not, and all were promised the protection of the union.

The same story was repeated on numerous other lines. It was among the switchmen that the American Railway Union was most strongly organized. Here the trouble usually originated and then other classes of employees would become involved.[35] The union as such merely refused to handle Pullman cars and did not declare strikes against the railroads. Such action was taken by the employees themselves on the various systems in retaliation for the dismissal of workers who refused to carry out orders relative to the inspecting, switching, or hauling of Pullman cars. Among the roads affected most seriously during the first two days of the boycott were the Illinois Central; the Chicago and Northwestern; the Chicago, Burlington, and Quincy; the Atchison, Topeka, and Santa Fe; and the Union Stock Yards and Transit Company. On June 28 not one of these roads had less than one thousand men on strike, while some had considerably more than three thousand. The total number of strikers was then estimated to be almost eighteen thousand.[36]

The movement in some respects was almost spontaneous, revealing on the part of many local unions a willingness to strike that greatly surprised Eugene Debs. Various committees and groups of men would call at Uhlich's Hall in Chicago and announce that their local unions had determined to strike until the difficulties at Pullman were adjusted. Thus strikes occurred on roads not included in the scope of the strategy planned by the executive board.[37] Many local unions viewed the situation as an opportune moment for giving expression to their own grievances. Many of the employees on the Chicago, Rock Island, and Pacific Railroad, for instance, were disgruntled over the application of rules relative to promotion and priority.[38] In the case of the local union at La Salle, Illinois, their representative, while in attendance at the convention of the American Railway Union, was either discharged for union activity or laid off because of slack work. A grievance committee was appointed to investigate the matter but received no satisfaction from the railroad officials.[39] These and other sources of friction sharpened sentiment on this system and caused the employees to welcome the boycott as an opportunity which might conceivably lead to a redress of some of their own grievances.

Eugene Debs did not enter the struggle with a light heart or with any delusions about an easy victory. He realized the portentous character of the conflict and the fighting capacity of his powerful antagonists and so endeavored at the outset to enlist in behalf of the American Railway Union the support of as many labor organizations as possible. On June 26 he telegraphed for assistance from the Benevolent Order of Switchmen, the United Mine Workers, the American Federation of Labor, and the four major railroad brotherhoods.[40] To the plea for help only President John McBride of the United Mine Workers seemed willing to pledge the full co-operation of his union. The others either ignored the communication or else replied evasively or negatively.[41]

More was at stake in this struggle than just the wages of Pullman employees. The very existence of the American Railway Union was in danger, as the battle lines were drawn more sharply and the two great giants measured swords in a contest in which no quarter was to be expected or given. For the Pullman workers there was boundless sympathy throughout the nation; but the struggle between the American Railway Union and the General Managers' Association was viewed by many in an entirely different light. The privileged classes were disposed to regard this industrial battle with strange misgivings and to shrink from its implications. As early as June 27 the *New York Times* declared:

> An effort will be made to unite all railroad employees in the country in one common effort to secure better wages, and while the boycott is ostensibly declared as a demonstration of sympathy in behalf of the strikers in the Pullman shops, it in reality will be a struggle between the greatest and most powerful railroad labor organization and the entire railroad capital. Success in the Pullman boycott means the permanent success of the one organization through which it is sought to unite all employees of railroads.[42]

The evolution of such a colossal labor organization aroused the full hostility of the General Managers' Association, whose predominant position was now believed to be menaced. As soon as the boycott was announced, the general managers prepared to meet the situation. The chairman, Everett St. John, issued a call for an emergency meeting in the Rookery Building, Chicago, on June 25. All railroads in the association were represented, and after a full discussion the members unanimously adopted a resolution setting forth the reasons why they would not tolerate such an "unjustifiable and unwarranted" procedure as was threatened by the American Railway Union. The boycott was not due to any grievances against the railroad companies but was because of "supposed" wrongs endured by a class of employees in an entirely different field of endeavor. The proposed course, it was explained, would embarrass the railroads, jeopardize existing contracts, and inconvenience the public; and, to prevent all this, firm action would be taken.[43]

In combating the boycott, the General Managers' Association was motivated by two major considerations, the first and more obvious of which was in defense of Pullman contracts. Under the terms of these agreements, the Pullman Company furnished palace cars to the railroads, and they in turn agreed to operate them, and no clause in any contract provided that during a strike either party would be released from its obligations. The Pullman Corporation could have instituted legal proceedings in the event that the general managers had submitted quietly to the boycott and permitted palace cars to be sidetracked; but whether or not the

Pullman interests would have brought suit against a score or more of railroads is problematic. The general managers, however, had no desire to circumvent their contractual obligations in this matter, particularly since, in so doing, they would have strengthened the growing influence of the American Railway Union. In the deep hostility of the railroads toward this new labor organization can be found the second determining factor. Toward the railroad brotherhoods no such antipathy was revealed, since they did not constitute a serious threat. It was otherwise with the American Railway Union, whose victory in the Great Northern Strike did little to allay the growing fears of the railroad managers that this union, if not checked, would be capable of doing them great harm. The determination to crush this labor organization, once and for all, was not disclosed in any resolution or statement of policy but is ascertainable from methods and techniques employed throughout the strike.[44]

Although allies, the Pullman Company and the General Managers' Association each pursued an independent course during the crisis. Upon invitation, Thomas H. Wickes was present at the important meeting of the general managers on June 25, and in the capacity of an observer followed carefully the deliberations, neither approving, dissenting, nor participating.[45] There is no evidence that any subsequent meeting of the association was attended by a Pullman official, although Wickes and Pullman did converse casually with some of the general managers. It does not appear that the Pullman Corporation asked for any assurances of support from the association, nor is there any reason to believe that the general managers conferred with the Pullman Company or even sought advice and assistance from it.[46]

From June 25 to July 15 the general managers held daily meetings for the purpose of supervising strategy and keeping abreast of the latest developments. It was the consensus on June 26 that any employee who refused to switch Pullman cars, even though willing to perform all other work, should be immediately discharged.[47] On the following day it was decided to appoint a manager who would devote his entire time to co-ordinating the anti-strike activities of the association and to prosecuting the campaign in a vigorous fashion, The post was unanimously offered to John M. Egan, who, prior to May, 1894, had been a member of the association for over six years and who for a long period of time had served as general manager of the Chicago and Great Western Railroad. He was no longer connected in an official capacity with any railroad system and was thus free to devote his full time to this heavy responsibility.[48]

At noon on June 28 John Egan assumed his new duties and without delay proceeded to the task of organizing his office in the Rookery Building along the most efficient lines. Telephone and telegraph instruments were set in place, sufficient clerks were employed, and arrangements were made to keep the office open twenty-four hours each day. Everett St. John, as chairman, continued to preside over all meetings of the association; while John Egan, as strike manager, was intrusted with the handling of details and the execution of all strike policies. The office of Egan remained the clearing house for reports on acts of violence, on interference with the movement of trains, on the need for protection, and on the hourly and daily aspects of the battle as it waxed and waned on all fronts. When calls for protection reached his office—and sometimes they came almost continuously—he would promptly relay them to the chief of police, the sheriff of Cook County, the United States marshal, or military officers. The men brought from the East to replace the strikers were received by this office and assigned to duty on the different lines. These and a multitude of other tasks were performed by John Egan in coordinating and integrating the fighting strength of the railroad corporations in the association.[49]

Each move of the General Managers' Association was planned with deliberation. The competitive rivalry that existed among some of the systems was now relegated to the background as they rallied in defense of their common interests. A bureau was established to furnish information to the press and thus create strong public sentiment for their cause. Detailed reports were submitted at the meetings of the association on the strength, influence, and strategy of the American Railway Union. In probing the inner workings of this labor organization, the association searched for weaknesses and for information that could be used against the union leaders.[50] Twenty or thirty detectives were employed to ferret out these facts and to ascertain the amount of violence and the identity of the perpetrators.[51]

All efforts of the general managers were directed toward one end—the complete annihilation of the American Railway Union. At no time was the association prepared to negotiate for an amicable solution of the dispute or to make even the slightest concessions in the interest of peace.[52] It was resolved on June 29 that any worker who was discharged for refusal to perform his duties or who quit work at the behest of the American Railway Union would never again be eligible for employment on any railroad represented by the General Managers' Association. Moreover, the men replacing the strikers would be given special protection and permitted to retain their positions permanently.[53] Few resolutions of the association were made public, but this one was, for the obvious purpose of discouraging men from striking or heeding the orders of the union. In carrying out the policies agreed upon, there was superb co-ordination among the general managers. In commenting on this unity, the Strike Commission said:

> Each road did what it could with its operating forces, but all the leadership, direction, and concentration of power, resources, and influences on the part of the railroads were centered in the General Managers' Association. That association stood for each and all of its combined members, and all that they could command, in fighting and crushing the strike.[54]

The need to replace all strikers promptly with new men was recognized from the outset as vital in the strategy of the general managers. On June 27 Committee No. 1 was instructed to secure sufficient men for this purpose. In keeping with previous arrangements, it was decided that the entire cost of transporting the men, as well as their board and wages until put to work, would be borne by the association. Railroad managers in numerous eastern cities were notified to establish agencies for the enrolment of switchmen, towermen, and yardmen. As needed, these men would be sent to Chicago.[55] In Pittsburgh, Philadelphia, Baltimore, Cleveland, New York, Buffalo, and elsewhere, employment offices were opened and hundreds of men enrolled. Because of the depression, the agencies were swamped with demands for work. At no time was there a lack of applicants; indeed, only a small part of those registered were actually called for duty.[56]

Typical of these employment offices was one established at the United States Hotel in New York City. A representative from Chicago aided by two clerks interviewed hundreds, if not thousands, of applicants, from whom experienced railroad men were selected and shipped west in groups of fifty workers or more. The applicants seemed not to have the slightest compunction about "scabbing" or "strikebreaking."[57] A few even appeared gleeful at the thought of replacing the strikers, for as they explained to a reporter: "We are going to settle an old account. We were strikers on the Gould roads under Martin Irons, and we haven't handled a switch since then. The men who are striking now are the men who helped fill our places then. Now we are going west to take their jobs."[58] All who received work were offered regular wages with the guaranty that they would not be supplanted by the strikers when conditions returned to normal.

The number of men daily employed in this manner and assigned to the roads fluctuated during the most violent phases of the strike from slightly over 100 to more than 250. In all, the association furnished about 2,500 workers. Although this may seem small in view of the character of the struggle, it must be remembered that each road through its own efforts employed new men, and only when this source proved inadequate would the assistance of Committee No. 1 be invoked. Through the channels of the association the Santa Fe secured 489 men; the Wabash, 247; the Chicago and Great Western, 244; but some railroads barely availed themselves of the service.[59] Precisely how much this service cost the General Managers' Association cannot be determined, but the total financial outlay of the organization for all purposes during the strike was thirty-six thousand dollars, and apparently most of it was spent by Committee No. 1. In apportioning these expenses, the association decided to assess each road on a basis of size. The thirteen largest lines were obliged to contribute 5 per cent, and the remaining ones a smaller amount.[60]

In determining what would be the most effective strategy, the

General Managers' Association sought advice from a distinguished group of railroad lawyers.[61] Before a special meeting on
June 30, George R. Peck, chairman of the legal committee, presented recommendations which, in the considerate judgment of
these corporation lawyers, would be tactically and judicially
sound. Several questions had been submitted to this committee,
and the answers, skilfully prepared, suggested the line of attack
best calculated to bring complete victory.

The report stressed the need for complete co-ordination among
the different railroads in their legal strategy against the American
Railroad Union and for this purpose suggested the appointment
of a legal subcommittee of seven members who would examine
all laws applicable to the strike and advise the railroad attorneys
as to which could be most appropriately utilized. Not only would
this subcommittee serve in an advisory capacity for all criminal
and civil prosecutions undertaken by any road, but it would also
seek to develop a "proper understanding" with the prosecuting
attorneys and other law-enforcing officers. While recommending
the prosecution of offenders under any law that could be found
applicable, the committee pointed out that the "action which can
be had under the federal laws will be more speedy and efficacious." For the present nothing was to be done against the union
officials under the conspiracy or boycott laws of Illinois. In the
federal domain, however, immediate prosecution was urged
against the American Railway Union for interference with mail
and interstate commerce; and such action, it was indicated,
should be instituted through the office of the United States district attorney in whatever manner he should direct.

In regard to civil suits against officers of the union and others
who might be culpable, the report suggested delay. But it proposed that such railroads as were advised by the subcommittee
should apply for injunctions to keep the strikers from trespassing
or from interfering with the employees. In the event that any
company applied for such a writ, all others were urged to co-
operate fully. It was further suggested that all proceedings begun
with the approval of this subcommittee should be carried on at
the expense of the association. The general managers were urged

to gather reliable information on overt acts against any railroad, to discover the identity of those guilty, and to obtain evidence connecting such acts with union officials.[62]

The report was unanimously received and the legal subcommittee duly established. On July 1 this group advised that injunction suits should be commenced by the different roads as soon as the situation warranted and that the time for such action on most roads had arrived. It was disclosed that some railroads already had filed or were preparing to file restraining orders against the strikers. The subcommittee further revealed that in addition to these individual suits the United States district attorney in Chicago, unless otherwise instructed, would very soon seek an injunction in behalf of the federal government to prohibit interference with mail trains, interstate trains, and interstate commerce not in transportation.[63] When the writ was issued on July 3, the subcommittee quickly explained to the association that all roads in this area were now protected but that elsewhere the railroads would have to prevail upon the government to secure similar writs. In view of the willingness of the Department of Justice to take such action, the subcommittee now felt that it was not advisable for the individual railroads as complainants to start injunction proceedings.[64]

A vital part of the strategy of the association was to draw the United States government into the struggle and then to make it appear that the battle was no longer between the workers and the railroads but between the workers and the government. The steps taken by the general managers to create the proper conditions favorable for federal intervention cannot be appraised accurately, since they involved a subterfuge. During the early phases of the crisis it was the policy of the roads not to alleviate the inconvenience in transportation but rather to aggravate this condition wherever possible, in order to arouse the anger of the traveling public and thus hasten action by the federal authorities.

On July 2 the general managers decided that the best strategy was not to accept freight for shipment. This policy combined with the gradual withdrawing of passenger trains from service would, it was hoped, force the government to furnish protection.[65] How extensively the stratagem was used cannot be determined, but the suspension of most of the remaining suburban rail service in Chicago at this time might indicate a genuine attempt to utilize such tactics.[66] So convinced were the union officials of the practice that they favored grand-jury action against the General Managers' Association. They claimed that the association sent out telegrams ordering certain railroad lines to suspend train movements in order to create the "desired effect."[67] It was further charged, although denied by the general managers, that, in order to incite the strikers, Pullman palace cars were attached to passenger and mail trains which had no need for such cars and normally traveled without them.[68] Such means were alleged to have been employed to provoke trouble, heighten the seriousness of an already critical situation, and arouse strong public sentiment against the American Railway Union.

In testifying before the Strike Commission, James R. Sovereign, grand master of the Knights of Labor, endeavored to support the charge that railroads deliberately delayed trains in order to develop public feeling against the strikers. From his own experiences he related how on July 6 he took passage on the Rock Island Railroad for Chicago, but when the train reached Blue Island, a suburb of Chicago, he and the other passengers were informed that the train could go no farther because of a large mob on the tracks ahead. Sovereign observed another train on the siding and was told by some of the passengers that it had been there twenty-six hours. This train was westward bound over the same tracks on which he had just come, and he had seen no evidence of trouble; but, as some of the employees revealed to him, the train was being voluntarily detained for the purpose of creating "sentiment." Impatient at all the delay, Sovereign went over to the Wisconsin Central station and boarded another train for Chicago, but after moving a short distance it likewise stopped. The conductor explained that because of a large mob further down the tracks it would be dangerous to proceed. Thereupon, Sovereign picked up his grip and started to walk along the tracks into Chicago, disregarding the protests of the conductor. During his entire journey on foot, he declared that he did not meet ten men on the road and saw no obstructions.[69]

As the struggle gained headway, the strikers displayed unbroken unity, grim determination, and a high degree of effectiveness. With a minimum of disorder they were able to paralyze a vast amount of railroad traffic.[70] Instead of minimizing all this, John Egan candidly and freely admitted it and on July 2 acknowledged that the railroads had been "fought to a standstill." He portrayed the situation in a manner as ominous and disturbing as possible in order to arouse the apprehension of the powerful "interests" and hasten federal participation. He boldly announced that the federal troops at Fort Sheridan should be called out, since there was no "other recourse left." With these troops, he explained, a breach could be made in the ranks of the strikers: ". . . . the strike would collapse like a punctured balloon. It is the government's duty to take this business in hand, restore law, suppress the riots, and restore to the public the service which it is now deprived of by conspirators and lawless men."[71]

When the carefully laid plans of the association were transformed into a campaign of active warfare, it became apparent that this organization had the support of a powerful ally. While maintaining the pretense of complete impartiality in its operations, the United States government, as further discussion will demonstrate, did precisely what was best calculated to bring victory to the railroads. The federal authorities utilized all the ponderous machinery of a powerful government, including injunctions and soldiery, to nullify completely the aims and activities of labor. As early as July 4 the association could jubilantly announce: ". . . . So far as the railroads are concerned with this fight, they are out of it. It has now become a fight between the United States Government and the American Railway Union, and we shall leave them to fight it out."[72]

NOTES

1. *U.S. Strike Commission Report*, pp. xxvii, 586, 587–89.

2. *Ibid.*, pp. 431, 432, 433.

3. *Ibid.*, pp. 6–7, 79, 433; *Chicago Times*, May 12, 1894, p. 1.

4. *Chicago Times*, May 12, 1894, p. 1; *U.S. Strike Commission Report*, pp. xxxvii, 417, 433, 586, 589; *Inter Ocean*, May 12, 1894, pp. 1, 2.

5. *Chicago Times*, May 12, 1894, p. 2, and May 13, 1894, p. 1; Carwardine, *op. cit.*, p. 41.

6. *U.S. Strike Commission Report*, pp. xxxvii, 417.

7. *Ibid.*, pp. 129–30.

8. Stead, *Chicago Today*, pp. 177–78 (quotation from speech of Eugene Debs, May 16, 1894).

9. Carwardine, *op. cit.*, pp. 41–44; *Chicago Times*, May 28, 1894, p. 2, June 1, 1894, p. 1, and June 15, 1894, p. 2.

10. *Biennial Report of the Adjutant General of Illinois* . . . . , *1893 and 1894*, p. xiv.

11. *Chicago Record*, May 12, 1894, p. 4, and May 18, 1894, p. 4.

12. *Chicago Tribune*, May 16, 1894, p. 6.

13. *Chicago Evening Journal*, May 14, 1894, p. 4.

14. *Chicago Times*, May 13, 1894, p. 20.

15. *Ibid.*, p. 1.

16. *U.S. Strike Commission Report*, pp. xxxix, 8, 130, 131; *Chicago Times*, June 13, 1894, p. 1.

17. *Chicago Times*, June 13, 1894, p. 2.

18. *Railway Times*, July 15, 1894, p. 3.

19. *Ibid.*, p. 1; "Record of Motions, Resolutions and Reports of the American Railway Union Relative to the Pullman Strike and Boycott, June 12 to 23," *U.S. Strike Commission Report*, pp. 87–94.

20. "Statement from the Pullman Strikers to the Convention of the American Railway Union, June 15, 1894," *U.S. Strike Commission Report*, pp. 87–91.

21. *Ibid.*, pp. 87–88.

22. McAlister Coleman, *Eugene Debs*, pp. 125–29; *Chicago Times*, June 16, 1894, p. 1.

23. *U.S. Strike Commission Report*, pp. 79–80; *Chicago Tribune*, June 16, 1894, p. 3.

24. *Inter Ocean*, June 17, 1894, p. 7; *U.S. Strike Commission Report*, pp. 80–81.

25. *U.S. Strike Commission Report*, pp. 93–94; *Chicago Times*, June 22, 1894, p. 1.

26. *Chicago Times*, June 22, 1894, p. 1; *Inter Ocean*, June 23, 1894, p. 1; *U.S. Strike Commission Report*, pp. 8, 17, 77, 94, 131–32.

27. *U.S. Strike Commission Report*, pp. xxxix, 17, 29; *New York Times*, June 30, 1894, p. 1.

28. *U.S. Strike Commission Report*, pp. 23, 132–35.

29. *Ibid.*, pp. xl, 6, 23, 64–65, 71–72, 120, 238–41.

30. *Ibid.*, pp. 136–37.

31. *Ibid.*, p. 136.

32. *Proceedings of the General Managers' Association* . . . . *1894*, pp. 94–95.

33. *Chicago Tribune*, June 23, 1894, p. 3.

34. *U.S. Strike Commission Report*, pp. 325–26; *Chicago Times*, June 26, 1894, p. 1, and June 27, 1894, p. 1; *New York Times*, June 27, 1894, p. 8.

35. *U.S. Strike Commission Report*, pp. 115, 116, 142.

36. *Ibid.*, pp. 325–26; *Chicago Tribune*, June 29, 1894, p. 1.

37. *U.S. Strike Commission Report*, p. xl.

38. *Ibid.*, pp. 59–60, 64, 238–41.

39. *Ibid.*, pp. 71–73, 236–37.

40. *Inter Ocean*, June 27, 1894, p. 3; *Chicago Times*, January 31, 1895, p. 3 (reprint of the telegram).

41. *Inter Ocean*, June 27, 1894, p. 3; *New York Times*, June 27, 1894, p. 8.

42. *New York Times*, June 27, 1894, p. 8.

43. *Chicago Tribune*, June 26, 1894, p. 8; *U.S. Strike Commission Report*, p. 250.

44. *U.S. Strike Commission Report*, pp. 47, 137.

45. *Ibid.*, p. 590.

46. *Ibid.*, pp. 252, 253, 625–26; *New York Times*, July 3, 1894, p. 2.

47. *Proceedings of the General Managers' Association* . . . . *1894*, pp. 97–99.

48. *Ibid.*, pp. 102, 107; *U.S. Strike Commission Report*, pp. 251, 269–70.

49. *U.S. Strike Commission Report*, pp. xlii–xliii, 269–70; "Report of John M. Egan," *Proceedings of the General Managers' Association* . . . . *1894*, pp. 221–27.

50. *Proceedings of the General Managers' Association* . . . . *1894*, pp. 92–219; *U.S. Strike Commission Report*, p. xliii.

51. *U.S. Strike Commission Report*, p. 252.

52. *New York Times*, June 29, 1894, p. 2, and July 3, 1894, p. 1.

53. *Proceedings of the General Managers' Association* . . . . *1894*, p. 114; *Chicago Tribune*, June 30, 1894, p. 1.

54. *U.S. Strike Commission Report*, p. xliii.

55. *Proceedings of the General Managers' Association* . . . . *1894*, pp. 102, 106–7.

56. *Ibid.*, pp. 106, 115, 145, 156, 171; *U.S. Strike Commission Report*, p. 252.

57. *New York Times*, July 1, 1894, p. 2, July 2, 1894, p. 2, and July 3, 1894, p. 2.

58. *Ibid.*, July 4, 1894, p. 2.

59. *Proceedings of the General Managers' Association* . . . . *1894*, pp. 226–27, 233–34.

60. *Ibid.*, pp. 232–33.

61. *Ibid.*, pp. 113–15.

62. *Ibid.*, pp. 123–26.

63. *Ibid.*, pp. 135–36.

64. *Ibid.*, p. 147.

65. *New York Times*, July 3, 1894, p. 2.

66. *Ibid.; Inter Ocean*, July 1, 1894, p. 1; *Chicago Times*, July 2, 1894, p. 1.

67. *New York World*, July 12, 1894, p. 2.

68. *U.S. Strike Commission Report*, p. 255.

69. *Ibid.*, p. 65.

70. *Biennial Report of the Adjutant General of Illinois* . . . . , *1893 and 1894*, p. 173; *Inter Ocean*, July 1, 1894, p. 1.

71. *Inter Ocean*, July 3, 1894, p. 3.

72. *New York Times*, July 5, 1894, p. 2.

CHAPTER VIII

FEDERAL INTERVENTION

FROM the outset the high officials of the federal government were disposed to view the situation with growing disquietude. In large measure they merely reflected the rising tide of apprehension which was permeating the propertied classes. The panic of 1893 had not only weakened the economic structure and sharply curtailed industrial profits, but it had also fostered an ominous restlessness among the underprivileged groups. The Coal Strike, the Commonweal movement, countless labor difficulties, and a growing tendency toward lawlessness were but symptoms of this upsurging of discontent. Never had labor been more vocal, and never had the "have nots" been more willing to flaunt their misery before a dismayed public.

Conditions led to greatly exaggerated fears and rumors, and when the Pullman Strike occurred—the culminating event in a series of unfortunate happenings—the upper class was prepared to believe the worst. By shamefully distorting the facts and greatly magnifying trivial incidents, the press was able to generate far more passion than circumstances justified. Nothing was done by the organs of propaganda to allay the fear that this was not an ordinary labor dispute but a mighty test of power between the forces of labor and capital. The implications of the struggle were all very vague, but even so it was widely felt that labor was seeking to dominate industry completely. The prophecy of certain alarmists that a life-and-death struggle between these two great forces was an inevitability seemed to be now in process of fulfilment. The American Railway Union was believed to be the rallying force, around which all labor would gather in a concerted effort to subordinate the economic machinery to their own ends. Some people shared the conviction that labor would not stop until it had seized control of the government and that the plight of the Pullman workers was merely a pretext for precipitating the conflict.[1] In an atmosphere thus charged with fears and forebodings, the vested interests looked to the federal government for swift and vigorous action.

The attorney-general of the United States was Richard Olney —a man peculiarly fitted to render immediate and decisive aid to the railroad corporations. Prior to his appointment he had held no political office and was virtually unknown. During his thirty-five years of law practice in Boston, Olney had developed an almost fanatical devotion to corporate law and property interests. He was the product of an era characterized by rapid industrial expansion and the growth of huge business monopolies and trusts. New England brains and financial resources had played an important part in the rise of big business; and, as legal adviser and director of several corporations, Richard Olney contributed his share to this great movement. Railroads were his specialty, and the list of his directorships was quite impressive, including the Atchison; the Chicago, Burlington, and Quincy; and the New York Central. Since he had served the railroad interests for several decades as a private citizen, it was hardly to be expected that in public life he would be any less solicitous about their well-being.

Richard Olney was not of the congenial, affable type but was inclined to be cold, brusque, and peremptory in his conduct. Reporters found him inaccessible and difficult to interview. When an emergency arose, he favored quick and forceful action, and this quality was exemplified repeatedly in his management of the legal department of the federal government. He was stubborn and endowed with an inflexible determination that seemed impervious to public pressure. To this man, Grover Cleveland intrusted the attorney-generalship in February, 1893, despite the fact that the two were almost strangers, having seen each other only once previous to the appointment.[2]

As head of the Department of Justice, Olney became the supreme strategist in directing the forces of the government against the American Railway Union. During the Commonweal movement, he not only acquired a rich and varied experience in resisting lawlessness but developed some of the techniques which later proved so effective in crushing the Pullman Strike. The speedy collapse of the Coxeyite movement seemed to justify, in his judgment, the summary procedure which he had followed.[3]

The outbreak of the Pullman struggle stirred up all Olney's latent resentment toward labor; and now he shifted his spleen from the dying cause of the Commonwealers to a new menace, the American Railway Union, which, being better organized, was considered all the more dangerous.[4] In his opinion the strike represented an attack against railroad property, corporate control, and all that his world held dear. In meeting the situation Olney was determined to act promptly and employ whatever means would prove most efficacious.[5] In view of the influence which he wielded as attorney-general, it might be almost said that suppressing the strike was his own affair. In exercising direct control over United States marshals and district attorneys he was able to create situations from which the federal government could extricate itself only by plunging deeper into the conflict. Most of the vital information concerning the strike was gathered by the Department of Justice from its agents throughout the nation.[6] This information proved a potent weapon in the hands of Olney, who was careful to use it in a manner best calculated to influence the judgment of Grover Cleveland.

During the strike there were daily Cabinet meetings, some lasting into the night, and among those in attendance none co-operated more closely than Grover Cleveland, Richard Olney, Major General John M. Schofield, and Secretary of War Daniel S. Lamont. As soon as federal troops were ordered to Chicago, direct communication by wire was opened between the military headquarters in that city and the office of the President. Numerous telegrams were received by and dispatched from the White House, which bustled with activity early and late. Cleveland followed the strike closely and permitted no important developments to escape his attention.[7] By no stretch of the imagination could it be said that he was the dupe of the attorney-general, although it is true that the guiding hand in shaping federal procedure was that of Richard Olney.

The attorney-general believed that Chicago's role in the struggle would be crucial. To one of his most trusted agents in that city he confided that "if the rights of the United States were vigorously asserted in Chicago, the origin and center of the demonstration, the result would be to make it a failure everywhere else and to prevent its spread over the entire country."[8] In keeping with this plan of action, the federal government proceeded with amazing speed, using every pretext and exploiting every situation in order to set in motion all its machinery of coercion. Every step, however, was defended on the grounds of necessity and legality, but to the propertied classes the best justification for this procedure could be found in its immediate and overwhelming effectiveness.

The entering wedge for federal intervention was furnished by disruption in the movement of United States mail. Ironically enough, the American Railway Union had no desire to interfere with anything so vital and even declared on several occasions that men would gladly be furnished to operate mail trains on condition that Pullman cars were not attached.[9] If the railroads had agreed to this provision, there would have been no interruption in the flow of mail, but such a course presumably would have involved the violation of Pullman contracts. Almost without exception, the railroad officials decided not to allow the operation of trains without the full complement of cars; and, since that usually included dining, parlor, or sleeping cars, such trains were often delayed or halted indefinitely because of the refusal of many employees to remain at work under such conditions. The general managers were not slow in turning this situation to their advantage, because, as they realized, it could be used to involve the federal government.[10]

The law did not clearly specify what constituted a mail train, nor did it require written contracts between the government and the railroads. Once a railroad was authorized to transport mail, it became the function of the division superintendent of the railway mail service in his district to determine what trains on the road should serve as carriers. Whenever a shift in trains was to be made or a new train assigned the duty of carrying mail, nothing more than a notice was served, although the matter was recorded in the office of the division superintendent and included in his report to the auditor. Any passenger train could be required to transport mail,[11] but was every car normally hauled in a train that carried mail an inviolate part of the mail train? If so, the law was silent about it. There was nothing in any statute, expressed or implied, that would indicate that mail trains as such necessitated the attachment of Pullman sleepers; and certainly the postmaster-general could legally have met the emergency by expressly providing that until the strike was terminated only passenger trains free of palace cars could be used for the transportation of mail. Such action would obviously have led to complications involving Pullman contracts; but, even if no difficulties impended, such a course would scarcely have appealed to a government committed to the full protection of all property interests.

In interpreting the law the Department of Justice in April, 1894, supplied its own definition of a mail train by ruling that it comprised all cars that are ordinarily hauled by such a train and that any person attempting to detach any part of it was guilty of obstructing the mail.[12] This construction of the law was comprehensive enough to hold any striker liable who endeavored to detach a palace car from a passenger train carrying mail or who in any way sought to delay the train because it included Pullman cars. That this was only an interpretation was evident by the fact that Postmaster-General W. S. Bissell recommended to Congress before and after the strike the need for a law clearly defining the character of a mail train. He advocated a definition similar to the interpretation rendered by Richard Olney. In the judgment of Bissell, if such a law, with suitable penalties, had been in effect at the time of the strike, there would have been less destruction of property and human life, and his department would have sustained a smaller loss of revenue.[13]

Shortly after the boycott took effect, the postmaster-general received notice of mail's being delayed at certain points throughout the west. One of the first communities so affected was Cairo, Illinois. When Louis L. Troy, division superintendent of the railway mail service at Chicago, protested about the matter to union officials on June 28, he was informed that it was not their intention to interfere with mail trains and that instructions to this effect would be issued to all strikers. On the following day the situation at Cairo seemed in no way improved, so Troy again visited union headquarters and warned the executive committee that under no circumstances should mail trains be molested. If necessary, he warned, the whole power of the government would be summoned to keep them moving. Debs explained that railroad strikers were not involved in the affair beyond peacefully withdrawing from work and that the union could not be held responsible for what outsiders did in their demonstrations.[14] Here, as elsewhere, the railroad officials were adamant in their determination not to permit the departure of a mail train without the full complement of cars. Any interference with Pullman cars on such a train was construed as obstructing the mail, and the incident was immediately brought to the attention of federal authorities.

As quickly as the office of postmaster-general received word of any interruption in the movement of mail, the matter was referred to the attorney-general, who immediately wired instructions to the proper United States district attorneys. They were urged to take all measures necessary to prevent the stoppage of mail and to punish those guilty. Warrants and any other available processes were to be procured from federal courts, the execution of which was intrusted to United States marshals. On June 29 mail was reported delayed in such scattered localities as Riverdale, Illinois; Hammond, Indiana; Hope, Idaho; and San Francisco, California. Other points were subsequently announced, and by July 5 the Department of Justice had deemed it advisable to instruct its district attorneys in nineteen states and territories to take the necessary steps to assure the unhindered movement of mail trains.[15] Considering the scope of the strike, it is remarkable that there was not greater paralysis in the movement of mail. In some cases mail reached its destination only after long delays, but, by rerouting it from the lines most seriously affected, most of it got through without great difficulty.[16]

Chicago was not involved in the obstruction of mail transportation during the earliest phase of the boycott, but the near-by communities of Riverdale and Hammond were; and the imminent danger of trouble spreading kept the Department of Justice alert to any emergency that might arise. On June 28 the United States attorney at Chicago, Thomas E. Milchrist, received from Richard Olney the same instructions that were being wired to other district attorneys in zones where the movement of mail was reported in jeopardy.[17] Milchrist promptly appeared before a meeting of the General Managers' Association and read Olney's telegram. Then he expressed a desire for the names of any who attempted to obstruct the passage of any train that contained a "mail car or a car carrying mail pouches, whether they cut off a Pullman car, or a dining car, or any other part of the train that is the regular and usual train in the carrying of mail." Warrants, he promised, would be quickly issued for the arrest of such offenders.[18]

On June 30 the situation in Chicago continued to be satisfactory, judging by the following dispatch which Lewis L. Troy sent to the authorities at Washington: "No mails have accumulated at Chicago so far. All regular trains are moving nearly on time with a few slight exceptions."[19] Milchrist, nevertheless, was becoming more apprehensive and recommended to the attorney-general that the federal marshal at Chicago be authorized to appoint at least fifty deputies.[20] This suggestion met with the hearty indorsement of Olney, who wired Marshal Arnold to deputize as many as were needed. To Milchrist he advised the procurement of all available processes and orders from the federal courts and cited many decisions considered apropos to the emergency. On the same day that these communications flew back and forth Milchrist conferred with the attorneys of the General Managers' Association and requested the names of all guilty parties interfering with the movement of mail and interstate freight. He explained that, if in his judgment the conspiracy section of the Interstate Commerce Law was applicable, he would invoke it in prosecuting those who obstructed interstate freight. At this, as well as the previous conference, gratification was expressed by the general managers and their lawyers for what Milchrist and Olney were doing in defense of law and order.[21]

One of the most incredible and perhaps least justifiable things which Olney did was to appoint on June 30 Edwin Walker as special attorney for the federal government at Chicago. The general managers were committed to the belief that one of their own lawyers, as special United States counsel, would give them a decisive advantage in suppressing the strike, and so they advised Olney that it was not only desirable but necessary to have the district attorney reinforced by expert counsel.[22] Their nominee for this position was a very clever corporation lawyer, who since 1870 had been general counsel for the Chicago, Milwaukee, and St. Paul Railroad. At the first outbreak of trouble, he was invited with others to serve the General Managers' Association in a legal advisory capacity.[23] In the role of federal prosecutor, such an individual could scarcely have possessed the qualities of a fair-minded, impartial agent of the law, seeking to promote justice irrespective of class interests. Somewhat ironically, Clarence Darrow observed that the federal government "might with as good grace have appointed the attorney for the American Railway Union to represent the United States."[24] To the corporation-minded Olney, such a choice was not in bad taste, and so he hastily carried out the recommendation of the general managers without even consulting Thomas Milchrist.[25]

The appointment of Walker was in no wise a reflection on the ability of Milchrist to perform the duties of his office, but was due to a firm conviction on the part of Olney that the exigencies of the situation demanded the selection of a highly resourceful lawyer who, as assistant to the United States attorney, would help to wage a more effective campaign against the strikers. To Olney, Chicago represented the heart of the union's cause, from which radiated all the impulses that kept the morale of the strikers intact. Convinced that the most adequate precaution should be taken here, he appointed Edwin Walker several days before the occurrence of any serious disorder in that city. As special counsel, Walker proved more than just an assistant to Milchrist; in a sense he became the director of affairs in Chicago for the Department of Justice.[26] During the heat of the conflict numerous telegrams and other communications were transmitted between Olney and Walker, some of which, because of their confidential nature, were sent in code. The attorney-general leaned heavily upon this special attorney for advice and information, and together they did much toward shaping the course which federal strategy took in Chicago.[27]

By July 1 the boycott was becoming increasingly effective in this city, but neither then nor for several days subsequently did any rioting or serious disturbance develop there. Unfortunately for the cause of labor, the same could not be said for the outlying village of Blue Island, where disorders were inspired by a riotous element.[28] Reports transmitted to the Department of Justice were anything but reassuring. The United States marshal on July 1 telegraphed to the attorney-general: "The situation here tonight is desperate. I have sworn in over 400 deputies, and many more will be needed to protect the mail trains. I expect great trouble. Shall I purchase 100 riot guns? . . . ."[29] The dispatch of Milchrist on the same day, no less disconcerting, revealed his determination to meet the situation by applying for an injunction. "The general paralysis," he announced, "warrants this course. Very little mail and no freight moving. Marshal is using all his force now owing to mob and obstruction of tracks, especially at Blue Island, Riverdale and other points. His force is clearly inadequate."[30]

These and other messages reinforced the determination of Richard Olney to resort to strong measures. To him a sweeping injunction had now become imperative, and to both Walker and Milchrist he immediately indicated the advisability of applying for such a writ. In his wire to Edwin Walker he explained that a restraining order could be secured under the Interstate Commerce Act, the Sherman Anti-trust Law, or on general grounds.[31] Perceiving the value of such a weapon, the General Managers' Association had already given it their fullest indorsement. Significantly, the strategy of that organization, as outlined by its legal subcommittee, was to be based upon the efficacy of restraining orders as issued by courts in equity. The decision of the United States government to apply for blanket injunctions relieved the railroads in most cases of the necessity for taking action in this field.[32]

The injunction was a comparatively new weapon in the strife between labor and capital. It is doubtful whether this procedure had been evoked in industrial disputes prior to the eighties. During the strike epidemic of 1886, court orders met with increasing favor; but not until 1894 did they come into their own as a powerful weapon that could be employed with devastating effect against labor. When the Commonweal movement was at its height, federal judges found it expedient to grant injunctions to protect railroad property in receivership. It was but a step in extending the writ to roads financially solvent, and soon they also became beneficiaries of this new-found instrument, whose application seemed not to be hedged by any special boundaries or restrictions. Its possibilities in labor controversies appeared to be limitless.[33] Forsaking the trodden path of precedence, judges issued the writs with such sweeping terminology that labor, wishing to strike or striking, found most of its customary avenues for redress of grievances closed. The extreme efficacy of such a writ lay in the fact that any attempt to violate its provisions meant a citation for contempt and summary punishment by the judge issuing the order. The accused was even denied benefit of jury trial.

The general pattern and form which the injunction assumed during the Pullman Strike was largely worked out in the early spring of 1894. The Northern Pacific Railroad, like many roads, had been forced into bankruptcy, and the receivers had decided to slash wages. Labor protested and evinced a determination to resist the proposed reduction by a strike. To prevent this, the receivers applied for and secured restraining orders from the federal courts at Milwaukee, St. Paul, and on the Pacific Coast. These injunctions were exceptionally broad, forbidding not only strikes on this road but any attempt, however peaceful, to foster sentiment for such action. The various officials of the railroad brotherhoods were among those enjoined, and so comprehensive was the St. Paul injunction that Chief Sargent of the Locomotive Firemen was reported as saying that he was prohibited "from even communicating with employees on the Northern Pacific."

It was by virtue of a rather extraordinary interpretation of the Sherman Anti-trust Law of 1890 that the right to issue these writs was justified.[34] In his decision of April, 1894, Federal Judge Jenkins of the circuit of Wisconsin upheld the injunction which he had issued at Milwaukee, on the grounds that a court in equity possessed the right under this law to forbid any combination of employees from quitting work in a body or in any way interfering with the operation of a railroad. In his opinion a strike when directed against a railroad was in restraint of interstate commerce, and hence illegal. Venting his spleen against strikes in general, he proclaimed:

A strike is essentially a conspiracy to extort by violence. . . . . I know of no peaceful strike. I think no strike was ever heard of that was or could be successful unaccompanied by intimidation and violence. . . . . The strike has become a serious evil, destructive to property, destructive to individual rights, injurious to the conspirators themselves and subversive of republican institutions. . . . . Whatever other doctrine may be asserted by reckless agitators, it must ever remain the duty of the courts, in the protection of society, and in the execution of the laws of the land, to condemn, prevent, and punish all such unlawful conspiracies and combinations.[35]

Richard Olney was in substantial agreement with the tenor of this decision and in a letter to Justice Harlan of the Seventh Federal Circuit Court of Appeals expressed the opinion that, even if the proposed strike on the Northern Pacific were to have developed peacefully, it would still remain the right and duty of the court to issue a restraining order. He explained that, whereas one person could lawfully quit work, such an act on the part of a large number of individuals might operate injuriously against public interest and hence be illegal. In comparing a public highway with a railroad, he pointed out that, just as the act of wilfully placing obstructions on the former could be enjoined, so it would be lawful to prohibit railroad workers from striking, since by such action they would have the same general effect of tying up traffic. In defending the unprecedented use made of the injunction, he contended that the courts were simply adapting the "established principles of equity to the new conditions of modern civilized life."[36]

It was not until after the Pullman Strike that the decision of Judge Jenkins was reversed by the federal circuit court of appeals. The reversal, however, proved little more than a modification of the basic ruling in the original decision. Although the court acknowledged that men could legitimately combine and withdraw peacefully from work, it emphatically denied to labor the right to unite for the purpose of inducing men to strike in violation of a contract of service or with the intent of injuring the employer. Such a course was branded by the judges as a conspiracy, against which the injunction could be freely used. Strong emphasis was placed upon the right of a court of equity to make unhesitating use of the writ to protect the right of property from wrongdoers.[37] In the light of this decision, it is most unlikely that Justice Harlan, one of the participating judges, could have been unsympathetic to the sentiments communicated to him previously by Richard Olney in the above-cited letter.

When Walker and Milchrist filed application for an injunction against the American Railway Union, they did so under the Sherman Antitrust Law. This act was enacted by Congress on July 2, 1890, as the result of years of increasing agitation against the evils of monopolistic control by big business. Rather ambiguous in its terminology, the law declared illegal "every contract, combination in the form of trust or otherwise, or conspiracy, in restraint of trade or commerce among the several states, or with foreign nations." Any person found guilty of engaging in such a combination or conspiracy could be punished by a fine of five thousand dollars or imprisonment for one year or both. The circuit courts of the United States were invested with the authority to issue restraining orders whenever, in their judgment, such action was deemed necessary to prevent violation of the law. Federal district attorneys, under the direction of the attorney-general, were empowered to institute proceedings in equity for the purpose of carrying out the intent of the law.[38]

An examination of the statute and of the debates which preceded enactment would furnish not the slightest evidence to show that Congress ever intended that this measure should be invoked against labor. When it was under consideration in the Senate, many speeches were delivered, an analysis of which clearly indicates that this legislation was designed to protect and safeguard competition in interstate trade and commerce against the attempt of powerful business combinations to throttle it.[39] The author of the bill, John Sherman, expressly stated that its purpose was not in any way directed against labor. He pointed out that "combinations of workingmen to promote their interests, promote their welfare, and to increase their pay, if you please, to get their fair share in the division of production, are not affected in the slightest degree, nor can they be included in the words or intent of the bill. . . . ."[40]

It was the duty of Richard Olney, as chief of the Department of Justice, to enforce the Sherman Anti-trust Law as vigorously as he could and in the manner comprehended by Congress. In view of his corporation background, however, he had no desire to attack combinations of great wealth. He was in no way disturbed about the evils of big business or the menace of trade conspiracies. His interpretation of this statute, as it applied to business monopolies, was considerably more narrow than was later propounded by the Supreme Court.[41] In scrutinizing the law he nevertheless was able to read into it a meaning never intended by Congress and to use it in legalizing a weapon destined to become the scourge of labor. The Sherman Anti-trust Law was thus cloaked in a new but strange garment and, ironical as it may seem, turned against the very people who had most enthusiastically applauded its adoption.

The refusal of Richard Olney to apply the law to illegal business combinations was unmistakably demonstrated as the Pullman Strike was drawing to a tragic close. George Denis, a federal attorney at Los Angeles, desired to apply for an injunction against the Southern Pacific Railroad on the grounds that it had unlawfully entered into conspiracy with several other roads. By outright purchase and through a system of long-term leases it was able to gain control of many competing railroads and to develop into a powerful monopoly. The combination included all three of the lines entering San Francisco: the California and Oregon Road, the Central Pacific, and the Southern Pacific. Provision was made for a division of expenses and earnings, irrespective of the volume of business carried by each. Rates became prohibitory on all but the Southern Pacific, in order to secure for this line the "long haul" from San Francisco east via New Orleans. In the judgment of George Denis and his assistant, Special United States Attorney Joseph H. Call, this was a flagrant conspiracy in restraint of interstate commerce. The monopolistic practices of this combination were so offensive that they had aroused strong popular resentment in California.[42] Despite all this, the attorney-general flatly refused to sanction equity proceedings in the matter. Rather lamely he contended that this consolidation had been formed prior to the adoption of the act of 1890 and that, since the law was "prospective in its operation," it could hardly be construed to "make crimes out of transactions long passed but not criminal when they occurred."[43] Such specious reasoning was not in the least convincing to Denis, who argued that the law was designed by Congress to render illegal all combinations in restraint of trade, regardless of whether they were organized before the enactment of the law or subsequently.[44]

The opening gun in the injunctive warfare during the Pullman Strike was fired in defense of the Santa Fe Railroad, then in federal receivership. On June 27 Henry C. Caldwell, United States circuit judge, issued a writ forbidding the strikers to interfere with the property or operation of this road within his circuit, which included the New Mexico area. Although conceding the right of an employee to quit work, the judge warned the strikers not to attempt enforcement of the boycott or to molest in any way those who remained at their jobs.[45] Such an order was enforcible only on that portion of the line within the jurisdiction of the judge issuing the writ; but on this road, as elsewhere, other judges responded whenever the emergency seemed to demand action. Federal Judge William Woods, for example, on June 29 threw the protective mantle of a restraining order over the Illinois division of the Santa Fe.[46] These injunctions were extremely modest in their scope, being granted upon petition of the receivers.

Far more drastic were the blanket injunctions secured at the behest of United States district attorneys upon the authorization

of Richard Olney. With such a restraining order, complete protection was furnished to all railroads within a given jurisdiction.
Whenever there seemed to be the need, these writs were quickly
sought, and invariably they followed the same general pattern of
that first omnibus injunction issued in Chicago on July 2 by Federal Judges William A. Woods and Peter S. Grosscup.

The bill for this injunction was largely the handiwork of
Thomas Milchrist, who labored on its preparation all night of
July 1. When submitted the following morning to Circuit Judge
Woods and District Judge Grosscup, certain recommended
changes were made. Present at this discussion was Edwin Walker,
who protested that the complaint should be given a broader basis.
Apparently, Milchrist had endeavored to establish the need for a
restraining order almost exclusively upon the dangers, threatened
and real, which confronted interstate commerce; but, upon the
suggestion of Walker, it was decided that interference with mail
trains should likewise become a prominent feature of the complaint.[47] In the revised form the document proved lengthy and
replete with numerous accusations and allegations. Twenty-two
railroads were listed as in urgent need of protection, all of them
engaged in interstate commerce. In disrupting the movement of
mail and interstate commerce the strikers were charged with conspiracy. Palace cars, it was claimed, were indispensable to the
successful operation of trains; but, even if this were not true, the
railroads could not very well refuse to use them, as such a policy
would lead to the violation of Pullman contracts. It was asserted
that force and intimidation were employed to discourage workers
from filling the vacancies of those who left their jobs. Violence
toward railroad property was also set forth as a deliberate weapon
of the strikers in pursuance of their conspiracy.[48]

With haste the writ was whipped into shape and ordered served
on the officials and members of the American Railway Union. In
reality it was a huge dragnet, applicable to all within the jurisdiction of the court who were involved in the attempt to obstruct the
movement of mail and interstate commerce on any of the twenty-
two railroads enumerated in the injunction. Such persons were
strictly forbidden to hinder or interfere in any manner with "mail

trains, express trains, or other trains, whether freight or passenger, engaged in interstate commerce, or carrying passengers or freight between or among the states." The strikers were further enjoined to stay away from the premises of the railroads and to refrain from molesting or damaging any property of these lines. Extremely important was the provision which forbade any striker or union representative to attempt by coercion, threats, or persuasion to induce any employee to abandon his job. Sending telegrams or any form of communication to workers for the purpose of encouraging them to forsake their duties as railroad employees was no longer permissible. Neither would the writ tolerate any attempt by threats or force to keep persons from accepting work on any road. All those involved in the conspiracy were warned to abstain from "ordering, directing, aiding, assisting, or abetting, in any manner whatever," any individual to commit any act proscribed by the injunction.[49]

For thoroughness and completeness, this writ left nothing to be desired. It was an ingenious weapon, whose terrible potentialities in the hands of a determined judiciary were soon revealed to the amazement and anger of labor. The *New York Times* referred to it as a "Gatling gun on paper," and as a

veritable dragnet in the matter of legal verbiage, one of these peculiar instruments that punishes an individual for doing a certain thing, and is equally merciless if he does not do it, so it is difficult to understand how the strikers can maintain their present policy and at the same time evade its operation or escape its influence.[50]

Since the great preponderance of newspapers was extremely hostile toward the strikers, it was not unnatural that they should accept the omnibus injunction as a skilfully contrived device, wholly necessary and completely within the law. A few papers, however, boldly attacked the writ as a usurpation of power. The *Chicago Times*, although acknowledging the wisdom of certain provisions, sharply denounced the part which denied to the strikers the right to promote their cause by peacefully campaigning among railroad workers. In the judgment of this paper, the writ was thus "a menace to liberty . . . . a weapon ever ready for the capitalist" and should be restricted as to use by law.[51] The

New York World was even more disturbed about the full implications of the injunction and without reservation condemned it as a dangerous violation of popular rights:

> So outrageous a stretch of federal power was not attempted during the Civil War, when amid the tumult of arms laws were silent. It is infinitely more harmful and dangerous than the stupid strike against which it is directed. . . . . The American people are long-suffering, but they are honest and they love justice. They will never consent that the power of the Federal Government shall be placed at the disposal of railroad managers when they quarrel with their employees, while the government recognizes no reciprocal obligation to secure the employees in the enjoyment of their rights and privileges.[52]

In serving the writ, various means were employed by the federal marshal and his deputy. Eugene Debs and some of the directors of the union were presented personally with copies, but general notice to all strikers was achieved through publication of the injunction in the newspapers of Chicago on July 3. Copies were also posted in public places and read to demonstrative crowds whenever the situation warranted. Such service was deemed adequate by Milchrist to place all people guilty of violating its provisions under the ban of the law.[53]

The large outpouring of humanity that overran the railroad yards at Blue Island on July 1 and 2 was partly spontaneous and certainly not motivated by the American Railway Union. Many of those who mingled in this noisy congregation of strike sympathizers did so out of idle curiosity, but some were grimly determined to enforce the boycott against Pullman cars. So serious did the situation become that the Rock Island Railroad was obliged to abandon all trains operating over these tracks.[54] To meet this lawless outbreak, Marshal Arnold, accompanied by some public officials, railroad attorneys, and deputy marshals, went to the scene of disturbance on the afternoon of July 2 and read the injunction to a milling, boisterous throng of two thousand people. Jibes, cheers, and groans greeted the reading, and when it was finished, the crowd seemed unwilling or unable to grasp the meaning of the order. John Arnold called on them in the name of the President of the United States to disperse and to resist no more the movement of trains. The injunction was read a second time but, as before, without results. The attorney for the Rock Island Road and the deputy sheriff of Cook County each, in turn, tried to explain the full meaning of the writ. In a parting speech Arnold issued a warning that sufficient force would be secured and that all trains would be moved regardless of consequences. He again urged them to avert trouble by retiring to their homes.[55]

So hopeless did conditions appear that on July 2 the marshal telegraphed to the attorney-general about his failure to disperse the rioters. "We have had a desperate time with them here all day," he professed, "and our force is inadequate, and in my judgment it is impossible to move trains here without having the Fifteenth Infantry from Fort Sheridan ordered here now."[56] This situation played directly into the hands of Olney and afforded him the opportunity to have federal troops rushed to Chicago. The avidity with which he favored this policy, without first seeking to exhaust all other means in suppressing disorders at Blue Island, including recourse to the state militia, raises the question as to Olney's basic motive for having the junction issued. Did he entertain the belief or hope that the enforcement of the writ would involve difficulties sufficient to furnish an excuse for military intervention? The *Chicago Times* seemed to think so. On July 2 the editor observed that "the object of the injunction is not so much to prevent interference with trains as to lay a foundation for calling out the United States troops. . . . . Declaration by the United States marshal that he is unable to execute the orders of the court might be alleged as the basis of a call for troops."[57]

Possibly the issuance of blanket injunctions from Michigan to California, occurring at approximately the same time, represented a concerted movement by the Department of Justice. Wherever any disturbances materialized, United States attorneys were at once notified by Richard Olney to apply for a restraining order, often upon the mere recommendation of some general manager or counsel for a railroad.[58] The slightest failure to enforce the writ led to the precipitate use of federal troops. The Chicago injunction, issued on July 2, was followed elsewhere by many similar court orders; and so quickly did events move that

by July 4 troops were already on active duty at four widely distributed points.[59] The execution of this strategy, characterized by
precision, revealed the closest co-operation between the railroads
and federal officials. Illustrative of this was the cordial relationship between Edwin Walker and the General Managers' Association. He was in frequent contact with railroad lawyers and was
greatly influenced by their judgment.[60] Shortly after the publication of the injunction, he attended a meeting of the general managers in the capacity of special United States attorney and explained at length the character and significance of the writ. The
members were urged to furnish any evidence of its violation. To
their extreme gratification, he revealed that federal soldiers
would soon be ordered out and that any suggestions from the rail-
ways as to how these troops should be distributed would be welcomed. Upon the conclusion of his remarks, the association tendered its thanks to him and expressed the hope that he would be
able to attend their meetings and give further advice.[61]

The first occurrence of trouble in the strike was met by a rapid
increase in the number of deputy marshals wherever conditions
seemed to indicate any need. United States marshals were
granted unrestricted freedom to recruit men, and many thousands of deputies were thus sworn in as temporary law-enforcing
agents. This policy did not necessarily mean that Richard Olney
was willing to repose much confidence in this arm of the government. The ineffectualness of federal deputies in suppressing the
Coxeyite disturbances was still vivid in his memory and doubtless
shook his faith in this force as a means of adequately protecting
mail and interstate commerce. Precisely what he expected from
these deputies is not known, but on June 30, when the first group
in Chicago was being commissioned for service, he disclosed to
Edwin Walker a complete absence of faith in the capacity of these
men to cope with the situation.[62] Perhaps he never intended that
they should suppress the strike but that by their inadequacy they
should demonstrate the need for federal troops.

In Chicago—hub of the strike—a total of about five thousand
deputy marshals were recruited, by far the greatest force of
United States deputies anywhere assembled during the struggle.

From the last day of June until July 5, John Arnold and his chief deputy, John Donnelly, swore in a continuous stream of these special officers, each of whom received a star as his insignia of authority. As to how many and what disposition should be made of them, Arnold was advised to consult with Milchrist and Walker. As quickly as the deputies received their commissions, they were taken in groups to whatever railroad area seemed to require their services. They were orally instructed to guard and protect interstate freight and passenger trains, as well as the movement of mail.[63]

This large aggregation of civil officers fell into two broad classifications: the regular force and those who were armed and paid by the railroads. The latter group, representing over two-thirds of all deputy marshals in Chicago, comprised those who were chosen by the railroad corporations and directly responsible to them. Any road desiring to have its own corps of deputy marshals would designate one of its officials as a sort of captain, to whom was intrusted the duty of choosing the men and directing their activities. The names of those selected for deputy service were submitted to the General Managers' Association, which in turn promptly transmitted them to the federal marshal with the recommendation that they be accepted. The men were then sent over to the marshal's office and commissioned without even the most superficial examination into their qualifications. Badges, but not guns, were supplied to these men by this office, which exercised no control over them and received no reports on their performance of duty. No effort was made to ascertain whether or not they were citizens. Many were regular employees of the railroad, and it was not unusual for the same hand that held the throttle of a locomotive to use a revolver in the name of the federal government. The engineers, firemen, and others, thus cloaked with this special authority, were in no wise relieved of their customary duties but were allowed to serve in a double capacity.[64] The Rock Island Road, typical of many, had a small army of five hundred deputy marshals, of whom one-half were employees of the company.[65] Concerning the propriety of all this, the Strike Commission commented: "It is placing officers of the Government under control of a combination of railroads. It is bad precedent, that might well lead to serious consequences."[66] The indiscriminate method of choosing deputy marshals may largely explain the unhappy record of these federal agents. Even the regular force of deputies was organized in a haphazard manner, many of whom were at first picked up off the streets. In the rush of rapid recruiting, applicants were accepted on their appearance, with the result that thugs, drunkards, and other disreputable individuals were placed in the role of maintaining law and order. Some did not know how to carry their authority and became extremely aggressive and provocative. Needless arrests were made and unnecessary trouble precipitated by a few of the more swaggering and arrogant of the deputy marshals. In certain cases freight cars were plundered and other railroad property destroyed by the very men employed to help prevent depredations.[67]

The superintendent of the Chicago police testified before the Strike Commission that the deputy marshals were "more in the way than of any service."[68] A reporter from the *Chicago Herald*, who for several days had occasion to observe two hundred deputies on duty, declared that in his opinion "they were a very low, contemptible set of men."[69] Another reporter, who represented the *Chicago Record*, was even more explicit in his remarks: "I must say that I saw more deputy sheriffs and deputy marshals drunk than I saw strikers drunk. . . . . After the troops came . . . . they became aggressive, ran around and made arrests on all sorts of provocations."[70] Although the more objectionable deputy marshals were weeded out and the quality of men somewhat improved as the strike continued, the general character of the force remained poor. The performance of these men must have sorely tried the patience of Walker, who on July 9 sent the following telegram to Olney: "At the risk of being thought meddlesome, I suggest that the marshal is appointing a mob of deputies that are worse than useless."[71] On the following day, the attorney-general wired Marshal Arnold: "Under the circumstances what is the use of the great mob of deputies which you seem to be employing? Are not a large proportion wholly unreliable? Do Messrs. Walker and Milchrist approve your action?"[72] In reply John Arnold explained that what he did was done with the approval of Milchrist but that he had already ceased swearing in deputies.[73]

In other localities the record of deputy marshals was no better. Against the use of such agents, sharp protests were lodged. None was more forceful than that of David H. Waite, governor of Colorado, who found the employment of deputy marshals in his state highly offensive. The marshal at Denver had instructed his deputies at La Junta and Trinidad, where trouble had arisen, to arrest without warrants all those who tried to induce railroad employees to quit work, who indulged in any talk on Sante Fe property tending to cause trouble, or who in any way violated the injunction of Federal Judge Moses Hallett. In complying with these orders, the deputies were advised to ignore completely the authority of all local officers and magistrates and to arrest them if they should seek to intervene. To Governor Waite such a policy was a usurpation of state's rights and a flagrant violation of the constitutional rights guaranteed to all citizens.[74] On July 8 he protested to Judge Hallett that a state of anarchy was being fostered in Colorado by the policy of his court which had

allowed the United States marshal to enlist a private army to suppress alleged state troubles, of which neither the county nor state authorities have any notice, and has called into active service United States troops without request or notice to the Governor of the State, and is waging an active war in Colorado without any declaration thereof by the United States, or notice or knowledge thereof by the state authorities, and utterly in violation of law.[75]

Although the maximum pay allowed to deputy marshals was $2.50 per day, with expenses not to exceed an additional $1.50, the cost to the federal government of this great army of civil officers during the Pullman strike was $375,000. In Chicago alone the outlay was $125,000.[76] Because this money was not immediately forthcoming, since it had to await appropriation by Congress, the marshals were placed in an embarrassing position when their deputies clamored for compensation. None found this situation more trying than John Arnold, whose force was extremely large and crowded with many in desperate need of money. The attorney-general advised him, as he did others, to borrow from a railroad or some other source until money was available from Congress. This course Arnold seemed reluctant to follow, apparently because he did not wish to assume personal responsibility for such a large loan.[77] He nevertheless believed that, since the deputies had been employed almost exclusively in defense of railroad property, the companies should at least pay the boarding and lodging bills of these men. The General Managers' Association, to whom he made this recommendation, took the position, shared by Richard Olney, that such expenses were incurred by the government for the "maintenance of Federal law and the authority of Federal Courts, and therefore ought no more to be paid by the railroads than by any individual citizen."[78]

In the light of this pronouncement it may seem somewhat contradictory that the railroads were willing enough to carry on their pay rolls during the strike those deputy marshals whom they selected and controlled.[79] This policy was due to the fact that a large proportion of these deputies were regular employees, while the remainder of them served the interests of the road no less completely. For the railroads to have insisted upon reimbursement would have put them in a very delicate position. Even so, Richard Olney was determined that the entire cost for all deputy marshals should be a charge against the federal treasury and demonstrated his adherence to this position when the question arose in connection with the Santa Fe Railroad. Here he held that the receivers of this road, who had already compensated their deputy marshals, should be reimbursed by the government. Such a course, he contended in a letter to Edwin Walker, was absolutely necessary in order to protect the government against any charge of partiality. If the railroads were permitted to share even a part of this cost, he explained, the government might then be denounced as the "paid agent and instrument of capital."[80] Judge Grosscup was inclined at first to take the opposite view but reconsidered after a conference with Walker and decided to follow Olney's advice in approving the proposed reimbursement.[81]

From the very beginning of the struggle it appears that the

attorney-general pondered the advisability of using federal troops. He realized that sweeping injunctions and the resulting difficulties of enforcement by federal marshals would create the proper conditions for an appeal to the military. The disorders at Blue Island, therefore, must have come to him as a welcome opportunity for immediate action. On July 3 he wired Edwin Walker that, whenever in his opinion the need for federal soldiers arose, they would be used "promptly and decisively." In demanding troops, Walker was urged to do so in co-operation with the United States judge, marshal, and district attorney.[82] The special district attorney immediately replied that it was of "utmost importance that soldiers should be distributed at certain points within the city. . . . ."[83]

Moving with alacrity and supported by the signatures of Judge Grosscup, Edwin Walker, and Thomas Milchrist, the United States marshal promptly sent a dispatch to the attorney-general stressing the urgency of the situation and asking for the aid of federal troops. He pointed out that the mob at Blue Island had ditched a mail train and upset several baggage cars, thereby blocking the movement of all trains, and that he had met with complete failure in trying to enforce the orders of the court.[84] To Richard Olney this communication was merely the final proof that the time for military intervention had arrived.

During the two or three preceding days, the attorney-general had done much to impress the President and his closest advisers with the seriousness of the situation and the need for drastic action. Telegrams and other pertinent dispatches, some rather alarming, had been submitted by Olney at the daily meetings of the Cabinet. All those in close touch with Grover Cleveland were genuinely disturbed over the alleged gravity of the situation. Precautionary steps were quickly taken to meet the emergency.[85] On July 2 confidential instructions were issued to the commanding officer at Fort Sheridan to make the necessary arrangements to move his men to Chicago at a moment's notice. A special train was sent to the fort and held in readiness.[86] During the evening of July 2 and the morning of July 3 the expediency of using federal troops was weighed at the White House. Prominent in these deliberations were President Cleveland, Secretary of War Lamont, Secretary of State Gresham, Richard Olney, Major General Schofield, and General Miles of Chicago.[87] When on July 3 Olney drew his trump card—the urgent request for troops by the federal marshal at Chicago—Cleveland decided to delay no longer. At four o'clock in the afternoon Colonel Crofton, in charge at Fort Sheridan, was ordered to move his entire command to Chicago for the purpose of enforcing the processes of the federal court, protecting the transportation of mail, and otherwise helping to execute the laws of the government.[88] Jubilantly the attorney-general announced: "The subject has now passed out of my hands. The filing of the injunction practically concluded my work, and it is for other branches to execute such action as the courts take."[89] This statement may have been designed to impress the public, but it certainly had no basis in fact, since he grew not less, but more, vigilant and zealous in his relentless campaign against the American Railway Union.

By express provision of the United States Constitution, the federal government was authorized to protect a state against domestic violence upon request for such aid by the legislature or, when the legislature was not in session, by the governor. It was not by invoking this clause that Grover Cleveland took action, since the legislature of Illinois was not in session and Governor Altgeld firmly believed the situation did not warrant such drastic measures. It was rather by virtue of the authority invested in the President's office by certain acts, referred to as Sections 5298 and 5299 of the *Revised Statutes of the United States*, that he sent troops to Chicago in complete disregard of the governor. These laws provided that whenever insurrection, conspiracies, or domestic violence obstructed the course of judicial proceedings and otherwise rendered impossible the execution of federal laws in any state by ordinary means, the President was empowered to call forth state troops or the regular army to suppress the disorders.[90] In meeting the situation at Chicago, neither Cleveland nor Olney seemed greatly concerned about the strictly legal aspects of their course but preferred to crush all opposition with an overwhelming force. In justifying the extraordinary use of troops, the President explained that it was necessary for the enforcement of judicial mandates and for the protection of mail, federal property, and interstate commerce.[91]

Chicago at this time was still free from riots. The confidential records of the General Managers' Association as well as the report of the Chicago superintendent of police show that prior to the arrival of troops the city was orderly, except for a few isolated and relatively unimportant acts of sabotage. Many trains did not move, but this was in no way due to threatening mobs but to insufficient crews. Blue Island experienced disorders, to be sure, but this locality was beyond the farthest limits of Chicago. Nevertheless, what happened in this suburb served as the basis for greatly exaggerated fears and the immediate concentration of troops in the great metropolis near by.[92] The impressive display of the military could hardly have been made because of what had actually transpired but because of forebodings and expectations of what might occur. The words of Grover Cleveland, written years after the struggle, would tend to confirm this fact:

> It was from the first anticipated that this [Chicago] would be the seat of the most serious complications, and the place where the strong arm of the law would be needed. In these circumstances, it would have been criminal neglect of duty if those charged with the protection of governmental agencies and the enforcement of orderly obedience and submission to federal authority, had been remiss in preparations for an emergency in that quarter.[93]

Even assuming that the situation on July 2 and 3 was becoming critical, why did the federal government not first avail itself of the Illinois militia? The use of these troops could easily have been effected upon application to the governor by the United States marshal precisely as was done not many weeks previously at Mount Olive, Illinois.[94] The record of John P. Altgeld shows conclusively that, where lawlessness threatened, he was willing to use troops.[95] The President, however, influenced as he was by the attorney-general, seemed to ignore almost completely the availability of the militia in Illinois, as elsewhere; but in a memorandum on July 5 he was belatedly reminded by Secretary of War Lamont that, in view of the limitations within which the federal government had to move and the comparatively small army at its disposal, the situation could be met more effectively by getting in touch with the governors of those states in which federal property was threatened.[96]

Within five hours after he received orders to move, Colonel Crofton and his troops were en route to Chicago. They arrived at 12:30 A.M. on July 4, and immediately the Colonel entered into a conference with Thomas Milchrist, John Egan, and Assistant United States Marshal Donnelly as to how the soldiers should be distributed.[97] The attorney-general intended that Walker, Milchrist, and Arnold should advise the military in such matters;[98] but none of these men proved more active in this respect than John Egan, strike manager of the General Managers' Association. As a result of this first conference, it was decided to concentrate the infantry at Blue Island and Grand Crossing and the artillery and cavalry at the Stock Yards. Before dawn all contingents, except those assigned to the Stock Yards, were at their posts; and after the break of day, the remaining ones were moved quickly to their new positions.[99]

Chicago was located within the Department of Missouri, and it was thus the duty of the commanding officer of this military area, Nelson A. Miles, to take charge of all federal troops concentrated in that city. Since the regular headquarters of the department were in Chicago, matters moved with smoothness, even though no troops were normally garrisoned there. When the omnibus injunction was issued at Chicago, General Miles was in the East, apparently not much disturbed about developments. He was promptly summoned to Washington, where on July 3 he took part in discussions relative to the need for military intervention. In his opinion such a course was not necessary then, but the President preferred to disregard this advice. Under orders, Miles left at once for his command and reached Chicago shortly before noon on July 4,[100] many hours after Colonel Crofton had completed the arrangement of his troops.

In a rapid survey of conditions, Miles had occasion to reverse his earlier judgment and even decided that the eleven companies already on duty were inadequate. To Major General Schofield he expressed a desire for more troops and alluded to what he believed would be the salutary effect at this time of moving additional soldiers to Chicago. The government was not adverse to such a suggestion and proceeded to rush new reserves to Chicago from Leavenworth, Kansas, and Fort Brady, Michigan. Subsequently, troops were also ordered from Madison Barracks, New York; Fort Riley, Kansas; and Fort Niobrara, Nebraska. The last of these contingents reached Chicago on July 10, increasing the total of federal troops there to 1,936 men. For fifteen days they remained on duty and were recalled only after the strike had been broken and all resistance had virtually disappeared.[101]

Like many federal officials, civil and military, General Miles reflected the strongest antagonism toward the American Railway Union. In helping to suppress the strike, he did so with the firm conviction that he was breaking the backbone of a force directly opposed to the government. He conferred frequently with general managers, especially John Egan, an action which, more than anything else, caused labor to view him as an ally of the railroads. He was particularly contemptuous of the white ribbon worn by strike sympathizers and revealed a strong antipathy toward Eugene Debs, whom he considered a dictator.[102] In an article on the strike, published in August, 1894, Miles pictured the struggle as between the forces of lawlessness and good government. He declared that "men must take sides either for anarchy, secret conclaves, unwritten law, mob violence, and universal chaos under the red or white flag of socialism on the one hand; or on the side of established government."[103]

The American Railway Union protested against military intervention, particularly because conditions in Chicago at that time did not in any way seem to justify such drastic measures. The appearance of regular soldiers served to arouse the anger of labor and, in the opinion of union officials, greatly to aggravate the situation.[104] At first Eugene Debs seemed to take the position that the use of troops would not jeopardize the cause of labor since soldiers could not themselves run trains and since they did not dare molest the strikers in their lawful and orderly conduct. He even indicated that soldiers might prove helpful to the cause of labor by preventing rioters from "destroying property, the stigma of which is placed by capital on labor."[105] On further reflection, however, he realized that these troops, under the guise of protecting interstate commerce and the processes of the courts, would be used in a manner highly prejudicial to the strikers. It was this unhappy contemplation that must have furnished the impetus for his extravagant statement to a United Press reporter:

The first shot fired by the regular soldiers at the mobs here will be the signal for a civil war. I believe this as firmly as I believe in the ultimate success of our course. Bloodshed will follow, and 90 per cent of the people of the United States will be arrayed against the other 10 per cent. And I would not care to be arrayed against the laboring people in the contest, or find myself out of the ranks of labor when the struggle ended. I do not say this as an alarmist, but calmly and thoughtfully.[106]

Chicago was not the first city to which federal troops were dispatched; they had already been ordered to Los Angeles, California; Raton, New Mexico; and Trinidad, Colorado. Together these communities disclosed a procedure that soon was invoked in other states and territories, whenever similar circumstances prevailed. United States judges, district attorneys, and marshals had only to reveal a need for federal troops, and the army was instructed to march. Expediency alone seemed to determine the course of the federal government, and it made no difference whether local officials or state executives believed themselves competent to meet the situation. The use of troops bore eloquent witness to the grimness of purpose which motivated those high in authority. Against the far-flung use of the military the strikers braced themselves, by no means abandoning faith in their cause.

NOTES

1. Robinson, *op. cit.*, pp. 195–201.
2. Henry James, *Richard Olney and His Public Service*, pp. 1–19, 26–27; Allan Nevins, *Grover Cleveland*, pp. 615–16.
3. *Annual Report of the Attorney General* . . . . *1894*, pp. xxx–xxxi.
4. *Ibid.*, p. xxxi.
5. Olney to Bellamy Storer, July 12, 1894, Olney Papers.
6. *Appendix to the* . . . . *Report of the Attorney General* . . . . *1896.*
7. *Inter Ocean*, July 4, 1894, p. 1; *New York Times,* July 6, 1894, pp. 2, 6, and July 9, 1894, p. 1; *Washington Post,* July 3, 1894, p. 2.
8. Olney to Edwin Walker, June 30, 1894, *Appendix to the* . . . . *Report of the Attorney General* . . . . *1896*, p. 60.

9. *U.S. Strike Commission Report*, p. 159; *Washington Post*, July 4, 1894, p. 2.

10. *Darrow, op. cit.*, p. 61; *U.S. Strike Commission Report*, pp. 159, 255.

11. Frank H. Jones (acting postmaster-general) to Olney, June 30, 1894, *Appendix to the . . . . Report of the Attorney General . . . . 1896*, pp. 248–50.

12. Frank H. Jones to Olney, June 28, 1894, *ibid.*, p. 245.

13. *Report of the Postmaster General, 1894: U.S. House Executive Document* (53d Cong., 3d sess., 1894–95), XIII, No. 1, Part 4, 396–98.

14. *Chicago Times*, June 29, 1894, p. 2, and June 30, 1894, p. 3.

15. *Appendix to the . . . . Report of the Attorney General . . . . 1896*, pp. 245–55; *Annual Report of the Attorney General . . . . 1894*, p. xxxi.

16. *Report of the Postmaster General, 1894*, p. 398.

17. Olney to Milchrist, June 28, 1894, *Appendix to the . . . . Report of the Attorney General . . . . 1896*, p. 55.

18. *Proceedings of the General Managers' Association . . . . 1894*, p. 113.

19. Altgeld, *op. cit.*, p. 658.

20. Milchrist to Olney, June 30, 1894. *Appendix to the . . . . Report of the Attorney General . . . . 1896*, p. 56.

21. *Ibid.*, pp. 57–58.

22. *Ibid.*, p. 57; *New York Times*, July 2, 1894, p. 2.

23. *Who's Who in America, 1899–1900*, p. 760; Darrow, *op. cit.*, p. 61.

24. Darrow, *op. cit.*, p. 61.

25. *Appendix to the . . . . Report of the Attorney General . . . . 1896*, pp. 59 and 60.

26. Olney to Walker, June 30, 1894, *ibid.*, p. 60.

27. *Ibid.*, pp. 60–75.

28. *Ibid.*, pp. 60–64.

29. Arnold to Olney, July 1, 1894, *ibid.*, p. 61.

30. Milchrist to Olney, July 1, 1894, *ibid.*, pp. 60–61.

31. Olney to Walker, July 1, 1894, *ibid.,* p. 61.

32. *Proceedings of the General Managers' Association . . . . 1894*, pp. 123–26, 135–36, 147.

33. Frankfurter and Greene, *The Labor Injunction*, pp. 21–24; *Reports of the Industrial Commission on Labor Organizations, Labor Disputes and Arbitration*, p. 602.

34. *The Railroad Gazette*, XXVI (1894), 12–13; *Federal Reporter*, LX, 803–24.

35. *Federal Reporter*, LX, 821–23.

36. Olney to Harlan, August 26, 1894, Olney Collection.

37. *Federal Reporter*, LXIII, 310–29.

38. *U.S. Statutes at Large*, XXVI (1889–1891), 209–10.

39. *Congressional Record*, XXI, Part 4 (51st Cong., 1st sess., 1890), 3146–47.

40. *Ibid.*, Part 3, p. 2562.

41. James, *op. cit.*, p. 29.

42. Denis to Olney, July 14, 1894, and August 2, 1894; Call to Olney, July 18, 1894, *Appendix to the . . . . Report of the Attorney General . . . . 1896*, pp. 33, 34–35, 37–40.

43. Olney to Denis, August 1, 1894, *ibid.*, pp. 36–37.

44. Denis to Olney, August 2, 1894, *ibid.*, pp. 37–38.

45. *Ibid.*, p. 154; *New York Times*, July 1, 1894, p. 2; *Chicago Times*, June 29, 1894, p. 1.

46. *Chicago Times*, June 30, 1894, p. 2.

47. *New York Times*, July 3, 1894, p. 2.

48. *U.S. Reports*, CLVIII, 565–69.

49. *The Federal Reporter*, LXIV, 726–27.

50. July 3, 1894, p. 1.

51. *Chicago Times*, July 4, 1894, p. 4.

52. July 4, 1894, p. 4.

53. *Federal Reporter*, LXIV, 727; *New York Times*, July 3, 1894, p. 1.

54. *Inter Ocean*, July 3, 1894, p. 4; *Chicago Times*, July 2, 1894, p. 1.

55. *U.S. Strike Commission Report*, p. 215; *Inter Ocean*, July 3, 1894, p. 4.

56. Arnold to Olney, July 2, 1894, *Appendix to the . . . . Report of the Attorney General . . . . 1896*, p. 62.

57. *Chicago Times*, July 3, 1894, p. 1.

58. *Appendix to the . . . . Report of the Attorney General . . . . 1896*, pp. 65, 69; *U.S. Strike Commission Report*, p. 143.

59. *New York Times*, July 5, 1894, p. 2.

60. R. Miller to H. Porter, July 9, 1894, Cleveland Papers.

61. *Proceedings of the General Managers' Association . . . . 1894*, p. 151.

62. Olney to Walker, June 30, 1894, *Appendix to the . . . . Report of the Attorney General . . . . 1896*, p. 60.

63. *New York Times*, July 2, 1894, p. 2; *Inter Ocean*, July 2, 1894, p. 2; *U.S. Strike Commission Report*, pp. 340–43.

64. *U.S. Strike Commission Report*, pp. xliv, 233, 270–71, 341, 343–44; George B. Harris (vice-president of Chicago, Burlington, and Quincy Railroad) to Olney, January 8, 1895, Olney Papers.

65. *U.S. Strike Commission Report*, p. 228.

66. *Ibid.*, p. xlv.

67. *Ibid.*, pp. 62, 341–42, 355–56, 366–67, 371; *Appendix to the . . . . Report of the Attorney General . . . . 1896*, pp. 67–68, 76–78.

68. *U.S. Strike Commission Report*, p. 355.

69. *Ibid.*, p. 371.

70. *Ibid.*, p. 367.

71. Walker to Olney, July 9, 1894, *Appendix to the . . . . Report of the Attorney General . . . . 1896*, p. 76.

72. Olney to Arnold, July 10, 1894, *ibid.*, p. 78.

73. Arnold to Olney, July 10, 1894, *ibid.*

74. *New York Times*, July 6, 1894, p. 2; *Inter Ocean*, July 7, 1894, p. 5.

75. *Inter Ocean*, July 7, 1894, p. 5.

76. *Appendix to the . . . . Report of the Attorney General . . . . 1896*, pp. 86, 100, 222.

77. *Ibid.*, pp. 86, 89, 97.

78. *Ibid.*, pp. 96–97.

79. Chester M. Dawes (railroad counsel) to G. B. Harris (vice-president of the Chicago, Burlington and Quincy), January 5, 1895, Olney Collection; *U.S. Strike Commission Report*, pp. 233, 340.

80. Olney to Walker, December 31, 1894, Olney Collection.

81. Walker to Olney, January 8, 1895, *ibid.*

82. Olney to Walker, July 3, 1894, *Appendix to the . . . . Report of the Attorney General . . . . 1896*, p. 66.

83. Walker to Olney, July 3, 1894, *ibid.*

84. *Annual Report of the Attorney General* . . . . *1894*, pp. xxxii–xxxiii.

85. *Washington Post*, July 3, 1894, p. 2, and July 4, 1894, p. 2.

86. Cleveland, *op. cit.*, p. 234; *New York Times*, July 2, 1894, p. 2.

87. *Washington Post*, July 3, 1894, p. 2; *Inter Ocean*, July 4, 1894, p. 1.

88. *U.S. Strike Commission Report*, p. 340.

89. *New York World*, July 4, 1894, p. 7.

90. *Revised Statutes of the United States* (1878), p. 1029; *U.S. Strike Commission Report*, p. xx.

91. *Ibid.*

92. *Report of the General Superintendent of Police of the City of Chicago* . . . . *1894*, pp. 11–13; *Proceedings of the General Managers' Association* . . . . *1894*, July 1–4.

93. *Op. cit.*, p. 232.

94. *Report of the Adjutant General of Illinois, 1893–94*, pp. xii–xiii.

95. *Ibid.*, p. xxxi.

96. Lamont to Cleveland, July 5, 1894, Cleveland Papers.

97. *Inter Ocean*, July 4, 1894, p. 1.

98. Olney to Walker, July 3, 1894, *Appendix to the* . . . . *Report of the Attorney General* . . . . *1896*, p. 67.

99. John M. Schofield, *Forty-six Years in the Army*, pp. 497–98; *Inter Ocean*, July 4, 1894, p. 1.

100. Schofield, *op. cit.*, pp. 494–97.

101. *Annual Report of the Secretary of War* . . . . , *1894*, I, 109; *Proceedings of the General Managers' Association* . . . . *1894*, pp. 222–23.

102. *U.S. Strike Commission Report*, pp. 144, 339; General Nelson A. Miles, "The Lesson of the Recent Strikes," *North American Review*, CLIX (1894), 180–88.

103. Miles, *op. cit.*, p. 187.

104. *U.S. Strike Commission Report*, pp. 39, 150.

105. *New York World*, July 4, 1894, p. 1.

106. *New York Times*, July 5, 1894, p. 2.

CHAPTER IX

THE POLICY OF ILLINOIS OFFICIALS

JOHN P. ALTGELD belonged to the Democratic party, the same political organization in control at Washington; but this fact did not cause him to share with the federal administration an exalted feeling toward big business. Motivated by deep-seated convictions, he endeavored during his term as governor to enforce the law impartially, without seeking to promote the interests of one class at the expense of another. He was never the pliant tool of corporate interests, nor did he ever permit his sympathy for labor to interfere with his official responsibilities. His extreme liberalism and humanitarianism were often construed by his enemies as a dangerous form of radicalism. In pardoning the three surviving Haymarket anarchists, he did so fully convinced of their innocence and absolutely indifferent to the political consequences of this act.[1] The storm of protest which greeted the announcement of clemency did not weaken his resolve to pursue any policy which, in his judgment, was dictated by reason and justice. The vested interests did not trust him because he was not subservient to their will and could not be induced to use troops for the purpose of smashing strikes.

It is not likely that John Altgeld ever forgot his lowly origin or the years of grinding toil which characterized his earlier life. He was born in Nieder Selters, Nassau, but was reared in Ohio, where he learned the meaning of poverty. After the Civil War he drifted around, working as a common laborer and schoolteacher. Denied a formal education, he nevertheless studied law and by dint of the most careful application succeeded in mastering the English language. In 1886 Altgeld was elected to the Superior Court of Cook County, Illinois, and subsequently became chief justice of this court. Although accumulating quite a fortune in real estate speculation (all of which he ultimately lost) and being otherwise successful by all the standards by which men judge success, he was never able to abandon the conviction that the underprivileged classes were at a great disadvantage in the struggle for existence. For the poor and lowly he revealed an instinctive sympathy, the more so because of a feeling that for them there was no equality of opportunity in American life.[2]

Election to the governorship in 1892 did not diminish his interest in the well-being of the lower classes or make him less willing to champion unpopular causes, if they appealed to his sense of justice. From his speeches as governor can be discerned his deep and abiding admiration for labor. Because he was unconventional in some of his views and unorthodox in certain of his executive acts, the upper class would have none of him. Vilified and scurrilously attacked by the press for giving freedom to the Haymarket anarchists and later for his part in the Pullman Strike, he became in a real sense a storm center; and the part he played, however valorous, at times seemed almost tragic. His appearance was not attractive or his features prepossessing. In describing him, a contemporary wrote:

. . . . the countenance was one made for the hands of the cartoonists, who in the brutal fury that was soon to blaze upon him and to continue to blaze until it had consumed him quite, could easily contort the features to the various purposes of an ugly partizanship; they gave it a peculiarly sinister quality, and it is one of the countless ironies of life that a face, sad with all the utter woe of humanity, should have become for a season, and in some minds remained forever, the type and symbol of all that is most abhorrent. There was a peculiar pallor in the countenance, and the face was such a blank mask of suffering and despair that, had it not been for the high intelligence that shone from his eyes, it must have impressed many as altogether lacking in expression.[3]

During the coal strike of April and May, 1894, and throughout the Pullman difficulties, Governor Altgeld was alert to the imperative need of preventing lawlessness. Wherever disorders warranted use of the militia, he acted promptly, often taking the initiative by inducing the sheriff or some other responsible official in the region affected to requisition for troops. The statutes of Illinois provided that whenever civil authorities were unable to maintain order the governor could employ the militia upon the application of either the sheriff, the coroner, the mayor, or the county judge. In calling out troops John Altgeld definitely op-

JOHN P. ALTGELD

posed their use for strikebreaking purposes.[4] In his determination to preserve domestic peace, however, he sometimes ordered out the militia even when suspicious that they were wanted primarily to undermine the position of labor or when, as he believed, the riots were faked by the subtle machination of railroads. To his very good friend, Henry D. Lloyd, he remarked on one occasion: "I have reason to fear that these troops are wanted at that place only to help the railroad defeat the demand of their men for higher wages, but I cannot refuse to send them in the face of allegations of public danger."[5]

On June 30 John Altgeld received a request from the Illinois Central Railroad for troops to protect its property at Cairo. The telegram stressed the imminent danger of violence and indicated that the sheriff had not furnished the necessary protection. Without delay the governor wired the sheriff for the facts and sent Colonel Hugh E. Bayle, assistant adjutant general, to Cairo for an investigation of conditions. Several companies of the militia were instructed to be ready for immediate transfer to this locality, but the disorders, if any, quickly subsided, and all need for troops disappeared.[6]

At other points more serious difficulties developed, often necessitating the prompt intervention of the military. On July 1 the governor received a wire for aid from Decatur, signed by a number of passengers whose train was detained because of obstructions. Upon inquiry Altgeld was informed by the sheriff of Macon County that he had been able to furnish sufficient protection for the traveling public but could do so no longer. Troops were promptly rushed to Decatur, and the sheriff was instructed to make certain that all trains illegally held were immediately released. On the same day the Chicago and Eastern Illinois Railroad Company informed the governor that its trains at Danville were forcibly detained and that the sheriff of Vermilion County would do nothing to relieve the situation. When asked about this, the sheriff acknowledged that conditions were becoming somewhat desperate and requested one hundred rifles. Altgeld, however, believed the emergency called for troops.[7] Disturbances likewise developed at Mounds, where three hundred and thirty-six soldiers were concentrated, as compared with two hundred and sixty-five at Decatur and two hundred and twenty at Danville. The fifth of July witnessed a substantial contingent of troops taking up its position at Springfield, and the eighth beheld another, smaller detachment moving into Spring Valley.[8] Within a few hours after orders were issued from Springfield, the soldiers were mobilized and moved to their destination, even though the distance covered was sometimes upward of two hundred miles.[9]

Every outburst of trouble was observed carefully by the governor, who conferred frequently with the adjutant general and other military officers. Numerous dispatches were received and sent by Altgeld relative to the movement of troops. For constant reference he kept in his executive office a large map of Illinois, showing with pins exactly where each company of the militia was located. Equally significant, he had a report prepared indicating precisely how many companies were available for service in Chicago, if the worst should develop. Realizing the crucial importance of this great metropolis, he kept his eyes constantly on the community as a potential source of trouble and was prepared to meet any request for assistance by concentrating thousands of troops there.[10]

Chicago was then a city of 1,800,000 people, covering an area of 186 square miles. Its importance as a railroad center was evidenced by the fact that within the city limits were approximately 3,000 miles of railway track and almost as many surface crossings. In addition, there were many yards, shops, roundhouses, signal towers, and complex switching systems that would require protection in the event of violence and rioting. Available for the safeguarding of this property was a regular police force of 3,000, and in reserve 500 substitutes.[11]

Even before the boycott took effect, steps were taken by the General Managers' Association to assure adequate police protection. On June 25 a representative of this organization conferred with Mayor Hopkins and on the following day with Michael Brennan, chief of police.[12] Whenever the occasion demanded, which was rather often, John Egan had extended conferences with Brennan about the measures most appropriate to meet the situation, and he always found the police executive willing to co-operate in any moves necessary to prevent disorders. On June 29 and again on the thirtieth John Egan explained to the general managers that it was the announced policy of Superintendent Brennan to remove any policeman who refused to perform his duty and that any officer guilty of negligence should be promptly reported. Egan further revealed that the chief of police was willing to use some of his men on outgoing and incoming trains for the purpose of facilitating the arrest of those who caused trouble.[13] In the determined stand of the police to resist lawlessness the mayor gave his unqualified support, making it very clear, however, that they were to be used only for checking disorders and protecting property and not for turning switches or making up trains.[14]

Wherever disturbances threatened, police detachments were quickly rushed to the scene of trouble; but often they would discover that conditions were peaceful and that Egan's hurried request for help was based on idle rumors. It was only after the arrival of federal troops that serious disorders developed in Chicago, and until then the municipal law-enforcing agencies handled all difficulties with relative ease.[15] Although the police were sympathetic toward labor, such sentiment did not, except in a few isolated cases, interfere with the performance of their duty. Whatever the assignment and however numerous the demands, they endeavored to meet the situation promptly and courageously. This was the verdict of the Strike Commission and others, including some of the general managers.[16] To some degree, but not materially, the police were aided by Sheriff Gilbert and two hundred and fifty special deputies, whose jurisdiction extended beyond the city limits of Chicago to all of Cook County.[17]

For reasons not difficult to understand, Edwin Walker was careful to portray John Hopkins and the police as pursuing a very lax policy toward the strikers and as being unwilling, prior to the arrival of federal troops, to take the necessary measures to enforce the laws. In a communication to the attorney-general on July 6, Walker declared:

The mayor of the city for the first time, last evening, apparently realized it was his duty to preserve order and protect property, and very rigid instructions were given to the police. Up to that time these outrages were committed in the presence of the police, no arrests were made, nor did the police make any effort in any direction except to disperse the mob.[18]

It was in building up a case for federal military intervention that Walker endeavored to establish the complete failure of the local government to perform its duty during the early phases of the crises. The fact that John Hopkins was sympathetic toward the Pullman workers, whom he felt had been shamefully exploited,[19] made the general managers suspicious of his motives and doubtless helped to discredit him in the eyes of the special United States attorney.

The *Railroad Gazette* took the position, shared by other publications, that, because of political considerations and owing to a personal grudge against George Pullman, the mayor wilfully neglected to use his police force to furnish sufficient protection to railroad property during the period prior to July 5.[20] In a very caustic editorial, entitled "Chicago's Evil Genius," the *Chicago Evening Journal* on July 10 charged that Hopkins did nothing during the early stages of the strike to prevent it from running into "riot, incendiarism and bloodshed." "For eight days," the paper charged, "the thoroughly Hopkinized police . . . . stood by and saw train men driven from their posts, switches blocked, locomotives 'killed,' trains ditched, railroad property destroyed and railway employees beaten and shamefully maltreated and abused."[21] In the attempt to justify the strong-arm tactics of the national government and to encourage it to furnish even more aid, the propertied interests and their organs of expression were disposed to paint a grossly distorted picture of conditions and completely to underrate the efficiency and effectiveness of the police force. After a thorough probing of the facts the Strike Commission reached the conclusion that the allegations of police negligence and incompetency during the strike were not proved.[22]

When federal soldiers were rushed to Chicago, Governor Altgeld was unaware of any need for troops there, having received no request for military aid in that city from any public official or pri-

vate citizen. Sheriff Gilbert, whose special deputies had been supplied with arms by the state, asserted on July 2 that he could see
no necessity for the militia. On the same day Chief of Police
Brennan announced that he had received no information of any
riot and that, until the strikers resorted to violence as a body,
there was no need for any other assistance. He seemed confident
that his men were equal to any emergency.[23]

Edwin Walker and other agents of the Department of Justice
were of a different opinion. Not only did they favor immediate
military intervention, but they wanted federal troops. The
United States marshal could have petitioned for the militia, and
Governor Altgeld would not have brushed aside the request. But
on July 2 and 3, the attorney-general remained supremely indifferent to the militia, and nothing was mentioned in any of his
dispatches about its availability. The general managers also
closed their eyes at this juncture to the efficacy of these troops,
because, like Olney, they preferred to believe that the emergency
required federal soldiers.[24] It was doubtless thought that more
could be expected from regular troops than from the militia,
whose commander-in-chief was a man the railroads could not
control or influence. Precisely why the President ignored the governor at this time, not even showing him the courtesy of serving
advance notice that federal troops were en route to Chicago, remains one of the unpleasant and inexplicable facts of the strike.
Not until the soldiers had entered the city did the governor learn
about the matter, and only after he had protested in ringing
terms did the White House take the trouble to inform him of the
reasons for this extraordinary course.

In his telegraphic protest to Grover Cleveland on July 5, Governor Altgeld in a forceful but dignified manner denounced the
use of federal troops as "unnecessary" and "unjustifiable." The
Illinois militia, he affirmed, was competent to meet any emergency within the state and, if necessary, could render assistance
to the United States government elsewhere. Reference was made
to the fact that in Chicago there was a substantial force of state
troops available for immediate use, including three regiments of
infantry, one battery, and one troop of cavalry. They had not

been ordered out, it was explained, because no one in Cook County had so much as intimated that it was advisable or necessary to do so. The governor referred to his record during the coal strike and his present policy toward railroad disturbances as evidence of his alertness in rushing troops wherever they were needed. He further revealed that the United States marshal for the southern district of Illinois had twice applied to him for aid in enforcing the processes of the federal court, that in each case troops had been quickly furnished, and that the same course of action was open to the marshal at Chicago.

Assuming that the federal government had acted without knowledge of the facts, John Altgeld endeavored to show in the dispatch that certain railroads were paralyzed, not because of obstructions, but because of their inability to get sufficient men to operate trains. These very railroads, he charged, sought to divert public attention from this fact by an outcry against obstructions. By way of proof he cited the recent experience of the Illinois militia when called upon to suppress alleged disorders. The officials of two railroads had reported that conditions at certain points bordered on anarchy. Troops were promptly sent to the designated railroad centers only to discover that the difficulty was due not to obstructions or threatening mobs but to the lack of adequate crews for the operation of trains. Altgeld acknowledged, however, that in some cases troublesome crowds formed, and in a few other cases Pullman cars were detached from trains; but he was careful to point out that, since the actual violence was slight and since the employees as a rule conducted themselves in an orderly manner, the situation could easily be handled by the authorities of the state. "The newspaper accounts," he affirmed, "have in some cases been pure fabrications and in others wild exaggerations."

In this message, which was adroitly and compactly worded, the governor further explained that the statute of 1861 could not be properly invoked under the circumstances, since the law authorized the use of regular soldiers within a state only when it was not practicable to enforce federal law by the ordinary judicial processes. This condition, he maintained, obviously did not exist in Illinois, as the local and state officials were equal to the task of controlling the few disturbances that had arisen. More important than anything else to Altgeld was the infringement upon the constitutional guaranty of local self-government. This he vigorously denounced:

> To absolutely ignore a local government in matters of this kind, when that government is ready to furnish any assistance needed, and is amply able to enforce the law, not only insults the people of the State by imputing to them an inability to govern themselves or unwillingness to enforce the law, but is in violation of a basic principle of our institutions. The question of Federal supremacy is in no way involved. No one disputes it for a moment, but under our Constitution Federal supremacy and local self-government must go hand-in-hand, and to ignore the latter is to do violence to the Constitution.

In conclusion the governor requested the immediate withdrawal of all United States troops from Chicago and gave assurance that, should conditions become uncontrollable, he would promptly apply for federal assistance.[25]

The reply of Grover Cleveland was singularly brief and confined merely to a bare statement of the reasons justifying the recent military policy of his administration. Without even deigning to comment on the major points raised by Altgeld, the President announced that the use of federal troops in Chicago was made upon the demand of the post office for the protection of the mails and upon the request of judicial officers who could not enforce by ordinary means the processes of the federal courts and because of evidence that conspiracies endangered the movement of interstate commerce. He explained flatly that what he did was strictly in harmony with the laws and Constitution of the United States and that he had no desire to interfere "with the plain duty of the local authorities to preserve the peace of that city."[26]

In the judgment of the Illinois governor, Cleveland's reply revealed some "startling conclusions" and evaded the real question at issue, which concerned the principle that "local self-government is just as fundamental in our institutions as that of federal supremacy." With masterful logic, John Altgeld on July 6 once more protested to the President, this time basing his arguments almost entirely upon constitutional grounds. He accused

Cleveland of assuming that his office possessed the legal right to send soldiers into a community to suppress the smallest disorder, even though the locality was fully prepared to meet the situation. Since the President was the sole judge as to whether or not disturbances existed anywhere in the country, he could thus, declared the governor, order federal troops into any locality and keep them there at his discretion.

The communication further contended that, except during a period of war, it was a basic principle of the government always to keep the civil authorities paramount to the military, and state troops were accordingly used only in conjunction with civil authorities and subordinate to them. But the federal soldiers in Chicago, it was asserted, were responsible to nobody except the army headquarters in Washington, and "in so far as these troops act at all it is military government." Equally significant was the explanation that the statute, which Cleveland invoked to justify his military policy, contemplated the use of federal troops in a state only under certain conditions, and even then not until the militia had first been used. The President not only ignored this, it was charged, but he broke completely with established practice by interfering with the industrial disputes of a state—a course which opened up a field so large as easily to absorb, with only a slight extension of authority, all details of local government.

In this constitutional analysis nothing was more striking than the observation that all the officers in Chicago who made representation for military aid were appointed by the President and for the most part could be removed at will by him. They were the agents of the President, and through one or more of them he could make application to himself for the sending of troops into that community. Since Grover Cleveland remained the only judge in the matter and in reality passed upon his own request, the governor protested the practice. This extraordinary and arbitrary use of power apparently was not subject to any check as far as Altgeld could determine, and against its exercise he registered strong objections:

This assumption as to the power of the Executive is certainly new, and I respectfully submit that it is not the law of the land. The jurists have told us that this is a Government of law, and not a Government by the caprice of individuals, and further, that, instead of being autocratic, it was a Government of limited power. Yet the autocrat of Russia could certainly not possess or claim to possess greater power than is possessed by the Executive of the United States, if your assumption is correct.

In this trend toward greater executive power Altgeld discerned a dangerous implication—the possibility that the President, who had final jurisdiction over state as well as federal troops, might become very ambitious and desire to establish a military government by ordering out the combined forces under the pretext of suppressing some local disturbances. While confining most of his remarks to principles and constitutional theory and devoting little space to actual conditions in Chicago, the governor referred briefly to the fact that federal troops in that city were proving an irritant to many people, who deeply resented interference in local self-government. Reiterating that these soldiers were unable to accomplish anything which the militia could not do, the executive of Illinois again demanded their recall.[27]

To what extent Cleveland was impressed by the logic of this second protest is not definitely known, but everything would indicate that it met with the same cold reception as the first one. Completely disregarding the weight of the governor's arguments, so carefully buttressed, the President deemed it better strategy to convey to the nation the impression that the present was no time to quibble over constitutional technicalities and that everybody should unite against the common danger of anarchy. In a communication, noteworthy for its brevity, the President replied to Altgeld's second protest by declaring:

> While I am still persuaded that I have neither transcended my authority nor duty in the emergency that confronts us, it seems to me that in this hour of danger and public distress discussion may well give way to active effort on the part of all in authority to restore obedience to law and to protect life and property.[28]

The attorney-general believed that the position of Altgeld rested on false premises and that the right of Grover Cleveland to act as he did was incontestable, since it was the plain duty of the chief executive to protect the courts and enforce the laws of the

United States. In the discharge of this duty Olney could see no reason why Cleveland should consult the mayor of Chicago or the governor of Illinois, nor could the attorney-general observe anything in the policy of the President that might be construed as an invasion of states' rights. Without hesitation, Olney repudiated the idea that the territory of any state was so sacred that the legitimate functions of the federal government could in any way be hampered or curtailed.[29]

Equally vigorous in defense of Cleveland's policy was Secretary of State Gresham, who possessed the same bias as Olney and who likewise misunderstood the tenor of Altgeld's arguments and the true implications of his position. With considerable force and even more feeling, he proclaimed:

The telegram of Governor Altgeld is State's rights gone mad. It is absurd. There is only one logical conclusion from the position which Governor Altgeld takes. If his demand means anything it means that the United States courts in the State of Illinois shall not be permitted to exercise their constitutional function of executing their processes except by special permission in each instance of Governor Altgeld. He takes the ground that the United States cannot maintain itself within the State of Illinois except by his permission. There is no other logical conclusion from this position. This is, of course, ridiculous. There can be no language too severe to characterize it. . . . .[30]

Among the propertied classes there was overwhelming support of Cleveland's policies and strong condemnation for the position of John Altgeld, whose patriotism and honesty of purpose were now openly questioned by many. The basis of the governor's protest was largely constitutional; but the legal profession, although traditionally conservative, seemed in no way disturbed at the new trends of national authority. Thomas M. Cooley, president of the American Bar Association, doubtless revealed the preponderant sentiment of his organization when he declared that the position taken by Governor Altgeld was not even plausible and, if anything, tended to keep the disorderly elements bold and defiant. In the judgment of this law professor and former chief justice of the Michigan Supreme Court, the President of the United States was required to execute federal law and, in doing so, was not subordinate to any state authority. "If the views of the governor were accepted as sound," propounded Thomas Cooley, "the mails might be stopped at Chicago, interstate commerce broken up, and the process of United States courts refused service, unless the governor, when disorder was dominant, saw fit to suppress it or to call upon the President to do so." It was the considered judgment of this distinguished lawyer that popular sentiment so completely supported the course followed by Grover Cleveland that "the question of constitutional law may be considered practically settled."[31]

The great majority of newspapers—Republican, Democratic, and Independent—not only applauded the policy of the federal government but struck out viciously at John Altgeld, often without regard to dignity or decency.[32] The *New York Times*, which had advocated the use of regular troops in Chicago as early as July 2,[33] denounced Altgeld five days later as "too thickhided and anarchistic to feel the sting of the President's reply to his second telegram." The editor contemptuously explained that the expression "law and order" meant something else to the Illinois governor than it did to civilized people. In presuming to question the authority by which the President acted, Altgeld was charged with sheer impudence.[34]

No less belligerent was the *Washington Post*, which accused both Altgeld and Hopkins of being in complete sympathy with Debs and desiring the success of his cause. The readers were reminded that, since the governor of Illinois was the same man who pardoned "the murderous anarchists of Haymarket notoriety" and Hopkins was the vindictive foe of the Pullman Company, little could be expected from such individuals. The real issue at stake, explained the paper, was not so much the transmission of mail as the preservation of civilization.[35]

Somewhat more rational in its approach was the *New York World*, which dispassionately pointed out that the federal troops were not sent to Chicago to preserve peace or usurp state authority but to render aid to the United States marshals in the enforcement of court decrees and the protection of mail and interstate commerce. Instead of splitting hairs over the theory of states' rights, all officials were urged to co-operate.[36] While glorifying the statesman-like qualities of Grover Cleveland, *Harper's Weekly* imputed to the Illinois executive, as a reason for seeking the recall of federal troops, the desire "to stand well with the lawless men who had incited the riot, and to secure their votes."[37] The *Nation* complimented President Cleveland for wasting no time in arguing with Altgeld, who, it was claimed, stood exposed by the President's terse reply as the "friend and champion of disorder." This magazine announced that Altgeld was as "unconscious of his own bad manners as he is of the bad odor of his principles; but boorish, impudent, and ignorant as he is, he can scarcely fail to wince under the treatment which he receives from the President."[38]

With few exceptions the power of the Chicago press turned against the Illinois governor with a ferocity that was borne of a hate that had smoldered ever since the anarchists were pardoned. Referring to the Illinois executive as the "dastardly Altgeld" and the "shameless governor," the *Chicago Tribune* asserted on July 7 that, if this official had not been derelict in his duties, there would have been little need for intervention by the President. The paper charged the governor with being a falsifier, when in his protest to Cleveland he minimized the importance of disturbances throughout the state. In this issue of the paper there was a battery of no less than three editorials, all directed against Altgeld and all of a highly inflammatory nature. One of them, in its closing tirade against the governor, asserted:

This lying, hypocritical, demagogical, sniveling Governor of Illinois does not want the law enforced. He is a sympathizer with riot, with violence, with anarchy. He should be impeached even if the legislature had to meet on its own motion to do it, and Lieutenant Governor Gill should be put in his place.[39]

The *Chicago Evening Journal* was just as fierce in its denunciation of the governor, characterizing him as a "petty, petulant demagogue, full of empty sounds and bad manners." Pitching its attack on a highly emotional plane, the paper charged Altgeld with "complete ignorance of constitutional law and the right of the Federal Government to protect national interests everywhere throughout the nation." "For two years longer," lamented the paper, "Illinois will have to endure the ignominy of having a demagogue and anarchist as its chief magistrate—a disgrace in times of peace, a menace and danger in days of turmoil and trial."⁴⁰

In sharp contrast to the above organs of expression was the *Chicago Times*, one of the few newspapers to condemn federal intervention. The use of United States troops was characterized in one editorial as unwarrantable and unlawful, and the President was charged with being a tool of the moneyed interests. The reader was reminded that the attorney-general was a railroad lawyer and stockholder and that he appointed another railroad counselor to assist the federal district attorney at Chicago. No less sensational was the allegation that Judge Grosscup owed his position largely to the fact that George Pullman made substantial contributions to the Harrison presidential campaign fund. If troops were needed, inquired the editorial, why was use not made of the militia? In denouncing Cleveland's policy, the paper proclaimed: "It is a damning record for the federal administration and one which will produce bitter results. If there be a cardinal precept in our national code it is the assertion of the right to local self-government, and that right is not to be overriden by railroads on the specious plea of interstate interests."⁴¹ In defense of the Illinois governor, the *Chicago Times* affirmed that his protests to Cleveland were "admirable state papers," which gave expression to incontestable principles of constitutional law. The editor held:

It was true patriotism for Governor Altgeld to courageously protest against the unwarrantable exercise of force by the United States authorities. The snarling pack of mercenaries yelping at his heels will have gone into oblivion long before his ringing letters to President Cleveland lose place as an epoch-making state paper.⁴²

On July 7 Eugene Debs joined with the chief executive of the Knights of Labor, James Sovereign, in a protest to Grover Cleveland against the exercise of federal authority in Chicago. The injunction was labeled "un-American," and the use of the regular army was denounced as being for the "support and protection of the railroad corporations in their determination to degrade and oppress their employees." It was explained that the Pullman

Strike occurred only after the plight of the Pullman workers had become desperate and their entreaties had been contemptuously spurned. Not until the Pullman Corporation had rejected all attempts at arbitration and conciliation did any railroad employee refuse to handle Pullman cars. The joint protest further argued that it was not the workers who were responsible for the interruption of mail transportation but the railway corporations, which refused to haul mail on any trains except those containing Pullman cars. Under the guise of protecting interstate commerce and the mail, federal soldiers were employed, it was charged, to coerce the workers into a "humiliating obedience to the will of their oppressors." In condemning the use of troops, the protest bitterly affirmed that there was "not an instance on record where in any conflict between the corporations and the people, the strong arm of the military power has been employed to protect the working people and the industrial masses from the ravages and persecution of corporate greed." In conclusion, Debs and Sovereign pledged their respective organizations to preserve peace and order and to aid in the arrest and prosecution of all violators of the law.[43]

In the opinion of Clarence Darrow, there was no need for federal soldiers at Chicago; and, even if there had been, the President did not possess the legal right to send them on his own motion. It was the conviction of this lawyer that the Constitution was pushed aside during the crisis, just as laws and customs are often ignored when people are sufficiently aroused.[44] Lyman Trumbull, eminent Illinois statesman, also opposed the strongarm tactics of the national government. When called upon by the leaders of the People's party in Chicago to prepare a declaration of principles for submission to the national convention of their party in December, 1894, Trumbull framed nine, one of which proclaimed that there was no power in the Constitution "to warrant the government in making use of a standing army in aiding monopolies in the oppression of their employees. When freemen unsheathe the sword it should be to strike for liberty, not for despotism, or to uphold privileged monopolies in the oppression of the poor."[45]

No direct protest was made by the mayor of Chicago against regular soldiers, although he firmly believed that if troops were needed the militia should have been used first. The precipitate use of the United States military, without any advance warning, came as a surprise to him, the more so because he was unaware that any railroad within the city suffered from insufficient protection.[46] Either because of deep resentment or a feeling that these soldiers were more or less useless, John Hopkins never expressed approbation for their performance in Chicago, although he was highly complimentary toward the police and national guard, to whom he believed was "due entirely the credit for restoring law and order in the city."[47] The chief of police deplored the use of federal soldiers and held that if they had not been called out on July 3, the police could have coped with all difficulties.[48]

Eager to avoid friction between the police and the regular army, the mayor and superintendent of police did everything possible to eliminate all causes for irritation between these forces. Instructions were promptly issued to the effect that the duty of preserving domestic peace and protecting life and property within the city devolved, as before, upon the police, who should, however, respect the authority exercised by United States civil and military officials. Whenever the occasion required, the ranking police officers were to ascertain what railroad property was under the control of federal authorities and then to act accordingly.[49] Edwin Walker was given assurance by Mayor Hopkins that no friction would occur between national and city officials.[50] The fact that United States soldiers and deputy marshals were spared unpleasant relations with the state and local forces during this extremely tense situation[51] was due in large measure to the forbearance and good judgment of the municipal authorities.

On the morning of July 5 the Rock Island Railroad announced that it was having trouble from mobs that obstructed the movement of trains. The matter was called to the attention of the mayor, who in the company of his corporation counsel visited the scene of rioting in order to observe the extent of damage. He saw a large body of people, mostly women and children and also a number of empty freight cars that had been turned over. Fully alert to the need of discouraging all such lawlessness, he promptly issued a proclamation, urging all citizens to remain peaceful, to avoid mingling in crowds, and to see that women and children kept off the public streets and railroad tracks. The people were reminded of the legal right of the mayor to call out the militia and, if necessary, to demand the services of every man in the city to help suppress disorder. Hopkins expressed his determination to preserve public peace and pledged himself to use every means available to achieve this purpose. The police force was authorized to break up all gatherings in the streets or near railroad tracks and to arrest any persons who refused to obey the command to disperse.[52]

In addition to this pronouncement, the mayor also ordered the superintendent of police to suspend all policemen on duty where these cars had been turned over. It was alleged that these men had been negligent in protecting railroad property; and, although Hopkins did not believe them guilty, he felt that, pending the investigation, such disciplinary action would have a salutary effect on the morale of the entire police force. Brennan was further instructed to remove in the future any officer who refused to do his full duty in enforcing the laws. The investigation revealed that the suspended policemen were not negligent but had been unable to keep adequate watch on all the rioters, some of whom would rush onto the tracks, push over a car, and then hurry away. The men were accordingly reinstated.[53] Nothing in the records would indicate that the police were lax in their duty or careless in the protection of property.

Immediately following Hopkins' visit to the scenes of disturbance, all substitute policemen were called into service, which increased the force to thirty-five hundred men. During the ensuing two weeks the police were almost continuously on duty, sleeping at the station but always remaining dressed and armed for action. The men frequently were at their posts as many as twenty hours during the day and while on duty were often compelled to eat hastily the rations brought to them. They endeavored to keep the right of way on railroads clear of people and, with the support of the militia, had the sole responsibility of breaking up mobs engaged in any kind of violence that did not involve the mail and interstate commerce. Among other duties shouldered by the police was that of helping to extinguish fires, of righting overturned cars, and of maintaining order throughout the city.[54] In responding to the menace of disorder, they performed yeoman service, but their capacity to cope with the situation was taxed to the limit. In commenting on the performance of his force, Michael Brennan revealed:

In all cases when the police were left to themselves peace was preserved, property was kept uninjured and the interference with the non-union men trifling. . . . . While the police made a number of charges on the crowd, escorted scores of trains through the most turbulent districts, guarded round houses, signal towers and right of ways, they killed no one. They used their clubs freely, vigorously and effectively; there were many cracked heads and sore spots where the policeman's club fell, but no human life was taken.[55]

With disorders becoming more pronounced on July 5, it may be asked why the mayor of Chicago did not at this time requisition for state troops? The primary reason seems to have been his conviction that the situation was then not serious enough to justify such drastic measures. Until there was the most urgent need for the militia, John Hopkins was reluctant to launch his administration on a course which he doubtless believed might lead to unpleasant political repercussions. His sympathy for the Pullman employees may have been a factor, since Hopkins believed that, once the troops were called out, the cause of labor would have slight chance of victory. Despite all this, he remained realistic about the matter. The First Regiment of Chicago was preparing at this time to go to its annual encampment at Springfield. When informed of this on July 5, the mayor telegraphed the governor that under the circumstances it would be advisable for these troops to be retained in Chicago, as they might be needed within twenty-four hours.[56] Although Altgeld agreed to do so, he expressed surprise at the request since nobody had indicated that the services of these troops might be needed and since they had completed all arrangements to go into training at Camp Lincoln for the week of July 7.[57]

On the morning of July 6 the governor of Illinois received

urgent telegrams from high officials of the Illinois Central Railroad, revealing a very critical condition on their line in Chicago. During the night forty-eight of their cars had been burned, and a passenger train had been boarded, the engine detached and permitted to run wild down the track. It was explained that a general state of lawlessness was rapidly developing, against which the civil authorities were powerless to act.[58] The president of this road was promptly advised by the governor to prevail upon Mayor Hopkins or Sheriff Gilbert to request military assistance and, should they refuse, troops would be forthcoming anyway. It was not necessary, however, for the railroad executive to make representations to Hopkins, since through other channels Altgeld had already reached the mayor.[59] Convinced of the need for immediate action, the governor had earlier wired his close friend and law partner, John W. Lanehart, to see Hopkins at once and stress the importance of acting with utmost speed. Four or five regiments, it was disclosed, would be rushed to Chicago as soon as the mayor made the request. The governor pointed out that federal soldiers had accomplished nothing and that, by moving swiftly, the city police and state troops could capture all credit for preserving order.[60]

Lanehart fulfilled his mission with success, and Hopkins, who was extremely friendly to the state administration, promptly requisitioned for five regiments. He acknowledged that the area of Chicago was too large and the police force too small to permit the civil authorities effectively to cope with riotous bodies of men that were operating within the city.[61] Upon receipt of this request, Altgeld promptly ordered General Horace Wheeler at Chicago to report to the mayor with his brigade and help in suppressing riots, preserving peace, and maintaining the law.[62] In another but confidential communication to General Wheeler, the governor stressed the importance of relieving the situation before federal reinforcements should reach the city. He urged the greatest caution in handling the people so as to avoid bloodshed. "There is no glory," he declared, "shooting at a ragged and hungry man. There is glory in being able to disperse a mob without bloodshed because it requires ability to do it." Experience has taught, he warned, that the men should keep their guns unloaded until it was necessary to fire, since men that kept their guns constantly loaded were more likely to fire without orders.[63]

The Illinois governor seemed convinced that Cleveland had ordered troops into Chicago for political reasons. This may explain why Altgeld was so anxious that the militia, co-operating with the police, should quickly terminate the disorders and thus deprive the President of all credit in the affair. In a second telegram to John Lanehart on the same day the governor stressed again the need for prompt action. The prestige which this would give to the administration of John Hoplins was emphasized. The mayor could do much, Altgeld pointed out, by personally directing things, since in a situation of this kind "executive ability, good judgment and quick action are the all important things." Lanehart was urged to show Hopkins the telegram and to impress him with the importance of following the suggested course of action.[64]

Within a comparatively short time thousands of state troops were poured into Chicago. The finest co-operation prevailed between the governor and the mayor,[65] the latter being given broad discretionary power as to the distribution of these soldiers. On one occasion Hopkins assigned to Sheriff Gilbert seven companies of state troops for duty outside of the city limits, and this move, with others, met with the cordial support of the governor.[66] There were 4,243 state troops concentrated in that great metropolis during the most crucial phase of the strike, and not until all danger was removed were the last of them recalled. Considering the fact that the maximum strength of the Illinois militia in 1894 comprised 5,705 men, it can readily be seen how large was the proportion on duty in Chicago. State troops remained in that city for a full month, occupying during this period more than fifty stations. The cost to the state of maintaining this great array of soldiery in Chicago was approximately $250,000.[67]

The willingness of John Altgeld to co-operate in suppressing disorders was well illustrated on July 8 when Governor Claude Matthews of Indiana made an unusual request. Serious disturbances had developed at Hammond—a city which had the misfortune of being divided by the Illinois-Indiana boundary. To cope with this situation, the governor of Indiana suggested that the troops of each state be permitted to cross the state line if necessary in preserving law and order.[68] In reply, Governor Altgeld expressed hearty accord, explaining that he had directed the Illinois troops to enter Indiana whenever the situation demanded and that the militia of Indiana would be granted reciprocal privileges in Illinois.[69]

John Altgeld was determined to go to the very limit in maintaining peace and on one occasion wired Hopkins that if necessary fifty thousand more men would be raised.[70] He was careful to explain, however, that as far as could be determined, the law did not authorize soldiers, deputy sheriffs, or city policemen to serve as "guards or custodians of private property." The duty of these men was to "keep the peace, quell riots and enforce the law." The position of the governor thus remained what it had been during the coal strike.[71] This policy could not have been welcomed by the vested interests and may explain why Altgeld was so calumniously abused by their mouthpieces. Despite all the fiery incriminations and bitter denunciations, the governor tried diligently to pursue an impartial course, without prejudice to any group or class of people.

NOTES

1. Barnard, *op. cit.*, pp. 234–35, 239–49.
2. *Dictionary of American Biography*, I, 231.
3. Brand Whitlock, *Forty Years of It*, pp. 65–66.
4. *Biennial Report of the Adjutant General of Illinois* . . . . , *1893 and 1894*, pp. vii–viii; Altgeld, *op. cit.*, p. 652.
5. Caroline A. Lloyd, *Henry Demarest Lloyd*, I, 148.
6. *Chicago Times*, June 30, 1894, p. 1; *Inter Ocean*, July 1, 1894, p. 2.
7. *Biennial Report of the Adjutant General of Illinois* . . . . , *1893 and 1894*, pp. xv–xvi.
8. *Ibid.*, p. xxxi.
9. *Ibid.*, p. xviii.
10. Caroline Lloyd, *op. cit.*, pp. 147–49.
11. *Report of the General Superintendent of Police of* . . . . *Chicago* . . . . *1894*, pp. 4, 18; *U.S. Strike Commission Report*, p. 349.
12. *U.S. Strike Commission Report*, p. 344.
13. *Proceedings of the General Managers' Association* . . . . *1894*, pp. 114–15, 126–27, 226.
14. *Inter Ocean*, July 3, 1894, p. 3.
15. *U.S. Strike Commission Report*, pp. 349, 353.

16. *Report of the General Superintendent of Police of* . . . . *Chicago* . . . . *1894*, pp. 16, 22; *U.S. Strike Commission Report*; pp. xliv, 346–47.

17. *U.S. Strike Commission Report*, p. xix.

18. Walker to Olney, July 6, 1894, *Appendix to the* . . . . *Report of the Attorney General* . . . . *1896*, pp. 71–72.

19. *U.S. Strike Commission Report*, pp. 348–49.

20. *Railroad Gazette*, XXVI (1894), 515.

21. *Chicago Evening Journal*, July 10, 1894, p. 4.

22. *U.S. Strike Commission Report*, p. xliv.

23. Altgeld, *op. cit.*, pp. 658, 668; *Inter Ocean*, July 3, 1894, p. 3.

24. *Inter Ocean*, July 3, 1894, p. 3.

25. Altgeld to Cleveland, July 5, 1894, Governor's Letter Book.

26. Cleveland to Altgeld, July 5, 1894, Cleveland Papers.

27. Altgeld to Cleveland, July 6, 1894, Governor's Letter Book.

28. Cleveland to Altgeld, July 6, 1894, Cleveland Papers.

29. *New York Times*, July 7, 1894, p. 4.

30. *Inter Ocean*, July 7, 1894, p. 4.

31. "Annual Address of the President of the American Bar Association," *Report of the Seventeenth Annual Meeting of the American Bar Association* (1894), pp. 225–33.

32. *Public Opinion*, XVII (1894), 329.

33. July 2, 1894, p. 4.

34. *New York Times*, July 7, 1894, p. 4.

35. July 7, 1894, p. 4.

36. July 7, 1894, p. 4.

37. XXXVIII (1894), 674.

38. LIX (1894), 19.

39. July 7, 1894, p. 12.

40. July 6, 1894, p. 4.

41. July 5, 1894, p. 4.

42. July 7, 1894, p. 4.

43. *New York World*, July 8, 1894, p. 3.

44. *Op. cit.*, pp. 62–63.

45. Horace White, *The Life of Lyman Trumbull*, pp. 415–16 (quotation from *Chicago Times*, December 27, 1894).

46. *U.S. Strike Commission Report*, p. 352.

47. *Biennial Report of the Adjutant General of Illinois* . . . . , *1893 and 1894*, p. xxvii.

48. *Report of the General Superintendent of Police of* . . . . *Chicago* . . . . *1894*, p. 13.

49. *Ibid.*, pp. 13–14.

50. Walker to Olney, July 6, 1894, *Appendix to* . . . . *the Report of the Attorney General* . . . . *1896*, pp. 71–72.

51. *Report of the General Superintendent of Police of* . . . . *Chicago* . . . . *1894*, p. 19; *U.S. Strike Commission Report*, p. 355.

52. *U.S. Strike Commission Report*, pp. 344–45, 357–58; *Inter Ocean*, July 6, 1894, p. 1.

53. *U.S. Strike Commission Report*, pp. xliv, 345, 358.

54. *Report of the General Superintendent of Police of* . . . . *Chicago* . . . . *1894*, pp. 18, 22.

55. *Ibid.*, p. 16.

56. Hopkins to Altgeld, July 5, 1894, Governor's Correspondence.

57. Altgeld to Hopkins, July 5, 1894, Governor's Letter Books.

58. Stuyvesant Fish (president of the Illinois Central Railroad) to Altgeld, July 6, 1894; S. W. Sullivan (general superintendent of the Illinois Central Railroad) to Altgeld, July 6, 1894, Governor's Correspondence.

59. Fish to Altgeld, July 6, 1894, ibid.

60. Altgeld to Lanehart, July 6, 1894, Governor's Letter Book.

61. Hopkins to Altgeld, July 6, 1894, Governor's Correspondence.

62. Altgeld to Wheeler, July 6, 1894, Governor's Letter Book.

63. Altgeld to Wheeler, July 6, 1894, ibid.

64. Altgeld to Lanehart, July 6, 1894, ibid.

65. Biennial Report of the Adjutant General of Illinois . . . . , 1893 and 1894, p. xxvi.

66. Hopkins to Altgeld, July 9, 1894, Governor's Correspondence; Altgeld to Hopkins, July 9, 1894, Governor's Letter Book.

67. Biennial Report of the Adjutant General of Illinois . . . . , 1893 and 1894, pp. iii, xxvii, xxxi; U.S. Strike Commission Report, pp. 347–48.

68. Matthews to Altgeld, July 8, 1894, Governor's Correspondence.

69. Biennial Report of the Adjutant General of Illinois . . . . , 1893 and 1894, p. xxv.

70. Ibid., p. xxvi.

71. Altgeld to Hopkins, July 27, 1894, Governor's Letter Book.

CHAPTER X

PROGRESS OF THE STRIKE IN CHICAGO

AMONG the twenty-six roads centering in Chicago, relatively few escaped involvement. As the struggle reached its crucial phases, freight transportation and suburban rail service were virtually suspended, and the movement of passenger trains was seriously disrupted. In canvassing the situation on July 5, General Miles discovered that thirteen railroads had been compelled to abandon all service in and out of the city,[1] while ten others were able to operate only passenger trains.[1] Slowly but inexorably the American Railway Union was tightening its grip on rail transportation, seeking to force a speedy settlement. Switch tenders, flagmen, towermen, yard clerks, and roundhouse men responded most readily to the appeal of Eugene Debs. Wholesale abandonment of work left the railroads helpless and caused the general managers to take alarm. The *New York Times* had already sounded an ominous note of warning when on June 29 it declared that the strike had "assumed the proportions of the greatest battle between labor and capital that has ever been inaugurated in the United States."[2]

Prior to July 4 the situation in Chicago did not go beyond some sabotage and an occasional demonstration that was quickly suppressed by the police. On June 26 at Grand Crossing in South Chicago a large throng had detained several trains for a few hours but had destroyed no property.[3] Not many days later an Illinois Central train, "the Diamond Special," was derailed near this point by an unknown person who had loosened spikes in the ties.[4] Such incidents proved the exception as the strike within the city continued to spread in a comparatively peaceful manner, while in the adjoining community of Blue Island traffic was brought to a standstill by a determined crowd that roamed at will over the tracks.[5]

Many railroads were seriously affected, but none more so than the Illinois Central, the Chicago, Milwaukee, and St. Paul, and the Chicago, Rock Island, and Pacific. In the case of the Illinois Central, the switchmen within the city and in the outlying regions struck almost simultaneously on June 26 and 27 and were joined by other workers. In a strategic move, barren of any notable results, this road served notice on the strikers to return to work by a certain time or be denied further employment with the company.[6] On the Rock Island Railroad the desire for a sympathetic strike was sharpened by local grievances. In a meeting at Blue Island on June 29, to which Debs and other strike leaders addressed fervid appeals, the workers decided to support the cause of the American Railway Union. Approximately forty-five hundred men, or more than one-third of all the employees on this line, responded to the call, leaving the road hopelessly crippled. Insufficient manpower, together with obstructions on the main tracks at Blue Island, forced the road on July 1 to announce the cancellation of all train service in Chicago. When the Rock Island, with the aid of four companies of United States infantry, tried to resume traffic on July 4, the difficulties proved so great that the attempt had to be abandoned.[7]

The Chicago, Rock Island, and Pacific Railroad shared with other lines the same strong resentment toward the industrial type of labor organization exemplified in the American Railway Union. This company, if anything, was more bitter than other roads toward the boycott of Pullman cars, since it owned jointly with the Pullman Company most of the sleepers used on its tracks—an arrangement distinctly contrary to the system by which the Pullman Corporation endeavored to maintain complete ownership of all palace cars that were in any way subject to its control. Originally the Rock Island owned all its sleepers but in 1880 sold a half-interest in them to the Pullman Company, with the understanding that profits and expenses on such cars be divided between the two corporations.[8] The boycotting of Pullman sleepers was thus a direct attack upon the property of the Rock Island Railroad, as well as a violation of its contracts with the Pullman Company. Everett St. John was general manager of this road and also chairman of the General Managers' Association, and in both capacities he bent every effort toward crushing the American Railway Union.

Fearful that major disturbances would develop any hour, the general managers had for several days been sending requests to the police for protection at various points, but prompt investigation usually proved the reported trouble to be groundless. Unwilling to admit that the paralysis of transportation was due primarily to insufficient crews,[9] the railroads preferred to attribute it to sabotage and violence and by this means to discredit the strikers and hasten military intervention. Although delayed, rioting and disorders finally broke out in Chicago, but not until after federal troops had been distributed at key points throughout the city.

What precipitated this lawlessness cannot be assigned to any one factor. The arrival of United States troops proved an irritant, but more important was the accumulated resentment shared by certain classes of people against the railroads. Within the city was an abnormally large group of hoodlums, tramps, and semicriminals, some of whom had been attracted to Chicago by the Columbian Exposition and left stranded by the depression. They were prepared to take advantage of any situation that would yield excitement and plunder. Unemployment and insecurity—products of the panic of 1893—had fostered a spirit of restlessness and despair, which in turn must have contributed to the recklessness of the crowds that assembled as much from curiosity as from any desire to do violence. In the movement of the mobs there was seldom any purpose or leadership. Most of the destruction was done wantonly and without premeditation.[10]

Owing to the increasing tenseness of the strike, people began to gather on railroad property and display an aggressive spirit during the evening of July 4. Cars were turned over and other acts of vandalism perpetrated. On the following day disturbances multiplied as large crowds roamed over the Rock Island tracks, pushing over freight cars, setting a few of them on fire, and otherwise blocking the movement of trains. Switches were thrown, signal lights changed, and trains stoned—much of the trouble being caused by half-grown boys who seemed to welcome the opportunity for excitement and deviltry. Mingling in the noisy gatherings was a large proportion of women and children. Although other roads suffered from this outbreak, the Rock Island sustained the brunt of the attack. The attempt on the part of the federal troops to clear the tracks failed, as did the efforts of the police to give adequate protection to railroad property; but no use at this time was made of firearms, although once or twice bayonets were employed. The largest mob, believed to number about ten thousand individuals, began its depredations at the Stock Yards and slowly moved eastward on Rock Island property, dispersing only with the approach of darkness.[11]

General Nelson A. Miles promptly communicated to Major General Schofield his fears that a most dangerous situation might develop unless the riotous gatherings were dispersed by the police or fired upon by the soldiers. He inquired as to whether or not his troops should be ordered to fire on mobs obstructing trains.[12] Only the day before, Miles had instructed his subordinate officers to use firearms, if necessary, against mobs that approached in a threatening manner,[13] but apparently he was not absolutely certain of his position in the matter and desired express authorization from his superior officer. In reply General Schofield chose to issue no instructions at this time for the dispersing of mobs but expressed strong disapproval of the manner in which federal troops had been utilized in Chicago. Instead of being concentrated in force at some central point for effective action wherever needed, they had been deployed at Blue Island, the Stock Yards, Grand Crossing, Forty-ninth Street, and the Lake Front. This was considered a strategic blunder by Schofield, who ordered the mistake rectified. Convinced that General Miles did not know precisely what purpose federal troops were expected to serve in Chicago, Schofield reminded him that the mere maintenance of peace and order in the city remained the function of the state and city authorities.[14]

In other ways John Schofield was displeased with the manner in which Miles handled the situation. Some weeks previously, in General Order No. 15, Schofield had implicitly instructed the

commanders of all military departments that when ordered out
to suppress insurrection they were to act only under the orders of
the President and high-ranking military officials and never under
the orders of any civil officer.[15] In distributing federal troops in
Chicago, the commanding officer was guided largely by the advice of Marshal Arnold and other civil officials. The policy was
not only in violation of instructions but led to tactical blunders.
Judging from the evidence presented by Schofield, the handling
of the federal armed forces in Chicago was characterized by
ineptness and insubordination.[16]

The disturbances of July 5 were climaxed in the evening by a
colossal fire which wrought great damage to the buildings of the
World's Columbian Exposition at Jackson Park. How the conflagration started remains a mystery. Handicapped by a scanty
water supply and a strong wind, the fire department was unable
to check the flames until seven structures had been consumed,
leaving "acres of black and smoking ruins." Although the fire
was believed to be of incendiary origin, there is no evidence that
this destruction was in any way related to the strike disorders.
But, occurring as it did at this critical juncture, many people felt
that it was the work of the same lawless mobs that were invading
the property of railroads. The press did nothing to allay this feeling but endeavored to create the impression that the fire was
perpetrated by strike sympathizers, if not by the strikers themselves.[17] While this conflagration was in progress, elsewhere and
at sundry points railroad cars were fired, thus multiplying the
burdens of a fire department greatly overworked.

The greatest havoc was caused on July 6 when mobs destroyed
railroad property valued at three hundred and forty thousand
dollars. This loss seems all the more appalling when compared
with the damage done on other crucial days, since neither before
nor subsequently did the maximum destruction of railroad property in Chicago for any day exceed four thousand dollars.[18] The
devastation on that ill-fated day was mostly the work of in-
cendiaries who ignited the cars with torches and waste taken from
axle boxes. Fanned by breezes, the flames swept through row
upon row of cars, tightly packed in the outlying yards, to which

fire hoses often would not reach. The Illinois Central was among the roads most seriously involved, owing to the fact that in the morning a railroad agent on this line shot two rioters—an act that inflamed the mob to madness. The fire department did its utmost to extinguish the flames, but the extensiveness of the fires and the scarcity of water made their task impossible.[19]

In the evening occurred the greatest devastation of all, when an epidemic of fires destroyed at least seven hundred cars at the Panhandle yards in South Chicago. Two miles long and a half-mile wide, these yards were crowded with cars. The rioters found the area unprotected, extremely accessible, and devoid of adequate water hydrants. In the vicinity was a Bohemian and Polish settlement, from whose dingy cottages many emerged to witness the spectacle and in some instances to profit by the plunder. The mob may have numbered six thousand, although comparatively few participated in the depredations.[20] In portraying the events of the night, the *Inter Ocean* vividly described the approach of the mob to the Panhandle yards and how the work of destruction was achieved:

From this moving mass of shouting rioters squads of a dozen or two departed, running toward the yards with fire brands in their hands. They looked in the gloaming like specters, their lighted torches bobbing about like will-o'-the-wisps. Soon from all parts of the yard flames shot up and billows of fire rolled over the cars, covering them with the red glow of destruction. The spectacle was a grand one. . . . . Before the cars were fired those filled with any cargoes were looted. . . . . The people were bold, shameless, and eager in their robbery. . . . . It was pandemonium let loose, the fire leaping along for miles and the men and women dancing with frenzy. It was a mad scene where riot became wanton and men and women became drunk on their excesses.[21]

The same day that witnessed this orgy of destruction also beheld the first movement of state troops into Chicago to combat a situation which had grown steadily worse despite the presence of federal soldiers. The militia was immediately deployed for the purpose of clearing the tracks, protecting property, and restoring order but in attempting to do so experienced serious difficulty.

While furnishing protection to a wrecking train on the afternoon of July 7, a company of the militia was assaulted by an angry mob on the Grand Trunk line at Forty-ninth and Loomis

BURNING OF SEVEN HUNDRED FREIGHT CARS ON PANHANDLE RAILROAD
SOUTH OF FIFTIETH STREET, CHICAGO, EVENING OF JULY 6, 1894

streets. Several thousand people had been following this train, and, as their number increased, many became bolder. Approaching Loomis Street, the train halted to remove an obstruction—an act which provoked the mob. The guards and crew were showered with abuse and assailed by bullets and a fusillade of stones. After warning the rioters to disperse, the commander ordered his troops to load their rifles. For the moment this seemed to have a salutary affect, causing a few women and children to leave, but in reality generating an uglier spirit among the rioters. Several soldiers were struck by stones. A bayonet charge was immediately ordered, during which some individuals were severely wounded but which cleared the railroad crossing of the tumultuous throng. More determined than ever to resist the progress of the train, the mob returned, some of whom in a quick sally upset a flat car which had just been righted. More missiles were hurled and some shots fired by the rioters, to which the deputies and a few of the police replied ineffectually with their revolvers. No reinforcements appeared; and, as four soldiers had already been severely wounded and the lieutenant felled, there seemed to be no alternative left to the commanding officer except to instruct his men to fire at will and to make it effective. Not until the streets were cleared did the firing cease, whereupon the car was righted and, the train permitted to proceed on its way. Although the mob reassembled later, it was again dispersed, but this time by the police and without any fatalities. In the Loomis Street fight, four rioters were killed and some twenty wounded, among whom were a few women. This affray marked the highest level of violence in the Chicago phase of the struggle.[22]

The action taken by lawless mobs furnished sensational and alarming news, but equally serious, although not so widely publicized, was the effect of the strike on the food and fuel situation. With a population approaching two million, Chicago was dependent on large daily shipments of fruit, vegetables, milk, and meat. The paralysis of transportation created an acute shortage in these commodities, forcing the prices of many items to almost prohibitive levels. The great perishable-produce mart on Water Street became almost deserted, while just outside the city there were miles of loaded cars containing foodstuffs rotting in the sun. The supply of coal began to run low,[23] although conditions did not persist long enough to create a fuel famine.

Between July 4 and July 10 not a carload of meat or livestock was moved at the Union Stock Yards, despite frequent attempts to do so by deputy marshals, deputy sheriffs, policemen, and federal troops. On July 5, for instance, two hundred soldiers and three hundred deputy marshals were able to move a trainload of livestock only one mile and were obliged to abandon the attempt and return the stock to their pens after a struggle of four hours.[24] The inability of farmers and other producers to market their products was an important factor in the rising tide of sentiment against the strikers.

Fully alert to the seriousness of the situation, the General Managers' Association on July 7 instructed John M. Egan to appoint a committee of three, with himself as chairman, for the purpose of conferring with the proper authorities relative to adequate protection for all points menaced by violence.[25] This committee called on Mayor Hopkins in the afternoon of the same day and suggested unity of action among the police, militia, and federal troops. Unimpressed with the need for closer co-ordination, the mayor emphatically refused to permit the national guard or police to act under General Miles, nor would he assume command of the United States soldiers.[26] The feasibility of such unified control was questionable, and Miles would undoubtedly have rejected it for jurisdictional reasons, but in his conferences with Edwin Walker and John Egan he seemed quite willing to co-operate with the general managers in their struggle against the American Railway Union.[27]

Assured by Egan that the railroads had sufficient men to move trains, General Miles and Marshal Arnold decided on July 7 to send an escort of forty deputy marshals and a contingent of United States troops with a mail train from each of the following depots: Union, Dearborn, Illinois Central, Rock Island, Grand Central, and the Chicago and Northwestern. Eight companies were detailed for this work, each soldier being equipped with one hundred rounds of ammunition and five days' rations. They were

"Harper's Weekly" (1894)

NATIONAL GUARDSMEN FIRING INTO THE MOB AT LOOMIS
AND FORTY-NINTH STREETS, CHICAGO, JULY 7, 1894

to assist the deputy marshals in clearing the roads for interstate commerce and were to use firearms, if necessary, in repelling all acts of hostility.[28]

The public could not view these developments in their true perspective. Calm, dispassionate reason gave way to panicky fears as the public read the sensational news stories. The disorders in Chicago occurred only on a portion of the railroad property, leaving all but a fraction of the great metropolis untouched by violence. The press, however, preferred to ignore this fact and to leave the impression that most of Chicago was convulsed in revolution.

The countless telegrams and letters that poured into the White House revealed the extreme agitation of many citizens. Some were concerned over the impending loss of their perishable crops because of the paralysis of transportation, while the majority seemed alarmed over the threat which the strike held for the security of life and property. Vigorous action was demanded of the federal authorities, including such proposals as martial law, wholesale arrests, and a presidential proclamation.[29] One Chicago businessman, typical of many, advised the President on July 6 to issue a proclamation in the interest of law and order and also to call on one hundred thousand volunteers to protect property. He warned:

Unless you take decided action at once the riot and rebellion will be entirely beyond your control and much property and blood will have to be sacrificed, and I fear we will never return to the peaceful years of the past. . . . . No half hearted measure will satisfy any one. If an officer of the army with a regiment of soldiers are placed in charge of the stockyards he should clear it of every striker and rioter or leave his men dead on the field as martyrs to liberty. I write for the interest of my wife and babies and pray God to guide you and show you the terrible volcano on which we stand.[30]

The White House was not indifferent to these pleas or to the latest developments.[31] Additional federal forces were ordered to Chicago, and on July 8 the President issued his proclamation against lawlessness in that city or anywhere in Illinois. Briefly he set forth the reasons for using federal troops and then admonished all citizens against encouraging or participating in any unlawful obstructions or assemblages. All persons involved in such activities were warned to disperse and retire quietly to their homes on or before noon of July 9. Those who ignored this warning and continued to resist the authority of the United States would be regarded as public enemies. It was explained that, in suppressing a riotous mob, the troops were to act promptly and energetically and hence could not discriminate between the guilty and those who were there in a spirit of idle curiosity.[32]

Had the situation permitted, the attorney-general would undoubtedly have gone further and induced the President to declare martial law in Chicago. This was apparent in an exchange of telegrams between Edwin Walker and Richard Olney on July 9. Although well pleased with the proclamation, Walker expressed the hope that, if mob disturbances persisted, the federal government would proclaim martial law. Although not unfavorable toward the suggestion, the attorney-general in reply expressed doubt as to the legality of such a course until Governor Altgeld was willing to invoke federal aid and thus place the United States in full control of matters.[33] The governor of Illinois was obviously unwilling to co-operate in such fashion. Whether Richard Olney would have devised some subterfuge to circumvent this obstacle, had matters continued to grow progressively worse, cannot be answered categorically.

Shortly after the publication of Cleveland's proclamation, Major General Schofield issued instructions as to the manner in which federal troops should resist rioters. The use of weapons against a mob was primarily a tactical question, to be determined by the immediate commander according to expediency and circumstances. Caution was to be exercised in using firearms, since vast numbers of innocent individuals usually mingled in riotous gatherings, and such people should be warned and given sufficient time to separate from the guilty. Bayonets were recommended against a mixed crowd in the first stages of a revolt, and only as a last resort should rifle and artillery fire be employed— and then only for the purpose of suppressing the disorders as quickly as possible. The soldiers were never to see how many casualties could be inflicted, but by effective blows to end all resistance quickly and then to stop the destruction of life immediately. "Punishment belongs not to the troops," declared the communiqué, "but to the courts of justice."[34]

The usefulness of federal troops was definitely circumscribed. As General Schofield made abundantly clear, they were to be used only for the protection of interstate commerce and mail routes and for the enforcement of judicial processes and the laws of the United States. The preservation of general law and order was not within their sphere of activity—a duty incumbent upon the state and municipal authorities. Despite all this and contrary to instructions, General Miles indicated on July 7 that, whenever Mayor Hopkins should make the request, federal troops would be ordered to help restore peace.[35] In an official communiqué to his officers two days later Miles explained that, should the state and local authorities fail to suppress lawlessness, the military forces would render assistance but not to the extent of leaving unguarded the property intrusted to their protection.[36] Such a policy met with the strong disapproval of Schofield, who believed that Miles had greatly exceeded his authority;[37] but there is no evidence that federal troops were used to help local officials as authorized by the Chicago commander.

The presence of United States soldiers did not relieve the marshal of the responsibility of arresting all who were guilty of violating the injunction or a federal statute. The troops were under orders to assist this official only when he was unable to discharge the duties of his office. Deputy marshals were thus sustained by the military, even though their deportment at times was discreditable.[38] Many of their arrests were made in a haphazard and indiscriminate fashion, on evidence that proved flimsy and unreliable. Of the one hundred and ninety arrests made in Chicago under federal statutes, only seventy-one resulted in indictments,[39] many of which were subsequently dismissed.

The conduct of the federal troops was exemplary. Unwelcomed by the state and municipal authorities and frowned upon by labor, these soldiers were in an unenviable position, which may explain why their conduct was characterized by such caution. Suppression of the riots was accomplished almost entirely by the police and the state militia, but this work was obviously not the responsibility of the United States Army. In the protection of mail and interstate commerce the regulars were expected to play an active part, but in carrying out this assignment they inflicted no casualties. Among the thirteen people killed and the fifty-three seriously wounded in Chicago during the strike, none were the victims of federal soldiers. The record of the police was as good, but the same cannot be said for the state troops, who killed five and seriously injured sixteen. The remaining casualties were accidental or attributable to marshals and other persons, some of whom remained unknown.[40]

To what extent United States troops served in restoring conditions to normal long remained a controversial issue. In the judgment of General Miles their presence in Chicago saved the "country from a serious rebellion";[41] but such a claim never elicited any support from the state and local officials of Illinois, who believed that all the credit for the suppression of disorder was due to the police and the militia. Whatever the merits of the respective arguments, it seems evident that Illinois could have done very well without federal aid; but it is equally true that this assistance proved a potent factor in the termination of the strike and the collapse of the American Railway Union.

Reference has already been made to the prejudice of General Miles against this union. How completely his officers shared his sentiments cannot be determined. One observer of this period, Brand Whitlock, referred in his book, *Forty Years of It*, to strike sympathizers and the white ribbon which they wore and mentioned a "Colonel of the regular army, in his cups at his club, who wished he might order a whole regiment to shoot them 'each man to take aim at a dirty white ribbon.' "[42] All federal soldiers on duty, officers as well as privates, were viewed by labor with the greatest suspicion and contempt. No such feeling was directed against the militia, whose presence in Chicago was recognized as necessary. Although Debs charged that some laborers were compelled to work at the point of federal bayonets, such tactics did not represent the policy of the army and were pursued, if at all, in only a few isolated cases, of which General Miles seemed not to have the slightest knowledge.[43]

"*Harper's Weekly*" (*1894*)

UNITED STATES INFANTRY IN THE CHICAGO STOCKYARDS

"TO HELL WITH THE UNITED STATES GOVERNMENT!"

At this point responsibility for the disturbances in Chicago might well be considered, since they weighed so heavily in the course which the strike took. It was vital to the interests of labor to prosecute the struggle peacefully. The Pullman workers had elicited widespread sympathy throughout the nation. Lawlessness would not only dispel this friendly feeling but would arouse public wrath and give to the railroads the opportunity to invoke the forces of organized society to suppress the strike. All this was well known to Eugene Debs, whose victory in the Great Northern Railroad strike, less than three months previously, had been due largely to the superb discipline and faultless behavior of the men. The Pullman Strike was a far greater struggle, and the scrupulous observance of the law even more necessary for a labor victory.

A strike peacefully waged would have been difficult to combat, particularly in view of the rapidly growing popularity of the American Railway Union and the capable leadership which it possessed. The railroads could hardly have been blind to the advantages which would accrue to their cause from public disturbances. Properly exploited by a friendly press, such a condition would win public support for the general managers and assure them ever increasing aid from the government. In examining the matter, there is hearsay evidence that the General Managers' Association employed *agents provocateurs* to incite the strikers to deeds of violence, but the facts are not sufficient to justify the suspicion that the railroads were a party to the destruction of their own property. Obviously such methods, if employed, were pursued in a manner so secretive as to render a full investigation impossible.

The railroads exhibited carelessness in leaving so many of their cars in yards that were unfenced, unprotected by private watchmen, beyond the fire limits, and easily accessible to marauders. In the destructive Panhandle fires there was not the slightest resistance offered to any of the rioters. This condition was true in other areas of the city—a fact which seemed very significant to John Hopkins.[44] Only a few of the cars destroyed were loaded, while most of them might be classified as old and dilapidated. Interestingly enough, no Pullman palace cars were where they could be burned.[45]

Extremely fragmentary and none too reliable is the evidence that men were hired by railroads to fire old boxcars and incite others to do so in order to make the strike unpopular. In Henry D. Lloyd's "Note Book" it was claimed that Mayor Hopkins procured forty affidavits proving that the burning of freight cars was the work of railroad agents.[46] Since John Hopkins never mentioned the matter and no other source confirmed it, the authenticity of the report is open to question. In writing to W. T. Stead in August, 1894, Lloyd declared:

If the people will not, out of their bovine peaceableness do the acts of violence that would afford the pretext for the "saviors of society" to keep possession, these latter will themselves commit the violence, and charge it upon the people. They did this in Chicago, I verily believe. They have done it in many preceding strikes. This is their winning card.[47]

Such a statement was an expression of opinion rather than of fact. More specific were the charges made by the vice-president of the American Railway Union, who, in his testimony before the Strike Commission, explained that he had supplied the detective department of Chicago with the names of men who were paid to destroy cars. In one particular case he referred to a railroad employee who allegedly received four hundred dollars for his work in igniting freight cars. As further proof, Howard submitted a letter from F. L. Horton, secretary of the Committee of Public Safety at Springfield, Illinois, to the effect that three men had been detected burning cars and one was overheard to remark that unless John Egan promptly paid the balance of the five hundred dollars promised to them for destroying those cars, the whole affair would be exposed.[48] This letter was forwarded to John Hopkins, who immediately had Horton brought to Chicago for questioning. So vague and inconclusive were the facts which he divulged that the whole story was discounted and the matter dropped.[49]

Carroll D. Wright, chairman of the Strike Commission, was reported by the *New England Magazine* in October, 1896, as telling a Boston newspaper that the destruction of the mass of cars in Chicago was instigated by the railroads as the surest way to involve federal troops and defeat the strikers.[50] As enlightening as this may seem, there is nothing in his famous report on the Pullman Strike to indicate that he had reached such a conclusion. The extreme reluctance of the railroads to seek damages from the city of Chicago for alleged negligence in furnishing adequate protection to their property was interpreted by some as evidence that they did not care to have the matter of incendiarism investigated.[51]

There is reason to believe that a few of the cars were fired by deputy marshals. James R. Sovereign, chief executive of the Knights of Labor, testified that he had seen in the files of the mayor's office a report prepared by secret police, whom Hopkins had placed among the deputies, proving that some of the federal agents had been guilty of arson.[52] In the judgment of Superintendent of Police Brennan there was strong suspicion that some of the fires were ignited by these deputies, who "hoped to retain their positions by keeping up a semblance of disorder." In his report for 1894 he explained that a large number of these deputies were "toughs, thieves, and ex-convicts," some of whom were arrested during the strike for the theft of property from railroad cars. On one occasion two of them were discovered under suspicious circumstances in proximity to a freight car that had just been ignited.[53]

Contrary to press reports, there was at no time a reign of terror in Chicago, although mobs overran railroad property and did considerable damage. Much of the destruction was perpetrated on the impulse of the moment by young hoodlums who enjoyed excitement. It was early discovered that freight cars could easily be overturned, since they were set upon central pivots on the tracks and could be teetered sidewise. It required but a moment for thirty or forty young toughs to line up with their shoulders against the lower edge of a car, and together start it swaying and then with an "Altogether, yo-heave-O" to send it crashing on to the opposite track. In this manner a gang could blockade three or four tracks and vanish before a soldier or policeman could arrive. Nothing less than a derrick could restore these cars to their former position. In the burning of cars, torches made by entwining some oily waste on the end of sticks were found to be quite serviceable.[54]

Most of the destruction represented a blind wave of recklessness that perhaps symbolized all too eloquently the enormities of the times.[55]

Judging by the number of arrests made by the police, conditions could not have been so bad as depicted by alarmists. Most of the offenses committed by the rioters—arson, murder, burglary, intimidation, assault, riot, and inciting to riot—came almost entirely under the jurisdiction of the local authorities. Even so, the number of arrests made in Chicago by the police as a result of the strike was only five hundred and fifteen.[56] Strangely enough, the turbulent year of 1894 revealed fewer arrests in that city than during the more peaceful years of 1892 or 1893, and the total amount of fines collected was considerably less than in either of the two preceding years.[57]

The general managers were quick to capitalize on conditions by boldly attributing to the strikers full responsibility for the disturbances.[58] The press rendered magnificent service to the railroads by building up the impression that the strikers not only perpetrated the violence but sought to establish a state of anarchy. Some newspapers contended that only by such a course could the strikers hope to win. In this fashion the *New York Times* argued the matter, holding that the only opportunity for a labor victory was by ruthlessly disregarding the law. The editor explained that whether the strikers committed the violence or induced others to do so mattered little, since all of it was chargeable to Eugene Debs and what he represented.[59]

In seeking to fix responsibility for the rioting the press and the general managers, either wilfully or in ignorance, indulged in a campaign of publicity that was based upon gross misrepresentation. The evidence on this point is abundantly clear—that the strikers had very little part in the disturbances. This was borne out in a most convincing manner by the testimony presented before the Strike Commission. John Egan acknowledged that very few of the names reported to him for lawlessness were those of railroad workers.[60] The chief deputy marshal of Chicago, John C. Donnelly, affirmed that he did not see any strikers take part in the disorders.[61] Mayor Hopkins and Superintendent of Police

Brennan shared the conviction that the riots were not caused by members of the American Railway Union.[62] Police Inspector Nicholas Hunt, who controlled one thousand policemen in an area where much of the rioting took place, revealed that those "caught in the act of doing some depredations were not railroad men."[63] Equally significant was the testimony of two assistant fire marshals, Joseph L. Kenyon and John Fitzgerald, who had jurisdiction in the territories most seriously affected by incendiarism. They found no evidence that would implicate the strikers in the burning of freight cars and other railroad property.[64]

The press representatives, who mingled with the rioters and for days followed the shifting events, were almost unanimous in their testimony before the Strike Commission that the turmoil and public disorders could not be ascribed to members of the American Railway Union. Some of these reporters did not take the pains to give proper emphasis to this fact during the riots, and others, having taken pains, had their work edited. Typical of the reporters was Harold I. Cleveland, from the *Chicago Herald*, who covered the Rock Island tracks. He possessed a wide acquaintance among the employees of this road but did not observe a single railroad man involved in the riots. In his opinion the disturbances were primarily due to the "rough, vicious and lawless elements" from the districts adjoining the tracks.[65] For approximately ten days Victor M. Harding of the *Chicago Times* observed conditions on the Illinois Central Road but found nothing to indicate that the strikers had any part in the destruction of property. In his presence, some of them sought to discourage the crowd from acts of vandalism.[66] Reporters from the *Chicago Record* and the United Press Association likewise observed that union members tried to persuade rioters to desist from their depredations and go home.[67]

So rapidly did events move and so swiftly did the strike spread that it was difficult for Debs and his lieutenants to keep the movement within their full control. The union members on each road were instructed not to take action unless they could make it effective and so were urged to strike only when such a course was sanctioned by a majority on the road. In the heat of battle, such advice was not always observed. In some cases militant minority groups would declare strikes, select committees and determine policies.[68] The strike aroused the greatest enthusiasm among the yard and shop employees. Many firemen and telegraph operators rallied to the cause as did some conductors, brakemen, and engineers; but, for the most part, the members of the brotherhoods responded rather coldly. From numerous roads and yards committees would visit union headquarters and confer with the officers. In order to rally the strikers and promote greater unity, daily meetings were held, at which the executives of the union made speeches.

The sessions at Uhlich's Hall were open to the public. Press representatives were especially welcomed, and every courtesy was extended to them. At no time did the city authorities find it necessary to maintain policemen in or near any of those meetings.[69] W. C. Roberts, of the *Chicago Dispatch*, who attended every meeting at Uhlich's Hall, declared that they were "generally of a conciliatory nature" and that at no time did he hear any incendiary language. All the speakers urged the men to stay away from every place of excitement and to conduct themselves as law-abiding citizens. The utterances of Debs and Howard impressed him as being very sincere. He pointed out that every effort was made to discover who the miscreants were that committed the violence and to turn them over to the authorities.[70] Among other reporters who covered the meetings was William K. McKay, of the *Chicago Evening Mail*. "All the speeches I heard," he affirmed, "counseled obedience to law and order, and my interviews with Mr. Debs and Mr. Howard were all the same way."[71]

It was clear to the American Railway Union that the only hope for victory lay in a strike free of overt acts and deeds of violence. Through the local committees, the union officials tried to ascertain whether or not any of the members were guilty of violating the law. Detectives were employed to help establish the identity of those criminally involved. The right of the railroads to hire whomever they pleased was freely recognized, and under no circumstances would the union sanction threats, intimidation, or violence against "scabs." From time to time manifestoes were issued by Eugene Debs, appealing to all strikers to countenance no violence and to keep off the property of railroad companies.[72] On July 7, for instance, he reminded the members:

We have repeatedly declared that we will respect law and order, and our conduct must conform to our profession. A man who commits violence in any form, whether a member of our order or not, should be promptly arrested and punished and we should be the first to apprehend the miscreant and bring him to justice. We must triumph as law abiding citizens or not at all. Those who engage in force or violence are our real enemies.[73]

Eugene Debs believed that the railroads would be unable to replace the strikers with sufficient men to permit the operation of trains and that in time the union would force these corporations to adopt a more conciliatory attitude. The American Railway Union denounced as false the claim of the general managers that the trains did not move because of interference from the strikers. Debs perceived clearly the strategy of the railroads—to attribute to these men responsibility for the rioting, and thus poison the public mind and invoke the forces of the government against labor.[74] He tried hard to counteract this stratagem, but without much success. In the judgment of the Chicago mayor, the railroads were unable to secure enough men to operate their trains but, anxious to conceal this fact, attributed the paralysis of transportation to the disturbances for which the strikers were blamed. Using this plea as a cloak to conceal their helplessness, the general managers called for aid, which, as Hopkins admitted, was really needed to suppress the disorderly gatherings. Although convinced that the strikers were not responsible for the riots, Hopkins nevertheless recognized in the lawlessness a force that would defeat the cause of labor.[75]

In the Great Northern Strike, the American Railway Union took definite steps to forestall violence, with the result that none occurred. Regular reliefs of union members were detailed to patrol the railroad property and prevent arson, thievery, the turning of switches, and other lawless acts. Instructions were issued to shoot the first person caught violating the law. The union intended to take similar measures in the Pullman Strike but was unable to do so because of the proportions which the struggle so quickly assumed. In a few places, however, local unions furnished some protection for railroad property prior to the arrival of troops.[76]

At no time did the union lose sight of the purpose for which the strike was being fostered. On July 5 Eugene Debs issued to the public a lengthy statement in justification of the policy pursued by the strikers. In reviewing the origin of the struggle, he related how the Pullman workers finally resorted to a strike after being shamefully exploited and denied the right to arbitrate their grievances. The American Railway Union was not fighting for recognition but simply to see that justice was done. He explained further that the Pullman workers were willing to abide by any reasonable proposition. "Let the spirit of conciliation, mutual concession and compromise," Debs pleaded, "animate and govern both sides, and there will be no trouble in reaching a settlement that will be satisfactory to all concerned." In order not to have his plea for conciliation mistaken for weakness, he then proceeded with more firmness:

It has been asked what sense is there in sympathetic strikes? Let the corporations answer. When one is assailed, all go to the rescue. They stand together, they supply each other with men, money and equipment. Labor in unifying its forces, simply follows their example. If the proceeding is vicious and indefensible, let them first abolish it. In this contest labor will stand by labor.[77]

In Chicago, hub of the great strike, labor demonstrated overwhelming support for the American Railway Union. On June 30, the Trades and Labor Assembly, representing the local trade-unions in that city with approximately one hundred and fifty thousand members, pledged its united strength in sustaining the fight against the Pullman Company and the General Managers' Association. A committee, appointed to confer with the officers of the American Railway Union, explained that, if circumstances required, every union man in Chicago would participate in a sympathetic strike. Debs, however, was unwilling at this time to countenance such extreme measures.[78]

As the tide of battle reached a crucial phase, with the prospects for a labor victory becoming somewhat doubtful, there developed a growing demand for a walkout of the trade-unions in Chicago.

It was the opinion of James Sovereign on July 6 that such an expression of solidarity on the part of labor would impress all with the urgent need for the settlement of the difficulties and would cause the people to rise "en masse in a demand for arbitration." Stressing the need for action, he explained that labor was engaged in a struggle for existence, and in the event of defeat would suffer in a manner from which recovery would be most difficult.[79] Such sentiments were shared by the vast majority of workers in Chicago, and steps were accordingly taken in the direction of a city-wide stoppage of industry. On July 7 the Building and Trades Council, representing a membership of twenty-five thousand workers, voted unanimously in favor of a strike but decided to delay action pending developments. This organization expressed itself in favor of a general cessation of all business throughout the country, unless the Pullman Company should accept the principle of arbitration.[80]

The trade-unions of Chicago now decided that the time for united action had arrived. A mass meeting was set for the evening of July 8 at Uhlich's Hall, to which each local union was advised to send three representatives with full instructions and authority to act. Only delegates with credentials were admitted to this meeting, and behind closed doors the representatives from more than one hundred unions in Chicago deliberated from eight o'clock in the evening until dawn the following morning. The chiefs of seven national labor organizations were there, including Debs of the American Railway Union, McBride of the coal miners, Sovereign of the Knights of Labor, Prescott of the Typographical Union, and O'Connell of the machinists. During the tense hours the delegates weighed carefully the question before the convention: "Shall the trade-unions of Chicago strike in sympathy with the Pullman boycott, to the end that the principle of arbitration may win?"

Many favored an immediate strike, while some objected because of existing agreements and contracts between certain unions and their employers. All opposition vanished, however, when press reports reached the delegates at midnight that Cleveland had issued a proclamation which, as they believed, would virtually place Chicago under martial law. Before taking the irrevocable step to paralyze Chicago by a city-wide strike, the congress of trade-unions decided that one last attempt should be made to induce the Pullman Company to accept arbitration. A committee of seven was chosen to confer with Mayor Hopkins and explore all possibilities that might lead to an amicable solution of the dispute. If the Pullman Strike, however, were not settled by four o'clock on Tuesday afternoon, July 10, the way then would be open for the general strike, to take effect the following morning. This arrangement was unanimously adopted by the convention. In the debates on this and related matters, bitter denunciations were voiced against Pullman, Cleveland, and the railroads.[81]

Several days prior to this convention, the mayor of Chicago had appointed a committee of aldermen, with John McGillen as chairman, to seek an equitable adjustment of the controversy. Its services were offered to all parties. To this group the American Railway Union set forth precisely what issues were involved. The General Managers' Association explained, when interviewed, that the struggle arose from a matter over which it could exercise no authority. To the council committee it seemed clear that, if the dispute between the Pullman Corporation and its employees could be solved, the railroad strike would quickly end. At this juncture the committee of seven from the Congress of Trade Unions called on the mayor and was referred to the McGillen Committee. After a careful appraisal of all facts, the two groups decided they would recommend the creation of a board which would seek to determine the validity of the contention so emphatically stressed by the Pullman Company—that there was nothing to arbitrate. Two of the members on this arbitral committee would be appointed by the Pullman Corporation, two others by the circuit court judges of Cook County, and together these four would select a fifth one. Paradoxical as it may seem, this committee was merely to arbitrate the question of whether or not there was anything to arbitrate.

A subcommittee of the two groups called upon the Pullman officials and presented the proposal. McGillen emphasized that the request was only a slight one and that, in view of the gravity of the situation, the company could not very well ignore it. Tragic consequences, he warned, might follow unless some settlement of the controversy were soon reached. To this, as to all appeals, the company was indifferent. In flatly rejecting the proposition, the Pullman officials explained there was nothing to arbitrate and that the company would not tolerate any interference in its private business affairs, either from the employees or from the state, federal, or local government.[82] Later, in reporting to the city council on the work and failure of his committee, McGillen spoke scornfully of Pullman's refusal to "listen to just and fair appeals when he alone is the cause of all this strife, of all this wreck and ruin which is imperiling the lives and property of this great city out of which he has reaped his harvest of millions."[83]

As soon as the committee of seven acknowledged failure, the chairman of the Trades and Labor Congress issued a proclamation calling upon all trade-unions in Chicago to launch the city-wide strike as planned. The local lodges of the Knights of Labor responded, as did several other unions, but the general strike did not materialize. Only a small portion of workers left their lathes and workbenches, certainly not more than twenty-five thousand.[84] It was not that labor had suffered any diminution of sympathy for the Pullman employees, but conditions were becoming less auspicious for the drastic step which had been contemplated with such enthusiasm only two days before. Eugene Debs and other executives of the American Railway Union had been arrested, and with the military so strongly intrenched in the city the trade-unions demonstrated unexpected caution when called upon to redeem their pledge. Perhaps they realized all too clearly that in a sympathetic strike at this eleventh hour they would be fighting for a lost cause. Some preferred to await the outcome of the executive conference of the American Federation of Labor, which was scheduled to meet in Chicago on July 12. Whatever reasons may have prompted the unceremonious retreat of these unions, after such ardent pledges of support, it appears that a general strike at this time would have done labor great harm without benefiting the dying cause of the American Railway Union.

On July 10 Debs was arrested for conspiracy, and shortly afterward the Briggs House conference convened—the last hope of a union already fighting a rear-guard action. At the Uhlich conference of trade-unions on July 8, it was decided that Samuel Gompers, president of the American Federation of Labor, should come to Chicago immediately. Since many of the trade-unions that joined in the request were affiliated with the federation, Gompers decided reluctantly to go, although convinced there was little he could do. After consulting with his closest advisers, he wired the members of the executive council of the federation, as well as fifteen or twenty executive officers of various other national and international unions, to meet in Chicago on July 12 for a full examination of the situation. The response was excellent, with twenty-four high union officials in attendance, including representatives from two of the brotherhoods. Meeting in the Briggs House, with Samuel Gompers as the presiding officer, the conference proceeded at once to a careful consideration of all aspects of the strike in order to determine what policy, if any, should be adopted.[85]

During the first session a committee from the Cigar Makers' Union of Chicago presented a strong plea for a general strike. Explaining that the struggle of the American Railway Union concerned the well-being of all workers, the committee stressed the need for the complete solidarity of all labor in the crisis. United action and the cessation of work everywhere, it was confidently stated, would force Pullman to arbitrate. Among others who pressed for such action was James Sovereign. The plea for this drastic course was viewed with extreme realism by the tried and experienced labor leaders of this conference, who understood the limitations and dangers of a sympathetic strike. They were, however, willing to explore all possibilities and in the afternoon session sent a telegram to President Cleveland, stressing the seriousness of the situation and urging that he use his influence to end the industrial crisis in a manner fair to all parties. He was asked to come to Chicago at once and join the conference or, if this were not possible, to send a representative. The President chose neither to answer nor to acknowledge the request.[86]

Upon invitation, Eugene Debs appeared before the conference in the evening, and in a calm and dispassionate manner discussed the origin and issues of the struggle. Many questions were raised and various angles of the situation analyzed. Although reluctant to give advice, Debs declared, when pressed by Gompers for a statement, that in his judgment all the forces of labor should be peaceably mustered to secure a satisfactory adjustment of the dispute. Debs labored under no delusions. He realized that not much could be expected, but he hoped that the prestige of this group might be used to help him salvage from the struggle at least the jobs which the members of his union had so willingly abandoned when they rallied to the support of the Pullman employees. He asked Gompers to deliver to the general managers a document from the American Railway Union proposing the termination of the boycott on condition that the strikers be permitted to return to their jobs. Debs suggested that, if the offer were rejected, a general strike should then be ordered.[87]

After Eugene Debs had finished his remarks and left, the labor executives weighed the matter. It was quite apparent that the American Railway Union was defeated, for otherwise Debs would not have been willing to terminate the strike on such terms. The members of his union were apparently no longer concerned with the boycott; they were now fighting for their jobs. In view of this, a general strike was deemed inauspicious. Even if the executive council of the federation had favored such a course, it possessed no power to order a general strike and could only have made a recommendation to that effect. The request that Gompers transmit to the general managers a communication from the American Railway Union was also rejected, presumably because such a course might involve the American Federation of Labor in a manner prejudicial to its best interests. Gompers and other members of the conference, however, agreed to accompany Debs and his associates on the mission—an offer which Eugene Debs obviously could not accept since he was personally offensive to the general managers.[88]

However feeble were its efforts to render assistance, the Briggs conference did not lack sympathy for the cause espoused by the

American Railway Union. Aside from the two representatives of the railroad brotherhoods, who refused to indorse the boycott, there was complete feeling of admiration for the courageous fight made by Debs. It was recommended that the executive council of the American Federation of Labor vote one thousand dollars toward his legal defense.[89] Before adjourning, the conference prepared a statement of policy, which, although friendly in spirit, gave to the American Railway Union no prospects of any real help. It was urged that sympathetic strikes be avoided as inexpedient and unwise and that any union of the federation participating in such action should abandon it immediately. The document explained that in view of the depression and because of the great array of armed force which had been summoned to sustain corporate interests, the odds were overwhelmingly against the policy of calling men out on a general or local strike. The press was singled out for special condemnation—charged with serving the vested interests by maliciously misrepresenting the facts.

With equal vehemence the statement denounced certain corporations for seeking to cloak themselves in the pretended garments of law and order while endeavoring to associate the strikers with lawlessness and anarchy. For years, it was recalled, the railroads had contemptuously violated the Interstate Commerce Law; but, when confronted by indignant labor, they quickly invoked the aid of the government. In this struggle, affirmed the report, the federal government supported by marshals, injunctions, bayonets, and a presidential proclamation had rushed to the protection of the corporations. In the action taken by the American Railway Union, the Briggs House Conference recognized "an impulsive, vigorous protest against the gathering, growing forces of plutocratic power and corporation rule."[90]

Although condemned by many for not pursuing a more vigorous course, this conference could not have done much else if it was to reflect the prudence of Samuel Gompers, who was more calculating and less daring than Eugene Debs. As chief executive of the American Federation of Labor, Gompers represented the principle of craft unions but, even so, seemed to bear no animus toward the American Railway Union. He believed, however, that the creation of a dual organization among railroad workers was unfortunate and that it would have been better if the brotherhoods had been permitted to correct their own mistakes.[91] Being himself cautious and conservative, he doubted the wisdom of so young a union inaugurating a strike of such colossal proportions. Sensitive to injustice, he admired the fearlessness with which this organization threw down the gauntlet to the Pullman Corporation and refused to retreat when challenged by the General Managers' Association. For George Pullman, Gompers entertained only scorn. He wrote:

It is indeed difficult to conceive a cause in which right was more on the side of those who were defeated. . . . . We hope to add to the contumely and contempt which every earnest, honest, liberty loving man, woman and child in the country must feel for the most consummate type of avaricious wealth absorber, tyrant and hypocrite this age, of that breed, has furnished—Pullman. . . . . The end is not yet. Labor will not down. It will triumph despite all the Pullmans combined; and as for Pullman, he has proven himself a public enemy. His name and memory are excoriated today and will be forever.[92]

Eager to end the strike, Debs and his associates requested Mayor Hopkins to deliver to the General Managers' Association the communication which Samuel Gompers had declined to transmit. Couched in conciliatory language, the dispatch stressed the menace which the struggle held for the security, peace, and prosperity of the nation. In view of this, and without reference to the differences that precipitated the battle, the American Railway Union indicated its willingness to meet the general managers halfway. The only condition laid down was the reinstatement of all strikers to their former positions except in the case of those, if there were any, who had been convicted of crime.[93]

In the company of Alderman McGillen, the mayor called upon the chairman of the General Managers' Association, Everett St. John, who seemed disinclined to accept the document but finally consented to do so out of courtesy to the office which Hopkins, as mayor, represented. The names affixed to the communication were extremely offensive to St. John, as well as to John Egan, who soon joined the group. The latter exclaimed that the mayor should not have permitted himself to become a messenger boy for those parties. Egan expressed confidence that the general managers were getting along all right and that any overtures from the American Railway Union were unwelcome. Nettled by this attitude, Hopkins explained that if the situation was so well in hand he would gladly have all the soldiers withdrawn, since the daily cost to Chicago of furnishing protection for railroad property was extraordinarily high. Egan quickly protested that troops were still needed.[94]

The document was subsequently returned to the mayor with the explanation that the general managers were unwilling to accept this or any other communication from the American Railway Union. Convinced that the union faced defeat, the railroads could see no advantage in making any concession, preferring instead to annihilate the organization.[95] While recognizing the right among themselves to form an association to promote their common interests, the railroads refused to accord to their employees the same privilege of collaboration.

The Pullman Company was just as adamant in its refusal to negotiate with the American Railway Union and equally determined to resist all proposals for arbitration. Reference has already been made to the efforts and failure of this union to induce the Pullman Corporation to accept arbitration. Every attempt of the Pullman employees to persuade their company to submit such grievances as rents and wages to an impartial board for settlement met with the same inhospitable treatment. The arbitral board suggested by these workers was to consist of three members—the employees and the Pullman Company each to select one, and these two a third individual.[96]

The Civic Federation of Chicago did its utmost to bring about an amicable solution by creating a conciliation board, to which Jane Addams was appointed a member. She visited the town of Pullman, examined the rentals, and discovered that, whereas wages had been placed on a competitive basis, the rent schedules remained unaffected by the business depression. Whether or not Pullman rentals were exorbitant was a matter which could be appropriately referred to experts, and so Jane Addams suggested to the strike committee at Pullman that the real estate board of Chicago appoint three men familiar with suburban rents to examine the facts and submit their estimate to the Pullman Company and to the employees as a basis for readjustment. The strike committee was anxious to have this done but did not care to give the impression that rentals constituted their only grievance and so declared themselves favorable to arbitration of any and all points. When the proposal was presented to the Pullman officials, it met with a cold reception, as did the suggestion that rents be placed on a competitive basis. Balked here, the conciliation board could go no further, although it had hoped that the question of rentals could be settled and then in turn other grievances.[97]

The mayor of Detroit, H. S. Pingree, tried also to effect a settlement. He dispatched telegrams to the mayors of fifty cities, asking them to join him in an appeal to George Pullman for arbitration. Fortified with their replies, Pingree went to Chicago on July 11 and, accompanied by John Hopkins and Erskine M. Phelps, a big manufacturer, called upon the Pullman officials. A lengthy conference ensued, during which the telegrams were produced. Although Pingree argued the matter forcibly and alluded to the adverse public sentiment which the company would have to face if arbitration were rejected, the Pullman authorities remained impervious to all entreaties, refusing to recede from their former position.[98]

At any time George Pullman could have terminated the conflict by merely agreeing to submit the grievances of his employees to an impartial board. This course Pullman unalterably opposed. He was firmly convinced that a great principle was involved in the strike—whether or not a capitalist should operate his factory in his own way, completely free from the dictation of labor or outside interests. The questions at issue, he asserted, were matters of fact and hence not suitable for arbitration. A matter of opinion, he affirmed, might be arbitrated, but not the question as to the advisability of operating the Pullman shops at a financial loss. In defending the wage policy of his company, Pullman explained that such matters were governed by the law of supply and demand.[99]

It will perhaps never be known how much influence, if any, was exerted upon George Pullman by the directors of his company. If any of them were critical of his refusal to arbitrate, there seems to be no convincing evidence. Among the railroad executives there may have been some sentiment against Pullman's recalcitrance in the matter; but, as members of the General Managers' Association, they were careful to assume a policy of complete aloofness in the labor difficulties of the Pullman Corporation. At the club, however, George Pullman engaged in casual conversation with some of the railroad managers, who agreed that the questions at issue should not be submitted to arbitration.[100] If the railroads had really desired to avoid a clash with labor, they could have encouraged or at least suggested to the Pullman Company a more conciliatory course. It thus appears that they welcomed the opportunity to destroy the American Railway Union[101] and would probably have frowned upon any attempt to terminate the struggle short of their objective.

George Pullman had no desire to remain in Chicago when signs were evident that serious disturbances might develop. On June 28, he and his family left the city for their palatial home on the seashore at Elberon, New Jersey, where he was out of all danger. During a part of the time he took refuge in his cottage "Castle Rest" on the St. Lawrence River at the Thousand Islands. Wherever he was, he remained in direct communication with his general offices, but to the press he pretended aloofness from the struggle, declaring that the whole matter was out of his hands.[102] In Chicago his home was placed under heavy guard. The women servants were removed to places of safety, and all valuable plate was deposited in the vaults of the Pullman Company.[103] Despite all the precaution, a dozen large plate-glass windows in the house were smashed on July 25 by an anarchist who, upon being arrested, cursed both the United States government and George Pullman.[104]

The conduct of the Pullman inhabitants during the struggle was highly commendable. While in some parts of Chicago rioting and disorders disturbed the peace, in the model town there was no trouble. On May 19, eight days after the employees had struck, the *Pullman Journal* declared, "In some respects the week here has seemed like a continuous Sunday."[105] This observation was equally true of every ensuing week. No injury was done or attempted against any property of the company. The mayor of Chicago revealed that not a pane of glass had been broken in that community during the twelve weeks of the strike and not one complaint of any kind had been filed with the city authorities by the Pullman Corporation.[106] The strikers, who scrupulously refrained from loitering on the streets of Pullman, held all their meetings in the near-by settlement of Kensington. Radical utterances were discouraged, and the strikers were repeatedly enjoined by their leaders to avoid saloons and to conduct themselves peacefully. On July 6 a regiment of the militia took up its position in the town of Pullman and remained there for several weeks, despite the splendid behavior of the people.[107] The nearest that violence approached the town was on July 5 and 6 when a mob, from South Chicago and Kensington, stopped trains and destroyed a number of boxcars on the Illinois Central tracks near Pullman. For a time the situation was critical, but it soon quieted down. In this riotous outbreak the Pullman inhabitants had no part[108] or in any other disturbance which occurred in Chicago.

By July 13 the strikers in Chicago had been virtually beaten. All rioting had disappeared, and train schedules were beginning to return to normal. On July 10 the militia had opened the way for the first train from the Stock Yards and successfully smashed the blockade.[109] The Rock Island Railroad began operation of suburban trains on July 10 and within two days resumed the movement of freight in the yards.[110] On other lines a similar story could be told. The rapid collapse of the strike was succinctly summarized by the Strike Commission in the following statement:

The action of the courts deprived the American Railway Union of leadership, enabled the General Managers' Association to disintegrate its forces, and

to make inroad into its ranks. The mob had worn out their fury, or had suc-
cumbed to the combined forces of the police, the United States troops and
marshals, and the state militia. The railroads were gradually repairing damages and resuming traffic with the aid of new men and with some of those
strikers who had not been offensively active or whose action was laid to intimidation or fear.[111]

At the height of the struggle there was in Chicago a mighty
array of more than fourteen thousand armed agents, including
the police, Illinois militia, deputy sheriffs, United States soldiers,
and deputy marshals.[112] Only after the situation had greatly
eased were these forces reduced. It was not until July 18 that
Richard Olney, after carefully canvassing the situation, recommended to President Cleveland that federal troops could safely
be retired from Chicago. Mayor Hopkins had given assurance
that the forces at his disposal were sufficient to preserve peace and
enforce the laws. At the last minute, however, Edwin Walker informed Olney that, since several thousand determined switchmen, supported by switch engineers and firemen, were still on
strike, the complete evacuation of the soldiers would be inadvisable. The attorney-general, notwithstanding his high regard for
Walker's judgment, remained unconvinced that the evacuation
order should be countermanded.[113] On the nineteenth of July
Hopkins was accordingly informed that all federal troops would
be withdrawn without further delay.[114] The same day witnessed
the withdrawal of the first contingent of state troops, but the
evacuation of the militia proceeded very gradually and was not
completed until August 7.[115]

Despite the odds, crushing as they were, Eugene Debs was
slow to admit defeat. Hopefully he looked to the West for continued support, as he vainly tried to rally the scattered forces of
his union for a last-ditch fight. With the conflict convulsing a
large part of the nation, Debs clung to the belief that the fortunes
of the battle in Chicago would not necessarily determine the final
outcome. Sustained by an indomitable will but not always a
master of realism, he grossly overrated the staying quality of the
strikers elsewhere, who were faced by the same pitiless opposition
that was sapping the vitality and undermining the morale of the

Chicago strikers. While others were abandoning all hope for the American Railway Union, Debs could still hurl defiance at the general managers. As late as July 15, he boldly asserted:

We will win our fight in the West because we are better organized there. There is brawn and energy in the West. Men there are loyal, fraternal and true. When they believe they are right, they all go out and stay out until the fight is over. . . . . We will show the general managers that the attempt to crush organized labor will result in receiverships for all their railroads.[116]

NOTES

1. Cleveland, *op. cit.*, pp. 236–37, quoting General Miles to the secretary of war, July 6, 1894.

2. June 29, 1894, p. 1.

3. *Chicago Tribune*, June 27, 1894, p. 2.

4. *Inter Ocean*, July 1, 1894, p. 1.

5. *Ibid.*, p. 2; *U.S. Strike Commission Report*, pp. 213–15.

6. *U.S. Strike Commission Report*, pp. 325–26.

7. *Ibid.*, pp. 213–16, 231, 238–41; *New York Times*, July 2, 1894, p. 2.

8. *U.S. Strike Commission Report*, p. 223.

9. *Ibid.*, p. 385; *Report of the General Superintendent of Police of . . . . Chicago . . . . 1894*, pp. 11–13, 14.

10. *Report of the General Superintendent of Police of . . . . Chicago . . . . 1894*, pp. 14–15.

11. *Ibid.; U.S. Strike Commission Report.*, pp. 216–17, 363–64; *Biennial Report of the Adjutant General of Illinois . . . . , 1893 and 1894*, p. 173; Schofield, *op. cit.*, pp. 500–501.

12. Schofield, *op. cit.*, pp. 499–500, quoting Miles to Schofield, July 5, 1894.

13. *Ibid.*, pp. 498, quoting Miles to Schofield, July 4, 1894.

14. *Ibid.*, pp. 499–501, quoting Schofield to Miles, July 5, 1894, and Miles to Schofield, July 6, 1894.

15. *Ibid.*, pp. 505–6.

16. *Ibid.*, pp. 494–95.

17. *Report of the Fire Marshal to the City Council of . . . . Chicago . . . . 1894*, pp. 90–91; *Inter Ocean*, July 6, 1894, p. 1.

18. *Journal of the Senate of the Thirty-ninth General Assembly of the State of Illinois* (1895), p. 32, governor's message, quoting from *Report of the Chicago Fire Department.*

19. *Inter Ocean*, July 7, 1894, p. 1; *Report of the Fire Marshal to the City Council of . . . . Chicago . . . . 1894*, pp. 91–92.

20. *Report of the Fire Marshal . . . . ,* p. 92; *Inter Ocean*, July 7, 1894, p. 1.

21. *Inter Ocean*, July 7, 1894, p. 1.

22. *Biennial Report of the Adjutant General of Illinois . . . . , 1893 and 1894*, pp. 174–76; *Report of the General Superintendent of Police of . . . . Chicago . . . . 1894*, pp. 15–16; *Inter Ocean*, July 8, 1894, pp. 1–2.

23. *New York Times*, July 1, 1894, p. 2, and July 4, 1894, p. 2; *Chicago Herald*, July 6, 1894, p. 4.

24. *Biennial Report of the Adjutant General of Illinois . . . . , 1893 and 1894*, p. xxvi; *Chicago Times*, July 6, 1894, p. 4.

25. *Proceedings of the General Managers' Association . . . . 1894*, p. 182.

26. *Inter Ocean*, July 8, 1894, p. 1.

27. *New York World*, July 9, 1894, p. 1.

28. *Ibid.*, July 8, 1894, p. 2; *Proceedings of the General Managers' Association . . . . 1894*, p. 180.

29. Cleveland Papers.

30. George A. Williams to Cleveland, July 6, 1894, *ibid.*

31. *New York Times*, July 9, 1894, p. 1.

32. James D. Richardson, *A Compilation of the Messages and Papers of the Presidents*, XII, 5931–32.

33. *Appendix to the . . . . Report of the Attorney General . . . . 1896*, p. 77.

34. Schofield, *op. cit.*, pp. 504–5.

35. *Inter Ocean*, July 8, 1894, p. 1.

36. Schofield, *op. cit.*, pp. 503–4, quoting "General Order No. 6," issued by General Miles.

37. *Ibid.*, p. 501.

38. *Ibid.*, p. 508.

39. *U.S. Strike Commission Report*, p. xviii.

40. *Report of the General Superintendent of Police of . . . . Chicago . . . .1894*, pp. 26–27.

41. *Annual Report of the Secretary of War . . . . 1894*, I, 109.

42. P. 93.

43. *U.S. Strike Commission Report*, pp. 144, 339.

44. *Chicago Times*, July 8, 1894, p. 1.

45. *Debs: His Life, Writings and Speeches*, pp. 192, 194.

46. Caroline Lloyd, *op. cit.*, I, 152.

47. *Ibid.*

48. *U.S. Strike Commission Report*, p. 20.

49. *Ibid.*, p. 350.

50. "Editor's Table," *New England Magazine*, XXI (1896), 254–55.

51. *Ibid.; Debs: His Life, Writings and Speeches*, p. 199.

52. *U.S. Strike Commission Report*, p. 62.

53. *Report of the General Superintendent of Police of . . . . Chicago . . . . 1894*, pp. 17–18.

54. *New York World*, July 10, 1894, p. 1.

55. *Report of the General Superintendent of Police of . . . . Chicago . . . . 1894*, pp. 5–6.

56. *U.S. Strike Commission Report*, p. xviii.

57. *Report of the General Superintendent of Police of . . . . Chicago . . . . 1894*, pp. 6, 28, 155.

58. *U.S. Strike Commission Report*, pp. 276, 327–28.

59. *New York Times*, July 12, 1894, p. 4.

60. *U.S. Strike Commission Report*, p. 276.

61. *Ibid.*, p. 341.

62. *Ibid.*, p. 357; *Chicago Times*, July 7, 1894, p. 1.

63. *U.S. Strike Commission Report*, p. 387.

64. *Ibid.*, pp. 390–93.

65. *Ibid.*, pp. 370–72.

66. *Ibid.*, pp. 374–76.
67. *Ibid.*, pp. 208–9, 360–62, 368–70.
68. *Ibid.*, p. 140.
69. *Ibid.*, pp. 140, 357.
70. *Ibid.*, pp. 383–84.
71. *Ibid.*, p. 384.
72. *Ibid.*, pp. 19–20, 25, 29–30, 47, 107, 140, 151, 209, 349–50.
73. *New York World*, July 7, 1894, p. 2.
74. *Ibid.*, July 5, 1894, p. 8, and July 7, 1894, p. 2.
75. *Chicago Times*, July 7, 1894, p. 1, and July 8, 1894, p. 1.
76. *U.S. Strike Commission Report*, pp. 26, 114.
77. *New York Times*, July 6, 1894, p. 2.
78. *Ibid.*, July 1, 1894, p. 1, and July 2, 1894, p. 2.
79. *Ibid.*, July 7, 1894, p. 2.
80. *Ibid.*, July 8, 1894, p. 2.
81. *Ibid.*, July 10, 1894, p. 1; *New York World*, July 10, 1894, p. 1; *Chicago Times*, July 9, 1894, p. 1; *Inter Ocean*, July 9, 1894, p. 1.
82. *New York Times*, July 10, 1894, p. 1; *Chicago Times*, July 10, 1894, p. 2; *U.S. Strike Commission Report*, pp. 350–51.
83. *Chicago Times*, July 10, 1894, p. 2.
84. *Ibid.*, July 12, 1894, p. 1, and July 13, 1894, p. 3; *Inter Ocean*, July 11, 1894, p. 1; *New York Times*, July 12, 1894, p. 1.
85. *U.S. Strike Commission Report*, pp. 189–90; "Proceedings of Briggs Conference," *American Federationist*, I (1894), 131–32.
86. "Proceedings of Briggs Conference," p. 132; *U.S. Strike Commission Report*, p. 190; Samuel Gompers, *Seventy Years of Life and Labor*, I, 414.
87. "Proceedings of Briggs Conference," p. 133; Gompers, *op. cit.*, I, 408–10; *U.S. Strike Commission Report*, pp. 154–55, 191.
88. *U.S. Strike Commission Report*, pp. 191–94; *American Federationist*, I (1894), 124; Gompers, *op. cit.*, I, 410–12.
89. "Proceedings of Briggs Conference," p. 133.
90. *Ibid.*, p. 125; *U.S. Strike Commission Report*, pp. 192–93.
91. *U.S. Strike Commission Report*, p. 195; Gompers, *op. cit.*, I, 404–5.
92. *American Federationist*, I (1894), 121–23.
93. *U.S. Strike Commission Report*, p. 58.
94. *Ibid.*, pp. 146–47, 255–56, 271, 274, 356.
95. *Ibid.*, pp. 256–58, 271–75.
96. *Ibid.*, p. 424.
97. *Ibid.*, pp. xxxix, 459–60, 590, 645–48.
98. *Ibid.*, pp. 351, 590; *New York World*, July 12, 1894, p. 2.
99. *U.S. Strike Commission Report*, pp. xxxix, 556–57, 585.
100. *Ibid.*, p. 562.
101. *New York Times*, July 3, 1894, p. 2; *Chicago Tribune*, June 29, 1894, p. 1.
102. *New York World*, July 4, 1894, p. 7; *New York Times*, July 4, 1894, p. 2, and July 12, 1894, p. 1.
103. *New York Times*, July 9, 1894, p. 2.
104. *Ibid.*, July 26, 1894, p. 4.

105. May 19, 1894, p. 8.

106. *U.S. Strike Commission Report*, p. 349.

107. *Report of the General Superintendent of Police of* . . . . *Chicago* . . . . *1894*, p. 21; Carwardine, *op. cit.*, pp. 38–40.

108. Carwardine, *op. cit.*, pp. 41–44; *Pullman Journal*, July 7, 1894, p. 8.

109. *Biennial Report of the Adjutant General of Illinois* . . . . , *1893 and 1894*, p. xxvi.

110. *U.S. Strike Commission Report*, pp. 218–19.

111. *Ibid.*, p. xlii.

112. *Ibid.*, p. xix.

113. *Appendix to the* . . . . *Report of the Attorney General* . . . . *1896*, pp. 86–87, 90–91, 256.

114. *U.S. Strike Commission Report*, p. 352.

115. *Report of the General Superintendent of Police of* . . . . *Chicago* . . . . *1894*, pp. 27–28.

116. *New York World*, July 16, 1894, p. 2.

CHAPTER XI

NATION-WIDE CHARACTER OF THE STRUGGLE

WHILE seeking to make the boycott against Pullman cars effective, the American Railway Union found itself involved in a struggle of gigantic proportions. The General Managers' Association, representing forty-one thousand miles of tracks, vigorously resisted the boycott, as did virtually all other lines that were in any way affected. With incredible speed the struggle swept over the country, involving twenty-seven states and territories. Although Chicago remained the heart of the disturbances, many of the railroads running east, north, and south were forced to operate intermittently, while all the transcontinental lines except the Great Northern were paralyzed by the blockade. In meeting the situation the federal government swore in many thousands of deputy marshals and invoked the assistance of troops from six of the eight military areas of the United States. The commanding officers of the departments of California, Colorado, Columbia, Missouri, the Dakotas, and the Platte were given authority to act in the emergency. Over sixteen thousand federal soldiers were thus made available to protect the railroads.[1]

When the boycott was launched, labor could not foresee how far reaching would be the scope of the conflict or what powerful forces would be mustered in defense of the railroads. With crusading ardor and unrestrained enthusiasm the convention of the American Railway Union had accepted the boycott as the only feasible means of forcing the Pullman Company to assume a more conciliatory policy toward labor. In response to the plea of Eugene Debs for support, tens of thousands of Railroad workers throughout the nation endeavored to halt the operation of Pullman palace cars. The employees who refused to handle such cars were summarily discharged, and this would generally precipitate an immediate strike among the switchmen, flagmen, and other categories of workers to whom the union of Eugene Debs had such a strong appeal. At St. Louis, for example, the employees of the Missouri Pacific Railroad filed notice that they would not handle Pullman sleepers. When one of their members, a switchman, was discharged for refusing to move one of these cars, the workers demanded his reinstatement and, upon being rebuffed, called a strike. The local union at Butte, Montana, demanded the cessation of sleeper service and then ordered the men to quit work when the warning was not heeded.[2] In this manner many of the strikes occurred.

If labor revealed unexpected unity, the railroads displayed even greater singleness of purpose. The right to boycott palace cars was denied, and every attempt to sidetrack these cars was resisted. Railroad after railroad was thus drawn into the conflict, even including some that did not handle Pullman cars. This situation was primarily due to the fact that in some of the large cities the switching was done by associations; and so interwoven were the relations of the railroads at these points that when one line was involved the others could not very well escape. Local grievances accentuated the difficulties and strengthened the desire for sympathetic action on the part of railroad workers who were not themselves directly involved in the boycott.[3]

The executives of the union advised against strikes on roads that did not use or would agree not to use Pullman cars, but in the heat of the struggle such advice was not always followed. The youthful character of the union and the nature of the struggle may explain why some of the local unions preferred to heed their own counsel. This was quite evident in the case of the Mobile and Ohio Railroad, which maintained Pullman sleeper service between St. Louis and New Orleans. Like many other roads, this line was quickly involved in a strike growing out of the boycott. Not anxious to make an issue of the matter, the Mobile and Ohio decided to make no further attempt to operate palace cars until after the affair was settled and so informed Eugene Debs on June 28. Since the road did not belong to the General Managers' Association, he promptly recommended that this strike be terminated. The local union, however, refused to comply on the grounds that such action would weaken the united front of labor.[4]

The situation on the Cleveland, Cincinnati, Chicago, and St. Louis Railroad—best known as the Big Four—presented a somewhat different picture. This line was neither a member of the General Managers' Association nor an operator of Pullman cars. Quite obviously a strike on such a road was not within the scope of the union's strategy, but one nevertheless occurred because of the dissatisfaction engendered by a 10 per cent reduction in wages. On July 3 the Big Four sent two representatives to confer with the directors of the American Railway Union for the purpose of making peace on terms agreeable to that organization. Distrust in the integrity of the road, however, caused the peace move to fail, even though a continuation of the strike could hardly be expected to serve the cause of the boycott.[5] This lack of confidence may have been justified, since the Big Four, on the very day it was making overtures for peace, wired Richard Olney about the "urgent" need for blanket injunctions in Indiana and southern Illinois. In response to this request the attorney-general promptly instructed the district attorneys in these states to apply to the courts for such writs.[6]

The willingness of strikers to permit mail trains to move without molestation, provided there were no Pullman cars attached,[7] found no favor in the eyes of either government or railroad officials. At Sacramento, California, for instance, a train was assembled on July 3 containing several mail cars and some sleepers. When the character of the train became known, members of the American Railway Union protested and then quickly uncoupled the objectionable cars and pushed them into the yards. The railroad officials now refused to permit the train to leave, although its departure would have met no further opposition from labor. Significantly, the postmaster at Sacramento on this occasion telegraphed Postmaster-General Bissell that a committee of union members had given assurance that their organization did not desire to interfere with the transportation of mail and would even furnish a crew to take the mail train to its destination.[8]

Local unions elsewhere revealed no disposition to impede the movement of mail, which, it was boldly asserted, could be transported without the use of Pullman sleepers. At Salt Lake City on

July 4 the American Railway Union even went so far as to apply to the federal district court for an injunction compelling the Union Pacific Railroad to operate trains without Pullman sleepers.[9] If such a court order could have been secured here and at other vital points, the movement of mail would have encountered little difficulty, and one of the most impelling causes for federal intervention would have been eliminated.

The omnibus injunction issued in Chicago on July 2 seemed to furnish the railroads with their greatest hope. This "Gatling gun on paper" was viewed by the general managers everywhere as a weapon of extraordinary potency. Without waiting for the government to decide where and when the injunction should be employed, the railroads urged the widest possible use of it and even presumed to counsel the Department of Justice precisely at what points it was needed. Such advice was by no means ignored. Prompted by Richard Olney, many district attorneys quickly prepared sweeping injunction bills, in some cases doing so with the co-operation of railroad lawyers.

In seeking this protection the railroads often preferred to place the matter squarely and bluntly before the attorney-general instead of intrusting to the district attorneys the exclusive right of doing so.[10] Special effort, however, was made by the railroad counsel to impress these lesser agents with the seriousness of the situation and the need for immediate action. It was thus not unusual for Richard Olney to receive almost simultaneously from the United States attorney and the railroad executives in a district the same urgent plea for restraining orders.

The technique employed was well illustrated in the case of two middle western railroads,[11] which notified Olney on July 5 that the movement of mail and interstate traffic in Missouri was seriously jeopardized. They requested that the federal attorney at Kansas City be directed to file an injunction similar to the one at Chicago. The legal advisers of the railroads had already convinced the district attorney that a dangerous situation existed. On July 6 he wired Olney about the need for an injunction and was promptly granted authority to apply for the writ. The railroad lawyers very obligingly offered to assist in the preparation and presentation of the bill—a course which the federal attorney did not deem necessary, although he did submit it to them for approval before filing it in the federal court.[12]

At Memphis, Tennessee, the United States attorney asked permission to secure a restraining order but made the request only after several railroads had urged him to do so.[13] Elsewhere similar pressure was applied and, flanked by railroads and a corporation-minded attorney-general, the district attorneys had virtually no choice of action. The federal attorney at Milwaukee was instructed to apply for a writ simply because Edwin Walker had proposed such a course. Later Walker recommended the appointment of a special assistant to aid this attorney and even nominated a man for the position.[14] Olney promptly granted both requests. The attorney-general seldom took the trouble to canvass the situation in order to determine what need really existed for a restraining order. His plan to blanket the entire nation, if necessary, with omnibus injunctions soon became apparent; and the extreme willingness on his part to authorize his agents to seek these writs, often upon the request of a railroad lawyer, bears eloquent proof of the unity of purpose which motivated the Department of Justice and the railroads.

In serving injunction writs the marshals and their deputies experienced trouble, since it was difficult for them to establish the identity of the offenders. The writs were so devised that unknown parties could be made defendants upon the discovery of their names. The experience of Henry Bohl, federal marshal for the southern district of Ohio, was no different from that of many others. He requested the railroads to supply the names and residences of the strikers and in addition to permit loyal employees to serve as special deputy marshals. Such men, it was explained, could render effective aid in recognizing the offenders and in serving judicial writs. The railroads did as requested, with results that seemed most gratifying. In disclosing to Richard Olney the strategy used, Bohl announced that, since these special deputies were paid by the railroads as regular employees, the government was under no obligation to compensate them.[15] To this position Olney took violent exception, declaring in a note bristling with indignation that the government asked no "charitable contributions from railroads or any other corporations or persons." All deputy marshals, he insisted, would be paid by the government, and payments already made by any railroad would be considered advances for which the company would be subsequently reimbursed by the federal treasury.[16]

As the battle lines lengthened, the executives of the American Railway Union were faced by the extremely difficult task of coordinating the activity of hundreds of local 'unions, many of which had but recently mushroomed into existence. Although strong in enthusiasm, most of these local groups were weak in experience and rather loosely knit. The democratic character of the American Railway Union, although exemplary, was perhaps a source of weakness, since so much freedom of action remained with each local organization. Quite obviously the task of directing all these units in a manner best calculated to promote victory was one which must have given Eugene Debs the greatest concern. It was necessary not only to issue instruction to scores of local unions in matters of strategy and policy but, equally important, to strengthen their morale against the extraordinary measures of the government and also against the avalanche of propaganda that poured with such virulence from the press.

In directing the strike Debs sent thousands of telegrams to all parts of the nation. None of the messages counseled violence, while many urged the men to remain firm but peaceful. In advising local unions to strike, Debs would instruct them first to select a committee to take charge and to forward the chairman's name to headquarters. By this method local groups could more easily be kept within bounds and would more likely remain subject to the guidance of the executive board. In seeking to bolster morale Debs injected an optimistic tone into all his communications, stressing the inevitability of victory and discounting the efficacy of measures taken by the government. Relative to the injunction, he was careful to explain that such an instrument could not possibly move trains. In the use of troops he recognized "an old method of intimidation" but emphatically denied that soldiers could operate trains.[17] Typical of many telegrams was the one which he sent to the local union at Clinton, Iowa, on July 4:

Pay no attention to rumors. We are gaining ground everywhere. Don't get scared by troops or otherwise. Stand pat. None will return to work until all return. If they do they are scabs and will be treated as such. Not men enough in world to fill vacancies and more occurring hourly.

On the same day Eugene Debs triumphantly announced to many local unions throughout the nation that the Illinois Central, Wabash, Monon, and the Big Four were now involved in a strike at virtually every point. Hoping that this news would spur the strikers on to greater endeavor, he counseled them to redouble their effort in persuading other categories of railroad employees to quit work. To all, whether members or not, was pledged the full protection of the union.[18] In one telegram Debs warned that "all who work are assisting capital to defeat labor."[19] On the sixth of July he advised:

Every true man must quit now and remain out until the fight is won. There can be no half way ground. Men must be for or against us. Our cause is gaining ground daily and our success is only a question of a few days. Do not falter in this hour. Stand erect. Proclaim your manhood. Labor must win now or never. Our victory will be positive and complete. Whatever happens, do not give credence to rumors and newspaper reports.[20]

The tactics of Eugene Debs were construed by the attorney-general as an attack upon organized society. On July 4 Olney declared: "We have been brought to the ragged edge of anarchy, and it is time to see whether the law is sufficiently strong to prevent this condition of affairs. If not, the sooner we know it the better, that it may be changed."[21] Neither in the law nor in himself did he at any time lose confidence. The technique which he employed varied little from district to district. In enforcing the injunction writs, each marshal was instructed to swear in as many deputies as were deemed necessary. In the event of difficulties the marshal was promptly advised to apply for the assistance of regular soldiers and in making the request to join, if possible, with the federal judge and district attorney. In response to this appeal United States troops were quickly rushed to the scene of trouble and the most energetic measures taken.

One of the first scenes of serious trouble was on the Santa Fe Railroad between La Junta, Colorado, and Las Vegas, New Mexico. Serious financial difficulties had forced the road into federal receivership, leaving wages between two and four months in arrears. The announcement of the boycott thus found many of the Santa Fe employees in a desperate condition and in an ugly mood and determined to follow the leadership of the American Railway Union.[22] Pullman cars were sidetracked, and the ensuing strike proved so effective in this area that traffic ceased. The communities most critically affected were Trinidad, Colorado, and Raton, New Mexico. Mail and passengers were detained, with considerable inconvenience to the latter, some of whom quickly exhausted their funds. In the Raton yards the passengers were fed by the railroad company.

With the first outbreak of trouble in this region on June 30, Richard Olney authorized the federal attorneys in Colorado and New Mexico to see that mail trains were unobstructed and to procure whatever warrants or other judicial processes were necessary.[23] When Attorney Hemingway at Santa Fe failed to acknowledge these instructions, Olney impatiently demanded to know the reason. Hemingway quickly explained that as far as he had been advised there was no obstruction of the mails in the Territory of New Mexico "but only a refusal of employees to work. . . . . I do not understand that the mere refusal to work," he protested, "is obstruction of the mail, but if in error advise me, and will proceed at once." The attorney-general removed all doubt about the matter when he bluntly ordered Hemingway on July 2 to secure at once a restraining order, if he had not already done so, and to instruct the marshal to furnish adequate protection for the operation of all trains.[24] In both Colorado and New Mexico deputy marshals were recruited to enforce the court orders, but they proved inept and unsuccessful. The quality of these men was poor, and the extraordinary scope of power which was theirs to exercise against the strikers and local officials benefited nobody and served only to aggravate the situation.[25]

At Trinidad—junction for the Santa Fe Road and the Union Pacific, Denver, and Gulf line—a large crowd surrounded and completely disarmed fifty-two deputy marshals as they approached the town on July 1. Whether this was accomplished by strikers, as charged by the press, cannot be determined, but it was evident that some of the mob carried arms. Sentiment at Trinidad was overwhelmingly in favor of the strikers. The restraining order posted here was torn up and the authority of the federal court in other ways flouted. Without notifying Governor David Waite of this situation or seeking any assistance from the state, the United States marshal and district judge of Colorado promptly laid the facts before Richard Olney, who in turn placed the matter before Grover Cleveland. Since both of the railroads involved were in federal receivership, the need for military intervention seemed very urgent. In a hastily summoned conference the President conferred with his closest advisers and decided to order General MacDonald McCook at Fort Logan, near Denver, to send a force to Trinidad.[26]

Early in the morning of July 2, five companies left Fort Logan. At the railroad junction of Pueblo they found the telegraph wires cut and all trains unable to move. After easing the situation here and seeing that the telegraph lines were partially restored, the troops pushed on to Trinidad, arriving in the late afternoon of the same day. The railroad tracks were quickly cleared of the mobs and order restored. Under the protection of bayonets the deputy marshals on July 4 arrested forty-eight "ringleaders," who in a meeting of the strikers had made what were construed to be "incendiary speeches." These men, together with twelve arrested at Pueblo, were promptly transferred to Denver, where they were jailed for contempt of court.[27]

In the meantime the situation at Raton, New Mexico, grew steadily worse. Here the American Railway Union lodge comprised about five hundred members. In enforcing the boycott they were supported by three hundred coal miners, mostly foreigners, who were already on strike. The sheriff of the county was sympathetic to labor and convinced that an invasion of deputy marshals might lead to a serious clash and so warned Marshal Hall not to enter Raton with armed deputies. Informed of this, Edward P. Seeds, associate justice of the Supreme Court in New

Mexico, wired Hall to ignore the sheriff and, if he interfered, to arrest him. Fortified with this authority, the marshal and eighty-five deputies entered Raton, where they were received with unconcealed hostility. In the hotels and wherever the deputies sought room and board, the servants quit, with the result that Hall was obliged to fill their places with deputy marshals.[28] Unable to move trains, the marshal, supported by Associate Justice Seeds, petitioned Olney for troops on July 2 and was promptly informed that the soldiers who had left Fort Logan for Trinidad would also be ordered to furnish protection at Raton.[29]

During the night of July 3 some rioters at the little mining town of Blossburg, three miles above Raton, turned sixteen cars loose, which, gaining speed on the heavy grade, crashed into Raton, littering the right of way with wreckage. It took most of the next day to clear the tracks, and in the evening Colonel Pearson with the Tenth Infantry arrived. Immediately the coal miners, some of whom were armed, left for their homes. Completely overawed, the strikers gave little trouble thereafter. Thirteen of the worst offenders were arrested for contempt of court and transferred to the jail at Santa Fe.[30] Troops were subsequently rushed to other points, including New Castle and Las Vegas. At the latter point four mail trains and two hundred and fifty passengers were being detained; but here, as elsewhere, all resistance was soon broken. Nevertheless, the railroads were unprepared to move trains immediately because of insufficient crews. It was not until July 11 that the Union Pacific, Denver, and Gulf Railroad resumed its regular train service, although the Santa Fe began operation somewhat earlier. While nobody was killed at any of these points, the danger of further trouble was considered so great that federal troops were kept on duty at Trinidad, Raton, Las Vegas, and New Castle during the rest of July and throughout August.[31]

In the Far West transportation was seriously disrupted as early as June 28. Here the American Railway Union enjoyed the sympathetic support of a large proportion of the population. This feeling was due in large measure to the fact that labor was arrayed in the struggle against the Southern Pacific Railroad—a corporation which had gained monopolistic control of virtually all rail facilities in California. Even the ferries plying across San Francisco Bay, as well as most of the streetcar lines in San Francisco, were subject to the control of this colossus. Transportation rates were exorbitant, and the policies of this corporation in every way seemed to reflect an attitude of supreme indifference to, if not contempt for, the public. By the bulk of people in the Pacific states this monopoly was viewed with suspicion and open hostility. Many condemned it as a flagrant violation of the Sherman Anti-trust Act. The refusal of the Department of Justice to raise a finger in the matter contributed to the growing impression that the laws of the United States were not enforced impartially as between the vested interests and labor unions.[32]

Popular support for the strikers and animosity for the Southern Pacific Railroad manifested itself in various ways. Unlike the newspapers in other states, the press in California revealed such a friendly attitude toward labor that the *Nation* on July 12 gloomily observed that there "does not seem to be a voice raised there in favor of law and civil government; and the inconvenience and losses to which the public are subjected seem to be accepted willingly, so long as the railroads suffer quite as much or more."[33] In seeking men to serve as deputies, the marshals encountered difficulty. Even more significant was the refusal of state troops, when mustered into service, to charge or fire upon the mobs.[34] Joseph Call, a special federal attorney at Los Angeles, became so apprehensive of public sentiment during the early stages of the strike that he believed open rebellion to be an imminent possibility. Even after the collapse of the strike Call faced the future with foreboding due to the deep-rooted bitterness toward the Southern Pacific and other monopolies. To Olney on July 18 he conveyed his fears:

> I do not hesitate to speak plainly when I say, that in my opinion, if the United States Government cannot protect the people of the Pacific states against these monopolies, it will require a larger standing army than the Government now possesses to uphold the power and dignity of the United States.[35]

The first trouble in California was the signal for Richard Olney to instruct the district attorneys at San Francisco and Los Angeles to take the necessary measures to prevent interference with the movement of mail and interstate commerce. Against the increasing effectiveness of the boycott, however, the marshals and their deputies seemed helpless; nor did the writs of injunction, secured at the behest of the attorney-general, improve the situation.[36]

Los Angeles was the first locality in the state to witness military intervention and under circumstances unlike any which characterized the use of troops elsewhere. The boycott had developed peacefully but effectively. Since the marshal was critically ill, Olney believed the situation required the services of the military; and, without waiting for the injunction to be filed and the customary demand for soldiers to be made, he prevailed upon the President on July 1 to issue the necessary orders. On the next day, Joseph Denis, United States attorney at Los Angeles, was duly informed of the action and instructed to co-operate with the soldiers when they arrived. On the fourth of July six companies of regulars reached the city only to find conditions very quiet but no trains moving.[37]

At no time, either before or after the arrival of these forces, was an overt act committed, except on July 10 when some cars were overturned at a railroad crossing. The commander of the troops, Colonel William R. Shafter, was nevertheless in receipt of rumors that the strikers were secretly arming and preparing to attack every train with a Pullman sleeper.[38] Some of the rumors caused the district attorney considerable anxiety, as evidenced by the cipher telegrams which he sent to Olney on the fourth of July. In one Denis divulged an alleged report that for the preceding ten days strike sympathizers, heavily armed, had been drifting into Los Angeles. He expressed the fear that in enforcing the injunction the government might encounter resistance from five thousand armed men. In another message Denis asked frantically for five hundred stands of arms and one hundred thousand rounds of ammunition to arm deputy marshals and "such citizens as have volunteered to conserve the peace."[39] The district attorney was afraid that the three hundred soldiers on duty would be unable to cope with the situation. On July 5, however, the tension seemed to have eased in the mind of Denis, judging by the reassuring dispatch which he sent to the attorney-general on that day.[40]

Under the protection of bayonets, enough men were secured to enable the railroads to resume service gradually. The first overland mail train for the East left Los Angeles without a mishap on July 7, and thereafter other trains departed, each carrying a small detachment of troops. By such means the route to San Francisco was subsequently opened. After July 15 the practice of using a military escort for each train was discontinued, but the troops remained on duty in the Los Angeles area until the middle of August.[41]

Elsewhere in California, particularly at Sacramento and Oakland, serious difficulties arose. Both of these cities were important railroad terminals, and in each of them the number of striking employees was exceptionally high. At Sacramento—the worst storm center in the state—there were twenty-five hundred railroad workers, of whom all but four hundred joined the strike. From Stockton, Lathrop, and other communities located on lines converging at Sacramento hundreds of railroad workers came to join those already on strike in this strategically important junction. One large party, many heavily armed, arrived from Dunsmuir by means of a train which they had seized. At least three thousand determined strikers thus gathered at Sacramento and, supported by a sympathetic public, quickly developed into a formidable force.[42] At Oakland the same situation prevailed, but on a somewhat smaller scale.

The first major incident occurred at Sacramento on July 3 when the United States marshal, Barry Baldwin, and his deputies endeavored to protect a mail train which was being assembled. Because it contained some Pullman cars, the strikers intervened and forcibly disconnected them. While trying to persuade the strikers to disperse, Baldwin was roughly handled and in seeking to make arrests was thwarted by a large and turbulent crowd. Convinced that further effort would prove futile, he promptly called upon the governor of California for help—a course distinctly contrary to that which was being followed by other marshals under similar circumstances. The response to the plea was immediate, and on the following morning two regiments of the state militia reached Sacramento. The troops, however, proved sympathetic to the strikers and wholly unreliable in any offensive operation. Some privates even left the ranks in open defiance of the orders, while the great body of these soldiers demonstrated an unwillingness to charge against or fire upon the strikers. In view of such disaffection the marshal could see no hope of relieving the situation without federal soldiers and so notified Charles A. Garter, the United States attorney at San Francisco.[43]

In the meantime conditions at Oakland were becoming critical. A large mob, which had taken possession of the railroad yards, adopted the practice of seizing live engines wherever they could be found and, by raking the fires and blowing off the steam, leaving them dead on the tracks.[44] Owing to conditions here and at Sacramento, Garter believed the time ripe for federal armed intervention and promptly dispatched to Richard Olney on July 5 several telegrams setting forth the imperative need for regular troops.[45]

The situation which so alarmed Garter was but one phase of the struggle extending throughout the entire length of the rail line from San Francisco to Omaha and cannot be treated apart from events occurring on this overland route. In response to the plea of Eugene Debs for concerted action, the employees on the Central Pacific and Union Pacific railroads promptly sidetracked Pullman cars and, in doing so, paralyzed transportation. Incidents arose, and in suppressing them the federal government developed a co-ordinated plan of military action.

The Union Pacific suffered little actual violence from the boycott in Nebraska and Wyoming. In the latter state the railroad ran through a sparsely settled country, and the population at some points consisted largely of railroad men engaged in the strike. Public sentiment was very favorable to the cause of labor —a condition which may explain why the city authorities at Rawlins, Wyoming, on one occasion ordered all the deputy marshals out of the town. Because of such sentiments the marshal for that state found it impossible to secure sufficient deputies to clear the tracks and enforce the orders of the court. Nor was the railroad company able to supply new men to operate the trains, allegedly because of the intimidating and threatening attitude of the strikers.[46]

At Ogden, Utah—western terminal of the Union Pacific—the strikers were in absolute control of the railroad yards and used force, whenever necessary, to uncouple Pullman cars. Some engines and cars were damaged when railroad officials persisted in the attempt to operate sleepers. Supported by public sentiment, the strikers flouted the court orders and in various ways defied the marshal, who was able to raise only a small force of deputies. When the omnibus injunction, secured by order of the attorney-general, was read to a large crowd on July 4, the feeling was one of open and contemptuous hostility. The marshal did not dare make any arrests for fear such action would precipitate a riot. All mail and interstate trains ceased to move—a situation which, in the judgment of railroad officials and federal agents, necessitated immediate intervention by the military.[47] Shortly before the arrival of troops, fires were set simultaneously in seven different places in Ogden, presumably for the purpose of burning the city, although the value of the property actually destroyed did not exceed one hundred thousand dollars. In the opinion of the United States district attorney, this was not the work of strikers but of thieves and criminals, "who take advantage of a strike or any outbreak of that kind to do their nefarious and wicked work."[48]

The Central Pacific was even more completely paralyzed than the Union Pacific. To Richard Olney the situation called for federal soldiers to be employed wherever needed in order to restore uninterrupted communication between Omaha and San Francisco. In justifying such a course the President held that troops were necessary not only to protect interstate commerce and the mails and to enforce the judicial processes but also to keep the Union Pacific and Central Pacific Roads open for military and other governmental purposes as contemplated by the congressional acts which chartered these companies. On July 7 Cleveland ordered the commanding officers of the Department of the Platte and the Department of California to act promptly in meeting the situation. The latter general, Thomas H. Ruger, was further authorized to consult with the governor of California relative to the availability of the militia and, whenever practicable, to co-operate with such troops. This somewhat extraordinary instruction was due to the belief that Ruger's command might not be adequate to cope with a situation which seemed desperate.[49]

Acting simultaneously, the two generals endeavored to carry out their instructions promptly. The commander of the Department of the Platte, John R. Brooke, experienced less difficulty than Ruger and by a vigorous show of force quickly suppressed all resistance east of Ogden. West of this city, however, he was compelled to move more cautiously. Nine companies of troops were ordered to that terminal, four of which were subsequently assigned the task of opening the Central Pacific in co-operation with a similar force that was to move east from Sacramento. The troops that left Ogden on July 11 were authorized to go as far as Truckee, California, and to leave small detachments at all division terminals. In California the task of restoring rail communication seemed more formidable. With 300 of his troops already at Los Angeles, General Ruger considered his remaining force inadequate for the work at hand and so asked for assistance from the Mare Island Navy Yard. On the eleventh of July, 542 soldiers reached Sacramento by boat, and on the following day 370 sailors and marines landed at Oakland.[50]

The larger force was concentrated at Sacramento, because the strikers there were more numerous and conditions more menacing. With sabers drawn and bayonets fixed, the cavalry and infantry were able to drive the mobs away from all railroad stations, yards, and shops in that city. In accomplishing this feat, not a shot was fired and not a single person wounded. This bloodless victory, however, was quickly followed by overt acts. On the same day a train, heavily guarded by troops, left for San Francisco but was derailed only a few miles from Sacramento. Some fish bars and spikes had been expertly removed, causing the rails to spread. The engineer and three soldiers were killed outright, while several soldiers were wounded, one mortally. Responsibility for this outrage was charged against the strikers. Two days later, while protecting some employees in the yards at Sacramento, the troops were provoked by angry strikers, who became abusive and threw missiles. A few shots were fired, killing one striker and wounding another.[51] Aside from these incidents no further blood was shed, neither here nor in Oakland, where open conflict between the strikers and soldiers was fully expected. Shortly before the arrival of troops at Oakland, the wives and mothers of the strikers, in anticipation of trouble, organized the Ladies' Relief Organization. Bandages were prepared and arrangements made to turn one of the public halls into a hospital.[52] That no bloodshed occurred here was due perhaps as much to the coolness of the military as to any other factor. The presence of the militia may have had a salutary effect, since its conduct was tempered by sympathy for labor.

The opening of the Central Pacific was not long delayed. On July 13 a force left Sacramento to form a junction with a force en route from Ogden. At various points soldiers were detailed to protect railroad property. At Carlin, Nevada, two small bridges had been burned but were quickly repaired; otherwise no serious trouble was experienced in fulfilling this assignment. Under the protection of military guards, trains now began to move; and on July 16 the first through train from Ogden reached San Francisco. Although the naval force was withdrawn during the latter part of July, it was not until almost a month later that the marines and soldiers were removed from duty on the Central Pacific Railroad.[53]

The Northern Pacific Railroad was seriously involved almost from the very beginning. On June 26 some switching crews were discharged for refusing to handle Pullman coaches, and on the following day other dismissals occurred. The American Railway Union immediately decided to tie up the road, and instructions were accordingly wired to all division points. Passenger and freight trains were halted at numerous places, and within a short time virtually all traffic between St. Paul and Puget Sound ceased.[54] West of Fargo, North Dakota, and particularly throughout Montana, the strikers demonstrated the greatest strength. Deputy marshals and strikebreakers were subject to abusive and threatening language, but the amount of actual violence was not large. A few engines were ditched, and some property was destroyed, including the burning of the bridge at Hell

Gate River. Precisely how much of this vandalism was perpetrated by nonstrikers cannot be determined, although it is known that the floating population contained some vicious elements.[55] The general pattern followed in suppressing difficulties on the Northern Pacific was similar to that used elsewhere,[56] although in some respects the technique varied. On July 3 Brigadier General Merritt, commander of the Department of the Dakotas, informed the secretary of war that not since June 25 had he received any mail from Forts Keogh and Custer, located on the Northern Pacific line, and that he was unable to send supplies or the paymaster to these posts.[57] The telegram was referred to Richard Olney, who explained that when this railroad was chartered in 1864 Congress provided that it should always be available for the transportation of mails, troops, and military supplies. Since Congress had subsidized this line and had designated it as a military road, Olney concluded that it was the duty of the President, as commander-in-chief of the armed forces, to keep it open.[58]

It was not the urgent pleas from United States marshals and district attorneys, important as they were, that finally decided Richard Olney to press for immediate action on this road, but a telegram from James McNaught, counsel for the receivers of the Northern Pacific. In alluding to the helplessness of the deputy marshals McNaught stressed the inadequacy of any protection short of troops. He explained that the Northern Pacific would like to start a train immediately from St. Paul and that, if military protection were provided, the road could be opened and the strike broken within a week.[59] The suggestion met with the hearty indorsement of the attorney-general, who promptly transmitted it to the secretary of war with the recommendation that it be acted upon. To both Cleveland and Lamont the proposed course seemed agreeable; and on the same day the commanders of the Department of the Dakotas and the Department of Columbia were ordered to use their forces to clear the tracks and open the Northern Pacific to commerce.[60]

Troops were quickly thrown around tunnels and bridges in the areas where violence threatened. Protected by two companies, the first train left St. Paul on July 6; and, as it proceeded west, the guard was changed at convenient points. At Livingston, Montana, the train received a noisy demonstration from angry strikers, but no overt act occurred; and on the twelfth, without mishap, it reached the burned bridge at Hell Gate River in western Montana and there met the eastbound train, which, under a heavy military escort, had come from the Pacific Coast. Other through trains, fully protected, began to move; and the service, which at first was fitful, gradually became more regular. In carrying out orders the soldiers experienced no difficulty, although they were sometimes showered with abuse. Because the situation was considered potentially dangerous, particularly in Montana, troops remained on duty long after the struggle on the Northern Pacific had subsided. Indeed, it was not until September that the last detachment was withdrawn.[61]

The Great Northern was the only transcontinental railroad that escaped involvement because it had no contracts with the Pullman Company and used no Pullman sleepers. At one time, however, the road was dangerously near embroilment. In order to relieve a rather critical situation at Helena, Montana, on July 9, General Merritt decided that four companies should be transferred to that city from Fort Assinniboine. Since these troops would have to be transported by the Great Northern, the local branch of the American Railway Union on this road threatened to call a strike if an attempt were made to haul these men. Fortunately, the emergency at Helena eased somewhat, and the order for these soldiers was countermanded;[62] otherwise a serious struggle might have ensued, since the union on this line was exceptionally strong and since James Hill was grimly determined not to bow to labor in the matter. When troops were finally moved by the Great Northern on July 17, the employees refused to take action as it was then too late to aid the cause of the American Railway Union, which was beginning to collapse everywhere.[63]

In surveying the nation-wide scope of the struggle one becomes bewildered at the multiplicity of incidents and the rapidity with which events transpired. On some lines the boycott was achieved with considerable violence, whereas on other roads it was accomplished with a minimum of disorder. The Atlantic and Pacific Railroad, for example, suffered from a serious disruption of traffic but very little from property damage. Although Olney received frantic appeals for troops at certain points on this line, the only noteworthy act of vandalism was the burning of a bridge.[64]

In the Cherokee strip of the Oklahoma Territory the most alarming form of terrorism was practiced. For weeks the Rock Island Road in this area had been the victim of outrages, and the advent of the great strike seemed to accelerate the amount of destruction. Bridges were blown up, trains derailed, and other means of sabotage employed. On the night of July 12 the piling was sawed from under a bridge and dynamite planted therein, and when the train crossed there was an explosion, wrecking thirteen cars of freight and severely injuring several members of the crew. Against such acts the deputy marshals appeared to be helpless, and so the governor of the territory requested the assistance of federal troops. At Enid and Pond Creek much of the trouble occurred, and here the deputy marshals and soldiers were concentrated in force. The conduct of the military, however, proved a source of irritation to the citizens at Enid, who protested about the matter to Richard Olney.[65]

Serious trouble flared up at some of the railroad junctions in Iowa, particularly Dubuque and Sioux City. Switches were spiked and other measures taken to halt transportation. So critical was the situation at Sioux City that the governor of the state ordered out six companies of the militia to suppress disturbances.[66] No human lives were sacrificed here, but the same cannot be said for Spring Valley, Illinois, where striking miners had become extremely aggressive. On July 10 a passenger train of the Rock Island, heavily protected by federal troops, pulled into the station where a fusillade of stones greeted the engineer and fireman. The soldiers were ordered to the station platform; and, when the mob refused to disperse or to stop hurling missiles, the command to fire was given. The rioters fled, leaving two of their number dead and several injured. In the evening of the same day the soldiers entrained for Chicago.[67]

Few localities were more seriously involved than Hammond,

Indiana—a vital railroad junction through which many of the great eastern roads from Chicago passed. From almost the very outset determined strikers at this point endeavored to enforce the boycott with a resoluteness that must have gratified the heart of Eugene Debs. As trains entered the yards, they were flagged down and the engines seized and held by strikers until all Pullman cars could be uncoupled and sidetracked. Assisted by thirty deputies, the sheriff tried to prevent this, but, being unable to do so, he wired for state troops on June 29. The governor, however, was unimpressed with the need for such stringent measures and showed no disposition to act at this time. The federal marshal and his deputies were not much more successful than the sheriff, although they did arrest some officials of the local union on a charge of obstructing the mails.[68] The situation went from bad to worse, despite the efforts of the strikers to conduct the boycott in an orderly fashion. Feeling ran high, and public sentiment favored the cause of labor. Large mobs formed, recruited in part from the hoodlums and toughs of South Chicago. Ranging over the tracks, the rioters attacked scabs, derailed engines and cars, and otherwise inaugurated a state of anarchy. Traffic, which had moved intermittently, ceased altogether on July 7. The crowning offense was the seizure of the telegraph office that evening, apparently in the attempt to forestall a further appeal for the militia.[69]

The government, both state and federal, was now determined to suppress the disturbances. The General Managers' Association had urged Governor Mathews to act[70] and, in the face of other frantic pleas, he could delay no longer. In a conference with the United States marshal, Mathews seemed to favor the use of federal troops but refused to call upon the President for such aid. This was a disappointment to Olney, who, for reasons of strategy and federal prestige, had hoped Governor Mathews would do so. On July 8 the attorney-general urged the district attorney at Indianapolis to suggest to the governor the advisability of such a course.[71] It may be that, in the hope that Mathews would do this, Olney had refrained from using federal troops earlier. The position of the Indiana executive in this matter remained unshaken, however; and the attorney-general was finally compelled to proceed, as in so many other states, without requisition by the governor for federal aid.

On July 8 six companies of the militia reached Hammond, and on the same day heavy contingents of regular soldiers from Chicago arrived. Moving slowly up and down the tracks, the federal troops fired indiscriminately at any who seemed engaged in suspicious activities. Several casualties resulted, including the death of Charles Fleischer, a highly respected carpenter, who had not the remotest connection with the strike. The father of four children, he had come to the tracks in search of his son and was accidentally killed.

Among the people of Hammond the action of the military aroused the keenest resentment. Mayor Reilly promptly wired the governor: "I would like to know by what authority United States troops come in here and shoot our citizens without the slightest warning." The president of the local branch of the American Railway Union joined with a leading citizen in the following wire to Mathews: "Federal troops shooting citizens down promiscuously without provocation. Cannot something be done to protect citizens? Act quickly." In reply, Governor Mathews explained that any resistance to authority had to be punished and that it would "be a matter of extreme regret should inoffensive citizens suffer." Warrants were sworn out before a local magistrate for the arrest of the troops involved in the shooting, which for obvious reasons were never served.[72] Public meetings were held in Hammond on July 9 and 16 for the purpose of denouncing the action of President Cleveland in sending troops to their city. Mayor Reilly was among the speakers. At the second meeting one of the ministers in the city, Rev. Herzberger, read an open letter to President Cleveland charging that without warning federal troops fired "wantonly into the midst of our peaceful citizens. . . . . I demand an investigation of this unlawful act . . . . the innocent blood of Charles Fleischer, like the blood of Abel, calls for vengeance and the just God will not let it cry in vain."[73]

The East was more or less successful in escaping from the conflict, because of the relatively small membership which the American Railway Union had in that area and because of the large army of unemployed railroad workers that crowded the eastern cities. Equally significant was the fact that several of the lines in the East had contracts with the Wagner Palace Car Company or the Monarch Sleeping Car Company and did not use Pullman sleepers. The extension of the boycott throughout the East was thus neither advisable nor necessary. But, whether east or west, all states felt the full impact of the crisis. Everywhere fear and apprehension gripped the minds of the people. Food costs soared.[74] In New York City peaches that sold for $1.00 per box before the strike retailed on July 5 for $3.60. Poultry prices increased $4\frac{1}{2}$ cents per pound wholesale; and, with other meat prices showing the same alarming trends, it was freely predicted that a meat and poultry famine would soon confront the city.[75] Had the paralysis in rail transportation continued for many more days, the food situation would indeed have become critical.

In meeting the crisis what part did the states play? Owing to circumstances prescribed largely by the federal government, most of the states were forced to pursue a negligible role. Not many made use of the militia; but in most cases those that did hoped by such action to preclude the necessity of federal soldiers. By the prompt employment of state troops, Iowa and Alabama escaped federal military intervention. In the latter state fourteen companies of the militia on July 8 were quickly rushed to Birmingham when transportation ceased and disorders threatened. The crowds which gathered on railroad property and adjacent streets in this city were quickly and effectively dispersed at the point of the bayonet.[76] Other states, among them Illinois, California, and Indiana, were less fortunate, being unable to avoid the use of federal soldiery even though they made extensive use of the militia. If the federal government had not moved so swiftly and boldly, refusing to consult state executives and denying to them the opportunity to act freely and fully in the crisis, these officials would have endeavored to cope with the situation by means of their own resources.

Some of the state executives made no attempt to conceal their resentment toward the President, among them being the governors of Illinois, Colorado, Kansas, Missouri, Oregon, Idaho, and Texas. Governor William Stone of Missouri was greatly disturbed when he protested to Cleveland for the "impertinent" interference of federal authorities in the local affairs of his state. In his opinion the deputy marshals did more to provoke riots than anything else. He characterized as an outrage "the practice of making interference with mails and interstate commerce a pretense for setting aside the state authorities without giving them an opportunity to assert themselves."[77] So aroused was Governor H. Waite of Colorado that he suggested to the governors of Illinois and Kansas on July 14 that the chief executives of all those states whose rights had thus been violated should confer together for the purpose of making a joint protest.[78] In reply John Altgeld revealed a willingness to co-operate in any move calculated to yield substantial results but indicated that in his judgment further protests would be futile until public feeling had subsided.[79]

The governor of Texas, J. S. Hogg, was equally opposed to federal intervention. Determined to have none of it in his state, he wired the President on July 11 that his state was both able and willing to protect all rights guaranteed by the state and federal constitutions. "You are thus notified," he warned, "that you may not feel called upon by the plea of an alarmist to use United States troops here unless requested by state authority."[80]

Governors Sylvester Pennoyer, of Oregon, Lorenzo D. Lewelling, of Kansas, and William J. McConnell, of Idaho, entertained the same strong feelings in the matter but were unable to check, reduce, or deflect in any way the course which the federal government had elected to pursue. The attitude of the press toward the public utterances and formal protests of these state executives was unfriendly and in some cases extremely hostile. On July 12, for instance, the *Nation* announced that were it not for the power of the federal government to intervene,

a Populist or anarchist governor like Altgeld of Illinois, Lewelling of Kansas, Waite of Colorado, or Pennoyer of Oregon might allow government to be overthrown in his state, and lawlessness to run riot, and still claim that there was no warrant for federal intervention. Happily the President is armed by statute with all the power needed not only to suppress mobs, but to overcome anarchist governors.[81]

The great majority of state executives preferred to remain noncommittal, although some openly defended Cleveland's course. In the Deep South, where strong sentiment for states' rights still flourished, Governor John M. Stone of Mississippi heartily indorsed the policy of using federal troops wherever necessity required.[82] But, whatever the attitude of the governors—whether friendly, critical, or indifferent—none of them cared to justify the strike or condone the disturbances, and some of them issued proclamations warning the people to preserve order and cease all interference with railroad traffic.[83]

In seeking to rally public sentiment against the strikers and to discourage disturbances, President Cleveland on July 9 addressed to the nation a proclamation somewhat similar to the one issued on the preceding day to Illinois. He proclaimed that within the states of North Dakota, Montana, Idaho, Colorado, Washington, Wyoming, California, and the territories of Utah and New Mexico it was impracticable to enforce federal law by the ordinary course of judicial procedure. For this reason, he revealed, military forces were being used. All persons engaged in any "unlawful obstructions, combinations, and assemblages" on any railroads in the above states and territories were solemnly warned to disperse and retire to their homes before three o'clock in the afternoon of July 10.[84]

Eugene Debs had hoped that all railroad workers would support the strike and sustain the boycott; but, to his chagrin, the brotherhoods, without exception, rejected his appeal for co-operation. This policy was not due to a lack of sympathy for the Pullman employees or to any feeling of esteem for the General Managers' Association. It was primarily because of a mounting fear that in case of victory the American Railway Union would continue its unprecedented growth and ultimately absorb all railroad unions into one mighty industrial organization. This goal was manifestly the aim of Eugene Debs, who believed that the growing solidarity of railroad corporate wealth rendered the system of craft and class unions obsolete.[85] The brotherhoods, however, were not anxious to be destroyed and consequently viewed with unrestrained hostility the ambitious program of Eugene Debs.

To them the idea of a sympathetic strike was preposterous. They could see no valid reason why their contracts with the railroads should be violated for a quarrel which was not their own, in order to aid a union that represented a real threat to their existence.[86] The situation was complicated by the fact that some members of the railroad brotherhoods belonged to the American Railway Union and, when asked to strike, did so without hesitation.[87] The brotherhoods did all they could to discourage this defection from their ranks, even threatening to expel those who struck.[88] When four hundred engineers on the Wabash road joined the strike, P. M. Arthur, grand chief of the Brotherhood of Locomotive Engineers, denounced this action as a clear violation of the rules of their union. Under the circumstances, he explained, unemployed engineers would be permitted to fill the vacancies created by the striking members.[89] To the General Managers' Association Arthur wrote on July 2 that the engineers would perform their duties regardless of what other employees might do and that it would make no difference to his organization whether a railroad company wished to employ union or nonunion firemen and switchmen. Any engineer, he declared, who refused to work under such conditions could be discharged and need expect no support from the brotherhood.[90]

Because Eugene Debs had for years served as grand secretary and treasurer of the Brotherhood of Locomotive Firemen and was still the editor of their journal, this organization pursued a more tactful course in opposing the strike. The *Locomotive Firemen's Magazine* was extraordinarily reticent about the struggle, except for some editorials that flayed Pullman and his corporation. The grand master of this union, however, made it very clear that his organization would have no part in the boycott and that any firemen who joined the strike would have to look to the American Railway Union for support, since the Brotherhood of Firemen could furnish none.[91]

The grand chief conductor of the Order of Railroad Conductors made no attempt to conceal the hostility which existed between his union and that of Eugene Debs.[92] Even more realistic was the grand master of the Switchmen's Union, who declared that, since the switchmen were always obliged to wage their own battles, alone and unaided, he could see no good reason why they should rush to the support of another organization with which they had nothing in common. Bitterly he recalled the treatment which the switchmen suffered during some of their strikes at the hands of other craft and railroad fraternities. He warned that members of his union who supported the boycott would be liable to expulsion.[93]

No organization displayed more venom than did the Brotherhood of Railroad Trainmen. Everything possible was done to prevent the members of this union from striking. Not content with doing just this, the executives of the organization lashed out viciously at the whole purpose and plan of the American Railway Union. Curiously enough, the grand master of this brotherhood, S. E. Wilkinson, actually defended the policy of the General Managers' Association in resisting the boycott. He held that the railroads took this action, not in support of the labor policies of George Pullman, but in defense of the contracts which they had with the Pullman Corporation.[94] The general managers appreciated this expression of good will as well as all other evidence of co-operation so abundantly demonstrated by the various brotherhoods. In return, the railroads made it quite apparent that they bore no animus against the old, established railway orders.[95]

Labor in general revealed a tremendous amount of sympathy for the strikers, and in the case of some organizations seemed willing to translate that feeling into co-operative action. Foremost among such unions was the Knights of Labor, which still wielded some influence with its one hundred and fifty thousand members. Organized along industrial lines, it bore a resemblance to the American Railway Union, in which was recognized a kindred spirit. When the convention of the American Railway Union assembled in June, James R. Sovereign, chief executive of the Knights of Labor, was invited to attend. He proposed that both unions affiliate, and after the matter was fully discussed an agreement providing for such an alliance was adopted by the executive boards of the two organizations. Although more nominal than anything else, this arrangement developed into a very cordial relationship.[96]

On June 27 Sovereign issued a manifesto urging the members

of his organization to render whatever assistance they could to the American Railway Union in its "fight against plutocratic enslavement."[97] Three days later he released another declaration in which he instructed all local officers of his union to call meetings for a discussion of the Pullman boycott. The traveling public was to be notified that those who patronized Pullman sleepers would not receive any patronage from the Knights of Labor. Above all, each member was urged to conduct himself peacefully in this struggle against "corporate greed."[98] Interestingly enough, Terence V. Powderly, the former executive of this union, was not at all in sympathy with the strike because of the injury it would do to the public, and on July 2 in an address made known his reasons for opposing the boycott.

In various cities throughout the East labor groups indorsed the boycott and denounced the Pullman Company. On July 1 the Central Labor Union in Boston, comprising forty-five trade-unions, adopted such resolutions and, in addition, urged the people not to patronize the cars of the Pullman Company until it was willing to accept arbitration. Similar action was taken on the same day by the Central Labor Union of New York City;[99] and then, on July 8, representatives of organized labor in that city reassembled, this time to condemn the federal government as well as the railroad brotherhoods—the latter disparagingly referred to as the "Benedict Arnolds of the labor movement."[100] The most eloquent indorsement of the strike, however, was made at Cooper Union Hall in New York City by a mass meeting of laborers on the night of July 12. Presided over by the president of the New York State branch of the American Federation of Labor, the meeting was addressed by a panel of noted speakers, including John Swinton and Henry George. On a large canvas strip, prominently displayed in the hall, was the following legend:

> They hanged and quartered John Ball
>   but Feudalism passed away.
> They hanged John Brown, but Chattel
>   Slavery passed away.
> They arrested Eugene Debs, and may kill him,
>   but White Slavery will pass away.
> Such Souls go marching on.

Although extremely tense, the meeting was free of incendiary remarks and clamorous appeals. Numerous resolutions were adopted denouncing federal intervention, the "arrogant" refusal of Pullman to arbitrate, the "perversion of the federal judiciary," and the control of the government by corporations. While we respect law and order, declared one resolution, we recognize that "the most vociferous shouters for law and order are they whose official actions have violated law and incited to disorder." Perhaps the most expressive of all remarks made was that uttered by Frank K. Foster, editor of a Boston labor newspaper, when he declared to that great gathering:

> George Pullman is but of today, Olney is but of today, and Grover Cleveland is but of today. But the cause of labor . . . . and the cause of American citizenship are for now and all time to come. We are not here as judges to draw the indictments against the real culprits of the land. This occasion is analogous to that which preceded the emancipation proclamation.[101]

These expressions of sympathy and good will were deeply appreciated by the strikers, but speeches and resolutions could not bring victory to embattled labor. The great need was complete and unbroken solidarity among all railroad workers, and with feverish haste Debs sought to realize this objective by seeking to make the cause which he represented the cause of all railroad employees. In this spirit he dispatched countless telegrams in trying to solicit the full co-operation of all. Typical of these communications was the one which he sent on July 8 to the president of the Central Labor Union of Buffalo:

> We ask your co-operation . . . . we are making a great fight for labor, and deserve the support of all railroad employees. Capital has combined to enslave labor. We must all stand together or go down in hopeless defeat. It is impossible for companies to fill vacancies. We can solve this problem only by quitting in a body and standing together, one for all and all for one, upon each and every road throughout the land.[102]

Whatever Debs could do to rally all railroad workers he did, but his efforts proved unavailing. Because of the recalcitrance of the brotherhoods, a large segment of the skilled workers opposed the boycott and for all practical purposes assisted the railroads in breaking the strike. The large amount of unemployment among railroad workers was another factor which served to undermine the strategy of Eugene Debs. Chauncey M. Depew, president of the New York Central Railroad, estimated that one-third of all railroad workers in the East were then out of work.[103] From this great reservoir of labor the railroads could recruit freely. The times were thus inauspicious, and the funds of the union quite inadequate for any contest of endurance. Structurally and otherwise, the American Railway Union was ill prepared to battle with the General Managers' Association, bolstered, as it was, by the full weight of the government. Supported by the military, the United States marshals sought to enforce the injunctions with a vengeance and did so by arresting union leaders at many key points. The arrest of Debs and other national officers of the union proved a serious blow; and, bereft of effective leadership, the resistance of the strikers began to disintegrate rapidly.

Eugene Debs was slow to abandon hope and with tenacity of spirit fought on, hoping somehow to turn defeat into victory. In the dispatches which he sent as late as July 16 there was no note of defeatism, even though the outlook for victory was becoming quite hopeless. In a message on that day he declared: "We have assurance that within 48 hours every labor organization will come to our rescue. The tide is on and the men are acquitting themselves like heroes. Here and there one weakens, but our cause is strengthened by others going out in their places."[104] Debs apparently believed that many labor unions would render support at the eleventh hour, and to them he now looked hopefully. Some had voiced resolutions to that effect; but, now that the struggle was taking such a tragic turn, it seemed that most of the enthusiasm for sympathetic strikes had suddenly yielded to the sober realization of the dangers and futility in such a course. The action of James Sovereign, in issuing a call on July 10 for a general strike of all the Knights of Labor, proved a futile and empty gesture.[105] Fearing the consequences or realizing the hopelessness of such a course, the Knights refused to act. Nor were other unions any more willing to risk their future in such a fashion.

It was for the Pullman employees that the conflagration raged, but throughout the struggle they remained quietly in the background. The great works at Pullman remained closed, but in the repair shops at Wilmington, Delaware; St. Louis, Missouri; and Ludlow, Kentucky, the Pullman Corporation was more fortunate. Although the American Railway Union sent organizers to all these plants, the one at Wilmington—largest of the three—resisted every attempt at unionization. Only a small minority of the men joined, and work here was at no time suspended. At the other two shops most of the employees became members of the union and on June 25 declared a strike. Moving resolutely, the Pullman officials proceeded to employ new men and continue operations. Within two weeks the St. Louis plant had returned to normal; but, owing to the threatening attitude of railroad strikers in Ludlow, the plant discreetly closed down on July 3 and did not reopen until two weeks later.[106]

In the town of Pullman the men were so completely unionized that the company was obliged to await the outcome of the railroad strike. By July 18 the cause of the American Railway Union seemed doomed and on that day the officials of the corporation posted a notice that as soon as a working force could be employed, the shops in Pullman would resume operation. The strike leaders and those otherwise offensive to the company were refused employment; but all others had the privilege of reapplying for work, on condition that they would surrender their membership card in the American Railway Union and sign a contract agreeing to have nothing more to do with this or any other labor union. The workers were further obliged to accept the old wage scale, against which they had struck, and the same rentals.[107] Forced by necessity, many of the strikers yielded to the will of the company and accepted the terms. Some, however, refused. When asked by one of the strike commissioners why he would not make application for work, Theodore Rhodie, a veteran employee of the Pullman Company, replied: "There is one reason, and that is I do not like to walk up there and hand up my membership in the American Railway Union; because when a man asks me to give up my principles, my rights as an American citizen, he might just as well ask me for my life."[108]

Although there was no real danger of violence, the First Regiment of the Illinois militia, as well as a large police force, stood by when the company accepted applications for re-employment. After twelve weeks of idleness, the repair shops were reopened on August 2 and subsequently other departments. By August 24 there were twenty-three hundred employees at work in Pullman, of whom five hundred and fifty were new men.[109]

A hastily summoned convention of the American Railway Union met in Chicago on August 2 and, faced by the cold logic of events, bowed to reality. The reports left no doubt in the minds of those present concerning the hopelessness of the struggle. All the telegrams from union headquarters had been seized by the government; but even more disheartening was the fact that Eugene Debs and other leaders had been arrested and now awaited prosecution. To continue resistance under such circumstances seemed worse than useless. Since the strike on each road had been inaugurated by the workers on that line, it was decided that they were the proper ones to call it off. Such action was soon taken on all railroads except the Santa Fe, where at certain points the strikers refused to capitulate.[110] In this fashion the dramatic action taken on June 22 by an enthusiastic, crusading convention was annulled. Official recognition was thus given to a defeat unrelieved by any compensating values save the realization that the fight had been waged in behalf of several thousand exploited workers at Pullman. Measured in terms of wages lost and of strikers that were blacklisted and denied employment, the price paid by labor was exceedingly high. Completely discredited and unable to retrieve anything from the struggle, the American Railway Union rapidly began to disintegrate. Never had labor suffered more disastrously; but, as if this were not enough, the government proceeded grimly and resolutely to the further task of prosecuting the leaders of this union.

NOTES

1. *Annual Report of the Secretary of War* . . . . *1894*, I, 4, 11, 57–58; *Report of the Postmaster General, 1894*, p. 25.
2. *U.S. Strike Commission Report*, pp. 115–16.
3. *Ibid.*, pp. 115–16, 159.
4. *Ibid.*, pp. 27–28; *Chicago Times*, June 29, 1894, pp. 1, 2, and June 30, 1894, p. 1; *New York Times*, June 30, 1894, p. 1.

5. *U.S. Strike Commission Report*, p. 159; *Ex Parte: In the matter of Eugene V. Debs et al.; Records and Briefs of the U.S. Supreme Court*, CLVIII, 2, 7.

6. *Appendix to the . . . . Report of the Attorney General . . . . 1896*, pp. 65, 69, 104–5.

7. *New York World*, July 4, 1894, p. 7.

8. *Washington Post*, July 4, 1894, p. 2.

9. *New York Times*, July 5, 1894, p. 2.

10. *Appendix to the . . . . Report of the Attorney General . . . . 1896*, pp. 65, 69, 73, 104–5, 171–73.

11. The Chicago and Alton, and the Kansas City, Fort Scott, and Memphis.

12. *Appendix to the . . . . Report of the Attorney General . . . . 1896*, pp. 70, 138–40.

13. *Ibid.*, p. 187.

14. *Ibid.*, pp. 69–70, 205.

15. Bohl to Olney, August 17, 1894, *ibid.*, p. 178.

16. Olney to Bohl, August 18, 1894, *ibid.*, p. 179.

17. *Ex Parte: In the matter of Eugene V. Debs et al.; Records and Briefs of the U.S. Supreme Court*, CLVIII, 1–10.

18. *Ibid.*, p. 5.

19. *Ibid.*, p. 6.

20. *Ibid.*, p. 8.

21. *New York Times*, July 5, 1894, p. 2.

22. *U.S. Strike Commission Report*, pp. 138–39.

23. *Appendix to the . . . . Report of the Attorney General . . . . 1896*, pp. 41, 154–55.

24. *Ibid.*, pp. 155–56.

25. *New York Times*, July 6, 1894, p. 2; *Inter Ocean*, July 7, 1894, p. 5.

26. *Appendix to the . . . . Report of the Attorney General . . . . 1896*, pp. 41–42; *New York Times*, July 2, 1894, p. 2.

27. *Annual Report of the Secretary of War . . . . 1894*, I, 136–38.

28. L. E. Hall to Olney, July 16, 1894, *Appendix to the . . . . Report of the Attorney General . . . . 1896*, pp. 160–62.

29. *Ibid.*, pp. 156–58.

30. *Ibid.*, p. 162.

31. *Annual Report of the Secretary of War . . . . 1894*, I, 138–40.

32. *Appendix to the . . . . Report of the Attorney General . . . . 1896*, pp. 34–35; *Nation*, LIX (1894), 23.

33. LIX (1894), 23.

34. *Appendix to the . . . . Report of the Attorney General . . . . 1896*, pp. 24, 26, 34.

35. Call to Olney, July 18, 1894, *ibid.*, pp. 34–35.

36. *Ibid.*, pp. 17–21.

37. *Ibid.*, p. 19; *Report of the Secretary of War . . . . 1894*, I, 111.

38. Shafter to Lamont, July 5, 1894, *Appendix to the . . . . Report of the Attorney General . . . . 1896*, pp. 228–29.

39. Denis to Olney, July 4, 1894, *ibid.*, p. 23.

40. Denis to Olney, July 5, 1894, *ibid.*, p. 24.

41. *Ibid.*, p. 234; *Annual Report of the Secretary of War . . . . 1894*, I, 111, 244.

42. *Annual Report of the Secretary of War . . . . 1894*, I, 112.

43. *Appendix to the . . . . Report of the Attorney General . . . . 1896*, pp. 22, 25–26.

44. *New York Times*, July 7, 1894, p. 2.

45. *Appendix to the . . . . Report of the Attorney General . . . . 1896*, pp. 25–26.

46. *Ibid.*, pp. 210–11.

47. *Ibid.*, pp. 192–95.

48. *Ibid.*, p. 197.

49. J. M. Schofield to Brigadier General Brooke, July 7, 1894; Schofield to Brigadier General Ruger, July 7, 1894, *ibid.*, pp. 230–32; *Annual Report of the Secretary of War* . . . . *1894*, I, 111–12.

50. *Ibid.*, pp. 112–14.

51. *Ibid.*, p. 114; *Appendix to the* . . . . *Report of the Attorney General* . . . . *1896*, p. 238.

52. *New York World*, July 9, 1894, pp. 2, 3.

53. *Annual Report of the Secretary of War* . . . . *1894*, I, 113, 114.

54. *Ibid.*, p. 125; *New York Times*, June 28, 1894, p. 1.

55. *Annual Report of the Secretary of War* . . . . *1894*, I, 125, 128; *Appendix to the* . . . . *Report of the Attorney General* . . . . *1896*, pp. 201, 239.

56. *Appendix to the* . . . . *Report of the Attorney General* . . . . *1896*, pp. 50–53, 146–48, 201.

57. *Ibid.*, p. 225.

58. Olney to Lamont, July 5, 1894, *ibid.*, p. 226.

59. James McNaught to Olney, July 6, 1894, *ibid.*, pp. 227–28.

60. *Ibid.*, pp. 227–33.

61. *Ibid.*, p. 239; *Annual Report of the Secretary of War* . . . . *1894*, I, 125–26, 129.

62. *Annual Report of the Secretary of War* . . . . *1894*, pp. 127–28.

63. *Ibid.*, p. 128.

64. *Appendix to the* . . . . *Report of the Attorney General* . . . . *1896*, pp. 6–8, 235–36.

65. *Ibid.*, pp. 111–12, 182–83, 240–42.

66. *Ibid.*, pp. 113–15.

67. *Chicago Record*, July 11, 1894, p. 3.

68. *Chicago Tribune*, June 30, 1894, p. 1; *Inter Ocean*, June 30, 1894, p. 1.

69. *Inter Ocean*, July 8, 1894, pp. 1, 4.

70. *Proceedings of the General Managers' Association* . . . . *1894*, pp. 189–90.

71. *Appendix to the* . . . . *Report of the Attorney General* . . . . *1896*, pp. 106–7.

72. *Chicago Times*, July 9, 1894, pp. 1, 2; *Inter Ocean*, July 9, 1894, p. 1.

73. *Inter Ocean*, July 17, 1894, p. 2.

74. *New York World*, July 4, 1894, p. 7.

75. *New York Times*, July 6, 1894, p. 1.

76. *New York World*, July 9, 1894, p. 3.

77. *Chicago Times*, July 7, 1894, p. 2.

78. Wait to Altgeld, July 14, 1894, Governor's Correspondence.

79. Altgeld to Waite, July 18, 1894, Governor's Letter Books.

80. Hogg to Cleveland, July 11, 1894, Cleveland Papers.

81. LIX (1894), 22–23.

82. *Ibid.*, p. 19.

83. *New York World*, July 8, 1894, p. 2.

84. Richardson, *op. cit.*, XII, 5932–33.

85. *U.S. Strike Commission Report*, pp. 153–54.

86. *Ibid.*, pp. 32–33, 154.

87. *New York Times*, July 1, 1894, pp. 1, 2; *Chicago Times*, June 30, 1894, p. 1.

88. *New York World*, July 8, 1894, p. 3.

89. *Railroad Gazette*, XXVI (1894), 524.
90. *Proceedings of the General Managers' Association* . . . . *1894*, p. 159.
91. *New York Times*, July 1, 1894, p. 2.
92. *U.S. Strike Commission Report*, pp. 185–87; *Chicago Tribune*, June 30, 1894, p. 1.
93. *Inter Ocean*, June 28, 1894, p. 3; *U.S. Strike Commission Report*, pp. 332–33.
94. *New York Times*, July 8, 1894, p. 2; *Railroad Trainmen's Journal*, XI (1894), 679–81.
95. *Railroad Trainmen's Journal*, XI (1894), 690.
96. *U.S. Strike Commission Report*, pp. 60–61, 156; *Chicago Times*, June 14, 1894, p. 1.
97. *New York Times*, June 28, 1894, p. 1.
98. *Ibid.*, July 1, 1894, p. 2.
99. *Ibid.*, July 2, 1894, p. 2.
100. *Ibid.*, July 9, 1894, p. 1.
101. *Ibid.*, July 13, 1894, pp. 1, 6.
102. *Ibid.*, July 9, 1894, p. 1.
103. *Ibid.*, July 7, 1894, p. 2.
104. *Debs: His Life, Writings and Speeches*, p. 52.
105. *New York Times*, July 11, 1894, p. 2.
106. *U.S. Strike Commission Report*, pp. 554, 571–72, 589; *Inter Ocean*, June 26, 1894, p. 3.
107. *U.S. Strike Commission Report*, pp. 422, 440, 441, 481, 564, 591.
108. *Ibid.*, p. 438.
109. *Ibid.*, p. 591; Pullman, *op. cit.*, pp. 40–41.
110. *U.S. Strike Commission Report*, p. 151.

CHAPTER XII

IN THE TOILS OF THE LAW

NOTHING contributed so much to the defeat of the strike as did the action taken by the federal courts. Between the Department of Justice and the federal judiciary there seemed to be a sympathetic understanding, and almost every move initiated by the former received the hearty support of the latter. Without this co-operation Richard Olney could not have blanketed every strike-infested region throughout the nation with an omnibus injunction—a weapon which proved very demoralizing to labor. From strike headquarters in Chicago, where the strategy of the American Railway Union was conceived, orders were issued to local organizations scattered over a wide area. Only in this manner could a united front be maintained and all activities co-ordinated among scores of striking groups from Michigan to California. As a result of the injunction, however, the central offices as well as all terminal offices of the union were restrained from performing many of the functions vital to the prosecution of the strike. For no less an offense than urging workers to join the struggle, union leaders were cited for contempt and arrested. Nor was this all, since the government quickly impaneled grand juries that indicted hundreds of strikers and their leaders for conspiracy.

In the judgment of Eugene Debs, the collapse of the strike was not achieved by the soldiers or railroad brotherhoods but by the federal courts, which paralyzed the leadership of the railway union. He explained:

Our men were in a position that never would have been shaken under any circumstances if we had been permitted to remain among them . . . . but once we were taken from the scene of action and restrained from sending telegrams or issuing the orders necessary, or answering questions; when the minions of the corporations would be put to work at such a place, for instance, as Nickerson, Kansas, where they would go and say to the men that the men at Newton had gone back to work, and Nickerson would wire me to ask if that were true; no

274

answer would come to the message because I was under arrest, and we were all under arrest. The headquarters were demoralized and abandoned, and we could not answer any messages. The men went back to work, and the ranks were broken up by the federal courts of the United States.[1]

The officials of the American Railway Union realized that lawlessness would destroy their cause, and for this reason exerted every effort to keep the strike free of such acts. In spite of all they could do, violence occurred; but most of it, as previous treatment has made abundantly clear, was the work of lawless elements over which the union could exercise no control. The strikers were nevertheless credited by an enraged press and an inflamed public with full responsibility for all the mischief done—a situation which made it easy for the government to employ boldly and without restraint a weapon which otherwise would have been used with greater caution. The injunction was so sweeping and all inclusive that the union leaders could not move without running afoul of it. The purpose of the writ was designed not so much to protect property as to crush the strike.

It is doubtful that labor realized the full import of the injunction when first issued, although Eugene Debs did consult some of the best constitutional lawyers in Chicago. They told him to proceed just as he had been doing, committing no violence and doing everything in his power to restrain men from lawlessness.[2] This Debs did, but he soon discovered that the courts placed a construction upon the writ which left him no freedom of action. That he did not perceive the true character of the injunction when it was first served is evident by the following observation which he made on July 4:

I cannot see the necessity for serving an injunction on me commanding me not to do that which the statutes of the state also require me not to do. It is an assumption that I am ignorant of the law. I again say that I have done absolutely nothing prohibited by the law. I shall not do so, nor will I countenance others doing so.[3]

In seeking evidence that the injunction had been violated, Milchrist urged the general managers to report the names of any who encouraged employees to strike or who in any way sought to discourage workers from performing their duty.[4] Significantly enough, the role played by Thomas Milchrist in shaping the judicial strategy was much less important than that of Edwin Walker, in whose judgment the attorney-general seemed to repose the most implicit confidence. As special district attorney, Walker was prepared to serve as liaison agent between the government and the railroads; and not only did he confer with railroad lawyers and executives whenever it suited his purpose, but he attended meetings of the General Managers' Association. In serving two masters he experienced little difficulty, since both sought the same broad objectives in the struggle.

From almost the very outset Walker favored both equity and criminal procedure against the strikers. Milchrist at first opposed the latter course because, as he claimed, it would be extremely difficult to obtain evidence for convictions; but, in the opinion of Walker, the mere calling of a grand jury and the securing of indictments would have a "greater restraining effect upon Debs and his followers than proceeding by injunction."[5] On July 3 Edwin Walker outlined his plan of action to the attorney-general. Equity proceedings would have to await the gathering of further evidence; but, as was confidently expected, sufficient proof of contempt would be assembled within a few days, and then Debs and his associates would be sent to jail. It was further indicated that in one week a grand jury would be summoned to indict the strike leaders for conspiracy. Walker was careful, however, to emphasize the dangers of precipitate action but explained that, since he had a thorough understanding with Judge Grosscup, everything would proceed as rapidly and effectively as circumstances warranted.[6] To Richard Olney this strategy seemed agreeable, although he was becoming impatient for action, and in reply he instructed the special assistant district attorney not to lose any time in calling a special session of the grand jury.[7]

On July 6 Walker informed the attorney-general that sufficient evidence had now been gathered for presentation to the grand jury which was scheduled to meet on July 10. He expressed the belief that the bail would be so large in the aggregate that Debs and his associates would have to go to jail and remain there until their cases were called up for trial. Walker explained:

We shall be able to show that this conspiracy has extended over the entire northwest, as well as the Pacific coast, and also east through Michigan, Indiana and Ohio, and I firmly believe that the result of these trials and the punishment of the leaders will be so serious that a general strike upon any railroad will not again occur for a series of years.[8]

The general managers seemed to think that the arrest of Eugene Debs was being needlessly delayed. This feeling Edwin Walker did not share, because of the belief that it would be inexpedient to arrest Debs before he was indicted and that contempt proceedings should await action by the grand jury. He felt that hasty action would prove dangerous and might influence the Knights of Labor to call a general strike. However logical may have been his position, the attorneys for the General Managers' Association assumed a very critical attitude in the matter.[9] They believed that the sooner Debs was behind bars, the quicker the strike would collapse. On July 9 the president of the Chicago, Milwaukee, and St. Paul Railroad revealed the nature of these criticisms to Walker, who seemed to take them quite seriously. He decided to confer immediately with some of these lawyers, including the chairman of the legal committee of the General Managers' Association, and agreed to advise Milchrist to order the arrest of Debs if these attorneys should recommend such a course.[10] What transpired at this conference is not known, but on the following day the grand jury assembled and took the action which Richard Olney and the general managers so fervently desired.

When Milchrist and Walker met the special grand jury on July 10, they asked for indictments against Eugene Debs and his co-officials on the grounds of conspiracy. Composed of out-of-town residents, the jury proved extremely amenable. In his instructions to this group Judge Grosscup smoothed the way for prompt action by leaving virtually no course open but the one demanded by the government. He pointed out that an agreement on the part of two or more individuals to stop trains unlawfully would have the effect of halting mail trains and interstate commerce, and this should be proof of the existence of a conspiracy.[11] The railroads, he explained, have a right to the service of each employee until he lawfully decides to quit and that concerted action to induce men to strike "under any effective penalty or threat . . . . to the injury of the mail service or the prompt transportation of interstate commerce" might be classified as conspiracy.[12]

With such advice the grand jury retired to hear evidence, which consisted principally of telegrams dispatched from the headquarters of the American Railway Union. The only witness was Edward M. Mulford, manager of the Western Union office in Chicago, who was subpoenaed to produce copies of these messages. At first he refused to make them available, on the grounds that, being "privileged communications," they should remain in the custody of his company. When Grosscup, however, threatened him with a jail sentence, he decided to yield to the will of the court.

Only the telegrams that seemed most incriminating were submitted to the jury. None advocated violence while some advised against it, but there were many which counseled the railroad workers to support the boycott. In view of what Judge Grosscup had said, such urgings were construed as evidence of conspiracy, and without delay the grand jury voted true bills for the four highest officials of the American Railway Union: President Eugene Debs, Vice-President George W. Howard, Secretary Sylvester Keliher, and Lewis W. Rogers, editor of the *Railway Times*. The jury was in session not more than two hours when this action was taken, and ten minutes later bench warrants were issued. With a speed that must have gladdened the hearts of Walker and Olney, the accused were quickly apprehended and brought into court. After a few hours of detention, they were released on bail, the bonds required for each being ten thousand dollars.[13]

While Debs and his associates were in the custody of the court, the union headquarters were raided by a squad of deputy marshals and deputy post-office inspectors. Every room was completely ransacked; and all books, papers, records, and correspondence, including the unopened personal mail of Eugene Debs, were seized and transferred to the office of the United States district attorney. Although conducted according to in-

structions from Thomas Milchrist, the raid was in complete violation of the subpoena issued for the occasion—a court order which
merely required that the private secretary of Debs and certain
other persons appear before the grand jury with the books and
papers of the union.[14] There was no authority to make any arrests or seizures. Realizing the illegality of the action, Judge
Grosscup quickly repudiated it and ordered all private papers
returned. At a special session of the court on July 11, he explained to Milchrist that Debs was charged with a serious crime
but possessed the same rights as any other accused citizen and
that his private papers could not be confiscated and used as evidence against him, any more than he could be incriminated by
his own testimony extracted under compulsion.[15]

The attorney-general viewed this raid as embarrassing to the
government. On July 11 he bluntly reminded Walker that the
seizure of Debs's papers was unlawful and that they should be
returned and the affair publicly disavowed. Olney was careful to
explain that, in enforcing the law, the government could not itself
afford to be lawless by violating personal rights. "The government is too strong," he admonished, "and its cause too righteous
to warrant or require anything of that nature."[16] Because the
press agents somehow got hold of this message in a garbled form,
Richard Olney released the whole thing for publication. This,
together with the character of the note, aroused the keenest resentment on the part of Walker, who refused to recognize the
enormity of the offense. He preferred to minimize the entire matter. To the attorney-general on July 12 he declared: "In this
matter Milchrist and myself acted in harmony. It is not the time,
in my opinion, to make public apologies to any officer of the
American Railway Union, and I cannot understand why your
telegram to me should be given to the public press, nor why my
action in this matter should be publicly censured."[17] Surprised
at the tenor of this dispatch, Olney replied that he did not hold
Walker responsible for the incident and hence did not deem him
censurable for it.[18]

Convinced that the strike leaders feared the grand jury more
than the presence of troops,[19] the prosecution made the greatest

possible use of this jury. Numerous arrests were made during the rioting in Chicago, and those who could not furnish bail were committed to jail. The grand jury indicted many of these and in all named sixty-nine persons in the omnibus indictments for conspiracy. Seven indictments were voted against Debs, Howard, and Rogers, but only three each against the full board of directors. So enthusiastic was the jury in probing the situation that Milchrist and Walker experienced some difficulty in confining the jury's work strictly to offenses against the transportation of mail and commerce. On July 19 the jury completed its investigation and was discharged.[20]

Elsewhere throughout the United States grand juries were summoned and numerous indictments for conspiracy drawn up, some of which were directed against large groups of strikers. At Salt Lake City, for example, one indictment charged forty-five strikers with obstructing the mail.[21] Many of the indictments were issued with such haste and on such flimsy evidence that they were subsequently dismissed by the government, but not until they had served their purpose, which was to spread fear and defeatism among the strikers. Many of the arrests, whether for conspiracy or contempt, were made on slight provocation; and, although prosecution in such cases was usually abandoned, the victims were often subject to great inconvenience. Some of them were transported a considerable distance and lodged in jail, only to be released after a few days. Those without funds were often obliged to beg their way home.[22] Among the hundreds arrested for contempt, only a very small proportion was actually found guilty. Erroneous arrests were to be expected in a struggle characterized by such tenseness; but it may be assumed that the general policy of making arrests represented a part of the strategy of the Department of Justice to undermine the morale of labor. According to the vice-president of the American Railway Union, the practice of the government in this respect was most objectionable.

Men have been arrested in Chicago because they refused to turn switches when told to; they were arrested when they refused to get on an engine and fire an engine; one man was arrested for going up and looking at a policeman's star;

in Albuquerque, New Mexico, they arrested a man and he was sentenced to fifteen days in jail for contempt of court because he refused to get on an engine and fire it when told; the fact that he did not get on the engine was considered contempt of court.[23]

Before the special grand jury in Chicago had completed its work, contempt proceedings were commenced. On July 17 two informations were filed in the federal district court against Debs, Howard, Keliher, and Rogers: one by George R. Peck in behalf of the receivers of the Santa Fe Road, and the other by Milchrist and Walker in behalf of the United States government. The defendants were charged with contempt and their immediate arrest demanded. The prosecution declared that the injunction of Judges Grosscup and Woods had been wilfully and deliberately violated by Debs and his co-officials, not once, but on numerous occasions. It was alleged that in open disregard of the writ, the defendants by telegram had continued to urge railroad employees on various lines to quit work. Hundreds of such messages were dispatched and many employees were induced to strike, often in a body, thus causing serious interference to the movement of interstate commerce. The government further charged that the strikers seized railroad property, fostered violence, and by physical force obstructed mail and interstate trains. Workers who refused to join the strike were intimidated. By this and other means the union was charged with seeking to establish unlawfully a boycott of Pullman sleepers. The prosecution contended that the directors of the American Railway Union possessed full authority to call the workers out on a strike and by the exercise of this power had flagrantly violated the injunction.[24]

In seeking to prove contempt the government submitted some telegrams to the court. When only a few had been read, the judge announced that sufficient evidence had been presented to indicate a deliberate violation of the injunction. The attorney for the American Railway Union, S. S. Gregory, vainly protested that the information failed to charge the defendants with personal participation in any violence and that the case as presented did not warrant jurisdiction by a court of equity. The government, he announced, was really using its power and authority to vindicate the property rights of the railroads. The judge, however, could see no need for further discussion at this time and ordered the arrest of the defendants but suspended service of the writs when assured that the accused would voluntarily surrender themselves. This Debs and his three associates did at the afternoon session of the court. Again Gregory endeavored to save his clients by declaring that if time permitted he could prove that the information failed to show any violation of the injunction and that until contempt had been proved there could be no punishment. He explained it was no offense for workers to quit work peacefully; and as for the allegation that threats and intimidation had been used by the accused—there was nothing in the information to bear this out.

Although unimpressed by these arguments, the court was willing to grant the defense sufficient time to answer the informations and accordingly deferred the hearing until July 23. This was done over the strenuous objections of Edwin Walker, who, being anxious to get away for his summer vacation, demanded an immediate hearing. The bail was fixed at three thousand dollars for each defendant; and, although there were several bondsmen present, Debs and his colleagues waived bail and were committed to jail. When interrogated about this, Debs explained that it was a matter of principle. "The poor striker who is arrested," he averred, "would be thrown in jail. We are no better than he."²⁵ The refusal of these men to accept bail came as a surprise to Walker, who was hardly prepared for such an extraordinary gesture. In explaining the matter to Richard Olney, he was at first inclined to characterize it as an act to arouse sympathy but later expressed the belief that it was done because Debs, confronted by defeat, felt the need for rest and seclusion from the excitement of office.²⁶ It may be that Debs believed that imprisonment at this juncture would popularize his cause and help to rally labor; but there is nothing to indicate that he had the slightest desire to shirk his duties or to escape from the full responsibilities of his office.

As scheduled, the hearing for contempt began on July 23, with Judges Grosscup and Woods presiding. The four defendants, each wearing a new white ribbon, appeared without showing any trace of their imprisonment. Gregory, who was now assisted by another attorney, W. W. Erwin, filed a joint answer to the contempt charges. All the allegations set forth by Milchrist and Walker were categorically denied. The defendants disclaimed any intention of violating the restraining order and emphatically declared that they had not done so. It was pointed out that the workers on each railroad, by a majority vote, alone possessed the power to call a strike and that the high officials of the union might advise but could exercise no authority in the matter. Those who struck, it was claimed, did so on their own accord and not because of any control or direction from the American Railway Union.

Did the accused interfere with the operation of trains carrying mail and interstate commerce or in any way seek to induce others to do so? Were the defendants or the members of the union involved in the violence and disorders? To every charge of this sort the defendants issued a flat denial, while emphasizing the fact that they had strongly urged the strikers to abstain from intimidation and other forms of lawlessness. It was even affirmed that in seeking not to violate the injunction, Eugene Debs had sought and scrupulously followed the advice of competent lawyers.[27]

The defense took the position that contempt and conspiracy would involve punishment for the same acts and that the prosecution should decide which of the two proceedings to abandon, since it would be illegal to punish a man twice for the same offense. Gregory asked the court to quash the equity charges and, should this be denied, at least to grant the defendants the benefit of a jury trial. The United States attorney vigorously opposed the suggestion by announcing that he had never known of a contempt case being tried by a jury and that just because the defendants had been indicted for the same acts which constituted contempt was their misfortune. The court sustained the prosecution by refusing to dismiss contempt proceedings or to permit a jury to hear the case. Before the hearing could progress further, however, Edwin Walker became ill, and the court decided on July 25 to postpone the case until September 5. The defendants were each required to post an additional bond of seven thousand dollars, which increased the aggregate amount of their guaranty for the contempt hearing to forty thousand dollars. This time Debs and his associates preferred not to waive bail and were released from custody.[28]

In the judgment of Richard Olney this delay in equity proceedings was extremely unfortunate since, as he believed, it would give the American Railway Union the opportunity to start another strike. He felt that freedom for Debs and his co-officials at this juncture would tend to create apprehension and alarm among the business classes.[29] Edwin Walker did not think so and at some length explained to the perturbed attorney-general why postponement was necessary and in what respects the government would benefit from this course. It was quite apparent that Walker's illness was not serious and nothing more than a case of mild indisposition. "The heat was really stifling," he wrote, "and the crowd of strikers present at the hearing made the air of the room intolerable." Overwhelmed by fatigue, he felt an impelling need for an immediate vacation at the seashore; but there were other reasons why he wanted the hearing deferred.

In a lengthy conference with Judge Woods the special district attorney was advised that the best interests of the government would be served by the proposed delay. Woods had to leave Chicago within a few days and could not possibly conclude the hearing before his departure; and so there seemed to remain no other course open to the prosecution, unless it had been willing to refer the matter to the master for proof—a procedure that would have kept all parties in the city during the entire summer. Walker could see no reason for doing this, particularly since the situation did not require haste. He believed the strike was already broken and the American Railway Union so badly demoralized that by September there would be little left of the organization. In seeking to quiet Olney's fears, he explained that, until the hearing was held, contempt proceedings would hang over the heads of the accused, and, as Judge Woods had warned, any repetition of the acts complained of would only aggravate the contempt.

Walker felt certain that labor considered the contempt proceedings as a test case involving the effectiveness of equity in controlling unions. In view of this he believed that the defendants would contest the case, if possible, even more strenuously than the indictments for conspiracy. The need for a government victory in the matter seemed imperative to him; and to Olney he explained: "If the courts sustain the position of the government, that equity has jurisdiction to restrain such confederations, and enforce the rule of non-interference with the transportation of the mails and interstate commerce, there would be no more boycotting, and no further violence, in aid of strikes."[30] While impressed with the importance of equity in prosecuting the union leaders, Walker was just as anxious to secure convictions under the indictments and for this reason believed that the contempt case should be delayed until fall since the same evidence would be used in both proceedings. He was inclined to believe that the government would commit a strategical blunder by showing its full hand in the civil case in advance of criminal proceedings.

Among other reasons for the delay in contempt proceedings was the belief that by waiting a few weeks some very damaging evidence would be made available by the *Chicago Herald*. This publication had agreed to aid in the prosecution of both the civil and criminal cases and had already furnished some evidence, the rest of which was expected by the first of September. With this proof Walker seemed confident that he would have "no trouble whatever in connecting the directors of the American Railway Union with all the violence and intimidation that was exercised over the employees that remained in the service of the different railway companies, as well as over new employees that were called to take the place of strikers."[31]

Whether the *Chicago Herald* was able to justify the enthusiastic expectations of Edwin Walker is doubtful, but it is clear that this paper was bitter toward the American Railway Union and editorially made malicious attacks against it.[32] According to the officials of the union, this hostility was primarily due to their refusal to deposit the funds of the union in the bank owned by John R. Walsh, who was also publisher of the *Chicago Herald*. Affidavits were made, purporting to show that when the American Railway

Union convention assembled in June a representative of this newspaper approached Eugene Debs and some of his associates, offering the support of this publication if the union would do business with Walsh's bank. By refusing, Debs presumably invoked the ill will of John Walsh.[33]

To the attorney-general the foregoing reasons seemed valid enough as a justification for the delay in equity proceedings, although he would have preferred to have the matter settled at once and the accused imprisoned. In wishing Walker a pleasant vacation, Olney was quite complimentary, thanking him "for the great ability and discretion, as well as zeal, which you have brought to the aid of the Government in the whole affair."[34]

The absence of Walker from Chicago did not deter the government from filing a second information on August 1, charging the remaining directors of the American Railway Union with the violation of the injunction. To the original four were added five more: James Hogan, William E. Burns, Roy M. Goodwin, J. F. McVean, and Martin J. Elliot. It was now affirmed that all the officers and directors of the union had entered into a conspiracy to promote the strike and boycott. The prosecution declared that the directors, in order more effectively to realize their aims, had divided the work among committees. To Debs and Howard had been assigned publicity; to Hogan, direction over all correspondence and telegrams; and to Rogers, Burns, and Goodwin supervision of meetings, speeches, and the organization of local lodges. Rogers was identified as the editor of the *Railway Times*—the official organ through which the directors were alleged to have counseled the members of the union and other railroad workers to disregard the injunction. These and other points were listed, some in repetition of those already set forth in the first information.[35]

In reply to this information the defendants filed a joint answer, which in many respects did not differ essentially from the one made by the original defendants. It was denied that any of them had entered into a conspiracy to paralyze the railroads until such companies would agree not to haul Pullman palace cars. Injecting a new note into their strategy, the defense expressed the belief that the railroads were the ones really guilty of conspiracy, since they had formed an illegal combination for the purpose of reducing wages and preventing the members of the American Railway Union from securing redress of grievances. The Pullman Company was alleged to be a partner to the conspiracy. It was claimed that in pursuance of this conspiracy, and for the purpose of supporting the Pullman Company in its struggle and in order to bring down upon labor the penalties of the law, the railroads invoked the action of the courts.

The defense denied that there was any specific or fixed division of duties among the officers and directors, although it was admitted that in practice "some tacit and occasional division actually occurred, but that the same was in no wise formally or generally observed." It was asserted that neither in the *Railway Times* nor anywhere else did the defendants counsel the slightest violation of the restraining order. All the telegrams set forth in the information were declared to have been sent for the purpose of lawfully and peacefully advising men voluntarily to quit work because of the "grievances done or threatened them, and by reason of the unlawful conspiracy of the railroads . . . . and the Pullman Palace Car Company." The defendants emphasized that the strike was "occasioned solely by the free, voluntary and peaceable action of the employees" in quitting work for the purpose of protecting their rights and that they took this action without control, assistance, or direction from the executives of the union.[36]

Clarence Darrow was invited to join in the defense of the accused and after some hesitation accepted, although aware that it would take a tremendous amount of time with little compensation. He did so out of sympathy for labor and because of the belief that the leaders of the American Railway Union were being unjustly prosecuted. When the strike broke out, he was counsel for the Chicago and Northwestern Railroad and was assigned to the legal committee of the General Managers' Association. Having no desire to be a party in the campaign to crush the strikers, he asked to be relieved of this responsibility. The president of the railroad, to whom Darrow explained his position so candidly, very generously permitted the lawyer to remain in the service of the road without having to use his talents against labor. Later, when Darrow decided to defend the officials of the American Railway Union, he was granted leave from his duties on this road.[37]

The problem of financing the costs of legal defense became exceedingly difficult in view of the straitened circumstances of the American Railway Union. The funds of the union, never very large, were now all gone. Since Debs and the other directors were unable to shoulder the expense, they were compelled to rely upon contributions. The *Railway Times* and the *American Federationist* appealed to labor organizations and union members everywhere to make donations to the Debs Legal Defense Fund. The executive council of the American Federation of Labor voted five hundred dollars and did what it could to solicit money from affiliated organizations. A minimum of $20,000 was deemed necessary, but the total collected by the middle of November from all sources did not exceed $2,000.[38] Despite all this, the defense went grimly ahead in its preparation to protect the accused from the vengeance of the government.

In the federal court at Chicago on September 5 William A. Woods, as presiding judge, began the hearing on contempt. The defense was represented by Erwin, Darrow, and Gregory, and the government by Walker and Milchrist. The latter, whose term of office had expired in August, was appointed by the attorney-general as special assistant in order that he might still continue to aid in the prosecution of the strike leaders. The receivers of the Santa Fe Railroad had also filed an information against four and then later all of the defendants, and since this case was identical to that of the United States, the court decided to hear both at the same time.

As the hearing progressed, it became apparent that the defense was pursuing a course at variance with what the government expected. Not only did the defendants avail themselves of the privilege not to testify, but they called no witnesses and offered no evidence in their behalf except parts of certain documents which were offered in connection with other parts presented by the prosecution.[39] Such a policy was doubtless dictated by the belief that it would be better strategy to save their witnesses and most of their evidence for the conspiracy trial, considered much more crucial. The counsel for the defense also may have questioned the wisdom of revealing their full case in a court where there was no jury and before a judge whose lack of sympathy for labor was mirrored in the injunction which he had helped to issue. The defense was, nevertheless, emphatic in denying that there had been any violation of the injunction. It was contended that the defendants did not favor interference with the movement of mail or interstate commerce, nor did they at any time urge the strikers to engage in lawlessness. The right of the court to issue the writ and to hear and determine the contempt case was seriously questioned. The court, it was held, had no authority under the Sherman Anti-trust Act to issue the injunction. The denial of trial by jury and the punishment of the accused for conspiracy and contempt—thus twice for the same offense—were declared to be unconstitutional.

In seeking to prove guilt the prosecution called numerous witnesses, most of whom were furnished by the railroads; and in addition submitted much documentary material, principally telegrams. As the hearing proceeded, Walker kept Olney well informed of developments and was in turn advised by the attorney-general. Walker acknowledged to Olney on the fourteenth of September that the defendants "did not personally or physically interfere with the movement of trains" and that they did "expressly warn all persons against violence and interference with the transportation of the mails." In the opinion of Walker, however, this fact did not lessen their guilt. As the railroads were being paralyzed and as disorders were spreading, he explained, the accused continued to dispatch orders "calling the men out and urging those who were not members of the union to join the strike." Walker confided to Olney the belief that, if the court should deny the legality of the injunction under the Sherman Anti-trust Act, the government could still invoke the writ to prevent unlawful interference with the transportation of the mail.[40]

In the judgment of Richard Olney, the Sherman Anti-trust

Law furnished the necessary authority for the writ; but, even without resort to this measure, the government was still able to protect the mail by equity proceedings. He believed, however, that the injunction could be sustained on broader grounds—the right of a court of equity to render protection against a public nuisance. In clarifying this point Olney explained to Walker that a railroad was nothing but "a peculiar species of a public highway" and that, if the courts could enjoin any obstruction or obstacle on a public highway, they could do the same for any railroad. By virtue of the Interstate Commerce Act, declared the attorney-general, all interstate railroads were subject to the jurisdiction of the United States, and any obstruction thereon could be enjoined by the federal government as a public nuisance. Nor did the obstruction necessarily have to be some physical obstacle; it could be a strike. By uniting the workers and simultaneously withdrawing them from an interstate railroad, the defendants obstructed the operation of the road and were guilty of creating a public nuisance. Such an action, averred Olney, was illegal and could be restrained by a court of equity.[41] Realizing the effectiveness of this contention, Walker gave it considerable emphasis in his closing arguments, without, however, overlooking the Sherman Anti-trust Act as a source of authority for the writ.[42]

Since Judge Woods viewed the Debs contempt case as a real opportunity, he was in no hurry to hand down the decision, which he desired to be an extremely able piece of work.[43] Although the final arguments were heard during the latter part of September, it was not until December 14 that the decision was rendered. In all respects it was a sweeping victory for the government. Every contention of the prosecution was sustained; and by numerous legal citations Woods endeavored to buttress his conclusions.

Concerning the applicability of the Sherman Anti-trust Act to this case, the judge entertained not the slightest doubt. While acknowledging that the "original measure, as proposed in the Senate, was directed wholly against trusts and not at organizations of labor in any form," he expressed the belief that the bill subsequently underwent modification. But, declared the judge, it was intended that the courts should perform the duty of interpreting the law and determining what combinations or conspiracies were in restraint of trade. In the opinion of Woods, the law was very comprehensive, embracing "all instrumentalities and subjects of transportation among the states." Applying the law to the matter at hand, he ruled that the boycott of Pullman cars and the interference with transportation represented a conspiracy within the meaning of the act.[44] The validity of the injunction under this law was thus fully upheld, but the court recognized other grounds as equally valid in sustaining the writ. Under the interstate commerce laws the government was also privileged to utilize the writ.[45]

The right to punish for contempt was held not to be an abridgment of the right of trial by jury. It was pointed out that the same act may be both a crime and a contempt of court—the former to be tried by a jury, the latter by the court of equity which issues the writ.[46]

Did the defendants violate the injunction? In the opinion of the court they did. By citing telegrams and by quoting remarks alleged to have been made by Eugene Debs, the judge endeavored to prove that the injunction did not cause the American Railway Union in any way to modify its course of action. The defendants, it was charged, had practical control of the organization and were largely responsible for its policies. Their original intention was only to boycott Pullman sleepers; but, when the railroads began to discharge the men who refused to handle these cars, the union officials decided to halt the movement of trains until their demands were granted. This action, averred the court, was taken as early as June 27; and from this time on, and in complete defiance of the injunction, the defendants did everything possible to stop transportation.[47]

As for the admonitions against violence—these the judge was disposed to discount, expressing the belief that they were primarily designed to win public support for labor. It is reasonable to infer, he exclaimed, that the defendants intended that "this strike should differ from others only in magnitude of design and boldness of execution, and that the accustomed accessories of intimidation and violence, so far at least as these were found essential to success, would not be omitted." While acknowledging that the accused may have opposed extreme violence, the court charged them with responsibility for much of the lawlessness that occurred.[48] In boycotting Pullman cars, which are "instrumentalities of commerce," the defendants were held to be guilty of a conspiracy in restraint of interstate commerce and thus to have violated the Sherman Anti-trust Act. By seeking to halt the movement of trains the leaders of the American Railway Union were charged with extending the conspiracy against transportation.[49]

Eugene Debs was sentenced by Judge Woods to six months' confinement, while the other defendants were given only three. Because of crowded conditions at the Cook County jail it was decided to commit the prisoners to the McHenry County jail at Woodstock, Illinois, where on January 8, 1895, they began serving their sentences for contempt.[50] Shortly thereafter the counsel for the defense applied to the United States Supreme Court for a writ of error and a writ of habeas corpus. While denying the former, the court consented to grant a hearing on the latter, which, however, was not held until March 26.

In pleading their case before this high tribunal, the defense counsel was strengthened by the addition of a distinguished statesman and lawyer, Lyman Trumbull, whose services were offered without compensation, although he did accept traveling expenses. Like Darrow, his sympathies were with labor. Extremely critical of Cleveland's policies during the strike, he was now eager to use his talents in behalf of the American Railway Union, whose leaders, he believed, were being persecuted. Despite his eighty-one years, Trumbull was still active and on this occasion acquitted himself in a very creditable manner. This great liberal, who throughout the years had fought the good fight, had slightly more than a year of life left.[51]

In addition to Trumbull, the petitioners were represented by Darrow and Gregory. The latter, in his arguments, explained that the Sherman Anti-trust Act was not applicable, but that, if it were, then Section 4, which authorizes such proceedings, was unconstitutional. Why? Because it committed to a court of equity the enforcement of a penal statute and denied to the accused trial by jury contrary to the Sixth Amendment. Gregory contended that

no more tyrannous and arbitrary government can be devised than the administration of criminal law by a single judge by means of injunction and proceedings in contempt. To extend this power generally to criminal cases would be absolutely destructive to liberty and intolerable to a free people. It would be worse than *ex post facto* legislation. No man could be safe; no limits could be prescribed to the acts which might be forbidden nor the punishment to be inflicted.[52]

In denying that the prisoners had engaged in any conspiracy, Lyman Trumbull argued that what they did was done to compel the Pullman Company to adopt a conciliatory policy toward its employees. It was for this purpose only that the American Railway Union launched the boycott and then urged its members to quit work on the railroads which persisted in operating Pullman cars. In pursuit of this lawful purpose, declared Trumbull, Eugene Debs and his associates are charged with obstructing commerce, but "refusing to work for a railroad is no crime, and, though such action may incidentally delay the mails or interfere with interstate commerce, it being a lawful act, and not done for the purpose, it is no offense." Relative to the injunction, the attorney flatly charged that it pertained to matters over which a court of equity has no jurisdiction. In clarifying this point, he explained that a restraining order could be used by a property-owner to protect himself against an "irreparable injury" but that it was contrary to time-honored practice for the government to invoke the writ to prevent interference with private property, even though it were done to safeguard interstate commerce. If the prisoners are guilty of interfering with the transportation of the mails, asserted Trumbull, they should be punished under the criminal statutes, but under no circumstances does an equity court have jurisdiction.[53]

Clarence Darrow contended that the prisoners were entitled to freedom because the court lacked authority to issue the injunction and because the acts complained of in the information were not illegal. Concerning the first point, Darrow probed very carefully the history of the Sherman Anti-trust Act. By analyzing the disposition of Congress at the time the bill was passed, he tried to prove that the law was intended to apply only to "combinations in the shape of trusts and pools." He revealed that at no place in the measure was "there any mention of any labor organization or strike or boycott or the slightest reference that would be construed by men of ordinary intelligence as an intention to apply this law to the combinations of laboring men, or strikes or boycotts." And yet, protested Darrow, the circuit court dared to use such a law as authority for the injunction.[54]

Relative to his second major contention, he sought to show that the defendants did not violate the injunction, nor did they do anything which the courts had the right to enjoin. It was pointed out that the telegrams dispatched by Debs and his co-officials furnished virtually the only allegation in the information pertinent to the violation of the injunction. Some of these dispatches urged the members of the American Railway Union to quit work and to induce others to do so. In prevailing upon the workers to follow such a course, Debs was merely exercising a right which the courts had recognized as belonging to labor. "The whole information," emphasized Darrow, "plainly shows that since the granting of the injunction not one act was committed by these defendants, or any of them, that was in any way unlawful, or that could be forbidden by the court if workingmen are to have the right to organize and the right to strike."[55]

It was denied that the disorders which occurred during the strike were even remotely perpetrated by the American Railway Union. No evidence was presented, not one single fact, proclaimed Darrow, to show that the union or any of its officials were connected with any unlawful acts. Just because disorders occurred during the strike, he exclaimed, is no reason why the defendants should be held responsible.[56] He further said:

If men could not do lawful acts because violence might possibly or reasonably result, then the most innocent deeds might be crimes. To make men responsible for the remote consequences of their acts would be to destroy individual liberty and make men slaves. . . . . If it is lawful for men to organize and in accordance with the organization to cease labor, they cannot be regarded

as criminals because violence, bloodshed or crime follows such a strike. . . . .
Strikes are deplorable, and so are their causes. All men who engage in them
hope for a time when better social relations will make them as unnecessary as
any other form of warfare will some day be. But under the present conditions of
industrial life, with the present conflicting interests of capital and labor, each
perhaps blindly seeking for more perfect social adjustments, strikes and lockouts
are incidents of industrial life. They are not justified because men love social
strife and industrial war, but because in the present system of industrial evolution to deprive workingmen of this power would be to strip and bind them and
leave them helpless as the prey of the great and strong.[57]

The government was represented by Attorney-General Olney,
Assistant Attorney-General Whitney, and Edwin Walker. So important did Richard Olney consider the case that, contrary to his
policy, he appeared before the tribunal. The only other time he
did this, while serving as attorney-general, was in arguing the
income tax case.[58] He was determined that the contempt decision should be sustained. His feeling for Debs was one of unmiti-
gated hatred. Olney was extremely anxious that this labor leader
be severely punished; but in a communication to Walker on
January 7, 1895, he expressed the fear that "no punishment he is
likely to get, if he is convicted and sentenced on all the pending
indictments, will be commensurate with his offense."[59]

Reserving for himself a major role in the hearing, Olney argued
eloquently that the injunction should rest upon broader grounds
than were set forth in the circuit court decision. While convinced
that complete authority for the writ was furnished by the Sherman Anti-trust Act and by the government's property interest in
the mail bags, he nevertheless believed a much better basis for the
injunction existed, and to this proposition devoted the greater
part of his plea. The federal government, he announced, had
complete jurisdiction over the railroads by virtue of the interstate
commerce law and other acts relating to post roads and the shipment of livestock. This legislation was construed by Olney to constitute an express prohibition against interference with interstate
rail transportation. Notwithstanding, many railroads were paralyzed, and much property was destroyed in July, 1894, the responsibility for which, in his judgment, belonged to the defendants, unless "it be true that man can wantonly touch the match

to powder and yet be blameless because not rightly realizing the ensuing devastation." In meeting the situation, explained the attorney-general, the state authorities acted slowly and ineffectively, thus aggravating the situation. But, even if Illinois had done otherwise, he averred, there was need for intervention by the United States government, since interstate commerce—a federal matter—was being assaulted.

What remedies did the government have? Irrespective of the Sherman Anti-trust Act, the United States could prosecute for conspiracy to obstruct the mails; but this method, he revealed, would not be very effective against large mobs, since the object was not so much to punish interference as to prevent it. The government could apply to the courts of equity for a restraining order against unlawful interruption of interstate rail transportation, and in doing so, insisted Olney, the government had no alternative because criminal prosecution was wholly inadequate in meeting the emergency. Just as a trustee has the right to protect the property intrusted to his care by resort to a court of equity, even though he has no private interest in the matter, so the United States—a trustee for all interests and parties concerned—was held to possess the power to render protection by all the means at its disposal, including equity proceedings. It was denied that the government needed expressed authorization from Congress to avail itself of this weapon. The executive branch of the government had received statutory power to protect interstate commerce and was under obligation "to carry the legislation into effect by all appropriate means at its command." Since the injunction was the most effective instrumentality in this case, Olney held that it was precisely the one which the government, as the guardian of public interests and rights, should employ.[60] Contempt proceedings, he pointed out, were essentially of a summary character requiring no indictment by grand jury or trial by petit jury. As to the charge that the defendants had been deprived of their constitutional rights, he pointed out that the same act may be a crime and yet involve contempt.[61]

Walker's brief and Whitney's oral arguments need not be discussed here as they produced little in the way of a new approach to the case but rather an attempt to strengthen arguments to which reference has already been made. The hearing required only two days, but not until May 27 did Justice Brewer deliver the unanimous opinion of the Supreme Court.

Two questions were propounded by the court: (1) Does the federal government possess the authority to prevent interference with the transportation of mails and interstate commerce? (2) If so, has the court of equity the jurisdiction to render assistance by issuing injunctions? In answer to the first question, it was held that Congress, having been invested by the Constitution with the power to control interstate commerce and the postal system, adopted various statutes pertaining to these matters. Since Congress has the power, affirmed the court, "it follows that the national government may prevent any unlawful and forcible interference therewith." How can this be accomplished? The authorities can punish those guilty by criminal action; but this might prove ineffective in enforcing freedom of interstate commerce, and without some other remedy the government would be impotent. The court announced:

But there is no such impotence in the National Government. The entire strength of the nation may be used to enforce in any part of the land the full and free exercise of all national powers and the security of all rights entrusted by the constitution to its care. . . . . If the emergency arises, the army of the nation, and all its militia, are at the service of the nation to compel obedience to its laws.[62]

In answering the second question the Supreme Court held that every government has the right to appeal to its own courts for assistance and, even though lacking pecuniary interest in the matter, may not be deterred from seeking such aid. A court of equity, it was explained, has jurisdiction over public nuisances and may be resorted to by the government to prevent them. During the Pullman Strike an intolerable situation arose. Interstate commerce and the mails were obstructed, and in meeting this public nuisance the courts of equity were held to have the authority to act. The same offense, it was asserted, may give rise to a civil action and a criminal prosecution. In derailing a train, for instance, the culprit would be punished by the criminal courts; but in committing this act he may also be guilty of disobeying an order of a civil court, issued for the protection of property rights, and would be punished for contempt without jury trial. In such procedure, affirmed the decision, there would be no violation of the right of trial by jury since the "power of a court to make an order carries with it the equal power to punish for disobedience of that order. . . . . To submit the question of disobedience to another tribunal, be it jury or another court, would operate to deprive the proceeding of half its efficiency."[63]

The court denied that the right of employees to quit work had been challenged. The purpose of the writ was rather "to restrain forcible obstructions of the highway along which interstate commerce travels and the mails are carried." Convinced that there was such an obstruction, the Supreme Court held that the circuit court possessed the authority to issue the injunction and to punish by fine or imprisonment all who were guilty of disobeying the order.[64] The writ of habeas corpus was thus denied and the decision of Judge Woods affirmed, but on broader grounds than had been advanced by the lower court.

In the judgment of Richard Olney, the decision left nothing to be desired; and by the business interests throughout the nation it was received with unconcealed enthusiasm. One week previously the Supreme Court had declared the federal income tax unconstitutional—a decision no less gratifying to the same moneyed interests. To the attorney-general and his friends the Debs decision was infinitely more significant; and in their elation over this victory they could quickly forget that the rich no longer were obliged to pay a tax on their income. Lawyers, industrialists, and many others showered Richard Olney with the heartiest congratulations over his success in the Debs case. None seemed more jubilant than George R. Peck, chairman of the legal committee of the General Managers' Association, who wired the attorney-general: "I congratulate you with all my heart on the Debs Decision. The Supreme Court seems to agree with you that 'the soil of Illinois is the soil of the United States.' "[65]

The decision proved offensive to workers everywhere. Its implications were all too clear, particularly as to the extraordinary power now recognized as available to the government in resisting the efforts of organized labor. The injunction had received from the Supreme Court a legal sanctity such as it had never had before. It is little wonder that this decision, coming as it did close upon the heels of the income tax ruling, caused many people to view that high tribunal as an exalted servant of the vested interests.[66]

Many liberals were extremely critical of the decision, but none was more so than Governor Altgeld, who viewed it as creating a form of government not hitherto known to men—government by injunction. A federal judge could now issue an order at the behest of some corporation attorney, prohibiting most anything, including that which the law did not forbid. Thus could the judge legislate and, having done so, proceed to arrest people and, without a jury trial, to imprison them, not for disobeying any statute but on the pretext that they had violated his injunction. In the Debs case, explained the governor, it was the judge who issued the injunction and who later sentenced the defendants to prison—the "judge being legislator, court and executioner." By such summary procedure, protested Altgeld, the constitutional guaranty that "no man shall be deprived of his liberty without a trial by an impartial jury" is virtually destroyed, as well as the theory that ours is a government of law.

The governor of Illinois was convinced that if the defendants had been given a jury trial they would have been released, since violation of the law was not proved against them. The subserviency of the federal judiciary to corporate interest was set forth as the cause for this deplorable condition of affairs. Altgeld believed that appointment to the bench was determined by the candidate's willingness to serve the propertied interests. Against this situation the governor impulsively cried out:

. . . . The corrupt money power has its withering finger on every pulse in the land and is destroying the rugged manhood and love of liberty which alone can carry a people through a great crisis. What, then, is the situation today? For over twenty years foreign and domestic capitalism has dominated. "It sits in the White House and legislates in the capitol. Courts of justice are its ministers and legislatures are its lackeys." And the whole machinery of fashionable society is its handmaid.[67]

Governor Altgeld made these remarks on June 2, 1895, less than a week after the Supreme Court had spoken. He uttered them with the full knowledge that Eugene Debs and his associates would not be convicted by a jury for conspiracy or any other crime. Four months earlier, or sixteen days after the defendants started serving their sentence for contempt, the trial for conspiracy began in the federal court of Judge Grosscup. From the Woodstock jail, some fifty miles northwest of Chicago, Debs and his fellow-prisoners were taken daily to that city for the trial which opened on January 24. The directors of the American Railway Union were not the only ones accused of conspiracy to obstruct and retard the mails. Originally sixty-nine had been indicted for this offense by the federal grand jury in Chicago, but the government decided, prior to the commencement of the trial, to proceed against only forty-five—a number which was shortly reduced to twenty.[68]

The attorneys for the defense consisted of Clarence Darrow and S. S. Gregory, while the prosecution comprised Edwin Walker, Thomas Milchrist, and the new federal district attorney, John C. Black. As the trial got under way, it became apparent to all that this was no ordinary case but one having far-reaching significance to labor. In the opinion of Darrow, it was a historical case—one which would count much for liberty or against liberty. The punishment for conspiracy carried a maximum penalty of two years' imprisonment or a fine of ten thousand dollars or both; but to Darrow it was not just a question of securing an acquittal for the defendants but of safeguarding the rights of labor.

The defense counsel had prepared their case with painstaking care and were quick to seize on any situation that would serve to undermine the government's position. At the very outset, for instance, Gregory objected to the participation of Walker in the case, on the grounds that, while representing the United States, he was also serving as counsel for the Chicago, Milwaukee, and St. Paul Railroad, one of the lines interested in the case. When Walker denied that part of the statement was true, Gregory demanded that an inquiry be made into the matter—a course which the court declined to follow. The judge explained somewhat lamely that it was not for the court to interfere with the right of the attorney-general to retain Walker in the case.[69]

Farmers predominated in the jury, which was selected with a minimum of delay. The government was careful to see that all workingmen were excluded, but the jury as constituted did not appear prejudiced against labor. Having disposed of the preliminaries, the court was now prepared for a statement from the prosecution and the defense.

Speaking in behalf of the former, Milchrist charged that the violence during the strike was the result of the conspiracy entered into by the defendants. In proving conspiracy, he denied that it was necessary to show that any of the accused had committed an overt act or that they had met together or formally organized for the purpose of carrying out the conspiracy. He declared that, since those who engage in conspiracy do so in secret, it would be impossible to prove it by direct evidence and that the "results of their acts must be taken as evidence of their intentions." The defendants, he charged, were guilty of conspiracy when they cut off Pullman cars which comprised a regular part of the trains carrying mail. Milchrist conceded that it was lawful for Debs to call out members of the American Railway Union but that in ordering others out he was guilty of conspiracy.[70]

Clarence Darrow in opening the case for the defense charged that Milchrist was a "puppet in the hands of the great railroad corporations in this persecution, not prosecution." In the three thousand dollars' worth of telegrams sent by the defendants, not one, it was affirmed, contained a word urging violence, although many exhorted the strikers to avoid lawlessness. No person, averred Darrow, can be convicted of conspiracy unless it is proved that he conspired to do the acts complained of; but Milchrist, refusing to recognize this, has contended that the accused conducted a strike during which lawlessness occurred, and that they are therefore responsible for it. It was explained that there were "two requisites to crime, intent and act" and that, in so far as the mail was concerned, there was not the slightest desire on the part of the defendants to interfere; indeed, they were anxious to haul the mails but would not allow the operation of Pullman cars.

The general managers, on the contrary, refused to permit the mail to move without these cars, preferring, as Darrow revealed, "to use the inconvenience of the public and the feeling of sanctity for the mails as a club to defeat the effort that was being made to better the condition of workingmen and women."

Darrow reminded the court that the right to strike has been acknowledged by the prosecution. The railroad workers, availing themselves of this right, quit work and very soon became engaged in a struggle of gigantic proportions. "Yet great as was the excitement stirred up by the fevered accounts of a fevered time," said Darrow, "scarcely any foolish words and not a single unlawful one can be charged to these men." He further declared: "The evidence will show that all the defendants did was in behalf of the employees of that man whose name is odious wherever men have a drop of blood, Mr. Pullman. No man or newspaper undertook to defend Mr. Pullman except the General Managers' Association, and their defense gives added proof of his infamy."⁷¹

In his interpretation of what comprised conspiracy, Judge Grosscup gave considerable comfort to the prosecution. In proving conspiracy it was necessary, he ruled, to "show an agreement of obstruction which is to retard the United States mails." In elucidating this, he expressed the belief that the government did not have to show that the agreement in so many words provided for interference with the mails. If the agreement did not infer obstruction but had the logical effect of causing interference with the mail—this would be an agreement of conspiracy. If the government, declared the judge, could prove that the defendants "had entered into an agreement unlawfully to stop all trains, and the natural and the logical and almost inevitable effect was the stoppage of the mail trains, such an agreement . . . . might be sufficient proof of the existence of the conspiracy."⁷²

As the trial progressed, numerous witnesses were summoned to testify. Edward M. Mulford, manager of Western Union in Chicago, revealed that nine thousand telegrams with Debs's signature were dispatched during the strike.⁷³ The most outstanding witness was Eugene Debs, who traced the part which the American Railway Union played in the strike. The origin, character, and aims of the union were set forth, as he endeavored to prove that it was scrupulously committed to a strict obedience of the law. There was nothing spectacular or sensational in his remarks, only a calm and dispassionate recital of the facts.[74]

George Pullman might have proved an interesting witness, had he been willing to testify. On February 6 the court issued a subpoena for him, but the deputy marshal, in calling at the Pullman Building to serve the writ, was informed, after some delay, that George Pullman was out. Thirty minutes previously, as the usher in the reception room later testified on the witness stand, George Pullman entered his office. When informed of the deputy's mission, however, Pullman quickly gave instructions that he was not in and by another exit hastily left the office and soon afterward the city.[75] It was not until after the jury had been dismissed that he returned to Chicago and, accompanied by his attorney, Robert Todd Lincoln, called upon Judge Grosscup.[76] Presumably the entire matter was quietly and amicably adjusted.

Among the witnesses were several railroad executives, but their testimony was not nearly so sensational as the minutes of the General Managers' Association, a copy of which Darrow managed to obtain. Using the document as evidence, he tried to show that the railroads had united in a powerful confederation for the purpose of uniformly reducing wages and otherwise pursuing a common policy toward labor.[77]

The progress of the trial was suddenly halted on February 8 by the illness of one of the jury. Being satisfied with developments, the defense was eager that some arrangement be made to resume the trial. It was proposed that a new jury be immediately impaneled, consisting of the eleven old jurors and one other, and that the evidence already taken be read to them. The judge, however, was inclined to question the legality of such procedure and accordingly dismissed the jury on February 12. This was done over the strenuous objections of the defense, which was convinced that the jury was growing more and more sympathetic to their side.[78] According to Darrow, the jury, when discharged, stood eleven to one for acquittal.[79] Convinced of the futility of prosecuting the accused, the district attorney continued the case for a year and then quietly entered nolle prosequi on the records, thus indicating that no further action would be taken.

After the abrupt ending of the conspiracy case, Eugene Debs still had the greater part of his contempt sentence to serve. From the outset he quickly adjusted himself to the routine of prison life. In his heart there was no bitterness toward society, although the injustice of the sentence rankled in his soul. This feeling was apparent in a manifesto which he issued immediately after entering the Woodstock jail. Declaring that he and his colleagues had no regrets or apologies to make, he characterized the entire proceedings of the circuit court as "infamous." He proclaimed:

> There is not a scrap of testimony to show that one of us violated any law whatsoever. If we are guilty of conspiracy, why are we punished for contempt? . . . . We are, by chance, the mere instrumentalities in the evolutionary processes in operation through which industrial slavery is to be abolished and economic freedom established. Then the starry banner will symbolize, as it was designed to symbolize, social, political, religious, and economic emancipation from the thraldom of tyranny, oppression and degradation.[80]

The months of imprisonment gave him the opportunity to read widely and to meditate deeply on the injustices and contradictions of the economic system. Slowly a transformation occurred in his mental processes; and, when he emerged from prison, he was unalterably committed to socialism as the only hope of mankind. To that cause he was thenceforth destined to devote the best years of his life.

The imprisonment of Debs had the further effect of making him a national character and in labor and liberal circles somewhat of a martyr. His mail at Woodstock was exceptionally heavy and when freed he was in demand almost everywhere as a public speaker. His release was the occasion for a mammoth celebration in Chicago by organized labor. Representatives of more than fifty unions journeyed in a special train to Woodstock in order to greet their hero and accompany him to Chicago. Upon their return, Debs was welcomed at the station by one hundred thousand people. Declining to ride in a carriage drawn by six white horses, he expressed a preference to walk in the parade held in his honor. That night he received a tremendous ovation in the great convention hall at Battery D, which overflowed with admirers and supporters.[81] Among the speakers was Henry D. Lloyd, who hailed Debs as the "most popular man among the real people today . . . . the victim of judicial lynch law, the repudiator of contempt of court as a substitute for the constitution of the United States, and of Gatling guns as harmonizer of labour and capital; the first rebel against government by injunction."[82]

Glad to be free and not ashamed of having been incarcerated, Eugene Debs declared to this great throng:

> I have borne with such composure as I could command the imprisonment which deprived me of my liberty. Were I a criminal, were I guilty of crimes meriting a prison cell, had I ever lifted my hand against the life or liberty of my fellowmen . . . . I could not be here. I would have fled from the haunts of civilization and taken up my residence in some cave where the voice of my kindred is never heard; but I am standing here with no self-accusation of crime or criminal intent festering in my conscience, in the sunlight, once more among my fellowmen.[83]

NOTES

1. *U.S. Strike Commission Report*, p. 146.
2. *Debs: His Life, Writings and Speeches*, pp. 17–18.
3. *New York World*, July 5, 1894, p. 8.
4. *Proceedings of the General Managers' Association . . . . 1894*, p. 192.
5. Walker to Olney, July 2, 1894, *Appendix to the . . . . Report of the Attorney General . . . . 1896*, pp. 63–64.
6. Walker to Olney, July 3, 1894, *ibid.*, pp. 67–68.
7. *Ibid.*, p. 70.
8. Walker to Olney, July 6, 1894, *ibid.*, pp. 71–72.
9. *Ibid.*, pp. 74–75.
10. Roswell R. Miller (president of the Chicago, Milwaukee, and St. Paul Railroad) to Henry H. Porter (president of the Chicago and Eastern Illinois Railroad), July 9, 1894, Cleveland Papers.
11. *Chicago Times*, July 11, 1894, pp. 1, 2; *Inter Ocean*, July 11, 1894, p. 2.
12. *Public Opinion*, XVII (1894), 359.
13. *New York Times*, July 11, 1894, pp. 1, 2; *Inter Ocean*, July 11, 1894, pp. 1, 2; *Appendix to the . . . . Report of the Attorney General . . . . 1896*, pp. 77, 78.
14. *Debs: His Life, Writings and Speeches*, p. 22; *Chicago Times*, July 11, 1894, pp. 1, 2.
15. *New York World*, July 12, 1894, p. 2; Walker to Olney, July 11, 1894, Cleveland Papers.
16. Olney to Walker, July 11, 1894, *Appendix to the . . . . Report of the Attorney General . . . . 1896*, p. 80.
17. Walker to Olney, July 12, 1894, *ibid.*, p. 81.
18. Olney to Walker, July 12, 1894, Cleveland Papers.

19. Walker to Olney, July 13, 1894, *ibid.*

20. *Debs: His Life, Writings and Speeches,* p. 23; *Appendix to the . . . . Report of the Attorney General . . . . 1896,* p. 91.

21. *Appendix to the . . . . Report of the Attorney General . . . . 1896,* p. 197.

22. Altgeld, *op. cit.,* pp. 681–82.

23. *U.S. Strike Commission Report,* p. 37.

24. *Federal Reporter,* LXIV, 727–30.

25. *New York Times,* July 18, 1894, pp. 1, 5; *Chicago Times,* July 18, 1894, p 1; *Appendix to the . . . . Report of the Attorney General . . . . 1896,* pp. 87, 92.

26. Walker to Olney, July 17, 1894, and July 20, 1894, *ibid.,* pp. 90, 91–93.

27. *Federal Reporter,* LXIV, 730–34.

28. *New York Times,* July 24, 1894, p. 5, July 25, 1894, p. 5, and July 26, 1894, p. 4; *Debs: His Life, Writings and Speeches,* p. 22.

29. Olney to Walker, July 26, 1894, *Appendix to the . . . . Report of the Attorney General . . . . 1896,* p. 94; Olney to Walker, July 28, 1894, Richard Olney Papers.

30. Walker to Olney, July 26, 1894 (first letter); Walker to Olney, July 26, 1894 (second letter), Richard Olney Papers.

31. *Ibid.*

32. *Chicago Herald,* July 23, 1894, p. 4.

33. *Chicago Times,* July 22, 1894, p. 1.

34. Olney to Walker, July 28, 1894, Richard Olney Papers.

35. *Federal Reporter,* LXIV, 734–35.

36. *Ibid.,* pp. 735–37.

37. Darrow, *op. cit.,* pp. 57–59, 61–62.

38. *American Federationist,* I (1894), 127, 193; *Railway Times,* September 1, 1894, p. 1; *Chicago Record,* January 26, 1895, p. 7.

39. *Federal Reporter,* LXIV, 793.

40. Walker to Olney, September 14, 1894, Richard Olney Papers.

41. Olney to Walker, September 24, 1894, *ibid.*

42. Walker to Olney, September 29, 1894, and February 27, 1895, *ibid.*

43. Walker to Olney, November 2, 1894, *ibid.*

44. *Federal Reporter,* LXIV, 745–55.

45. *Ibid.,* pp. 739–45.

46. *Ibid.,* pp. 745–46.

47. *Ibid.,* pp. 755–56, 759–64.

48. *Ibid.,* pp. 756–59.

49. *Ibid.,* pp. 764–65.

50. "Petition for Habeas Corpus and Certiorari," pp. 2, 6, *Ex parte In the Matter of Eugene V. Debs et al., Records and Briefs of the U.S. Supreme Court,* Vol. CLVIII.

51. White, *op. cit.,* pp. 414, 418–19.

52. "Argument for Petitioners (S. S. Gregory)," pp. 1–69, *Ex parte In the Matter of Eugene V. Debs et al., Records and Briefs of the U.S. Supreme Court,* Vol. CLVIII.

53. "Brief by Lyman Trumbull," pp. 1–8, *ibid.*

54. "Arguments for Petitioners (Clarence Darrow)," pp. 1–51, *ibid.*

55. *Ibid.,* pp. 63–73.

56. *Ibid.,* pp. 73–85.

57. *Ibid.,* pp. 85–97.

58. James, *op. cit.,* pp. 26–27.

59. Olney to Walker, January 7, 1895, Richard Olney Papers.

60. "Oral Arguments of Richard Olney," pp. 1–17, *Ex parte In the matter of Eugene V. Debs et al.*, *Records and Briefs of the U.S. Supreme Court*, Vol. CLVIII.

61. *Ibid.*, pp. 17–21.

62. *United States Reports*, CLVIII, 578–82.

63. *Ibid.*, pp. 582–98.

64. *Ibid.*, pp. 598–600.

65. George R. Peck to Olney, May 27, 1895, Richard Olney Papers.

66. Charles Warren, *The Supreme Court in the United States*, III, 423–24.

67. Altgeld, *op. cit.*, pp. 459–61.

68. *Debs: His Life, Writings and Speeches*, pp. 13, 23; *Chicago Record*, January 26, 1895, p. 7.

69. *Chicago Record*, January 25, 1895, p. 5; *Chicago Times*, January 25, 1895, p. 7.

70. *Chicago Times*, January 27, 1895, p. 7.

71. *Ibid.*

72. *Ibid.*, January 30, 1895, p. 9.

73. *Chicago Record*, January 31, 1895, p. 7.

74. *Debs: His Life, Writings and Speeches*, pp. 25–29.

75. *Chicago Record*, February 8, 1895, p. 7.

76. *Debs: His Life, Writings and Speeches*, pp. 183–84.

77. *Ibid.*, p. 25.

78. *Chicago Times*, February 9, 1895, p. 9, February 12, 1895, p. 9, and February 13, 1895, p. 9.

79. *Op. cit.*, p. 66.

80. *Debs: His Life, Writings and Speeches*, p. 41.

81. *Ibid.*, pp. 41–49; Darrow, *op. cit.*, pp. 67–68.

82. Henry D. Lloyd, *Men, the Workers*, p. 183.

83. *Debs: His Life, Writings and Speeches*, pp. 46–47.

CHAPTER XIII

PUBLIC OPINION AND THE PRESS

FROM the scattered references that have already been made to the press it is apparent that the newspapers of the nation were inclined to be very hostile toward the American Railway Union. Measured in terms of accuracy and fairness, journalism was woefully lacking during this period. Sensationalism, misrepresentation, and other techniques of yellow journalism were abundantly revealed in the news stories that crowded the pages of numerous metropolitan newspapers. Controlled by capitalistic influence, these publications were unable to view the struggle in a detached or disinterested frame of mind. The same fears and misgivings that disturbed the propertied classes during that hectic year of 1894 caused the press to portray the Pullman Strike in a manner calculated to arouse the strongest ill will against labor.

The newspapers in Chicago most violently opposed to the American Railway Union were the *Chicago Herald, Inter Ocean, Chicago Tribune, Chicago Journal,* and *Chicago Evening Post.* Reporters discovered that their stories on the strike, when published, were garbled, colored, and distorted. The interviews granted by Eugene Debs to press representatives were subject to deliberate misrepresentation; and statements falsely attributed to him were used as a basis for vicious editorial attacks. It was even charged before the United States Strike Commission that the Chicago press actually hired falsifiers to manufacture reports designed to bring the union officials into disrepute.[1]

A reporter on the *Chicago Tribune* was dismissed from his job because he refused before the grand jury to declare as authentic a distorted version of an interview which he had with Eugene Debs. The statement was so garbled that the reporter was not even able to recognize it, nor would he perjure himself in order to retain his position. Another example of falsification occurred

when Debs left Chicago during the strike for a visit to his home in
Terre Haute. Although he scrupulously refrained from riding in
Pullman sleepers, it was immediately reported over the Associated Press wires that Debs on this occasion secured accommodations in one and from the car waived adieus to his friends. In
commenting on this alleged incident, the press queried: "When
will you fellows stop following that humbug who appeals to the
public not to patronize Pullman cars and then rides away in one
himself?" Several hundred letters of inquiry were received by
Debs concerning this charge, which he indignantly refuted.[2]

The press was so successful in misrepresenting conditions that,
when Mayor Pingree of Detroit arrived in Chicago on July 11, he
expected to see one half of the city in flames and the other half
convulsed by rioting.[3] All over the nation during the early July
days the impression grew that Chicago was torn by civil strife—a
feeling in large measure fostered by the news stories. No less effective were cartoons and sketches, whose appeal to the unthink-
ing classes must have been tremendous. Often appearing on the
front page, these drawings showed railroad cars and buildings in
flames; troops with fixed bayonets grimly holding back angry
crowds; boxcars being pushed over and other acts of vandalism
perpetrated; troops and police firing and charging upon the
mobs; and men and women plundering cars and carrying away
the loot, while other people with torches were pursuing their incendiary activities. Some of the sketches sought to establish the
impression that Chicago was under the control of anarchists and
that pitched battles were of frequent occurrence. The cartoonists
endeavored to place the responsibility for this disorder upon the
strikers, and to this end the drawings were largely directed.
Many of the most influential newspapers thus utilized every
means at their command for the molding of public opinion; and,
whether in the news columns, by the aid of sketches, or through
editorial expression, they were guilty of perverting the facts,
clothing ominous rumors in the garb of plausibility, and otherwise seeking to convince the reader that anarchy was rampant in
Chicago.

A few representative headlines will illustrate one of the most important techniques used by the press in arousing public sentiment against the strikers. The *Chicago Tribune* on June 30 captioned its major news story with "MOB IS IN CONTROL"; and on the next day used an even more dramatic heading: "MOB BENT ON RUIN—DEBS' STRIKERS BEGIN WORK OF DESTRUCTION." On July 5 the following headline appeared: "GUNS AWE THEM NOT—DRUNKEN STOCKYARD RIOTERS DEFY UNCLE SAM'S TROOPS—MOBS INVITE DEATH." The headlines for the *New York Sun* on July 6 were: "COULDN'T MASTER MOBS—REGULARS POWERLESS BEFORE CHICAGO'S RIOTOUS ARMY—SOME SOLDIERS WANT MARTIAL LAW"; and on July 7: "WILD RIOT IN CHICAGO—HUNDREDS OF FREIGHT CARS BURNED BY STRIKERS—THE TORCH IN GENERAL USE." The *Chicago Herald* on July 6 declared in heavy type: "MOB WILL IS LAW—CONDITIONS AMOUNTING TO ANARCHY PREVAIL IN THE STOCKYARD DISTRICT—ALL AUTHORITY SET AT NAUGHT BY A CROWD OF RIOTERS NUMBERING THOUSANDS." Even more startling were the headlines of the *Inter Ocean* on July 7: "FLAMES MAKE HAVOC—UNPARALLELED SCENES OF RIOT, TERROR AND PILLAGE"; "ANARCHY IS RAMPANT—MOBS AT PULLMAN AND BURNSIDE APPLY THE TORCH"; "CITY AN ARMED CAMP—U.S. TROOPS AND MILITIA AT THE DANGER POINTS PREPARED TO FIGHT."

Sensational as were these headlines, the details which followed were no less so, often representing an exaggerated description of events combined with extravagant allusions to imminent dangers. The *Washington Post*, for example, on July 7, carried prominently the following story:

FIRED BY THE MOB
CHICAGO AT THE MERCY OF THE INCENDIARY'S TORCH

PANDEMONIUM OF DISORDER

OVER 350 CARS BURNED AND MANY OTHER CONFLAGRATIONS STARTED

Bloody Work Expected Today. Thus Far the Mob Had Everything Its Own Way—Whole Trains Set on Fire and the Hose Cut—Fire Department and Police Alike Powerless—Frenzied Delight of the Victorious Rioters—The Officials and Military Realize the Solemnity of the Crisis—Anarchists and Socialists Said To Be Planning the Destruction and Looting of the Treasury—Active Preparations for the Emergency

CHICAGO, ILL., July 6.—The situation tonight is more alarming than at anytime since the trouble began. War of the bloodiest kind in Chicago is imminent, and before tomorrow goes by the railroad lines and yards may be turned into battle fields strewn with hundreds of dead and wounded. Lawlessness of the most violent kind was the order of things today. . . . . Chicago was never before the scene of such wild and desperate acts as were witnessed today and tonight. Furious mobs have for hours at a time been in complete control of certain sections of the city, and acts of lawlessness were committed without molestation. . . . . The 100,000 or more idle men in Chicago, in addition to the strikers, are taking advantage of the situation, and tonight it came to the knowledge of the Federal authorities here that the anarchists and socialist element, made up largely of the unemployed, were preparing to blow up the South end of the Federal building and take possession of the millions in money now stored in the treasury vaults.[4]

In their editorial columns the newspapers were at liberty to make a more frontal attack against the strike and, in doing so, demonstrated the utmost ruthlessness. In the opinion of many editors the struggle represented anarchy; to others it was nothing less than a rebellion; but by nearly all it was viewed as a serious upheaval which should be pitilessly suppressed. On July 3 the *Chicago Herald* expressed growing alarm that so much of the nation was in the throes of anarchy and that "we [the people] should tolerate anarchists like Debs and let him go on disintegrating the institutions of this country without realizing that we are paving the way to what might be violent convulsions."[5] According to the *New York Sun*, the American Railway Union desired to usurp absolute control over all railroads. It was charged that the president of the union had "hoisted a new flag, the flag of the American Railway Union, and while Debs' flag is aloft, the flag of the American Union has to come down."[6]

The *New York World* on July 9 asserted that the strike had obtained the proportions of a rebellion but seemed at a loss to know why Illinois should "submit even for a day to the terrors of mob law" or permit Debs from his headquarters to direct "open war against the state." In the opinion of this paper there was sufficient force within reasonable distance of Chicago to suppress all mob violence immediately and to open every railroad to traffic, and failure to utilize this force was a crime.[7] No publication was more outspoken than the *New York Times*. In seeking to discourage labor from co-operating with the "anarchists" at Chicago, this paper on July 9 bluntly charged that those who quit work out of sympathy for Debs or in support of the strike become criminals. With extreme bitterness, the editorial declared that Debs was a "lawbreaker at large, an enemy of the human race. . . . . It is time to cease mouthings. . . . . Debs should be jailed, if there are jails in his neighborhood, and the disorder his bad teachings has engendered must be squelched."[8]

Harper's Weekly characterized the boycott and ensuing strike as "blackmail on the largest scale." It was pointed out that in "suppressing such a blackmailing conspiracy as the boycott of the Pullman cars by the American Railway Union, the nation is fighting for its own existence just as truly as in suppressing the great rebellion."[9] In mid-July this journal warned that a powerful conspiracy was at work over a large portion of the nation seeking to overthrow the government of law and in its place to substitute the "decrees of conspirators." It was charged that the object of the American Railway Union was to gain mastery over all commerce and to subjugate the American people. "Until the rebellion is suppressed," proclaimed the editor, "all differences of opinion concerning its origin, or the merits of the parties to the dispute out of which it grew, are irrelevant to the issue of the hour, and must wait the future."[10]

The position of the *Independent*, a journal of some influence, differed little from that of *Harper's Weekly*. On July 5 the *Independent* deplored the fact that one man, not an employee of any railroad, possessed the power to paralyze transportation on so many lines. The American Railway Union was declared to be engaged in a gigantic conspiracy against both the railroads and the public. "We hope," asserted the editorial, "to see this rebellion . . . . speedily put down. It must be put down. The railroad companies must resist it to the bitter end."[11] In the next issue the *Independent* announced that the men engaging in the rebellion were "villains and dupes," who should be promptly suppressed and whose leaders deserved life-sentences in the penitentiary. It was further claimed that "all mischief done by irresponsible capitalistic trusts in twenty years does not amount to the wreck and waste of the anarchy of the Pullman Strike."[12]

Against Eugene Debs, personally, the press lashed out in a most savage manner. He was in large measure blamed for the situation, not only for the strike itself but for all the violence and disturbances which accompanied the struggle. Particularly vicious in their denunciation of this labor leader were certain Chicago papers. On July 2 the *Chicago Herald* charged that, in blocking mail and commerce, Debs and his associates were making war on the United States. "Short work," exclaimed the editor, "should be made of this reckless, ranting, contumacious, impudent braggadocio and law breaker. If the United States authorites perform their duty, he will issue his strike orders—if he issues any hereafter—from Cook County Jail."[13]

The *Chicago Tribune* on July 3 proclaimed that the struggle had attained the "dignity of an insurrection" and that it was now "Dictator Debs versus the Federal Government." The editor, however, hastened to point out that just as "that insurrection, wide, powerful and vast, was put down so will this one be. For if the marshals or deputies cannot quell it and the regular army cannot, then the President can call out the militia of the different states—a million men if need be—and crush it into the dust."[14] In the opinion of the *Inter Ocean* Debs should not be dealt with as a labor leader but as a criminal. The paper averred: He is as much a criminal as are the outlaws who hold up trains in the far west. It is time that the law take hold of this bold outlaw of the American Railway Union and make him feel the responsibility for the leadership of the mobs that are rioting in this city, destroying property for which the city will have to pay."[15]

In seeking to discredit Eugene Debs, the *New York Times* on July 9 raised the question of his sanity. Two years previously, it was affirmed, he had become afflicted with dipsomania and was compelled to undergo treatment. It was further claimed that his memory was then impaired and his will power virtually gone but that under the care of Dr. T. S. Robertson, of New York City, the patient was finally restored to health. As authority for the story, the physician himself was cited, who in an interview expressed personal admiration for Debs but strong antipathy for the strike. Whatever may have been his motive, Robertson sent Debs a telegram at this time urging him to cease his strike activities. "The condition of your nervous system and the great strain upon it," warned the physician, "make you irresponsible for your own orders." In presenting all this to the reader, the *New York Times* did so in such a manner as to cast reflection upon the mental and physical fitness of Eugene Debs. "Those who knew Debs well while he was in this city," declared the paper, "believe that his present conduct is in large measure, if not wholly, due to the disordered condition of his mind and body, brought about by the liquor habit, for which he was under treatment such a short time ago."[16]

The *New York World* likewise raised the question: "Is Eugene V. Debs responsible for his actions, or, indeed, is any man who once suffered from dipsomania a competent leader of his fellow men?"[17] The *Nation* appeared greatly astonished but not disappointed over the revelation. In exploiting the allegation for all it was worth, this journal took the position that it was indeed extraordinary that a man of Debs's "physical and mental condition should be able to paralyze great railway systems" and precipitate such a state of anarchy as to necessitate the use of the United States army. "It puts this country," concluded the editorial, "before the world as the sport of lunatics and madmen."[18]

Cartoons played their part in the strategy of the press to discredit Eugene Debs and the American Railway Union. The one appearing on the front page of the *Chicago Tribune*, July 4, pictured Debs in a chair with his feet cocked up on a desk. Under his boots was a crumpled copy of the Declaration of Independence, while on his head rested a crown bearing the words: "Dictator by the Grace of Gall." On the wall above his head was a banner with the inscription: "The union forever." The middle word, however, had been crossed out and just above were substituted the letters: "A.R.U." In the foreground an eagle, with feet and beak securely tied, was tethered to a spittoon. Two boys with firecrackers in their hands were talking to Debs. In reply to their questions, "Please, sir, may we celebrate Independence day," he answered with a snarl, "There ain't no Independence day. I've changed all that."

The *Chicago Herald* carried on July 2 a prominently displayed cartoon entitled: "The Dictator's Dream." It pictured a large man, personifying the American Railway Union, sitting brazenly on a throne with his feet sprawled out on a large cushion labeled: "Labor Rank and File." Standing humbly in front, with hat removed and shoulders bent, was Uncle Sam who was tendering to the "dictator" a plucked eagle on a platter. On the wall were several inscriptions, one declaring: "License to do just as you D——n please if you are a member of the A.R.U." and another: "We have a monopoly of all rights—the A.R.U."

The front cover of *Harper's Weekly* for July 21 carried an impressive cartoon entitled the "Vanguard of Anarchy." The drawing depicted a parade led by several well-known figures, all dressed in clownish costumes. Among them were a Populist United States senator, William Peffer, and three governors: John P. Altgeld, David H. Waite, and Sylvester Pennoyer. Some of the paraders supported a litter on which sat Eugene V. Debs, wearing a crown. Further back in the procession was a banner with the inscription: "Anarchy," above which, securely attached to the staff, were a skull, torch, and dagger. Peering from behind the banner were hideous monsters bearing torches and revolvers.

In every conceivable way the press thus tried to promote a psychosis of fear in the public mind. The desire to increase circulation figures may have played some part in the journalistic technique during this epochal struggle. Eager for news of the most colorful and dramatic sort, the great majority of newspapers were inclined to embellish their reports without much regard to actual facts. As the superintendent of the Chicago police explained, "The chasing of a crowd of boys off the railroad tracks was magnified into a riot in which thousands were ready to kill, burn, and pillage." This type of journalism proved so offensive that the Chicago police were instructed to prevent the newsboys from crying the sensational and incendiary headlines of certain publications.[19] Newspapers at a great distance from this strike-torn city were even worse offenders, and everywhere people were seized by a mounting fear of what the rising tide of "anarchy" might do. Typical of many people was Mrs. Walter Q. Gresham, wife of the secretary of state, who later revealed how apprehensive she became during this period from reading the accounts of the Chicago riots. She believed the loss of life and property would be tremendous, and she feared for the lives of her two grandchildren who resided there. She confided these fears to her husband, who assured her that the attorney-general and the secretary of war had the matter well in hand and would soon end the disturbances.[20]

On July 9 a special correspondent of the *New York World* arrived in Chicago to find that conditions were not at all as represented in the press. His report was in striking contrast to the inflamed stories that had been crowding the newspapers for days. He wrote:

> There is no sign of mob or riot or strike, even, about the main part of the city. Business goes on as usual. The streets and shops are thronged with women gayly dressed, laughing and chatting. . . . . There is no indication anywhere of dread or fear. No throngs gather to talk at street corners, and the strike is scarcely mentioned in the casual conversation one hears about hotels and other public places. Small boys yell constantly, "Extra! Full account o' de bloody riot!" but nobody except countrymen and New Yorkers just come to town buy the papers. It is day before yesterday's riot and yesterday's news warmed over.
>
> The mass of people evidently do not bother about the strike. . . . . Of mob rule and riot, in the sense in which it is generally understood—that of reckless and wanton destruction of life and property regardless of ownership—there has been none. The violence has been directed solely against railroad property. There has been a deplorable lot of it, but the tales of its extent have been greatly exaggerated.[21]

Realizing the importance of public opinion, the union resented keenly the highly prejudicial treatment which the strikers suffered at the hands of the press. The extreme hostility of such newspapers as the *Chicago Herald, Inter Ocean,* and *Chicago Tribune* toward the American Railway Union proved so offensive that on July 2 the directors of the union decided to urge a boycott against these publications. The journals were charged with debauching public opinion, and all citizens were accordingly asked to cease reading them. An appeal was made to merchants to stop advertising in these papers, while newsboys were requested not to sell them. This resolution was directed primarily against the editorial hostility of these newspapers and not against their reporters, who continued to receive courteous treatment at the headquarters of the union.[22] Convinced that the press did not accurately reflect public sentiment in Chicago, the union executives on July 2 decided to call on the people to display their sympathy for the cause of labor by wearing a small piece of white ribbon on their lapel until the struggle was over. The next day witnessed an epidemic of white ribbon worn by union members and strike sympathizers.[23]

Not all newspapers were unfair to labor or guilty of deliberate misrepresentation. Among those in Chicago that pursued a policy of impartiality to both sides were the *Chicago Daily News* and the *Chicago Record*. The *Chicago Dispatch*, *Chicago Mail*, and *Chicago Times* were inclined to espouse the cause of the strikers, but these publications could hardly compare in circulation, prestige, or influence with those which were antilabor.[24] A distinction was drawn by some newspapers between the struggle waged by the American Railway Union and the local strike conducted by the Pullman employees. The labor policy of George Pullman was condemned sharply by some papers, although the majority, without defending the Pullman Corporation, apparently felt that any criticism of that company would tend to weaken their case against the American Railway Union.

The *Chicago Herald* was among the newspapers which denounced with vehemence both George Pullman and the American Railway Union. In a sharp editorial on July 4 this paper emphasized that the harsh and unjust treatment received by the Pullman employees would not be forgotten in the court of public opinion, even though the plight of these workers was being pushed into the background by the titanic struggle that was then enveloping the railroads. George Pullman was warned not to mistake "hostility to lawbreakers and rioters for hostility to his ill-fed, under-paid employees." The editor proclaimed:

The termination of this struggle will not affect by one jot or tittle the standing of George Pullman in the court of public opinion. . . . . The patent fact that the American Railway Union was utterly wrong will not put the Pullman Company right. The case remains unadjudicated. It has not been decided; it has merely been postponed.[25]

The *Chicago Tribune* had no sympathy for the American Railway Union, but neither was this paper willing to condone Pullman's rejection of arbitration. The editor pointed out that the fact that certain labor leaders had sinned greatly did not relieve Pullman of responsibility in not seeking a peaceful solution of the conflict.[26] The *New York World* held that if Pullman was losing money in the construction of cars, as he claimed, the arbitrators would discover the fact and decide in his favor and he would have nothing to lose by arbitration. It was charged that, because of his refusal to follow such a course, "many thousand dollars worth of property has been destroyed. The trade of half the continent has been paralyzed and human life has been sacrificed, while the menace of bloody riot hangs like a pall over the second city of the country."[27]

No paper entertained more contempt for George Pullman than did the *Chicago Times*, which, unlike most publications, championed the cause of the American Railway Union. In the front-page cartoon of July 2 this newspaper caricatured Pullman in the role of Richard III—very obese and possessed with an evil countenance. He was pictured pacing slowly in front of his tent and repeating these lines:

My conscience hath a thousand several tongues,
And every tongue brings in a several tale
And every tale condemns me for a villain.

In a subsequent edition the *Chicago Times* described Pullman as a cold-hearted, cold-blooded autocrat. . . . . He wears no mask. His character is reflected in his countenance. He has a fat pudgy face. His hair is now gray and upon his square chin he wears a set of gray whiskers which the street urchins describe as "daubers." A pair of small, piggish eyes gleam out from above the puffed cheeks, and the glitter of avarice is plainly apparent in their depths. Mr. Pullman's usual expression is one of supercilious contempt for the world at large, mingled with traces of self-satisfaction at his own comfortable state.[28]

Editors were not alone in pointing the accusing finger of guilt at this wealthy sleeping-car magnate. Marcus Hanna, for instance, was particularly pungent in his comments. Successful as a politician, Hanna understood the psychology of the laborer. Convinced that Pullman's policy was anything but judicious, he once exploded: "The damned idiot ought to arbitrate, arbitrate, arbitrate! What, for God's sake, did the manufacturer think he was doing?" To a statement of a friend that George Pullman had done fine things for his employees, Hanna replied: "Oh, hell! Model——! Go and live in Pullman and find out how much Pullman gets sellin' city water and gas ten per cent higher to those poor fools. A man who won't meet his men half-way is a God-damn fool!"[29]

A very revealing letter was written on July 16 by Erskine M. Phelps, prominent industrialist in Chicago, to his friend, Walter Q. Gresham, secretary of state, relative to the culpability of the Pullman Company in the struggle. Phelps explained that in conversing with all classes of businessmen, including railroad executives, he had discovered that it was the almost universal opinion that, if Pullman had treated his men differently, the strike might have been averted. The manufacturer further divulged that even among railroad executives George Pullman had few friends and that because of his obstinacy the Pullman Company would undoubtedly suffer.[30]

No indictment of George Pullman was so caustic or damning as that written by the pen of John Swinton. Although this author did not reflect public opinion, he tried hard to influence it by his incisive, acrid, and biting style. He exclaimed:

> Pullman cared no more for the cries of his victims than the butchers of the Chicago shambles care for the cries of theirs. If the mothers and the children, as well as the fathers were crushed, what was that to him? . . . . Pullmanism is selfishness at its worst. It is extortion, venality and churlishness. It is one of the most execrable manifestations of the capitalist despotism that has ever been seen. . . . . That despotism must fall if man is to rise.[31]

Most people, however, were too absorbed in the great struggle sweeping the nation and too concerned about its implications to give much thought to George Pullman. As the conflict grew more intense, the plight of the Pullman employees seemed almost forgotten and the role of Pullman in the drama no longer of any great consequence. In most news stories during those stirring July days, he was mentioned, if at all, only casually. Popular sympathy for the Pullman employees quickly yielded to uneasiness and fear over the trend of events. To many alarmed souls the specter of anarchy in the United States was at last becoming a reality. The assassination of Sadi Carnot, the beloved president of France, by an anarchist on June 24, 1894, added to the misgivings of many Americans concerning the real menace of anarchy to their own country. On July 1, at St. Matthew's Church in Washington, D.C., congressmen, senators, and high executive officials united in a solemn memorial service for President Carnot; and on that occasion, according to the *Inter Ocean,*

many of these public men felt that it was inconsistent for the government to express sympathy with the sufferers from the fruits of anarchy in the old world and do nothing to check the rising tide of anarchy in the new world. For it is a fact, which the representative public men of this government have been very slow to acknowledge, that the audacious assumptions of labor agitators of this country are only another form of anarchy.[32]

From the pulpit ministers joined in the cry against Eugene Debs and the American Railway Union. They dilated upon the threatening aspects of the strike and the retributive justice which society should visit upon the "miscreants." Among the ministers in New York City who thundered against the strikers on Sunday, July 8, was Rev. John A. B. Wilson of the Eighteenth Street Methodist Episcopal Church. In discussing his theme, "The Strike and Its Terrors," he placed full responsibility for the situation upon Eugene Debs, who was characterized as a "demagogue," the "son of a saloon keeper, a man reared and educated upon the proceeds of human ruin." "This is the man," cried the minister, "who is able to bring death to hundreds, ruin to thousands and starvation to hundreds of thousands."[33]

On the same day, in the Prohibition Park Auditorium at Port Richmond, Staten Island, the Rev. A. B. Leonard, general missionary of the Methodist Episcopal church, demanded in a sermon the imprisonment of Eugene Debs and Governor John Altgeld as enemies of society. More forcible was the statement made to reporters by Dr. Herrick Johnson, professor at the Presbyterian Theological Seminary in Chicago, just before he ascended the pulpit of the Central Congregational Church in Brooklyn on July 8. He said:

There is but one way to deal with these troubles now and that is by violence. . . . . The time has come when forbearance has ceased to be a virtue. There must be some shooting, men must be killed, and then there will be an end of this defiance of law and destruction of property. Violence must be met by violence. The soldiers must use their guns. They must shoot to kill.[34]

Analysis of public sentiment makes it apparent that the majority of people fully supported the action taken by the federal government. Among the business, professional, and agricultural classes there seemed to be little opposition to the policies of the President. With the possible exception of the railroad brotherhoods, organized labor, however, was alert to the full implications of federal strategy and unwilling to indorse it. In the White House mail, unusually heavy during the crisis, there were letters of fulsome praise and sharp condemnation. The former predominated, some of which disclosed profound gratitude and a prayerful appreciation for the energetic measures which President Cleveland took to suppress the strike. From Chicago, for instance, Mrs. Edward Roby, president of the Ladies of the Grand Army of the Republic, expressed to Grover Cleveland a feeling of relief that members of her organization could "sleep nights assured that the pilot is true to his trust, and that you, and not our anarchist governor, are shaping and guiding our ship of state."[35] The acting president of the Chicago Bar Association, who represented the sentiment of that organization, was one of many in the legal profession to register complete indorsement of Cleveland's course.[36]

Businessmen from all parts of the nation sent congratulations to the President. One executive in New York City wrote that no businessman in the state could fail "to approve of the courageous and able way with which you have met the trying labor crisis."[37] Educators and literary men were no less fervent in commending the chief executive of the nation. The president of Leland Stanford University wrote tersely: "It is not often that an American citizen feels called upon to congratulate the President of the United States as having done his plain duty. In view of the present conditions, perhaps you may pardon me for doing this."[38] The editor of the *Century Magazine* revealed to the President that from all sources—friends as well as former enemies—nothing was now heard but praise and gratitude at "your patriotic and fearless action."[39]

Of an entirely different character were the communications dispatched from labor unions. Particularly trenchant were the resolutions adopted by numerous local lodges of the Knights of Labor. One of the local assemblies at Chicago, for instance, protested to Cleveland on July 10 against the "un-American" attitude which he had assumed in the struggle and against the presence in the Cabinet of Richard Olney, "known of all men as a railroad attorney and an owner of railroad stock." "We cannot," it was asserted, "fail to regard the pernicious activity of this pliant tool of corporations, who appears to be your closest adviser, as a most sinister omen, and as evidence that it is not in your heart or in your policy to act as the chief executive of all the people, whose interests are opposed to those of the corporations." In criticizing the policies of the federal government the resolutions were unsparing in their condemnation of the omnibus injunctions, arbitrary arrests, and the use of United States troops.[40]

Some of the protests received by President Cleveland breathed defiance of a dangerous sort. One such letter was written by John Cuthbertson, who had previously served as the supreme chancellor of the Commercial Telegraphers. Abandoning all caution, he proclaimed that the

people of the country cannot longer be deceived and unless "justice" is secured at this time, they will arise in their might within the next three years, and through a reign of terror, secure that which our present laws do not afford (justice to all). This strike may possibly be overcome by the federal troops, who are the present cause for loss of life and destruction of property, but it will only be of short duration and all the military power of the land will be powerless to stay the revolt.[41]

Neither the President nor the attorney-general was inclined to undervalue the importance of public opinion, and for this reason they endeavored not to antagonize labor unnecessarily. They wanted to create the impression that the policy of the government was not directed against labor but against the violence and lawlessness fostered by a small segment of misguided workers. As the force of the strike reached its crest and began to recede, sentiment among the laboring class, however, became increasingly hostile toward the government, and more specifically against Richard Olney, who, in the opinion of many, was the evil genius back of Grover Cleveland. Anxious to dispel such an attitude, Olney appeared suddenly in the role of a friend to the older and more conservative unions.

In the case of *In re Platt* v. *Philadelphia and Reading Railroad Company* he intervened dramatically in behalf of the Railway Trainmen. It had been the policy of this road to prevent its employees from organizing. In order to secure work on this line applicants were required to sign an agreement that if affiliated with a union they would immediately cancel their membership. During the panic of 1893 this railroad passed into federal receivership. In the meantime many of the employees had quietly joined the Brotherhood of Railway Trainmen; but, when this came to the knowledge of the receivers, the men were warned that unless they severed their connection with that union by October 8, 1894, they would be dismissed. Those who were thus threatened petitioned the court for an injunction to restrain the receivers from taking such action.[42] Before the hearing could be held, Richard Olney dispatched to the judge of the federal court at Philadelphia a lengthy statement in defense of the petitioners.

The attorney-general explained that, since the railroad was in receivership, the federal court and not the company possessed the authority to determine whether or not the members of the Brotherhood of Trainmen should be dismissed. In the opinion of Richard Olney, the court should refrain from taking such action, since the union was lawful and served a very laudable purpose. Its policy in regard to strikes was characterized as "eminently conservative." Strikes, Olney conceded, were legal if they did not involve "a malicious intent followed by actual injury, intimidation, violence, the creation of a public nuisance, or a breach of the peace of any sort." He insisted that the receivers would not remove the danger of strikes by discharging these union members, since unorganized workers, when aggrieved, could easily unite. With a considerable show of liberalism he announced that the right of a man to join a union is a legal right—"a right he may deem essential to his safety and welfare." Going even further, the attorney-general recommended arbitration as the best "mode for the settlement of contests between capital and labor."[43]

Although the court decided against labor, thus rejecting the advice proffered in this extraordinary communication,[44] Richard Olney had the satisfaction of receiving the hearty thanks of the Railroad Trainmen for the support which he rendered to them. The journal of this union even proclaimed that the "Attorney General can be credited with doing the right thing at the right time and while corporations stand aghast at his expression, the general public admires and applauds the vigorous protest against the enforcement of an unjust rule and the hearty commendation of the aims and purposes of proper labor organizations."[45] Such sentiment, however, was not shared by labor in general.

The mail of the attorney-general, as in the case of the President, was mostly of a friendly, complimentary character, although some of the communications were extremely bitter and provocative. Alfred Russell, attorney for the Wabash Railroad, was among those who warmly congratulated Richard Olney for his accomplishments. With fervor he exclaimed: "To have suppressed a rebellion, to have practically opened a new development of the Principle of Equity . . . . is glory enough for any one Attorney General."[46] On another occasion Russell sent Olney a poem, with the comment: "These rhymes may help to soften the asperities of office." The verses were inscribed to R.O., with the motto: "The Public Be Debbed!" The third stanza was as follows:

> Olney is up
> For any pup
> About your size, O Debs.
> He has a cell
> Will hold you well.
> Strike's tide—how quick it ebbs![47]

Richard Olney seemed delighted with this poetic outburst and in reply expressed the belief that "brother Debs and his associates might say there is 'more reason than rhyme' about this administration."[48]

In protest against Olney's course in the Pullman Strike, many labor groups dispatched sharply worded resolutions. On July 8, for instance, three thousand persons gathered on the Boston Common for the purpose of censuring the action taken against the strikers. A copy of the resolutions adopted was forwarded to Richard Olney, together with an explanatory letter, in which it was asserted that almost the entire working population of the nation regarded the course of the federal authorities "as an unblushing alliance of the government with the capitalist class, and a desperate usurpation of authority by the government." The resolutions characterized the proclamation of the President as a "Proclamation of Civil War." They emphasized that in the interest of peace and justice he should issue another proclamation, offering equal protection to the strikers in the enjoyment of their right to strike peacefully. The government should also compel George Pullman to arbitrate. "These measures," it was explained, "will bring all classes of citizens in harmony and all rioting will cease through sheer force of public opinion." The statement warned that

if the working people are treated to wholesale repression without any reference to their rights and grievances, it is to be feared that a worse mode of warfare than any yet resorted to may be developed on this soil. . . . . If the government sheds blood today it murders, and a Republic cannot murder its citizens with impunity.[49]

In the opinion of the executive officials of the Knights of Labor, Richard Olney was guilty of "high crimes and misdemeanors" and should be impeached. A petition, addressed to the House of Representatives, was accordingly drafted, setting forth the reasons for such action. With six congressmen and three senators affiliated with the Knights, it was hoped that the recommendation for impeachment would not be completely brushed aside. The memorial charged Olney with several offenses: subordinating the civil authority of the states to the military power of the federal government; sending United States troops into states without application for such aid by the governors or state legislatures; causing the federal courts to issue processes contrary to the American Constitution; and perverting the meaning of the laws, particularly the Sherman Anti-trust Act, which was designed to protect citizens against the injustices of monopolistic control. The "pretenses" advanced by the government in justification of these "unlawful usurpations" were declared to be "wholly unfounded."[50]

Congress was in no mood to entertain such a proposal. Owing to the explosive character of the times, this body had become increasingly conservative and less sympathetic toward the aspirations of labor. In both houses there was overwhelming support for Olney's tactics. The situation, it was felt, warranted strong measures, even though they should represent a new technique based upon a different interpretation of the prerogatives of the federal government. In the Senate on July 11 and in the House of Representatives five days later resolutions were adopted expressing full indorsement of the measures taken by the President and his administration in suppressing disorders, enforcing federal law, and in preventing interference with the movement of mail and interstate commerce.[51]

In the Senate the resolution evoked scarcely any criticism, not even from the states'-rights Democrats. An attempt was made, however, to add an amendment, recommending the use of arbitration in all labor disputes and condemning the refusal of any party in the Pullman Strike to submit their differences to arbitration. Although not expressly stated, this was obviously "a covert condemnation of the Pullman Company for its refusal to arbitrate." In defense of the amendment, Senator John W. Daniel (Democrat from Virginia) explained that in the act of October 1, 1888, Congress had already approved the principle of arbitration and should now commend it to all as an effective substitute for force in the settlement of controversies between labor and capital. Most senators responded coldly to this proposal, which they considered to be irrelevant and as tending to detract from the original resolution. It was pointed out that the law referred to never was and could never be enforced and that it was passed "as many things are passed by Congress, to please somebody or other."

Senator Joseph N. Dolph (Republican from Oregon) wanted to know why the Senate should seek, by extolling arbitration, "to conciliate the elements which are seeking to overthrow local government and to set the laws at defiance." In the judgment of Senator Orville H. Platt (Republican from Connecticut) no other question should be injected into the discussion except that of voicing approval for what the administration did to meet the situation. He declared:

The question is whether the person we have elected to be our Chief Executive is the Chief Executive of the United States or whether a man who calls himself President Debs is the President and Chief Executive of the United States. . . . . I object to anything except the straight, square, manly indorsement of what President Cleveland has done.

This attitude was shared by the great bulk of the Senate, irrespective of party lines; and without modification the original resolution was passed.[52]

The attorney-general deemed such a resolution to be extremely desirable; and, when he heard that Bellamy Storer (Republican from Ohio) proposed to introduce one in the lower house of Congress, he wrote immediately to the congressman expressing gratification that in this matter politics were being subordinated to patriotism. Olney assured Storer that the action pursued by the administration was prompted entirely by "its duty to the entire people of the country irrespective of party." "I believe too," he explained, "that the administration has done its best to hold an entirely even hand as between the strikers on the one hand and capital on the other." In proof of this, Olney mentioned how quickly he had intervened in Debs's behalf when the papers of this union leader were unjustly seized.[53]

Debate on the resolution in the House of Representatives was restricted to thirty minutes, the time being equally divided between the opposition and those who supported the measure. As spokesmen for the opposition, Lafe Pence (Populist from Colorado) and Richard P. Bland (Democrat from Missouri) were able to rally only a small following. While recognizing that under certain conditions it might be proper for the federal government to resort to injunctions, indictments, and federal troops, Pence denied that the American people would ever wish that the attorney-general who invoked such measures should be connected with any of the corporations involved in the difficulties. The congressman further inquired whether it was a decent thing for Olney to appoint a railroad attorney to serve as his special deputy in Chicago?[54]

In denouncing the resolution Bland appealed fervently to the doctrine of states' rights. The suppression of violence, he contended, was the duty of state authority, and the United States government should not interfere except to protect the mails and federal property. In the present situation, he explained, the federal government intervened in states where little or no violence arose or where the state authorities were able and willing to suppress it. "The whole country," he emphasized, "was flooded with deputy marshals; sheriffs were arrested, state authority was overthrown and the strong arm of the federal government took possession of matters properly belonging to the states." Appealing to the Democratic party, Bland warned that any who supported the resolution would be surrendering the "Democratic principle of local self-government." If this union is to be maintained, he pleaded, "it is to be maintained by maintaining and respecting the rights and the authority of the people of the states."[55]

In defense of the resolution two Democrats spoke: James B. McCreary, from Kentucky, and Thomas C. Catchings, from Mississippi. The former, in opening the arguments for his side, declared that the question involved in the discussion was whether law and order should be maintained or "mobocracy" and anarchy should triumph. Something higher was at stake, he affirmed, than the rights of capitalists, railroad corporations, or laboring men—it was the freedom and prosperity of the American people and the perpetuity of their national government. He seemed confident that all of the sixty-five million Americans were grateful that the President had courageously compelled the agitators and lawbreakers to submit to the authority of the government. In protecting the mails and interstate commerce the President, insisted McCreary, was merely fulfilling his duty as chief executive; and in doing this he employed the lawful means at his disposal.[56]

Congressman Catchings denied emphatically that the question

of states' rights was in any way involved in the matter. Everything done by President Cleveland, he maintained, was for the
purpose of upholding the dignity of the Constitution and federal
law. In defending the character of Richard Olney, the representative contended that this man was "an able lawyer, a brilliant
and distinguished member of the legal profession" and that "he
could not have done less than he has done and at the same time
have discharged his duty to his country." In conclusion Catchings expressed the hope that the courageous action of the administration has "taught a lesson to men like Debs and others who
choose to organize within the body of our citizenship a special
class which claims the right to lay its heavy hand upon the business of the country and disturb it." Immediately upon the completion of his remarks, the resolution was submitted to an un-
recorded vote and adopted by an estimated two-thirds majority.[57]

Less than a month later another spirited clash over the merits
of federal intervention developed in the House of Representatives,
which, however, died away almost as quickly as it flared up. The
occasion for this outburst was a debate, August 9, on a bill to promote the efficiency of the militia. In defending the bill, Adolph
Meyer (Democrat from Louisiana) was questioned by George W.
Fithian (Democrat from Illinois), who inquired whether or not
the gentleman thought the authorities of Illinois were unable to
maintain law and order within the state at the time federal troops
intervened? The fact, declared Fithian, is that the governor of
the state at that time had received no request for troops from
either the mayor of Chicago or the sheriff of Cook County, but,
when the demand was made, he promptly ordered the militia to
that city. The congressman from Illinois further explained that
at the time of federal intervention the local officials were preserving the peace; but, had the situation warranted, the governor
would have requisitioned federal soldiers. It is a democratic doctrine, he averred, that the chief executive of the United States has
no right to dispatch soldiers into a state without being requested
to do so by the legislature or governor, and "any gentleman who
takes the contrary position on the floor of this House is flying in

the face of Democratic doctrine that has been adhered to ever since the organization of the Democratic Party."[58]

Congressman Meyer, in reply, declared that if the President had not acted when he did there would have been "greater riots and greater destruction and possibly civil war in the city of Chicago and the state of Illinois." There is, he affirmed, a well-founded conviction among many people that the governor of Illinois did not rise to the emergency; for this reason and because the President was exercising his constitutional rights the measures which he took were ratified by the nation.[59] With even greater zest did Joseph G. Cannon (Republican from Illinois) defend federal intervention. He pointed out that, when the President acted, the federal courts were being defied, United States civil officers were unable to enforce the laws, interstate commerce was paralyzed, and the mobs were in control of Cook County. The President, he held, possessed the authority to end this intolerable situation, and the mayor of Chicago and the governor of Illinois had no power to stand in the way. Irrespective of parties, the enforcement of the law, he asserted, should be the "shibboleth for all the people." In ringing terms Cannon dared Fithian to make an issue of the matter in the next election, explaining that if he should do so "he will find me and he will find the Republican party endorsing the action of the President of the United States in the performance of his sworn duty and condemning the unpatriotic course of the governor of the state of Illinois."[60]

The prestige which Richard Olney wielded in Congress was clearly demonstrated at the time that Senator William V. Allen (Populist from Nebraska) endeavored to make the strike correspondence of the Department of Justice available to the Senate. On July 25, 1894, Allen submitted a resolution, proposing that the attorney-general transmit to the Senate copies of all telegrams and other correspondence (from June 1 to the present date) that had been sent and received by his office relative to the strike. On the following day the resolution was adopted and forwarded to Olney, who apparently had not been forewarned. Without delay he notified Senator William F. Vilas (Democrat from Wisconsin) that the resolution was highly objectionable, since it would have the purpose of revealing the case of the government in proceedings that were pending or about to be commenced in the United States courts. Olney suggested that perhaps the resolution had been adopted without due consideration. Vilas immediately explained the matter to the chairman of the Judiciary Committee, James L. Pugh (Democrat from Alabama), who on July 27 moved that the Senate reconsider its vote in the matter. Without any discussion, the president pro tempore declared quickly: "It is so ordered, if there be no objection. It is so ordered."[61]

Not until December 10, 1894, did Senator Pugh feel obliged to divulge to the Senate the reason for this action. He did so by explaining that it was unfair to require the attorney-general to transmit to the Senate and make public information upon which rested the criminal prosecutions of the federal government. This explanation did not prove convincing to William Allen, who could see no reason why the correspondence should not be published. He expressed inability to understand, for instance, how communications sent to the prosecuting attorney at Chicago could be used in criminal proceedings since they "would be clearly hearsay" and "would be clearly incompetent and irrelevant to any prosecution" that might be undertaken. But, assuming that they might be material, then, inquired Allen, does the chairman of the Judiciary Committee "assert as a proposition of law that the Government, like a thief in the night, has the right to withhold any fact essential to the defense as well as to the prosecution of a case under the statutes of the United States." The defendant, it was reiterated, has a "right to this knowledge. . . . . He has a right to file a motion for a bill of particulars setting forth everything essential to be proved by the United States and everything that may be essential to the preservation of his rights." All this, declared Senator Allen, the chairman of the Judiciary Committee should know.

Why then, inquired the senator, did Richard Olney desire to keep this correspondence secret? If it were aboveboard, why should he be unwilling to have it published? If it were surreptitious and unlawful, exclaimed Allen, then it should most certainly be scrutinized by the Senate. "In my judgment," he ventured, "it is an attempt upon the part of the chief law officer of the Government to keep the people of the United States ignorant of the position taken by him during that event and the questionable position occupied by the Government with reference to that transaction."[62]

The efforts of the Populist senator proved unavailing, with the result that the strike correspondence was allowed to remain a mystery for several years—until much of the heat and passion engendered by the struggle had subsided. In January, 1897, both houses of Congress adopted a concurrent resolution that the attorney-general publish, as an appendix to his 1896 report, copies of all telegraphic and other correspondence received and dispatched by the Department of Justice in 1894 pertaining to the Pullman Strike.[63] In compliance with this request a tremendous amount of vital material was released for publication, which sheds considerable light upon the strategy employed by Richard Olney during that epochal struggle. The published documents, however, can hardly be considered as complete. It is possible that some of the more revealing dispatches were conveniently destroyed; but there can be no doubt that a few were deleted and others withheld from publication. Among the published documents gaps seem to appear; and buried among the papers of Richard Olney are pertinent communications which do not appear in print. It is quite probable that the story of the Pullman Strike could be told in a more revealing manner and Olney's role portrayed more audaciously if all the communications, official and private, sent and received by this attorney-general were extant and accessible.

NOTES

1. *U.S. Strike Commission Report*, p. 157.
2. *Ibid.*, pp. 156–58; *Chicago Times*, July 22, 1894, p. 1.
3. *U.S. Strike Commission Report*, p. 158.
4. P. 1.
5. July 3, 1894, p. 6.
6. July 3, 1894, p. 6.
7. July 9, 1894, p. 4.
8. July 9, 1894, p. 4.
9. XXXVIII (1894), 627.

10. *Ibid.*, pp. 650–51.
11. XLVI (1894), 10.
12. *Ibid.*, p. 16.
13. July 2, 1894, p. 6.
14. July 3, 1894, p. 6.
15. July 8, 1894, p. 18.
16. July 9, 1894, p. 5.
17. July 9, 1894, p. 1.
18. LIX (1894), 20.
19. *Report of the General Superintendent of Police of Chicago . . . . 1894*, p. 17.
20. Matilda Gresham, *Life of Walter Q. Gresham*, I, 418–19.
21. *New York World*, July 10, 1894, p. 1.
22. *Chicago Times*, July 3, 1894, p. 1.
23. *Ibid.; U.S. Strike Commission Report*, p. 363.
24. *Public Opinion*, XVIII (1894), 329.
25. *Chicago Herald*, July 4, 1894, p. 6.
26. July 10, 1894, p. 6.
27. July 12, 1894, p. 4.
28. July 4, 1894, p. 9.
29. Thomas Beer, *Hanna*, pp. 132–33.
30. Phelps to Gresham, July 16, 1894, Walter Q. Gresham Papers.
31. *Op. git.*, pp. 262–66.
32. July 2, 1894, p. 7.
33. *New York Times*, July 9, 1894, p. 3.
34. *Ibid.*
35. Mrs. Roby to Cleveland, July 12, 1894, Cleveland Papers.
36. William J. English to Cleveland, July 12, 1894, *ibid.*
37. J. Edward Simmons to Cleveland, July 11, 1894, *ibid.*
38. David S. Jordan to Cleveland, July 18, 1894, *ibid.*
39. R. W. Gilder to Cleveland, July 11, 1894, *ibid.*
40. Patrick J. Dalton and John F. Chorangel (master-workmen) to Cleveland July 10, 1894, *ibid.*
41. Cuthbertson to Thurber (private secretary to Cleveland), July 8, 1894, *ibid.*
42. *Federal Reporter*, LXV, 660–67.
43. Olney to Judge George M. Dallas, November 3, 1894, Richard Olney Papers.
44. *Federal Reporter*, LXV, 667.
45. *Railroad Trainmen's Journal*, XI (1894), 1071–74.
46. Russell to Olney, July 8, 1895, Richard Olney Papers.
47. Russell to Olney, July 9, 1894, *ibid.*
48. Olney to Russell, July 13, 1894, *ibid.*
49. Morrison Swift to Olney, July 9, 1894, *ibid.*
50. *New York Times*, July 12, 1894, p. 1.
51. *Congressional Record*, XXVI, Part VII (53d Cong., 2d sess., 1894), p. 7282; Part VIII, p. 7544.
52. *Ibid.*, Part VIII, pp. 7281–84.
53. Olney to Storer, July 12, 1894, Richard Olney Papers.
54. *Congressional Record*, XXVI, Part VIII, 7544.
55. *Ibid.*, p. 7545.

56. *Ibid.*, p. 7544.
57. *Ibid.*, pp. 7545–46.
58. *Ibid.*, pp. 8340, 8341.
59. *Ibid.*, p. 8341.
60. *Ibid.*, pp. 8346–47.
61. *Ibid.*, pp. 7846, 7879; XXVII, Part I (53d Cong., 3d Sess., 1894–95), p. 154.
62. *Ibid.*, pp. 154–55.
63. *Appendix to the . . . . Report of the Attorney General . . . . 1896*, p. 3.

CHAPTER XIV

REPERCUSSIONS

WHAT the Pullman Strike cost the nation in dollars, human misery, and class bitterness cannot very easily be measured. On a front covering two-thirds of the United States the struggle surged to and fro for many days. Few people were spared the effects, but those who suffered most acutely were the participants and those dependent upon rail transportation. The railroads sustained substantial property damage at the hands of unruly mobs but experienced far greater loss in reduced earnings. In forfeited wages, unemployment, and suffering the strikers likewise paid a heavy price. Producers, shippers, merchants, and consumers were inconvenienced and even forced to undergo pecuniary losses wherever the wheels of commerce were slowed up or blocked. How much the business of the country actually suffered will never be known, although it has been estimated that the losses were not less than eighty million dollars.

In preserving law and order the taxpayer played an inactive but extremely important part. Throughout the nation many thousands of federal soldiers and deputy marshals endeavored to protect interstate commerce, while in those states where conditions required it the militia and the police tried to keep the peace. In Chicago alone the military and civilian law-enforcing agencies had at their disposal more than fourteen thousand men. Precisely what this force cost the government cannot be determined, but it is known that the outlay for the militia and deputy marshals in that city required almost four hundred thousand dollars.[1]

On the basis of the testimony presented before the United States Strike Commission, the total loss sustained by the railroads centering at Chicago was reckoned at $5,360,000. Less than $700,000 of this amount comprised property losses, such as perishable goods and rolling stock. The balance represented the loss in earnings, which proved infinitely more important than the depredations of lawless elements. In considering individual railroads the one most seriously affected was the Illinois Central, whose property losses aggregated more than $100,000 and whose earnings declined $500,000. Extra operating expenses swelled the total cost of the strike for this road to $730,000. The Rock Island and the Chicago, Milwaukee, and St. Paul each sustained property damages of less than $15,000; but, in the matter of earnings, the former lost $460,000 and the latter $618,000. The Santa Fe and the Chicago and Northwestern escaped with even less destruction of property but experienced business losses of $500,000 each. On some roads the property damages were almost negligible, but all lines, even the smallest, suffered from reduced earnings.[2] Significantly, neither the strike nor the financial losses had a very demoralizing effect on railroad stock, which declined an average of only $1\frac{1}{2}$ per cent during the struggle.[3]

Did labor suffer proportionately? The employees upon the roads centering at Chicago forfeited $1,400,000 in wages, while the strikers at Pullman lost $350,000.[4] What the tens of thousands of railroad workers throughout the nation sacrificed in earnings is not known. The majority of these employees had little, if any, reserve and were soon faced by want and privation. Nor did the American Railway Union possess a strike fund to which the members could turn. The strikers had fought courageously, but the realization of having done so could give them little satisfaction as they surveyed the consequences of their action. Their union, which had been launched with such high hopes, was now doomed to disintegration. The cause of the Pullman workers, for which much had been risked, no longer challenged their heroism. In abandoning that cause they were also inclined to relinquish all hope for a new and better era for labor. If this were all, perhaps it would not have been quite so bad; but, hungry and poverty-stricken, many strikers were denied work wherever they went.

The old practice of circulating the blacklist of each railroad among all systems had fallen into disuse except on the smaller roads. A new method, no less effective, had been adopted, by which an employee, upon being discharged, would receive clearance papers which stated the cause for dismissal. All division superintendents on the line were notified. In seeking employment on some other system the applicant would be asked for his papers; and, if he withheld them, the railroad would then secure the facts from the road where he had last worked. Such information was freely exchanged, and any worker discharged because of strike activity would receive no consideration. Since this was deemed to be a matter of detail for each road, the General Managers' Association did not bother to keep a record of the strikers.[5]

Although triumphant, the railroad executives were in an ugly mood. For instance, the general superintendent of the Southern Pacific Railroad proclaimed his determination to refuse employment to all strikers on his railroad and to follow them wherever they might go—throughout the United States and Canada—in order to keep them from securing work.[6] Most of the general managers no doubt applauded such sentiments but found it inadvisable to proceed so harshly. In practice not all the strikers were refused work or blacklisted. A distinction was drawn between those who had quit under duress or through fear and those who did so voluntarily. The former were re-employed; and even among the latter some were restored to their positions, depending on how inoffensive their conduct had been and how badly their services were needed. Detectives, employed by each railroad, gathered careful data on all strike activity, and upon the basis of this information the general manager largely determined what treatment should be accorded to each striker.

The Illinois Central Railroad re-employed approximately two-thirds of all employees who quit work during the strike and presumably blacklisted the remainder.[7] The Rock Island was even more generous, if its statement is to be accepted, since, out of the forty-five hundred workers who were willingly or unwillingly involved in the struggle, all but four hundred and fifty were finally forgiven.[8] Rather than jeopardize its own best interests by refusing employment to such a large army of workers, many of them highly skilled, this road found it better policy to retaliate only against those who had served the American Railway Union in an active and militant role. Other systems pursued a somewhat similar course, despite their threats of wholesale vengeance against all strikers. Nevertheless, thousands were blacklisted throughout the nation, and the plight of these men, vainly seeking work, was indeed tragic.[9]

Since Eugene Debs was primarily responsible for the creation of the American Railway Union, he, more than anybody else, did not want to see it perish. He wanted to make himself believe that it would live and, in doing so, closed his eyes to reality. On August 20, 1894, less than three weeks after defeat was officially acknowledged by his union, he expressed the conviction that it "is stronger today, numerically and in every other way, than it ever was since its organization."[10] Only wishful thinking could have prompted such an expression. The struggle had left the union shattered and broken and with a constantly dwindling membership. The officials of the union were not even free to save the union at a time when leadership was most desperately needed. Faced by contempt and indictment proceedings and then months of imprisonment, they were helpless to act, if action could have averted disaster.

What could be done was nevertheless done. Shortly before Debs entered Woodstock jail, the offices of the American Railway Union were transferred from Chicago to Terre Haute, Indiana, and assurance given that the work of reorganizing and strengthening the union would be "pushed with unabated vigor."[11] In prison Debs was alert to the obstacles that would confront any unionization drive and so endeavored, in conjunction with his fellow-directors, to formulate plans that would surmount these difficulties. In order to counteract the methods employed by the railroads, secrecy was considered extremely necessary in recruiting members. Timid workers were to be approached quietly at their homes or at some convenient place by carefully selected organizers. In joining the American Railway Union a person was not required to attend meetings or do anything that would reveal his membership. In this manner members would be protected against company spies and spotters.[12]

Such methods were used but without much success. According to Eugene Debs, railroad detectives were put upon his trail soon after his release from prison, and for two years they shadowed

him. Men whom he organized and those suspected of being affiliated with the union were summarily dismissed. In the spring
of 1897 Debs realized that further effort was useless. He seemed
convinced that the only hope for labor lay in political action.
From the remnants of the American Railway Union, assembled
in its last convention at Chicago in June of that year, was organized the Social Democratic party—the foreruner of the Socialist party of America.[13]

The strike left the Pullman workers in a demoralized condition.
Although many had found work by the middle of August, 1894,
a large proportion still remained jobless. The Pullman shops required only three-fourths as many men as before the strike—a
condition serious in itself but which was aggravated by the company's policy of employing hundreds of new men. For three
months public charity had borne the relief burden in the model
town, but this was now exhausted, and in despair the destitute of
Pullman appealed to the governor of Illinois on August 17. The
petition declared:

> We, the people of Pullman, who by the greed and oppression of George Pull-
> man, have been brought to a condition where starvation stares us in the face,
> do hereby appeal to you for aid in this our hour of need. We have been refused
> employment and have no means of leaving this vicinity, and our families are
> starving. Our places have been filled with workmen from all over the United
> States brought here by the Pullman Company. . . . . There are over sixteen
> hundred families here in destitution and want, and their condition is pitiful.[14]

Upon receipt of this request John Altgeld immediately wrote a
letter to George Pullman reviewing the plight of these people and
urging him to alleviate their suffering. The governor explained:

> These people live in your town and were your employees. Some of them
> have worked for your company for many years. They must be people of char-
> acter and industry or you would not have kept them. Many of them have prac-
> tically given their lives to you. It is claimed they struck because after years of
> toil their loaves were so reduced that their children went hungry. Assuming
> that they were wrong and foolish, they had yet served you long and well and
> you must feel some interest in them. . . . . The State of Illinois has not the least
> desire to meddle in the affairs of your company, but it cannot allow a whole
> community within its borders to perish of hunger.

Since the protection of Pullman property during the strike had cost the state fifty thousand dollars, Altgeld expressed the opinion that the Pullman Company should meet the situation and not put the state to any more expense. Should George Pullman refuse, the governor threatened to call a special session of the legislature or issue an appeal to the people of Illinois for aid.[15]

Proceeding to the model town, Governor Altgeld made a personal inspection of conditions. The ramshackle shanties in the brickyards were discovered to be overcrowded, one of them housing eight Italians. Poverty and hunger were found to have reached alarming proportions. Several days previously the relief committee had exhausted its resources in giving to each family two pounds of oatmeal and the same amount of corn meal. Deeply impressed, the governor again appealed to George Pullman for assistance. He pleaded: "The men are hungry and the women and children are actually suffering. They have been living on charity for a number of months and it is exhausted. Men who have worked for your company for more than ten years had to apply to the relief society in two weeks after the work stopped." In meeting the situation, Altgeld suggested that Pullman cancel all rent prior to October 1 and stagger the work in the shops so that the sixteen hundred families in destitution could buy bread.[16]

The reply of George Pullman was characteristic of the man. While minimizing the amount of poverty, he placed all responsibility upon the workers themselves. Had they remained at work, he pointed out, they would have received over three hundred thousand dollars in wages. When the shops resumed operation, many of the strikers refused to return to work, thereby necessitating, he explained, the employment of outsiders. He denied that the cancellation of rent would ease the situation. As for the staggering of work—this, he protested, was tried before the strike occurred but served only to create a false impression as to the true character of Pullman wages.[17] To John Altgeld the contentions of George Pullman were not very convincing. In a final communication to the sleeping-car magnate, the governor explained that "it is not my business to fix the moral responsibility in this case." But, he emphasized, there are

nearly six thousand people suffering for the want of food—they were your employees—four-fifths of them women and children—some of these people have been working for you for more than twelve years. I assumed that even if they were strong and had been foolish, you would not be willing to see them perish.[18]

In a lengthy proclamation, Governor Altgeld appealed to the people of Illinois in behalf of the Pullman inhabitants.[19] Various Chicago newspapers responded magnificently by vividly portraying conditions in the model town. An investigation proved to the county commissioners that the situation was even worse than that pictured in the press, and immediately they ordered one thousand sacks of flour and four thousand pounds of rice for that community. Contributions poured in from all quarters.[20] During the ensuing months many of the inhabitants moved away, and conditions in Pullman slowly improved. With the return of better times, the model town recovered in some degree its former position. The scars of the great struggle, however, were not easily eradicated, and the bitterness engendered had a deadening effect upon the entire community. The strike served to emphasize the commercial basis of the town, to expose Pullman's lack of genuine interest in the welfare of labor, and to magnify the inherent weaknesses of the Pullman experiment. The model town, which George Pullman "loved like one of his children" stood condemned, but he did not live to see it disintegrate.

Within three years following the great strike, the builder and guardian of the town of Pullman died. So closely was the town associated with the life of George Pullman that his demise jeopardized its existence and removed an influence that would have resisted the forces bent upon terminating the experiment. His death came unexpectedly from a severe heart attack on October 19, 1897, at the age of sixty-six years.[21] His passing was the occasion for lengthy obituaries, occupying many columns in the leading newspapers. In the town of Pullman flags were lowered to half-mast and resolutions of sympathy were expressed by various organizations. The impression seemed to prevail among his closest acquaintances that he was grossly misunderstood. A few of the observations were critical, but none breathed the hate or animosity which had characterized so many of the utterances about the man during the great strike. Even Eugene Debs, the most implacable foe of Pullman, made only this remark: "Peace be to his ashes. Mr. Pullman would not arbitrate when 'he had nothi ng to arbitrate.' He is on an equality with toilers now."[22]

The Pullman experiment had now reached the point where its continuation was no longer justifiable. The Supreme Court of Illinois delivered the death blow; but, even if the judiciary had not acted, the venture could not have survived many years. The action which doomed the town as a model community was initiated in the circuit court of Cook County by Maurice T. Maloney, attorney-general of Illinois, shortly after the conclusion of the strike. The Pullman Palace Car Company was charged with the violation of its corporate rights and the forfeiture of its charter was demanded. This company, averred Maloney, was authorized to build, lease, and sell railway cars but not to acquire large real estate holdings or to establish and manage a town. Such measures, being unnecessary to the successful operation of the company's business, were, he protested, a usurpation of the privileges granted under the law of incorporation.[23]

Precisely why the attorney-general of Illinois started proceedings against the Pullman Company is not known, although the action was undoubtedly the outgrowth of the Pullman Strike. Fourteen years had elapsed since the model town was established, and during this period the legality of the enterprise had never been questioned. The Pullman officials had been advised by legal counsel that the purchase of real estate and the erection of homes for the employees would be within the charter rights of the corporation.[24] With the outbreak of the strike, however, attention was focused on the Pullman Corporation. The fact that the Democratic administration of the state was sympathetic to labor and none too friendly toward George Pullman may explain why the suit was instituted. But the charge that Mayor Hopkins and Eugene Debs were leading spirits back of the action or that it was a political move to win the support of labor for the Democratic party cannot be substantiated.

The case came up originally for a hearing in the circuit court of Judge John Gibbons, who, six years previously, had written a book, *Tenure and Toil*, in which he severely criticized the town of Pullman. Afraid that impartial treatment could not be had under such a judge, the defense petitioned for a change of venue. In reply to the charge of being prejudiced, Gibbons defied anybody to say that he had criticized in his book a legitimate corporation. "I did condemn those pseudo corporations which existed purely for the purpose of robbing innocent people, and I also condemn corporate aggression or trusts," he declared, "but no man can show that I am opposed to a legitimate corporation." Gibbons nevertheless granted the petition, and the case was transferred to the court of Judge Frank Baker.[25]

Determined to save its charter, the Pullman Corporation engaged the best legal talent available. The right to construct tenements in order to house workers was held by the company to be essential for the success of its manufacturing enterprise. The defense explained that, since the site of the town was originally an open prairie, it was necessary to build a town; and in order to attract a high class of workers it was important that the community be attractively designed and strictly modern. It was further emphasized that the construction of homes and the building of the Pullman shops were "undertaken at the same time and as a part of a single harmonious scheme."[26] These and other contentions proved convincing to the court of Judge Baker, which overruled the attorney-general and on virtually all points sustained the Pullman Company in its interpretation of the charter.[27]

The Supreme Court of Illinois, to which the case was finally appealed, reversed the findings of the lower court in a four-to-three decision in October, 1898. In disregarding the plea that it was imperative for the company to construct a town the judges ruled that private capital and individual initiative would have met the situation by building homes, churches, stores, and other accommodations and that the laws of the state would have guaranteed the schools. The decision denounced paternalism in strong terms, affirming that the existence of a town or city where all the property belonged exclusively to a corporation was "opposed to good public policy and incompatible with the theory and spirit of our institutions."[28] The case was promptly remanded to the circuit court, where the Pullman Company was ordered to cease within one year the performance of all municipal functions, and within five years to dispose of all property designated by the Supreme Court as not required in the manufacturing business. This period was subsequently extended for another five years upon petition of the Pullman Company, which contended that because of a rather sluggish demand for real estate more time was needed.[29]

Strangely enough, the decision of the Illinois Supreme Court was received without any apparent resentment by the Pullman officials, who did not even take the trouble to ask for a rehearing on the case. According to one prominent newspaper, the only reason why the Pullman Company contested the suit at all was "to sustain its charter and to vindicate the lawfulness of its action." The largest shareholders, it was explained, welcomed the decision in so far as it affected the town of Pullman.[30] It is not improbable that, had George Pullman been alive, some attempt would have been made to circumvent the decision. One source revealed that it was his intention, in case of an adverse decision, to form a new company completely separate from the Pullman Palace Car Corporation, the stock of which, representing real estate, was to be distributed as a bonus to stockholders of the Pullman Company.[31] Death prevented the realization of this or any other stratagem which he might have planned. With the defender of the model town no longer at the helm, the Pullman Company was quite willing to permit the paternalistic experiment to pass into the limbo of unsuccessful ventures.

Governed only by the determination to realize the maximum from its property, the company proceeded with haste to liquidate all phases of the experiment. The interest of the corporation in the beauty of the town quickly disappeared. The policy of caring for the lawns of the inhabitants was discontinued, and the maintenance of shrubbery and flowers no longer remained the solicitous concern of Pullman authorities. Lake Vista was drained, and the surrounding park with its greensward, flower beds, and gravel walks was destroyed, the entire site being utilized for industrial

purposes. The public playground and the athletic island were
similarly appropriated to meet the needs of a company which was
experiencing a new era of industrial expansion.[32] Under such a
program the aesthetic features of the town gradually vanished.
The appearance of bare ground in front of the tenement blocks
and the absence of care for the shrubs and trees tended to emphasize the monotonous architecture of the homes. Pullman
ceased to be a "show place" for visitors.[33]

The various enterprises in the town were disposed of as quickly as
conditions would permit. The Florence Hotel was leased in 1901
and subsequently sold for seventy-five thousand dollars. Owing to
the lack of adequate fire-escape facilities, the Arcade Theatre was
condemned and permanently closed in 1902. The city of Chicago
had already assumed control of the police and fire departments
and now extended jurisdiction over such matters as sewerage,
maintenance of streets, and the collection of water bills. With the
abandonment of the old sewage farm, the sewage was emptied
into Lake Michigan through the Calumet River, but later discharged into the Chicago Sanitary Canal.[34] Following the death
of Duane Doty in November, 1902, the office of town agent was
discontinued; and the remaining functions of the office, pending
the final liquidation of the town, were transferred to the president
of the Pullman Loan and Savings Bank. The various departments of the town were gradually abolished, the last to go being
the Repair Department in 1907.[35] In 1899 the acreage holdings
of the Pullman Company were platted, but not until July, 1907,
was the plat of the town submitted to the city commissioner of
public works, thereby officially terminating the existence of the
model town as a separate community from Chicago.[36]

More fortunate than most of the enterprises was the Pullman
Library, whose cost of operation was guaranteed by Mrs. George
Pullman when the company withdrew all support. In doing this,
as in purchasing the Arcade, she was prompted by sentiment.
Very graciously she delegated the management of the library to a
committee of Pullman citizens, who immediately reduced the library fee to two dollars and subsequently abolished it altogether.[37]

The offer of the company to sell the school building to the Chicago Board of Education for forty thousand dollars was rejected. In 1889 the board would have gladly purchased it, but the Pullman officials would not then alienate any part of the town. The structure was now considered too antiquated for further use, and so it was decided to build a new one on a tract of land diagonally opposite from the old building. The property was condemned; but, instead of paying the forty thousand dollars demanded for it, the board of education carried the matter into the court of Judge John Gibbons, where the jury awarded the Pullman Company only fourteen thousand two hundred dollars.[38] On this site was erected a modern building which the directors voted to call the "Henry George School." Because this name evoked considerable criticism on the part of those who favored that of George Pullman, the board reconsidered and decided to honor the founder of the model town instead.[39]

Most of the property in the town was thrown on the market during the spring and summer of 1907—a period of unprecedented prosperity. The Pullman shops then employed over nine thousand men, or twice as many as were normally needed. The sale was conducted by officials of the Pullman bank, who for several weeks restricted the right of purchase to the residents of Pullman.[40] Prices ranged from fourteen hundred to six thousand dollars—the amount for each house being equal to one hundred times its monthly rental. The terms were comparatively easy: one-sixth of the price in cash and the balance in small monthly payments. Many Pullman employees purchased homes, although the largest acquisitions were made by outsiders, often for speculative purposes.[41] The tenement blocks on Fulton Avenue were purchased for three hundred and forty-two thousand dollars by Mrs. Florence Pullman Lowden, who explained that she was very glad to become identified with the town which her father had established. The Greenstone Church, occupied by the Presbyterians for twenty-three years, was acquired by the Methodists for fifteen thousand dollars. The Presbyterians intended to make the purchase but hesitated too long.[42] The homes and public buildings were thus disposed of in an amazingly rapid manner. By October, 1907, this gigantic transaction in real estate was virtually completed; and the model town, which originally cost eight million dollars, had now passed out of the hands of corporate ownership.[43]

With the company no longer identified with the town, it sank to the commonplace of the ordinary industrial community. The attempt of prominent citizens to prevent this was foredoomed to failure, and gradually most of them established their residences elsewhere. In 1910 the population was less than eight thousand people.[44] The lethargy which enveloped the spirit of the community proved incurable. As the Pullman shops underwent enormous expansion and reached new heights of industrial efficiency, the model town slumped lower and lower in the trough of decay. The town stands today a ghost of its former glory—a pathetic and ironical reminder of the dreams of George Pullman to inaugurate a new era of industrial harmony.

The weaknesses and contradictions of the experiment, obvious from the outset to only a few, became known to many during the great strike; and after Pullman's death virtually every appraisal of the venture was a pronouncement of failure and impracticability. At no time, however, did the newspapers deny the value of the sanitary and aesthetic features of the town. Even when it was generally recognized that the venture could not survive, the press still paid tribute to the fact that model homes, parks, streets, and other conveniences had been established to elevate the employee. Concerning all other aspects, however, press comments were no longer friendly. What the newspapers said about the experiment, as it approached its unhappy end, furnish an excellent commentary on why it perished.

Of major importance was the labor policy of George Pullman, which many papers strongly deprecated. The *New York Times* proclaimed that all illusions relative to the idealism of George Pullman in operating the model town were quickly shattered by his drastic wage policy of 1893 and 1894. "He stood revealed," declared the editorial, "as a 'hard man' and his extremely business-like behavior was much more fiercely resented than if no pretensions had ever been made on his behalf."[45] In the opinion of the *Chicago Journal*, George Pullman had failed miserably in understanding the proper relationship between employer and employee. "He was quite as hard and cold," affirmed this paper, "as any other employer in dealing with his factory hands. He paid the 'market value' and laid off men when work was slack. Landlord Pullman was not lenient when President Pullman reduced wages."[46] The *Chicago Evening Post* concurred with other organs of expression when it asserted that, in his policy toward labor, George Pullman consulted his own will, ignoring completely the demands of his employees.[47]

The absence of democracy and the existence of arbitrary control provoked criticisms no less trenchant. Fifteen years have elapsed, declared the *Inter Ocean*, since Andrew D. White, the ambassador to Germany, referred to the model town as the "probable solution of one of the knottiest problems of modern civilization." In explaining why White erred and the Pullman venture ended in melancholy failure, the editor alluded to the many restrictions imposed upon personal liberty.[48] The *Chicago Record* viewed the Pullman experiment as paternalistic, feudalistic, undemocratic, and contrary to American institutions.[49] The *Chicago Evening Post* expressed the opinion that "in Europe the town of Pullman would have been an unquestioned triumph of beneficent thoughtfulness for the well-being of the workingmen. In America, and more particularly in Chicago, it is an old world anachronism, and always will be."[50] Liberty, announced the *New York Journal*, "has its price, but it is better to pay it. Self-dependence has its trials, but they beget strength, which is better than helplessness. Pullman's personal motives may have been good, but the model town of his corporation was a gilded cage that imprisoned the manhood of its denizens."[51]

The editor of the *Calumet Record*,[52] who had long been an ardent supporter of the model town, was now willing to acknowledge the passing of the experiment as something for which all concerned were devoutly thankful. In his judgment the policy of ownership and control by the Pullman Company was primarily responsible for the instability of the population and business enterprises in the town. He explained that, aside from the Pullman bank, only two stores had retained their identity under the same management

for more than fifteen years and that the families which had resided continuously in Pullman for that period could be counted
on the fingers.[53] The *Chicago Times Herald*, in commenting on the
absence of homeownership, declared:

> The first ambition of the American workingman is to "own his own home"—
> an ambition that has done more to steady him than all laws and trade union
> regulations. It may be a poor thing, but he says proudly: "It is my own."
> The twenty-five foot lot with the little one story cottage stands for his share in
> the edifice of the Republic. It is his "stake" in the country. Mr. Pullman over-
> looked this sentiment. . . . . He mingled the relations of the employer and the
> landlord—an unpopular relation.[54]

Perhaps no indictment of the model town was more sweeping
than that pronounced by the *Chicago Journal:*

> Politically it was a rotten borough, socially a travesty on feudalism. It was
> the source of scandal for years, and in time it was the provocation of the out-
> break in 1894 that left a scar not soon to be removed. . . . . In other and even
> less pleasing aspects the "model town" wore the colors of statistical philan-
> thropy. Pullman was school master and preacher; sanitary officer, supplier of
> water, light and fuel, guardian of the peace and censor of everything from flower
> pots in windows to domestic morality. And the American workingman, being
> neither a slave nor a fool, rejected the money grabbing philanthropy of the
> "model town" and poor Mr. Pullman, a person of good intentions, lived to see
> his plan held up to public scorn and himself denounced as an enemy of labor.[55]

The ending of the "noble experiment" did not occasion among
the writers any expression of regret. The logic of circumstances
had convinced the idealists and theorists that they would have to
search elsewhere for a solution of industrial problems. Paternalism, instead of promoting better relations between employees and
employer, had actually provided the laborer with new grievances
and placed in the path of industrial peace an insuperable barrier.
Improved living conditions and a favorable environment contributed only in part to contentment of labor. Freedom of action
and the right of self-expression were equally important. The
strike of 1894, more than anything else, stamped indelibly on the
mind of the laborer the true character of the experiment. Convinced that the Pullman Corporation had no genuine interest in
his fate, the worker became cynical toward the whole venture.
The model town thus became a source of bitter disillusionment

and finally, exposed with all its frailties and contradictions, collapsed, joining many other social experiments designed to promote the well-being of the human race.

The passing of the model town was only one incident in the chain of events that flowed from the Pullman Strike. In so far as most workers were concerned, the liquidation of the experiment possessed little significance, since they had never reposed any real hope in the venture as a possible corrective for the ills of labor. The strike had given rise to new and "dangerous" antilabor weapons; and these, with all their implications, now challenged the full attention of organized labor. In the use of equity proceedings and federal troops the United States government had established precedents considered dangerous for the future welfare of the workers. The "unholy" alliance between the federal authorities and the railroads was viewed apprehensively. Was the government the servile tool of corporate interests? What rights did labor have? To what would all this lead?

When the outlook seemed gloomiest, the labor unions were able to derive comfort from the *Report of the United States Strike Commission*, based upon a searching investigation of the causes of the great struggle. The work of this commission was rendered possible by the Arbitration Act of 1888—a law sponsored by Grover Cleveland in the interest of industrial peace. Designed for labor disputes on interestate railroads, the act provided for voluntary arbitration and for a temporary fact-finding commission. Since arbitration was applicable only when both parties were willing and even then with no assurance that the award would prove binding, this mode of settling disputes proved highly ineffective. The commission of inquiry, however, could be invoked by either party or by the governor of the state or upon the discretion of the chief executive of the nation. Composed of the United States commissioner of labor and two other members appointed by the President, this board possessed the authority to subpoena witnesses and administer oaths in seeking to determine the nature and causes for the controversy.[56]

On July 12, 1894, a committee of officials from the Knights of Labor called upon Grover Cleveland for the purpose of invoking

the Arbitration Act of 1888. They came as representatives of the
strikers and were accompanied by United States Senator James
K. Kyle. The President promised that as soon as the rioting and
disorders ceased at Chicago he would appoint a commission to
make the investigation.[57] Cleveland was not, however, in any
hurry, although some of the labor leaders, including Eugene
Debs, opposed delay, on the grounds that quick action would aid
materially in quieting labor everywhere.[58] Not until July 26 did
President Cleveland announce that Nicholas E. Worthington of
Illinois and John D. Kernan of New York would join with Carroll
D. Wright, United States commissioner of labor, in an inquiry
into the recent labor strife on the Illinois Central and the Rock
Island railroads.[59] Lyman Trumbull was invited to serve on the
commission but declined for the reason that the scope of the
inquiry was too narrow.[60]

Hearings were held in Chicago during the last two weeks in
August and in Washington, D.C., on September 26. Only two
railroads were specifically listed for investigation, but so numerous were the ramifications that virtually all aspects of the struggle
in Chicago were scrutinized by the commission before its work
was concluded. More than one hundred witnesses were examined—and in a manner which reflected absolute impartiality.
If George Pullman and Everett St. John were subject to a searching and exhaustive interrogation, so were Eugene Debs and
George W. Howard. The commissioners were relentless in their
quest for facts. Those among the workers who took the witness
stand were candid in their remarks, but it was claimed that the
danger of being blacklisted kept many material witnesses from the
courtroom.[61] From the carefully sifted evidence the commission
prepared its recommendations. In November, 1894, the report,
including all testimony, was submitted to President Cleveland,
who in turn transmitted it to Congress.

The commission was vitally concerned with measures that
might be taken to avert or discourage future railroad strikes, and
to this end each witness was carefully interrogated. Numerous
suggestions were proffered, many of which represented measures
unsuited to the period or the times. Virtually all the labor leaders

seemed to favor government ownership of railroads as the best hope for preserving industrial peace. Eugene Debs expressed the sentiment of many when he declared that "government ownership of railroads is decidedly better for the people than railroad ownership of the government." It was his conviction that if the railroads were operated by the people in their own interest, instead of for private gain, train service would be better, the condition of the workers greatly improved, and the likelihood of strikes removed.[62] George W. Howard pointed out that, since 30 per cent of the railroads were already in federal receivership, government ownership would not be difficult to achieve. Such a step, he explained, would not only mean justice for labor but would eliminate the various evils which have flourished under private management.[63] Among others who supported the proposal were Samuel Gompers, James Sovereign, and P. H. Morrissy of the Railway Trainmen.[64] From railroad executives, however, the suggestion elicited not the slightest support.

Very little sentiment was voiced by labor or capital for compulsory arbitration. Eugene Debs felt that such an instrument would not promote harmonious relations between the employer and employee, but he was willing to concede that in the case of the Pullman Strike it might have proved efficacious.[65] Although most of the labor leaders concurred with Debs, a few expressed support for compulsory arbitration, if it could be impartially conducted and would not infringe upon the constitutional rights of the parties involved.[66] The general managers of the Rock Island and Illinois Central were adamant in their opposition to this method of settling disputes, contending that it would prove objectionable to the employees and disastrous to the employers and could not work until labor organizations became responsible.[67]

One of the officials of the General Managers' Association, John M. Egan, favored licenses for all railroad employees. This system, he explained, would be controlled by the government; and no man who could not meet the requirements and secure a license would be eligible to work. A code of rules and a schedule of wages would be uniformly enforced in a given area. All difficulties would be amicably adjusted between the railroads and their employees, and, in case of a strike, the licenses of the strikers would be revoked. This method, he averred, would obviate the necessity for arbitration, strikes, and labor organizers.[68] In commenting on the proposal, Everett St. John, chairman of the association, questioned its workability. In his judgment nothing should be permitted to interfere with the law of supply and demand. "It is," he asserted, "a principle as old as government itself, and has proven in the years past effective as applied to both employer and employee."[69]

Eugene V. Debs clung to the belief, which he emphasized before the Strike Commission, that more harmony and stability in capital-labor relations would occur if the workers were organized. A small amount of power is dangerous, he exclaimed, and a weak union is drawn into premature or needless strikes, often by a provocative employer; but, with strength and power, the union would be more cautious and conservative. Then, proclaimed Debs, the employer would be more willing to make concessions, knowing the full strength of labor. Each would be more disposed to respect the rights of the others.[70]

Among other remedies proposed were restriction of immigration; monetary legislation; suppression of business monopolies; settlement of labor controversies by the courts; control of wages and hours by the United States Labor Commission; a system of pensions for employees; and the determination by statute of maximum hours and minimum wage rates.[71] In all there was an impressive array of proposals, but very few made any impression on the Strike Commission. Most of the suggestions were too impractical or too irrelevant, and the only ones that received any serious consideration were arbitration, government regulation of industrial relations, government ownership of railroads, and the need for labor unions.

On all matters the commission tried to be eminently fair but utterly fearless. Contrary to popular expectation, responsibility for the violence was not placed upon the strikers. Impartial observers, asserted the *Report*, were becoming more and more convinced that the "real responsibility for these disorders rests with the people themselves and with the Government for not adequately controlling monopolies and corporations, and for failing to reasonably protect the rights of labor and redress its wrongs."[72] Toward labor conflicts the commissioners assumed a very critical attitude but seemed encouraged that even among union leaders there was general agreement that boycotts, lockouts, and strikes should be condemned as "barbarism unfit for the intelligence of this age." With pitiless logic the *Report* denounced all these weapons of industrial strife:

> They are war—internecine war—and call for progress to a higher plane of education and intelligence in adjusting the relations of capital and labor. These barbarisms waste the products of both capital and labor, defy law and order, disturb society, intimidate capital, convert industrial paths where there ought to be plenty into highways of poverty and crime, bear as their fruit the arrogant flush of victory and the humiliating sting of defeat, and lead to preparations for greater and more destructive conflicts.[73]

The commission not only defended the right of labor to organize but stressed the importance to society of strongly organized unions. It was explained that, because of the growth of railroad combinations, competition no longer protected the employees as to wages or shippers as to rates. While competition had thus greatly diminished among those who employed labor, it had rapidly increased among those who sought work. In illustration of this the *Report* cited the elimination of the competitive demand for switchmen among the twenty-four railroads at Chicago. Through the General Managers' Association these roads no longer had to compete against one another in hiring such workers, for whom competition had become unmercifully severe. Elsewhere, it was indicated, the same tendency had revealed itself. "In view of this progressive perversion of the laws of supply and demand by capital and changed conditions," proclaimed the commission, "no man can well deny the right nor dispute the wisdom of unity for legislative and protective purposes among those who supply labor."

Since unions are here to stay and will grow more powerful, is it not advisable, inquired the *Report*, "to fully recognize them by law; to admit their necessity as labor guides and protectors, to conserve their usefulness, increase their responsibilities, and to prevent their follies and aggressions by conferring upon them the privileges enjoyed by corporations with like proper restrictions and regulations?" Just as corporations have attained extraordinary power and responsibility, so, exclaimed the commissioners, it would not be surprising if labor, during the next half-century, were to attain a similar position of prestige. By acquiring equal status, labor and capital would then enjoy more harmonious relations since they would be in a position to respect each other's rights. While not identical, the interests of the two were held to be reciprocal. Employers were accordingly urged to recognize the right of labor to organize and bargain collectively.[74] The refusal of the Pullman Corporation to do so provoked the following comment:

> The company does not recognize that labor organizations have any place or necessity in Pullman, where the company fixes wages and rents, and refuses to treat with labor organizations. The laborer can work or quit on the terms offered; that is the limit of his rights. To join a labor organization in order to secure the protection of the union against wrongs, real or imaginary, is over stepping the limits and arouses hostility. This position secures all the advantage of the concentration of capital, power and control for the company in its labor dealings, and deprives the employees of any such advantage or protection as a labor union might afford. In this respect the Pullman Company is behind the age.[75]

In weighing the merits of government ownership of the railroads, the Strike Commission was unwilling to grant the immediate need for such a socialistic remedy. The *Report* pointed out, however, that if railroad combinations continued to grow until there were only half a dozen or less, then the question of government ownership would be pushed to the front. As monopolies expand, it was emphasized, there will need to be at least greater government regulation. Whenever a country, inquired the commissioners,

> finds itself in such relation to a railroad that its investments therein must be either lost or protected by ownership, would it not be wise that the road be taken and the experiment be tried as an object lesson in Government ownership? . . . . We need to fear everything revolutionary and wrong, but we need fear nothing that any nation can successfully attempt in directions made necessary by changed economic or industrial conditions.[76]

The refusal of the Pullman Company and the General Managers' Association to submit to arbitration or conciliation was greatly deplored by the Strike Commission, which expressed the belief that a "different policy would have prevented the loss of life and great loss of property and wages occasioned by the strike."[77] In the opinion of the commissioners, something more than ordinary arbitration was necessary to prevent future conflicts; indeed, nothing less than the interposition of the federal government would be sufficient. It was pointed out that, since railroads are quasi-public corporations, such matters as pooling, rates, and industrial relations were within the regulatory jurisdiction of the federal government. In safeguarding the interests of the shipper, the Interstate Commerce Commission was established—a tribunal to which both the railroad and shipper could appeal on equal terms. A similar commission, contended the *Report*, was necessary in order to investigate and adjudicate disputes between the railroads and their employees. The power to enforce its decisions would be intrusted to the United States courts, and, pending appeals, there should be no delay in complying with the ruling of the commission.

This commission, consisting of three members, would be permanent and possess sufficient power to determine wages and any other matter involved in a labor controversy on an interstate railroad. It was recommended that this tribunal be permitted to intervene in a dispute upon its own discretion or when invited by either or both parties. Each side in the controversy would be given the right to nominate one person to join with the other members on the commission in "hearing, adjusting and determining that particular controversy," providing the labor organization involved was a national trade-union incorporated under federal or state laws. Otherwise, only the permanent members would function. This provision, it was believed, would have the effect of creating greater confidence in the commission and of inducing labor organizations to seek incorporation.

During the investigation it would be unlawful for railroads to discharge employees except for inefficiency, negligence, or lawlessness, nor could unions resort to a strike or boycott. After the decision was rendered and for the ensuing six months, railroads could not dismiss employees except for these causes, and during the same period the workers were not privileged to quit work without giving thirty days' advance notice in writing. The Strike Commission recognized that the law would not operate reciprocally, since compliance on the part of labor could not always be enforced; but this was not viewed as a serious defect because the railroads derived all their privileges from the state and hence should be compelled to do whatever would best serve the public interest. Even if some of the employees should stop work because of dissatisfaction over a decision, the railroads would have no trouble, it was affirmed, in filling the vacancies from the abundant labor supply in the country.[78]

Whatever may have been the merits of this proposal to adjust labor difficulties on interstate railroads, there was virtually no sentiment for its adoption. Neither the press nor Congress revealed enthusiasm for a plan so contrary to the prevailing tenets of industrial freedom. Public thought was unprepared to support it, and even labor remained unimpressed. Concerning the other conclusions reached by the Strike Commission, there was a sharp cleavage of opinion. To most people, including the propertied classes, the *Report* proved a great disappointment. Instead of seeking to glorify or justify the part played by the government and the General Managers' Association, the commissioners sought only to reveal the unembellished facts, some of which reflected unpleasantly upon the policies employed in suppressing the American Railway Union. Striking labor was portrayed in a manner entirely different from that revealed during the strike by the capitalistically controlled organs of public expression. For this, if for nothing else, the powerful interests and the press could not view the *Report* with equanimity. But no less objectionable was the advocacy of labor's right to organize and bargain collectively—a position which was bitter as gall to the "rugged individualists" of this era.

The *Nation* referred to the *Report of the Strike Commission* as "a disappointing, in some respects a very discouraging document." The editor warmly defended the refusal of George Pullman and the General Managers' Association to arbitrate and otherwise took issue with the conclusions of the commission. Referring to the strike as a "social convulsion" and a "civil war," he protested that the use of arbitration would have been fatal. The whole idea of compulsory arbitration was rejected on the grounds that labor disputes should be left to the parties themselves for solution. Thoroughly nettled by the tenor of the *Report*, the editor finally exclaimed that "one good result of the report will be increased hesitation about appointing commissions to inquire into the origin and causes of labor troubles."[79]

Other comments were no more friendly. Only among labor was there rejoicing, and here unstinted praise was voiced for a report which dealt sympathetically with their aspirations and hopes. Eugene Debs explained that the *Report* "is eminently fair and impartial and meets with the unqualified approval of not only the American Railway Union, but of all people who believe in the American spirit of fair play and desire the enthronement of justice." In his opinion the result was a "triumphant vindication of the American Railway Union."[80] The American Federation of Labor was just as enthusiastic in indorsing what it chose to call a very "lucid and conscientious" report. The document seemed to impart to that organization a renewed determination to protect the rights of labor. We are more convinced than ever, proclaimed the *American Federationist*, "that this country has entered on the most perilous period of her history, and that nothing can save this people and nation from despotism and anarchy but the wisest and most energetic action on the part of her trade unions."[81]

The *Report* of the commission emphasized what the strike had already taught labor—that only through powerfully organized unions could it hope to maintain its rights and command the respect of the employer. Although the unionization movement was retarded and crippled by the struggle, such ill effects were only temporary. It was Debs who said that the general managers "might as well try to stop Niagara with a feather as to crush the spirit of organization in this country."[82] Neither he nor the other labor leaders were willing to abandon faith in the ultimate triumph of labor, although the immediate future was most discouraging.

Henry D. Lloyd, author and lawyer, believed the policy of the vested interests to be pregnant with the greatest danger for the status quo. Viewing the situation as a friend of labor, he took the position in a communication to Clarence Darrow in November, 1894, that the plutocrats were wrong in their supposition that they could cure the evil of strikes by force. He explained:

They are as blind as the fools of power have always been. . . . . It is only by the aggressions of the enemy that the people can be united. Events must be our leaders, and we will have them. I am not discouraged. The radicalism of the fanatics of wealth fills me with hope. They are likely to do for us what the South did for the North in 1861.[83]

Lloyd rebelled against the economic philosophy which so completely dominated the business world and which influenced so greatly the policy of the government. This philosophy was exemplified by the captains of industry who were committed to rugged individualism and who hotly resented interference from any source. They were unwilling to acknowledge the right of labor to unionize or to bargain collectively. They preferred to view labor as a commodity to be controlled by market conditions. The Pullman Strike was the logical outgrowth of conditions fostered in large part by the "hard and unsocial" principles of the vested interests. George Pullman and Richard Olney were the products of that age. Their creed was the creed of the moneyed interests— that property was the highest good and the chief end of society. They believed that social justice and human rights should remain forever subordinate to considerations of property. Both men lived as they believed and, in ignoring the yearnings of the workers, typified an era in which the rights of labor received scant recognition.

As the years slipped by and the memories of the Pullman Strike grew dimmer and dimmer, it became abundantly clear that labor had not suffered irreparably in that struggle. Fourteen years had elapsed when there appeared in the *Journal of the Switchmen's Union* an article in retrospect. The author affirmed that, although the railroads had emerged triumphant from the struggle and had proclaimed the annihilation of the American Railway Union, the principle of that organization still lived and was stronger than ever before.

There have been many changes since that great struggle against slavery, degradation and privation. . . . . Labor unions have again become . . . . stronger than ever. Many an honest workingman and woman went hungry in 1894 for daring to rebel against the humiliating conditions that existed at Pullman. Many a union man went to jail for disobeying the injunction of Judges Grosscup, Woods and Taft, but today we find Pullman has passed to the Great Beyond, where all are supposed to be equal; Woods is dead; Cleveland is dead; Egan has disappeared to God knows where; Grosscup has been under indictment; St. John has passed into the shadowy valley, but Eugene Debs still lives, loved by his fellowmen because of his honesty, for his many sacrifices to the cause of humanity. The cause of the working class is still here and here to stay and will be crowned gloriously triumphant long after the oppressors and tyrants and all their fawning retainers have gone the way of flesh and passed from memory.[84]

From 1894 on, labor strove diligently to circumscribe the use of the injunction and otherwise to secure from legislative bodies a fair measure of protection against judicial and corporate tyranny. The odds were great, but the forces of labor persisted. In 1896 the Democratic party protested against the arbitrary interference by federal authorities in local affairs and denounced "government by injunction as a new and highly dangerous form of oppression by which Federal Judges in contempt of the laws of the states and the rights of citizens, become at once legislators, judges and executioners."[85] It was not, however, until the adoption of the Clayton Anti-trust Act in 1914 that labor unions received some measure of protection from the injunction and were expressly exempted from the operation of the Sherman Anti-trust Act. The right to strike, picket, and boycott was held not to violate any federal law. Although these gains were gratifying, they were subsequently reduced in value by judicial interpretation. Undaunted, labor fought on and in time was able to implement this law and obtain other vital pro-labor enactments—until at length the workers had gained far more legislative protection and assistance than the strike-weary men of 1894 could have dreamed was possible. In the matter of settling railroad disputes, extraordinary progress was likewise made, although the compulsory plan of arbitration, which the Strike Commission advocated, was never destined to gain acceptance.

In scrutinizing the tremendous gains achieved by labor since that strife-ridden year of 1894, it is not possible to say with finality that any part of them had its origin in the Pullman Strike. But certainly from that struggle impulses were set in motion which affected the whole course of labor history. The Pullman Strike was more than just an industrial clash; it was an upheaval which shook the nation to its very depths and led to extraordinary applications of old laws and the creation of highly effective anti-labor weapons. In the heat of the struggle precedents were established that required long years to nullify. From that crisis labor gained rich experience and learned valuable lessons. In seeking the more abundant life, the workers were becoming more and more determined to secure for themselves a fairer share from the fruits of their toil.

In the face of overwhelming defeat the American Railway Union expressed no murmur of despair and no regret for its part in the drama. The cause, for which so much had been given and from which so little had been asked, was now finished. The men had fought well and suffered much. Were their sacrifices in vain and the struggle a catastrophic loss to labor? The American Railway Union did not choose to think so. With perhaps a greater measure of truth than was then realized, this union bravely proclaimed: "No, it was not a defeat—this ending of the most momentuous strike of modern times. It could not be, when we are so near a century that is to surely see the rights of the masses take that place in the policies of nations which is now basely devoted to the privileges of classes."[86]

NOTES

1. *Appendix to the . . . . Report of the Attorney General . . . . 1896*, p. 100; *Biennial Report of the Adjutant General of Illinois . . . . 1893 and 1894*, p. xxxi.
2. *U.S. Strike Commission Report*, pp. xviii, 330, 412, 416.
3. *Railroad Gazette*, XXVI (1894), 524.
4. *U.S. Strike Commission Report*, p. xviii.
5. *Ibid.*, pp. 176, 210, 221–22, 260.
6. *Ibid.*, p. 49.
7. *Ibid.*, p. 328.
8. *Ibid.*, pp. 219–20, 231.
9. *Ibid.*, pp. 22, 48–49, 86, 102, 104.

10. *Ibid.*, p. 175.

11. *Railway Times,* January 1, 1895, p. 1.

12. *Chicago Record,* October 8, 1895, p. 8.

13. *Debs: His Life, Writings and Speeches,* pp. 13, 20.

14. Altgeld, *op. cit.*, p. 421.

15. *Ibid.*, pp. 421–22.

16. *Ibid.*, pp. 422–23; *Chicago Tribune,* August 21, 1894, p. 1.

17. *Chicago Tribune,* August 22, 1894, p. 2.

18. Altgeld, *op. cit.*, p. 424.

19. *Chicago Tribune,* August 22, 1894, p. 13.

20. *Ibid.*, August 23, 1894, p. 1, and August 24, 1894, p. 1.

21. *Ibid.*, October 20, 1897, p. 1.

22. *Inter Ocean,* October 20, 1897, p. 2.

23. *Reports of Cases at Law and in Chancery Argued and Determined in the Supreme Court of Illinois,* CLXXV (1899), 129–33.

24. *Chicago Tribune,* August 12, 1894, p. 7.

25. *Ibid.*, October 25, 1894, p. 12, and November 18, 1894, p. 13.

26. *Report of Cases at Law and in Chancery Argued and Determined in the Supreme Court of Illinois,* CLXXV (1899), 143–49.

27. *Chicago Tribune,* June 2, 1895, p. 6.

28. *Reports of Cases at Law and in Chancery Argued and Determined in the Supreme Court of Illinois,* CLXXV (1899), 150–59.

29. J. Seymour Currey, *Chicago: Its History and Its Builders,* III, 205; *Calumet Record,* February 18, 1894, p. 1.

30. *Chicago Tribune,* October 25, 1898, p. 7.

31. *Ibid.*, October 26, 1898, p. 9.

32. *Inter Ocean,* April 29, 1899, p. 5.

33. Taylor, *Satellite Cities,* pp. 37–38.

34. *Ibid.*, p. 57; *Calumet Record,* July 17, 1902, p. 1.

35. *Calumet Record,* December 4, 1902, p. 1, and November 14, 1907, p. 5.

36. *Ibid.*, July 11, 1907, pp. 1, 5.

37. Ludlum, "History of the Pullman Library," pp. 5–6; Mrs. George Pullman to Bertha S. Ludlum, December 12, 1907, Pullman Collection, Pullman Branch Library.

38. Taylor, *op. cit.*, p. 56; *Calumet Record,* December 28, 1905, p. 1.

39. *Calumet Record,* June 13, 1907, p. 4, and July 4, 1907, p. 1.

40. *Ibid.*, May 16, 1907, p. 1, and October 3, 1907, p. 1.

41. *Ibid.*, July 11, 1907, p. 1; Taylor, *op. cit.*, p. 38; *Weekly Index,* May 9, 1907, p. 1.

42. *Calumet Record,* July 11, 1907, p. 1, and October 31, 1907, p. 1.

43. *Ibid.*, October 10, 1907, p. 1.

44. *Ibid.*, January 24, 1908, p. 5, and February 6, 1908, p. 5; Taylor, *op. cit.*, p. 58.

45. October 20, 1897, p. 6.

46. October 26, 1898, p. 4.

47. October 10, 1897, p. 4.

48. April 30, 1899, p. 16.

49. January 9, 1899, p. 5.

50. October 10, 1897, p. 4.

51. *Inter Ocean*, October 20, 1897, p. 2 (reprint of article from the *New York Journal*, October 19, 1897).

52. This paper was published in South Chicago by Henry Lee, whose father helped survey the town of Pullman.

53. *Calumet Record*, November 25, 1903, p. 10.

54. October 20, 1897, p. 6.

55. October 26, 1898, p. 4.

56. *United States Statutes at Large*, XXV, 501–4.

57. *New York World*, July 13, 1894, p. 1.

58. John W. Hayes to Cleveland, July 14, 1894; James H. Kyle to William H. T. Thurber (secretary to the president), July 19, 1894, Cleveland Papers.

59. *U.S. Strike Commission Report*, p. xv.

60. Trumbull to Cleveland, July 24, 1894, Cleveland Papers.

61. *U.S. Strike Commission Report*, pp. 122, 123.

62. *Ibid.*, p. 163.

63. *Ibid.*, pp. 33–34.

64. *Ibid.*, pp. 64, 184, 201.

65. *Ibid.*, pp. 163–64.

66. *Ibid.*, pp. 40, 63, 74, 83, 184, 186, 201, 430.

67. *Ibid.*, pp. 253, 334.

68. *Ibid.*, pp. 277–78.

69. *Ibid.*, pp. 253–54.

70. *Ibid.*, pp. 172–74.

71. *Ibid.*, p. xlix.

72. *Ibid.*, p. xlvi.

73. *Ibid.*

74. *Ibid.*, pp. xlvii–xlviii, liv.

75. *Ibid.*, p. xxvii.

76. *Ibid.*, p. xlix.

77. *Ibid.*, p. xlii.

78. *Ibid.*, pp. l–liv.

79. *Nation*, LIX (1894), 376.

80. *Debs: His Life, Writings and Speeches*, p. 57.

81. I (1894), 231–33.

82. *U.S. Strike Commission Report*, p. 163.

83. Lloyd to Darrow, November 23, 1894, Caroline Lloyd, *op. cit.*, pp. 145–46.

84. *Debs: His Life, Writings and Speeches*, pp. 39–40, quoted from the *Journal of Switchmen's Union*, July, 1908.

85. *Democratic Campaign Book . . . . 1896*, p. 5.

86. *Railway Times*, August 15, 1894, p. 2.

BIBLIOGRAPHY

MANUSCRIPTS

ALTGELD COLLECTION. Illinois State Historical Society, Springfield.

"Annual Reports of the Pullman Palace Car Company, 1883–1921." Library of Congress. (Mimeographed.)

CLEVELAND, GROVER, PAPERS. Library of Congress.

DOTY, DUANE. "The Arcade at Pullman" (1883). Pullman Collection, John Crerar Library.

————, "The Arcade Theatre" (1883). Pullman Collection, John Crerar Library.

————, "The Market at Pullman" (1883). Pullman Collection, John Crerar Library

GOVERNOR'S LETTER BOOKS: JOHN P. ALTGELD. State Archives, Springfield.

GOVERNOR'S CORRESPONDENCE: JOHN P. ALTGELD. State Archives, Springfield.

WALTER Q. GRESHAM PAPERS. Library of Congress.

DANIEL S. LAMONT PAPERS. Library of Congress.

LUDLUM, BERTHA S., "History of the Pullman Library," Pullman Collection, Pullman Branch Library.

OLNEY, RICHARD, PAPERS. Library of Congress.

"Pay Rolls of the Pullman Company, October, 1882—January, 1883." Pullman Company, Chicago.

PULLMAN COLLECTION. John Crerar Library.

PULLMAN COLLECTION. Pullman Branch Library, Chicago.

"Report to the State of Illinois on the Status of the Town of Pullman Relative to Housing, Population, Sewerage, Water Supply, Plumbing, Streets, Public Health and Etc., 1885." Pullman Collection. Pullman Branch Library.

"Town of Pullman Pay Rolls, March 15, 1886—March 31, 1887." Pullman Company.

"Visitors' Register for the Town of Pullman," Pullman Collection, Pullman Branch Library.

WALDRON, JOHN. "History of the Parish of Holy Rosary Church." Chicago: Holy Rosary Church, 1883.

NEWSPAPER AND PERIODICAL LITERATURE

American Federationist, Vol. I (1894–95).

ANONYMOUS. "The Arcadian City of Pullman," *Agricultural Review*, III (1883), 69–89.

————. "An Industrial City," *Scientific American*, L (1884), 279–80.

———. "Saltaire and Its Founder," *Harper's Magazine*, XLIV (1872), 827–35.

———. "Sir Titus Salt," *Chamber's Journal*, LV (1878), 545–47.

Calumet Record. A weekly newspaper published in South Chicago by Henry Lee, whose father helped to survey the town of Pullman. This paper, in certain respects, was the successor to the *Pullman Journal*, which ceased publication in 1898.)

Chicago Chronicle.

Chicago Daily News.

Chicago Evening Post.

Chicago Herald.

Chicago Journal.

Chicago News Record. (Between 1892 and 1893 this paper was called the *Chicago Record.*)

Chicago Times.

Chicago Tribune.

CLEVELAND, GROVER. "The Government in the Chicago Strike of 1894," *McClure's Magazine*, XXIII (1904), 227–40.

DICKENS, CHARLES. "A Yorkshire Colony," *All the Year Around*, XXV (1871), 185–87.

EATON, CHARLES H. "Pullman and Paternalism," *American Journal of Politics*, V (1894), 571–79.

———. "Pullman: A Social Experiment," *Today*, II (1895), 1–10.

"Editor's Table," *New England Magazine*, XXI (1896), 251–56.

ELY, RICHARD L. "Pullman: A Social Study," *Harper's Monthly*, LXX (1885), 452–66.

GRANT, THOMAS B. "Pullman and Its Lessons," *American Journal of Politics*, V (1894), 190–204.

Harper's Weekly, Vol. XXXVIII (1894).

Independent, Vol. XLVI (1894).

Inter Ocean.

Locomotive Firemen's Magazine, Vol. XVIII (1894).

MILES, NELSON A. "The Lesson of the Recent Strikes," *North American Review*, CLIX (1894), 180–88.

Nation, Vol. LIX (1894).

New York Sun.

New York Times.

New York World.

POND, IRVING. "America's First Planned Industrial Town," *Illinois Society of Architect's Monthly Bulletin*, June–July, 1934, pp. 6–8.

PORTER, HORACE. "Railway Passenger Travel," *Scribner's Magazine*, IV (1888), 296–318.

Public Opinion, XVII (1894).

Pullman Journal. (During the first two and one-half years of this paper's existence [1889–92] it was called the *Arcade Journal.* In 1898 the *Pullman Journal* was discontinued.)

Railroad Gazette, Vol. XXVI (1894).

Railroad Trainmen's Journal, XI (1894).

Railway Times. (This was the official organ of the American Railway Union and was published between 1894 and 1897.)

ROBINSON, HARRY P. "The Lesson of the Recent Strikes," *North American Review,* CLIX (1894), 195–201.

San Francisco Chronicle.

STEAD, WILLIAM T. "How Pullman Was Built," *Socialist Economist,* VII (1894), 85–88.

WARNER, CHARLES D. "Chicago," *Harper's Magazine,* LXXVII (1888), 116–27.

Washington Post.

Weekly Index. (This newspaper at present goes under the title, *Calumet Index.*)

PUBLISHED SOURCES, STUDIES, AND OTHER MATERIAL

ADAMIC, LOUIS. *Dynamite.* New York: Viking Press, 1931.

ADDAMS, JANE. *Democracy and Social Ethics.* New York: Macmillan Co., 1913.

——. *Twenty Years at Hull House.* New York: Macmillan Co., 1910.

ALTGELD, JOHN P. *Live Questions.* Chicago: George S. Brown & Son, 1899.

ANDREAS, A. T. *History of Cook County, Illinois.* Chicago: A. T. Andreas Co., 1884.

Annual Report of the Attorney General of the United States for the Year of 1894. Washington: Government Printing Office, 1894.

Annual Report of the Secretary of War for the Year of 1894. 3 vols. Washington: Government Printing Office, 1894.

Annual Reports of the President and Village Officers of the Village of Hyde Park. Chicago, 1882–89.

Appendix to the Annual Report of the Attorney General of the United States for the Year 1896. Washington: Government Printing Office, 1896.

Appleton's Annual Cyclopaedia, Vol. XIX. New York: D. Appleton & Co., 1880.

BANCROFT, EDGAR A. *The Chicago Strike of 1894.* Chicago: Gunthorp-Warren Printing Co., 1895.

BARNARD, HARRY. *Eagle Forgotten: The Life of John Peter Altgeld.* New York: Bobbs-Merrill Co., 1938.

BEER, THOMAS. *Hanna.* New York: Alfred A. Knopf, 1929.

——. *The Mauve Decade.* New York: Alfred A. Knopf, 1926.

Biennial Report of the Adjutant General of Illinois to the Governor and Commander-in-Chief, 1893 and 1894. Springfield: Ed. F. Hartman, 1895.

BROWNE, WALDO R. *Altgeld of Illinois.* New York: B. W. Huebsch Co., 1924.

BUCK, SOLON J. *The Agrarian Crusade.* ("Chronicles of America Series," Vol. XLV.) New Haven: Yale University Press, 1920.

BURNS, W. F. *The Pullman Boycott.* St. Paul: McGill Printing Co., 1894.

CARWARDINE, WILLIAM. *The Pullman Strike.* Chicago: Charles H. Kerr & Co., 1894.

CLEVELAND, GROVER. *The Government in the Chicago Strike of 1894.* Princeton: Princeton University Press, 1913.

COLE, ARTHUR C. *The Era of the Civil War.* ("Centennial History of Illinois," Vol. III.) Springfield: Illinois Centennial Commission, 1919.

COLEMAN, MCALISTER. *Eugene V. Debs.* New York: Greenberg, 1930.

Congressional Record (51st Cong., 1st sess.), Vol. XXI, Parts III and IV. Washington: Government Printing Office, 1890; (53d Cong., 2d Sess.), Vol. XXVI, Parts VII and VIII. Washington: Government Printing Office, 1894.

COOK, FREDERICK F. *By Gone Days in Chicago.* Chicago: A. C. McClurg & Co., 1910.

CURREY, J. SEYMOUR. *Chicago: Its History and Its Builders.* 5 vols. Chicago: S. J. Clarke, 1912.

DARROW, CLARENCE. *The Story of My Life.* New York and London: Charles Scribner's Sons, 1932.

DEBS, EUGENE V. *Debs: His Life, Writings and Speeches.* Chicago: Charles H. Kerr & Co., 1908.

———. *The Federal Government and the Chicago Strike.* (A pamphlet answering Grover Cleveland.) Chicago, 1910.

———. *The Great Strike of 1894 and Its Features.* New York: Morning Advertiser, 1894.

DE FOREST, ROBERT W., and VEILLER, LAWRENCE (eds.). *The Tenement House Problem: Including the Report of the New York State Tenement House Commission of 1900.* 2 vols. New York: Macmillan Co., 1903.

Democratic Campaign Book—Presidential Election of 1896. Washington: Hartman & Cadick, 1896.

DEWEY, DAVIS R. *National Problems.* ("The American Nation: A History," Vol. XXIV.) New York and London: Harper & Bros., 1907.

DE WOLF, OSCAR C. *Pullman from a State Medicine Point of View.* (Reprinted from *American Public Health Association Procedure,* IX, 290 ff.) Concord, N.H.: Republican Press Association, 1894.

DOTY, MRS. DUANE. *The Town of Pullman.* Pullman: T. P. Struksacher, 1893.

ELY, RICHARD T. *The Labor Movement in America.* New York: Thomas Y. Crowell & Co., 1886.

Federal Reporter
   Farmer's Loan and Trust Co. v. *Northern Pacific R. Co. et al.,* 60 at 803 (1894); 63 at 310 (1894).
   U.S. v. *Debs et al.,* 64 at 724 (1895).
   Platt v. *Philadelphia and Reading R. Co.,* 65 at 660 (1895).

FISH, CARL R. *The Rise of the Common Man, 1830–1850.* ("A History of American Life," Vol. VI.) New York: Macmillan Co., 1927.

FORD, HENRY J. *The Cleveland Era.* ("Chronicles of America Series," Vol. XLIV.) New Haven: Yale University Press, 1919.

FRANKFURTER, FELIX, and GREENE, NATHAN. *The Labor Injunction.* New York: Macmillan Co., 1930.

GIBBONS, JOHN. *Tenure and Toil.* Philadelphia: J. B. Lippincott & Co., 1888.

GOMPERS, SAMUEL. *Seventy Years of Life and Labor.* 2 vols. New York: E. P. Dutton & Co., 1925.

GRESHAM, MATILDA. *Life of Walter Q. Gresham.* 2 vols. Chicago: Rand, McNally & Co., 1919.

GROSSER, HUGO S. *Chicago: A Review of Its Government History.* Chicago: League of American Municipalities, 1906.

HENDRICK, BURTON J. *The Age of Big Business.* ("Chronicles of America Series," Vol. XXXIX.) New Haven: Yale University Press, 1919.

HOUGHTON, WALTER R. *Kings of Fortune.* Chicago: Loomis National Library Assoc., 1888.

HOURWICH, ISAAC A. *Immigration and Labor.* New York and London: G. P. Putnam's Sons, 1912.

HUSBAND, JOSEPH. *The Story of the Pullman Car.* Chicago: A. C. McClurg & Co., 1917.

Hyde Park Directory. Chicago: R. R. Donnelley & Sons., 1887 and 1888.

Is This Equal Taxation? (A campaign document published by the Tax Payer's party of Hyde Park.) Chicago: Rand, McNally & Co., 1885.

JAMES, HENRY. *Richard Olney and His Public Service.* Boston and New York: Houghton Mifflin Co., 1923.

Journal of the Senate of the Thirty-ninth General Assembly of the State of Illinois. Springfield: Ed. F. Hartman, 1896.

KARSNER, DAVID. *Debs: His Authorized Life and Letters from Woodstock Prison to Atlanta.* New York: Boni & Liveright, 1919.

KIRKLAND, JOSEPH. *The Story of Chicago.* Chicago: Dibble Pub. Co., 1892.

LLOYD, CAROLINE A. *Henry Demarest Lloyd.* 2 vols. New York and London: G. P. Putnam's Press, 1912.

LLOYD, HENRY D. *Men, the Workers.* New York: Doubleday, Page & Co., 1909.

McELROY, ROBERT. *Grover Cleveland: The Man and the Statesman.* New York: Harper & Bros., 1923.

McLEAN, JOHN. *One Hundred Years in Illinois, 1818–1918.* Chicago: Peterson Linotyping Co., 1919.

McMURRY, DONALD LeCRONE. *Coxey's Army: A Study of the Industrial Army Movement of 1894.* Boston: Little, Brown & Co., 1929.

Municipal Code of the Village of Hyde Park Together with General Laws. Hyde Park: Hyde Park Pub. Co., 1887.

NEVINS, ALLAN. *The Emergence of Modern America, 1865–1878.* ("A History of American Life," Vol. VIII.) New York: Macmillan Co., 1928.

———. *Grover Cleveland: A Study in Courage.* New York: Dodd, Mead & Co., 1932.

———. *Letters of Grover Cleveland.* New York: Houghton Mifflin Co., 1933.

ORTH, SAMUEL P. *The Armies of Labor.* ("Chronicles of America Series," Vol. XL.) New Haven: Yale University Press, 1919.

———. *Our Foreigners.* ("Chronicles of America Series," Vol. XXXV.) New Haven: Yale University Press, 1920.

PECK, HARRY THURSTON. *Twenty Years of the Republic, 1885–1905.* New York: Dodd, Mead & Co., 1913.

PERLMAN, SELIG. *History of Trade Unionism in the United States.* New York: Macmillan Co., 1922.

The Pride of Pullman. (A pamphlet, reprinted from an article in the *Inter Ocean,* January 10, 1883, concerning the opening of the Arcade Theatre.) Pullman, 1883.

Private Laws of the State of Illinois Passed by the Twenty-fifth General Assembly. 2 vols. Springfield: Baker, Bailhache & Co., 1867.

Proceedings of the General Managers' Association of Chicago, 1893 and 1894. Chicago: Knight, Leonard & Co., 1893 and 1894.

PULLMAN, GEORGE M. *The Strike at Pullman* (containing statements of President George M. Pullman and Second Vice-president T. H. Wickes before the U.S. Strike Commission). Chicago, 1894.

READ, CHARLES. *Put Yourself in His Place.* New York: Harper & Bros., 1897.

Report of the Bureau of Labor Statistics of the State of Illinois. Springfield: Phillips Bros., 1902.

Report of the Fire Marshal to the City Council of the City of Chicago for the Fiscal Year Ending December 31, 1894. Chicago: Cameron, Amberg & Co., 1895.

Report of the General Superintendent of Police of the City of Chicago to the City Council for the Year Ending December 31, 1894. Chicago: M. B. McAbee Printing Co., 1895.

Report of the Postmaster-General, 1894. (U.S. House Executive Docs., Vol. XIII, No. 1, Part IV [53d Cong., 3d sess., 1894–95].) Washington: Government Printing Office, 1895.

Report of the Seventeenth Annual Meeting of the American Bar Association. Philadelphia: Dando Printing & Pub. Co., 1894.

Reports of Cases at Law and in Chancery Argued and Determined in the Supreme Court of Illinois, CLXXV, 150–82. Springfield: Phillips & Co., 1899.

Reports of the Industrial Commission on Labor Organizations, Labor Disputes and Arbitration and on Railroad Labor. (U.S. House of Representative Doc. No. 186 [57th Cong., 1st sess.].) Washington: Government Printing Office, 1901.

Revised Statutes of the State of Illinois. Chicago: E. B. Myers & Co., 1898.

Revised Statutes of the United States. Washington: Government Printing Office, 1878.

RICHARDSON, JAMES D. *A Compilation of the Messages and Papers of the Presidents,* Vol. XII (1894). 20 vols. New York: Bureau of National Literature, 1897–1927.

Riis, Jacob A. *How the Other Half Lives*. New York: Charles Scribner's Sons, 1890.

Schofield, John M. *Forty-six Years in the Army*. New York: Century Co., 1897.

Sixth Annual Report of the Bureau of Statistics of Labor, 1875. Boston: Wright & Potter, 1875.

Sparks, Edwin E. *National Development*. ("The American Nation: A History," Vol. XXIII.) New York and London: Harper & Bros., 1907.

Stead, William T. *Chicago Today*. London: William Clowes & Sons, 1894.

———. *If Christ Came to Chicago*. Chicago: Laird & Lee, 1894.

Story of Pullman, The. (A pamphlet distributed by the Pullman Company at its exhibit at the World's Columbian Exposition.) Chicago, 1893.

Swinton, John. *Striking for Life: Or Labor's Side of the Labor Question*. Philadelphia: A. R. Keller Co., 1894.

Tarbell, Ida M. *The History of the Standard Oil Company*. 2 vols. New York: McClure, Phillips & Co., 1904.

Taylor, Graham R. *Pioneering on Social Frontiers*. Chicago: University of Chicago Press, 1930.

———. *Satellite Cities*. New York and London: D. Appleton & Co., 1915.

United States Reports: In re Debs, CLVIII, 564. New York and Albany: Banks & Bros., 1895.

United States Statutes at Large, Vol. XXV (1887–89). Washington: Government Printing Office, 1899.

United States Statutes at Large, Vol. XXVI (1889–91). Washington: Government Printing Office, 1891.

United States Strike Commission Report. (Senate Executive Doc. No. 7 [53d Cong., 3d sess.].) Washington: Government Printing Office, 1895. (This report, which was submitted to President Cleveland on November 14, 1894, by an investigating commission of three members, furnishes the most valuable source available for a study of the Pullman Strike.)

United States Supreme Court Records and Briefs: In re Debs. Vol. CLVIII. Washington, 1895.

Warren, Charles. *The Supreme Court in United States History*. 3 vols. Boston: Little, Brown & Co., 1922.

White, Horace. *The Life of Lyman Trumbull*. Boston and New York: Houghton Mifflin Co., 1913.

Whitlock, Brand. *Forty Years of It*. New York and London: D. Appleton & Co., 1914.

Wright, Carroll D., and Others. "An Attractive Industrial Experiment." *Massachusetts Labor Report, 1885*, Part I, pp. 1–26. Boston, 1885.

INDEX

PHOENIX BOOKS

in Political Science

PHOENIX BOOKS
in History